PRINCIPAL SIGHTS

★★★ Highly recommended
★★ Recommended
★ Interesting

S. POLO   Name and boundaries of quarter (sestiere)

Vaporetto line and stop

2   Map number

MURANO ★★
TORCELLO ★★
BURANO ★★
S. FRANCESCO
D. DESERTO ★
Treporti
Punta Sabbioni

Accademia (Ponte dell')	3	S. Maurizio (Campo)	55
Bandiera e Moro (Campo)	6	San Moisè (Salizzada)	58
Capello (Ramo)	10	San Salvador (Merceria)	61
Gallina (Calle Larga G.)	18	San Samuele (Campo)	64
Leoncini (Piazzetta dei)	21	San Simeon Profeta (Campo)	66
Libertà (Ponte della)	24	San Zulian (Merceria)	67
Nuova (Strada)	28	Sant'Angelo (Campo)	70
Orologio (Merceria dell')	31	Santi Apostoli (Rio Terà dei)	75
Pescaria (Campo della)	34	Sauro Nazario (Campo)	76
San Bartolomeo (Campo)	39	Seriman (Salizzada)	78
San Giovanni Crisostomo (Salizzada)	43	Traghetto (Campo dei)	79
San Lorenzo (Calle Larga)	46	Verona (Calle della)	82
San Marco (Calle Larga)	49	2 Aprile (Via)	85
San Marco (Piazzetta)	52		

A   Palazzo dei Camerlenghi
B   Palazzo Balbi (Pal. della Regione)
E   Palazzo Lando Corner Spinelli
H   Palazzo Loredan (Municipio)
M   Museo diocesano di arte sacra

M5 Fondaco dei Turchi (Museo di Storia Naturale)
N   Torre dell'Orologio
P   Pal. Corner della Ca' Granda (Prefettura)
Q   Campanile
T1 Teatro Goldoni

LIDO
S. Elena   11

★ S. FRANCESCO DELLA VIGNA

CASTELLO

★ ARSENALE

Torri d. Arsenale

ISOLA DI S. PIETRO

S. PIETRO DI CASTELLO ★

S. ELENA e S. PIETRO ★

★ MUSEO STORICO NAVALE

Campo S. Biagio

V. Garibaldi

Riva dei 7 Martiri

CANALE DI SAN MARCO

Riva dei Partigiani

Biennale

ISOLA DI S. ELENA

D0684206

OCT -- 2013   LIDO

S. LAZZARO DEGLI ARMENI ★

INDEX OF STREET NAMES

THE VENETO

VENEZIA	★ ★ ★	Vaut le voyage
Padova	★ ★	Mérite un détour
Treviso	★	Intéressant
Conegliano		Autre site décrit dans ce guide

Venice and the Veneto

The Discovering section of this guide is split between **Venice**, Venice's **outlying islands** and the administrative region of the **Veneto**. A full list of maps can be found on page 286.

VENICE
AND THE VENETO

Porta della Carta / Basilica di San Marco / © Nicola Muraro / iStockphoto

Editorial Director   Cynthia Clayton Ochterbeck

THE GREEN GUIDE VENICE AND THE VENETO

Produced by   Jonathan P. Gilbert, Azalay Media
Contributing Writer   Judy Edelhoff
Cartography   Michèle Cana
Production Manager   Natasha G. George
Picture Research   Sean Sachon
Interior Design   Chris Bell
Cover Design   Chris Bell, Christelle Le Déan
Layout   Michelin Travel Partner
Cover Layout   Natasha G. George

Contact Us   Michelin Travel and Lifestyle North America
                One Parkway South
                Greenville, SC 29615
                USA
                travel.lifestyle@us.michelin.com
                www.michelintravel.com

                Michelin Travel Partner
                Hannay House
                39 Clarendon Road
                Watford, Herts WD17 1JA
                UK
                ☎01923 205240
                travelpubsales@uk.michelin.com
                www.ViaMichelin.com

Special Sales   For information regarding bulk sales,
                customized editions and premium sales,
                please contact us at:
                travel.lifestyle@us.michelin.com
                www.michelintravel.com

One Team…
A Commitment to Quality

There's just one reason our team is dedicated to producing quality travel publications—you, our reader.

Throughout our guides we offer **practical information, touring tips** and **suggestions** for finding the best places for a break.

Michelin driving tours help you hit the highlights and quickly absorb the best of the region. Our descriptive **walking tours** make you your own guide, armed with directions, maps and expert information.

We scout out the attractions, classify them with **star ratings**, and describe in detail what you will find when you visit them.

Michelin maps featured throughout the guide offer vibrant, detailed and easy-to-follow outlines of everything from close-up museum plans to international maps.

Places to stay and eat are always a big part of travel, so we research **hotels and restaurants** that we think convey the essence of the destination and arrange them by geographic area and price. We walk you through the best shopping districts and point you towards the host of entertainment and recreation possibilities available.

We **test, retest, check and recheck** to make sure that our guidebooks are truly just that: a personalized guide to help you make the most of your visit. And if you still want a speaking guide, we list local tour guides who will lead you on all the boat, bus, guided, historical, culinary, and other tours you shouldn't miss.

In short, we remove the guesswork involved with travel. After all, we want you to enjoy exploring with Michelin as much as we do.

The Michelin Green Guide Team

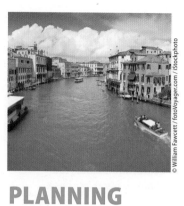

© William Fawcett / fotoVoyager.com / iStockphoto

PLANNING YOUR TRIP

WELCOME TO THE CITY

© Silvio Verrecchia / iStockphoto

CONTENTS

© Peter Barritt / age fotostock

EXPLORING THE CITY

YOUR STAY IN THE CITY

© Gwen Cannon / MICHELIN

HOW TO USE THIS GUIDE

PLANNING YOUR TRIP

The blue-tabbed PLANNING YOUR TRIP section at the front of the guide gives you **ideas for your trip** and **practical information** to help you organise it. You'll find tours, a host of breaks in the great outdoors, a calendar of events, information on shopping, sightseeing, kids' activities and more.

INTRODUCTION

The orange-tabbed INTRODUCTION section explores **Nature** from the lagoon to the impact of the built environment. The **History** section spans from the state's foundation to its ultimate decline. The **Art and Culture** section covers architecture, art, literature, traditions and folklore, while the **City Today** delves into modern Venice and the Veneto.

DISCOVERING

The green-tabbed DISCOVERING section features Venice and the Veneto's Principal Sights, arranged by region, featuring the most interesting local **Sights**, **Walking Tours**, nearby **Excursions**, and detailed **Driving Tours**.

🛈 Contact information, ⌦ admission charges, 🕓 hours of operation, and a host of other **visitor information** is given wherever possible. Admission prices shown are normally for a single adult.

STAR RATINGS★★★

Michelin has given star ratings for more than 100 years. If you're pressed for time, we recommend you visit the ★★★, or ★★ sights first:

★★★ Highly recommended
★★ Recommended
★ Interesting

Sidebars

Throughout the guide you will find peach-coloured text boxes (like this one), with lively anecdotes, detailed history and background information.

Address Books - Where to Stay, Eat and more...

WHERE TO STAY

We've made a selection of hotels and arranged them within the districts by price (🛌 *to fit all budgets, see the Legend on the cover flap for an explanation of the price categories*). For the most part, we've selected accommodations based on their unique regional quality, their regional feel, as it were. The hotels are marked on each map in this guide, accompanied by a simple key; wherever you want to go in Venice, you will be able to find a hotel nearby.
🛌 *See the district maps in DISCOVERING for hotel listings, and Where to Stay at the back of the guide for full reviews.*

WHERE TO EAT

We thought you'd like to know Venice's popular eating spots. So, we selected restaurants that capture the regional experience—those that have a unique regional flavor (🍴 *see the Legend on the cover flap for an explanation of the price categories*). We're not rating the quality of the food per se; as we did with the hotels, we selected restaurants for different districts and categorized them by price to appeal to all wallets, and featured them on our maps.
🍴 *See the district maps in DISCOVERING for restaurant listings, and Where to Eat at the back of the guide for full reviews.*

MAPS

- 🕭 **Venice maps** with Principal Sights listed.
- 🕭 **Veneto map**, **town plans** and **driving tours** in the Dolomites for trips out of La Serenissima.

All maps in this guide are oriented north, unless otherwise indicated by a directional arrow. The term "Local Map" refers to a map within the chapter or Tourism Region. A complete list of the maps found in the guide appears at the back

of this book, as well as a comprehensive index and list of restaurants and accommodations.

🕭 *See the map Legend at the back of the guide for an explanation of map symbols.*

ORIENT PANELS

Vital statistics are given for each principal sight in the DISCOVERING section:

- 🅸 **Information**: Tourist Office/Sight contact details.
- ▶ **Orient Yourself:** Geographic location of the sight with reference to surrounding boroughs, towns and roads.
- 🅿 **Parking:** Where to park.
- 🕭 **Don't Miss:** Unmissable things to do.
- 🕙 **Organising Your Time:** Tips on organising your stay; what to see first, how long to spend, crowd avoidance, market days and more.
- 🄺🄸🄳🅂 **Especially for Kids:** Sights of particular interest to children.
- 🕭 **Also See:** Nearby PRINCIPAL SIGHTS featured elsewhere in the guide.

SYMBOLS

🅂🅿🄰	**Spa Facilities**	🏖	**Tours**
🄺🄸🄳🅂	**Interesting for Children**	🅿	**On-site Parking**
🕭	**Also See**	▶	**Directions**
🅸	**Tourist Information**	✕	**On-site eating Facilities**
🕙	**Hours of Operation**	🏊	**Swimming Pool**
🕙	**Periods of Closure**	⛺	**Camping Facilities**
🔒	**Closed to the Public**	🏖	**Beaches**
💶	**Entry Fees**	☕	**Breakfast Included**
🚫	**Credit Cards not Accepted**	🕭	**A Bit of Advice**
♿	**Wheelchair Accessible**	🕭	**Warning**

Contact - Addresses, phone numbers, opening hours and prices published in this guide are accurate at the time of press. We welcome corrections and suggestions that may assist us in preparing the next edition. Please send your comments to:

UK
Michelin Maps and Guides
Hannay House
39 Clarendon Road
Watford, Herts WD17 1JA
travelpubsales@uk.michelin.com
www.michelin.co.uk

USA
Michelin Maps and Guides
Editorial Department
P.O. Box 19001
Greenville, SC 29602-9001
michelin.guides@us.michelin.com
www.michelintravel.com

VENEZIA

0   100   200   300   400 m

1 / 7000

5

S. Michele

CIMITERO

Cimitero

ISOLA
DI S. MICHELE

S. CRISTOFORO

CANALE

S

T

FOND. NOVE

F O N D A M E N T A

Fondamenta

C. Larga d. Botteri

C. d. Fumo

Calle Terà dei Birri

C. d. Stella

C. d. Squero

Rio Terà d. Testa

FOND. d. MENDICANTI

OSPEDALE

Nove

N O V E

OSPEDALI CIVILI

RIUNITI DI VENEZIA

C. L. G. Gallina

★ SCUOLA GRANDE
DI S. MARCO

S. ZANIPÒLO ★★

Campo di
S. S. Giovanni e Paolo

Salizz. S. S. Giovanni
e Paolo

Barbaria d. Tole

C. S. Marina

C. Calle

Rio d. Provolo

Rio d. S. Giovanni Laterano

Campo
S. Maria
Formosa

C. Lunga

C. S. M. Formosa

C. L. S. Lorenzo

Ruga Giuffa

Rio di S. Severo

Fond. di S. Lorenzo

Fond. d. S. Lorenzo

50

S. Maria
Formosa

C. d.
Bande

FONDAZIONE
QUERINI STAMPALIA ✝

Fond. Rimedio

Salizz. Zorzi

C. d. Chiesa

C. d. Corona

S. GIOVANNI
NOVO.

Fondamenta
dell'Osmarin

Cpo

C. d. Cappuccine

C. d. S. Giustina

S. Giustina

C. d. Cappuccine

C. S. Francesco

Fond. S. Francesco

★ S. FRANCESCO
D. VIGNA

68

C. Zen

17

Cpo S. Giustina

Cpo d.
Confraternita

Salizz. S. Giustina

132

S. LORENZO

Cpo
S. Lorenzo

47

42

Corte Nuova

118

C. d. Lion

POL.

10

CELESTIA

Sagredo

C.

Cpo d.
Celestia

U

Rio di Celestia

d. Gatte

Salizz.

SCUOLA DI S. GIORGIO
DEGLI SCHIAVONI ★★★

23

108

139

S. Giorgio
dei Greci

S. Antonin

Salizz.
S. Anto

Rio Ternita

V

G

R

10

CELESTIA

BACINI

★ S. FRANCESCO
D. VIGNA

Francesco
-17
68

Giustina
Cpo d.
Confraternita

Cpo d.
Celestia

Rio di
z. S. Giustina
-47
132

e Nuova

d. Gatte

Salizz.

Rio di S. Francesco

Rio di S. Ternita

DARSENA

UOLA DI S. GIORGIO
GLI SCHIAVONI ★★★

-23

ARSENALE ★

S. Antonin

Darsena

Arsenale Vecchio

GRANDE

Rio delle

izz
onik

Salizz.

d.

Pignater

Bandiera
e Moro

S. GIOVANNI
IN BRAGORA ★

Fond. d. Fronte

● Torri dell' Arsenale

C A S T E L L O

Schiavoni

Rio Ca'

Riva Ca' di Dio

ARSENALE

★ MUSEO STORICO
NAVALE

111

Cpo

della

Tana

della

Cpo S. Biagio

Riva
S. Biagio

PALAZZETTO
DELLO
SPORT

Rio

Fondamenta

della

Tana

S. FRANCESCA
DI PAOLA

Fond.

X

Via

Garibaldi

Calle
Correra

C A N A L E

Riva

dei

Sette

Martiri

Viale

Garibaldi

Sacco

100

Cpo
S. Giuseppe

D I

Giardini

Pubblici

GIARDINI
ESPOSIZIONE

Riva

dei

Viale

Partigiani

S A N

GIARDINI
BIENNALE

Y

M A R C O

H

J

TRIESTE

PORTOGRUARO

Caposile

PIAVE

SILE

Zero

S 14

DESE

Jesolo

LAGUNA   MORTA

BACINO DI LIDO

SILE

LIDO DI
JESOLO ♨♨

O.POLO

TORCELLO ★★

I. Mazzorbo ▲ **BURANO** ★★

Cavallino

Porto di
Piave Vecchia

VIVA

★**S. Francesco** ▲
d. Deserto

Lazzaretto Nuovo
▲

Treporti

Ca' Savio

CAVALLINO

S. Erasmo

Le Vignole
▲

Punta
Sabbioni

LITORALE   DEL

S. Servolo

LIDO ♨♨

PORTO DI LIDO

S. Lazzaro d. Armeni ★

Lazzaretto Vecchio

DI LIDO

M A R E

O DI MALAMOCCO

A D R I A T I C O

GGIA

THE VENETIAN LAGOON

0   5 km

——	Dykes
⬭	Sandbanks
⌐	Fishing
🏛	Palazzo or villa
▲	Campsite
⛵	Marina
🏄	Beach
☼	Industrial area
🗼	Lighthouse

Bacino : .... Basin

Laguna morta : .... Lagoon with minimal tide

Laguna viva : .... Lagoon with full tide

Porto : .... Harbour

Grand Canal from Ponte dell'Accademia
© William Fawcett / fotoVoyager.com / iStockphoto

MICHELIN DRIVING TOURS

The Veneto

ITALY ROUTE 4. *See the Michelin Guide Italy for even more driving tours in the surrounding regions of Lombardy and Romagna, and all the way south to Sicily.*

FROM THE DOLOMITES TO VENICE AND TRIESTE

This spectacular route combines the natural majesty of the Dolomite mountains with the cultural treasures of the Veneto and the Friuli-Venezia Giulia region – the latter occupying the north eastern corner of Italy with Trieste as its capital.

Local Veneto Trips

See the Veneto section of the guide for more routes and maps:

VILLAS OF THE BRENTA
◆**Padua to Fusina, via Mirano**

DOLOMITI
◆**Strada delle Dolomiti★★★**
◆**Val Pusteria area**

The route is approximately 500mi/ 800km long and requires at least 10 days, at least two of which should ideally be spent in Venice. From Venice head north to **Treviso**; the old centre, surrounded by waterways and what remains of the city walls, is a delight. From here **Portogruaro** has maintained the original layout of its old town and is justly famous for its Roman remains. In Friuli Venezia Giulia (*see ITALY Green Guide*) there are more fine Roman relics to enjoy at **Aquileia** before calling in at the seaside resort of **Grado**. Follow the coastline from here to **Trieste** with its blend of Italian and Central European culture. Be sure to savour the literary atmosphere in Caffè San Marco. Heading back north **Udine** boasts some excellent architecture. Back in the Veneto, pretty **Belluno**'s spectacular location is the gateway to the Dolomites. The route continues through the harsh and atmospheric **Dolomites** between its "capitals" of **Cortina d'Ampezzo** and **Bolzano**, ringing with the sounds of the German- and Latin-accented local dialect, before descending to **Trent**, dominated by the Buonconsiglio castle. The itinerary concludes in the beautiful Palladian town of **Vicenza**.

WHEN AND WHERE TO GO

When to Go

Although Venice has its attractions all year round, **Spring** (mid-Apr–Jun) and **Autumn** (Sept–Oct) are the ideal times to visit. Mild temperatures (60°–70°F/15°–21°C) make sightseeing comfortable, although still crowded. The highlight of Winter is **Carnevale**, a moveable and highly colourful feast, leading up to Lent, but do note that hotels (and restaurants) are booked months in advance, and room prices reflect its popularity.

Summer brings hot, often humid, weather with intense sunlight, though at least the sea breezes mean it is not as scorching as on the mainland. Unless you are on the tightest budget, find a hotel with air-conditioned rooms and don't forget to bring along your anti-mosquito devices. As well as insects, the city attracts the greater part of its 15 million visitors in summertime; the crowds threaten to overwhelm the city and make the main thoroughfares almost unbearable at peak periods. Make hotel reservations well in advance and expect very long lines at the main sights. Yet despite the crowds, the season's lengthy days and extended hours of operation are major draws.

Winter temperatures usually range from 30°F to 40°F and from just below freezing point to a few degrees above with overcast skies. Many connoisseurs of the city insist that this is the best time to see La Serenissima. The mists and fogs and even the floods (see NATURE; and box opposite) make the city particularly atmospheric, not to say downright melancholic, and of course the crowds have thinned out. On the other hand the cold and clinging damp can be uncomfortable and visitor opening hours may be reduced, with some establishments closing altogether for a week or two at a time. However, crisp clear winter days reward brave winter tourists.

Christmas in Venice is a magical time, with many churches festively decorated. Once again you will need to book well ahead and expect expensive room rates

October through December are the wettest months, however it's unlikely that the *acqua alta* will be more than a mild nuisance during your stay. Having lived with the sea as their neighbour for all their lives, the Venetians are prepared.

Where to Go

VENICE

It would be a shame to visit Venice and do nothing more than merely tick off an itinerary of great sights. As the French author, Jean-Louis Vaudoyer, once observed, "Nothing is simpler than to lose oneself in Venice and nothing is more fun than to be in this labyrinth." Yet, there are certain places and sights that demand a visit. If you only have a few days to spare here, we have made a few suggestions for making the most of *La Serenissima*. After ticking off the sights below we suggest simply wandering around the area you are in, exploring churches, bars and shops at will. You will almost certainly get lost in the narrow alleyways just as certainly as you will soon find your way back to a landmark.

Wellington boots

It is a curious and highly memorable sight to see the *Acqua Alta* (High Water) flooding the streets of Venice. The more flood-prone streets and squares are criss-crossed with wooden walkways and the city, which is usually so stylish, sees inhabitants and visitors alike wearing ungainly wellingtons, plastic boots, hip boots, and even plastic bags around their feet in an effort to keep dry.

Grand Canal★★★ and Piazza San Marco★★★

Go to the railway station and hop aboard Line 1 or the new (launched 2012) Art Vaporetto. If the weather is good, sit at the back in the open and watch the most glorious city High Street in the world go past. Get off at the Piazza San Marco.

After marvelling at the architecture surrounding you from canal, then ground level, ascend the campanile to get a birds-eye view of the piazza. Take a tour of **St Mark's Basilica**★★★ and/or the **Doges Palace**★★★, but only do both in one day if you have but a single day in Venice – otherwise it's a surfeit of riches in a few hours. Take a seat for a drink at one of the **grand cafes** in the piazza, but for value and the chance to mix with the locals, eat outside the square, snacking on *cichetti* in a *bacaro*.

Rialto★★

Go to the Rialto early in the morning, walk over the famous **Ponte di Rialto**★★ and watch the markets in progress. Pop into one of the little bars around here and enjoy a coffee or a glass of wine at a ridiculously early hour, among the locals. From here it's just a five minute walk to the **Frari** church and almost opposite the **Scuola Grande di San Rocco**. Between them these two institutions are a pantheon of Venetian art.

Dorsoduro

The **Accademia**★★★ is the city's main art gallery and houses a wonderful collection of Venetian paintings. If you don't know your Veronese from your Tiepolo, you can opt to watch seafaring vessels along the Zattere. Or wander over to the **Peggy Guggenheim Collection**★★, showing exclusively Modern and Contemporary Art, a two minute walk along the Grand Canal, and the second-most visited museum in the city, with not a Venetian Master in sight.

A five minute walk west brings you to the landmark church of **Santa Maria della Salute**, while a five minute walk south is the much-less visited **Squero di San Trovaso** where from across the canal you can glimpse gondolas being built and restored.

OUTLYING ISLANDS

Some tour representatives around the city will urge you to visit the island of **Murano**, world famous for its centuries-old glass blowing tradition. You definitely should go, though not with a glass company. Visit the excellent Glass Museum, a workshop, then the atmospheric Church of **Santi Maria e Donato**, perhaps the oldest in the lagoon.

You also have to make time for at least two more islands – a couple of hours on each will suffice. **Burano**, "the pearl of the lagoon" is like a tiny Venice washed in a glorious rainbow of pastel shades with the occasional eye-popping colour scheme.

Torcello, by contrast, is the island that time forgot, a dreamy overgrown, almost deserted place with a thousand-year old cathedral that is heart-achingly beautiful.

Finally, make the short journey across the lagoon to the church and monastery that you've seen countless times before in pictures of Venice, Palladio's splendid **San Giorgio Maggiore**. From the top of its campanile is the finest view in all Venice.

THE VENETO AND BEYOND

After a few days, particularly in crowds, Venice can start to feel claustrophobic. The hinterland is so full of cultural treasures and, if you have a little more time, natural scenery to explore, that it would be a shame not to venture out.

Day Trips

The richest city within easy distance of Venice is **Padova** (Padua)★★. Its historic centre is home to some of the most stunning historical and artistic sights in the Veneto, while its large student population gives it a lively buzz. You need two days to do it justice but an early start and late finish will cram in the highlights.

Guided Tours

There are any number of conventional guided tours of the city that are available to visitors, most of which include a guided walking tour and the option of a gondola ride. If you do hanker to ride in the city's most famous mode of transport then this is the cheapest way to do it, rather than negotiating for a private tour.

More unusual guided tours include: "Spicy Venice" – walking through the Rialto area, listening to the stories of Casanova and of libertine Venice in the 18C; and "Venetian Legends" – a walk through the districts of Castello and Cannaregio discovering the 'dark' side of the Venetian tradition.

🎫 Tickets can be bought at the tourist office – wear comfortable walking shoes!

Padua is linked to the city by the **Brenta Canal**, an attraction for its very popular day trip. Aboard a slow boat explore a selection of the great Italian **Villas of the Brenta**★★, which line this peaceful waterway (however, you cannot combine the Brenta and Padua in a single day).

If you are a fan of the Brenta Canal villas head for **Vicenza**★★, home of the great architect **Palladio**, where you can study more of his work. A small city, it can be seen easily in a day. **Verona**★★ is slightly further afield (75mi/120km) and like Padua requires two days to see it properly. It is the biggest city in the Veneto after Venice, and also the region's second richest artistic centre. A visit to the Roman Arena, Juliet's House and its scores of beautiful palazzi make the trip worthwhile.

Further afield

If you want to escape the dominance of Venice – which is prevalent in most of the Veneto – and swap narrow alleyways for mountains and meadows, then head north to the **Dolomiti**★★★.

Allow at least three nights of touring to see this majestic region. Call at the beautiful towns of **Bassano della Grappa**★★ and **Belluno**★ and the hilltop town of **Asolo**★. **Bolzano**★ is the principal city of the Dolomites and is well worth a visit. **Cortina d'Ampezzo**★★★ is an excellent base for exploring the region, whether hillwalking in summer, or skiing in winter.

KNOW BEFORE YOU GO

Useful Websites

www.turismovenezia.it
This is the official website of Venice with useful links to the official websites of adjacent areas such as the Riviera del Brenta; a very good resource for events, attractions, etc.

www.comune.venezia.it
The official website of Venice town council is excellent for visitors as well as locals with interesting news items as well as its Tourism section.

www.hellovenezia.com
A lively site giving details of events, tourist passes, and transport.

www.gondolavenezia.it
Everything you ever wanted to know about this elegant mode of travel.

www.veniceworld.com
A hotel booking service that provides links to restaurants, transportation, events, entertainment.

Italian Tourist Board

The Italian Tourist Board is known as **Ente Nazionale Italiano per il Turismo** (ENIT). www.enit.it.

UK

1 Princes St., London W1B 2AY; ☎020 08 1254.

USA

630 Fifth Ave., New York, Suite 1965, NY NY 10111. ☎(212) 245 5618.

10850 Wilshire Blvd, Los Angeles CA 90025. ☎(310) 820 1898.

500, North Michigan Avenue, Suite 506 Chicago IL 60611. ☎(312) 644 0996.

Canada

110 Yonge Street, Suite 503. South Tower, Toronto, Ontario M5C 1T4. ☎(416) 925 4882.

TOURIST OFFICES IN VENICE

The **Azienda Promozione Turismo (APT)** and its branches provide brochures, maps and lists of hotels, youth hostels and campsites free of charge. The main tourist office is the **Venice Pavilion** (☎041 529 87 11.

www.turismovenezia.it), situated near the Giardini Reali and St. Mark's Square. As well as providing tourist information, this office also sells novels, travel literature and other literary works on Venice in several languages. Other city centre tourist offices are located at the west end of the Procuratie Nuove, off Piazza San Marco; Piazzale Roma (Garage San Marco); and Santa Lucia Railway Station. All have the same telephone number as the main office.

Other useful offices are **Lido** (Gran Viale, ☎041 529 87 11, open Jun–Sept only) and **Marco Polo Airport** (☎041 541 5133).

International Visitors

ITALIAN EMBASSIES ABROAD

- ◆ 14 Three Kings Yard, London W1Y 2EH, UK. ☎020 7312 2200. www.embitaly.org.uk.
- ◆ 3000 Whitehaven St, NW Washington, DC 20008, USA. ☎(202) 612 4400. www.italyemb.org.
- ◆ 275 Slater Street, 21st floor, Ottawa, Ontario K1P 5H9, Canada; ☎(613) 232 2401/2/3. www.ambottawa.esteri.it.

ITALIAN CONSULATES ABROAD

- ◆ 38 Eaton Place, London SW1X 8AN, UK. ☎(020) 7235 9371. www.embitaly.org.uk.
- ◆ 32 Melville Street, Edinburgh EH3 7HA, UK. ☎(0131) 226 3631. www.consedimburgo.esteri.it.
- ◆ 690 Park Avenue, New York, NY 10065, USA. ☎(212) 737 9100.
- ◆ 3489 Drummond Street, Montreal, Quebec H3G 1X6 Canada. ☎(514) 849 8351.
- ◆ 136 Beverley Street, Toronto, Ontario, M5T 1Y5, Canada; ☎(416) 977 1566. www.constoronto.esteri.it.

Tourist Office

© Gwen Cannon / MICHELIN

FOREIGN EMBASSIES AND CONSULATES IN ITALY

Australia
- **Consulate general**: 3rd Floor, Via Borgogna 2, Milan. ☎ 02 777 04 217.
- **Embassy**: Via Antonio Bosio 5, Rome. ☎ 06 85 27 21. www.italy.embassy.gov.au.

Canada
- **Consulate**: Riviera Ruvvante 25, 35129 Padova. ☎ 049 87 64 833.
- **Embassy**: Via Zara 30, Rome. ☎ 06 85 44 42 911.

Ireland
- For **consulate** see UK below.
- **Embassy**: Via Giacomo Medici 1, Rome. ☎ 06 58 52 381. www.ambasciata-irlanda.it.

UK
- **Honorary consulate** in Venice: Piazzale Donatori di Sangue 2/5, Mestre. ☎ 041 5055 990 .
- **British embassy**: Via XX Settembre 80a, Rome. ☎ 06 42 20 00 01. www.italiantouristboard.co.uk.

USA
- **Consulate**: Via Principe Amedeo 2/10, 20121 Milan. ☎ 02 290 351. http://milan.usconsulate.gov.
- **Embassy**: Via Veneto 119a, 00187 Rome. ☎ 06 46 741. http://italy.usembassy.gov.

ENTRY REQUIREMENTS

British visitors travelling to Italy must be in possession of a valid national passport. Citizens of other European Union countries need only a national identity card. In case of loss or theft report to the embassy or consulate and the local police.

Entry visas are required for Australian, New Zealand, Canadian and US citizens (if the intended stay exceeds three months). Apply to the Italian Consulate (visa may be issued same day to personal callers; delay if submitted by mail).

US citizens may find the website www.travel.state.gov/travel useful for information on visa requirements, customs regulations, medical care, etc.

CUSTOMS REGULATIONS

For the most up-to-date information on what you can and cannot import and export and duty-free allowances on alcohol, tobacco and other goods, visit www.hmce.gov.uk (and enter "Travel" in the Search option).

US citizens should visit www.customs.gov for equivalent information.

HEALTH

As the UK is a member of the European Union, British subjects should obtain a **European Health Insurance Card (EHIC)** available from main post offices, before leaving home.

However the EHIC card only covers minimum medical expenses so separate travel and medical insurance is highly recommended.

Accessibility

Sights in this guide marked with the ♿ symbol have full or near full access for wheelchairs. However, it is highly recommended that you call the sight in advance to determine the extent of their facilities. Quite understandably many Venetian historic monuments and attractions do not have lifts or wheelchair facilities. Wheelchairs may be loaded onto the vaporettos but not onto the gondolas. Information on accessibility for wheelchair visitors is available online at the Venice City Council website, http://www.comune.venezia.it. This is an excellent resource (in English) listing suitable public transport, accommodation and attractions in some detail; for example if there are ramps, whether there are accessible public toilets, and so on. It also says whether there are aids for blind or visually impaired visitors.

There is more information on visitors with **impaired vision** on the City

Council website at www.comune.venezia.it/letturagevolata, although this is only in Italian.

UK travellers should contact:

- **Tourism for All UK** (formerly Holiday Care), ☎0845 124 9971. www.tourismforall.org.uk).

- **RADAR** (Royal Association for Disability and Rehabilitation), 12 City Forum, 250 City Road, London EC1V 8AF. ☎020 7250 3222. www.radar.org.uk.

GETTING THERE AND GETTING AROUND

See p45 for details of accommodation taxes and Venice's unique definition of high and low season.

By Plane

Venice is served by dozens of international and domestic flights arriving at **Marco Polo Airport** (including budget Easyjet flights from the UK), about 10km/6mi (*20min*) from the city by vehicle. ☎041 26 06 111, www.veniceairport.it.

Six budget airlines, including Ryanair, use Treviso S Angelo airport (☎0422 315 111. www.trevisoairport.it) which is 30km/18mi north of Venice.

AIRPORT TRANSFERS

By Bus: Marco Polo airport is linked to Venice's Piazzale Roma by **ACTV bus no 5** (€6; www.actv.it) and an **ATVO shuttle coach** (www.atvo.it).

From Treviso airport ATVO buses run to Mestre Railway station and Venice (in advance €6, on bus €7). Piazzale Roma) in time with departures and arrivals of Ryanair and Ttansavia flights. The journey takes around 1hr 10min.

By Taxi: Taxis are available from Marco Polo to Piazzale Roma (€40; www.radiotaxivenezia.com).

By Water: Alilaguna boats cross the lagoon with a choice of two routes; the Red Line or the Blue Line, which between them serve all major parts

of the city, including the Lido and Murano. The dock for Alilaguna (and private water taxis) is a 5 minute walk from the airport, or a 1 minute ride on the airport shuttle (€1).

As a rough guide as to the speed and cost of the service, it takes 70 minutes to reach Piazza San Marco and costs €15. For more detailed information on ticket prices and timetables, visit www.alilaguna.it.

Private **water taxis** offer a much faster 35 minute door-to-door service, but are very expensive (expect to pay at least €110).

By Ship

Venice Ferry Port is the busiest and most popular Southern European entrance to the Adriatic and Mediterranean Sea, handling around 500 major ship departures and 700 000 cruise passengers per year (most services run Apr–Oct only).

Venezia Lines (www.venezialines.com) operates from Venice to Slovenia (Piran, 2hr 30min) and several ports in Croatia: Mali Losinj 4hr 30min; Pula 3hr (then onto Lussino); Umago and Porec, 2hr 30mins; Rovinj, 2hr 45min; Rabac 4hr.

Viamare (www.viamare.com) also run ferries between Venice and Rabac.

Both **Anek Lines** and **Minoan Lines** (www.minoan.gr) operate ferries from Venice to Patras and Igoumenitsa on the Greek mainland, and also to Corfu. Book for all services with www.directferries.co.uk, or www.aferry.

co.uk. Many large **cruise operators** also call in at Venice. Some passenger cruise lines are Celebrity, MSC Italian Cruises, Princess, Carnival, Crystal, Cunard, Holland America, and Sea Cloud. Large ships generally use the main Marittima terminal. It's about a 15min walk or a 5min taxi or shuttle-bus ride from the Piazzale Roma. Smaller ships also use this cruise terminal but if more than three ships are in port at one time, they may use San Basilio terminal, on the Zattere promenade, fronting the Giudecca Canal, which is within easy walking distance or a short vaporetto ride from the Piazza.

By Train

The main line from Milan to Trieste via Brescia, Verona, Vicenza and Padova passes through Venice. Trenitalia is the Italian state railroad. See "offerte" or "offers" for discount options on www.trenitalia.com. A more luxurious

☺ Arriving in Venice ☺

The final stop in Venice for buses, taxis and cars is Piazzale Roma. From here you will have to walk with your luggage to the hotel. You can take the vaporetto service, but boats can be crowded and there's a fee for more than one bag.

alternative is the **Venice Simplon-Orient-Express Ltd**. Travelling at a leisurely pace in original 1920s and '30s carriages, the VSOE leaves from London and stops in Paris, Innsbruck, Verona and Venice (☺ *see Box below*).

By Coach/Bus

Coach services from Victoria Coach Station, London, are organised by National Express/Eurolines. ☎ 08717 818 181. www.eurolines.co.uk. Alternatively visit your nearest National Express office or agent.

Venice Simplon-Orient-Express

The Orient Express was the brainchild of the Belgian **Georges Nagelmackers**, who inaugurated the service in 1883. In 1906 the Simplon tunnel was excavated through the mountains between Switzerland and Italy (19.8km/12mi). The route could extend from Milan to Venice and on to Constantinople (56hr from Paris). After World War II, the legendary luxury train's financial problems eventually forced its closure in 1977. Revived in 1982, the trains have been restored to their former splendour, and include wood panelling, Lalique glass and Art Deco-style lamps. The Venice Simplon-Orient-Express leaves from London for Venice stopping in Paris, Innsbruck and Verona. The full trip takes about 32hr, covering 1 715km/1 065mi. Other London routes go through Budapest, Prague or Vienna. Venice trains also depart for Istanbul; in 2013 a new Venice-Copenhagen-Stockholm route was launched. For details, contact the office of **Venice Simplon-Orient-Express Ltd.** in the UK: ☎ 44 (0) 0845 217 0799 or 020 3117 1300, or www.orient-express.com.

The piano bar on board the Venice Simplon-Orient-Express

© Venice Simplon-Orient-Express

Highway Code

- In Italy vehicles drive on the **right-hand side** of the road.
- The **minimum driving age** is 18 years.
- **Seat belts** must be worn in the front and back of the vehicle. Drivers must wear **shoes**, carry **spare lights** and have a **red triangle** to be displayed in the event of a breakdown or accident.
- Emergency **road-rescue services** are offered by the **Automobile Club Italiano (ACI)**, ☎116.
- **Motorways** (*autostrade* – subject to tolls) and dual carriageways (*super-strade*) are indicated by green signs, ordinary roads by blue signs, and tourist sights by yellow or brown signs.
- Italian **motorway tolls** can be paid for with cash or with the **Viacard**, a magnetic card that is sold in Italy at the entrances and exits of motorways, in Autogrill restaurants and in the offices of the ACI (Automobile Club Italiano).
- The following **speed restrictions** are enforced:
  - 50kph/31mph in built-up areas.
  - 90–110kph/56–69mph on open country roads.
  - 90kph/56mph (600cc) to 130kph/81mph (excess of 1 000cc) on motorways, depending on engine capacity.
- **Fuel** is sold as *super* (4 star), *senza piombo* (unleaded 95 octane), *super plus* or *Euro plus* (unleaded 98 octane) and *gasolio* (diesel). Petrol (US: Gas) stations are usually open from 7am to 7pm. Many close at lunch time (12.30–3pm), as well as on Sundays and public holidays; many refuse payment by credit card.

By Car

FORMALITIES

Nationals of the European Union require a valid **national driving licence**. Nationals of non-EU countries should get an **international driving licence**, obtainable in the US from the American Automobile Association (www.aaa.com). Other documents required include the vehicle's current **registration document** and a **green card** for insurance.

MAIN ROADS

Venice is situated off the A 4 Torino–Trieste road, reached from the south by the A 13 Bologna to Padua road. Exit at Mestre onto the SS 11, then cross the Ponte della Libertà to Piazzale Roma.

MAPS

Michelin Tourist and Motoring Atlas Italy and Michelin Maps *no. 705* Europe (1:3 000 000), *no. 735* Italy (1:1 000 000) and *no. 562* Northeast Italy (1:400 000) will make route planning easier.

PARKING

Piazzale Roma

The municipal **ASM garage** (☎041 27 27 211. www.asmvenezia.it) at Piazzale Roma charges a daily rate of €26. Another possibility at Piazzale Roma is the **Garage San Marco** (☎041 52 32 213. www.garagesanmarco.it), which charges €26 for 12hr and €30 for 24hr.

Tronchetto

To the west of Piazzale Roma, Interparking Italia (☎041 52 07 555. www.veniceparking.it) on the island of **Tronchetto**—exit from the Liberty Bridge, serviced by vapo-retto—charges cars, camper-vans and caravans around €21 for 24hr.

On Foot

The easiest way of getting around is on foot. Always carry a map but don't worry if you get lost—everyone does, and soon finds their way again. It is all part of the Venice experience. Venice's system of house numbers can reach remarkable heights (up to almost 7 000), as these numbers refer to individually numbered addresses within the whole **sestière** rather than to a particular street or square. Even numbers are not always on one side of the street or odd ones on the other! Watch for the closest campo (square) and for yellow signs with directional arrows to major sights like the Rialto and Piazza San Marco.

On Water

VAPORETTO (WATERBUS)

See map of vaporetto routes on the inside back cover of the guide.

As conventional cities use conventional buses, so Venice is served by **waterbuses,** run by **ACTV** (☎041 27 22 111. www.actv.it). These come in two kinds: the lumbering *vaporetto* (plural, *vaporetti*), and, for longer distances, the faster *motoscafo* (motor boat, plural *motoscafi*).

Visitors should note that the name of a vaporetto stop does not necessarily mean that the waterbus will stop outside the monument after which it

is named – however it will always be in the close vicinity. Traffic on the Grand Canal is often congested and services may sometimes be erratic.

A reduced service operates at night: it's best to check the timetables on display or visit www.actv.it for all timetable enquiries.

Single tickets may be purchased from kiosks or machines at each landing stage, from Hellovenezia ticket desks, and from shops displaying the ACTV sign. A single ticket costs €7 and allows 1hr of travel including a change in the same direction of travel, but *not* a return trip. Unless you are making a very fleeting visit it makes sense to buy a Tourist Travel Card (*biglietto turistico*), which allows unlimited travel for the following prices: 12hr €18; 24hr €20; 36hr €25; 48hr €30; 72hr €35; 7 days €50.

A three-day "youth card" is available to anyone aged between 15 and 29 in possession of a Rolling Venice Card (on sale at the Hellovenezia ticket desks for €4) and allows 72 hours of travel for €18.

If you board without a ticket, you must request one immediately from the *marinaio* (sailor/attendant) in charge of the boarding gate. On-the-spot fines may be levied against passengers without a ticket.

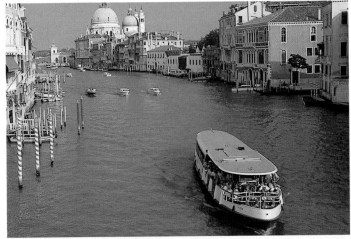

Vaporetto on the Grand Canal between the Salute and Accademia

Line 1 runs from Piazzale Roma and the railway station, the full length of the Grand Canal (14 stops) to Piazza San Marco and on to the Lido. It is known as the *accelerato*, although in some ways this is the slowest line.

Line 82 follows the same route as Line 1, but makes fewer stops and is therefore quicker. It runs from Tronchetto to Piazzale Roma, Giudecca, San Giorgio, San Marco and on to the Lido.

Art Vaporetto launched in 2012, runs during part of the year (www.vaporettoarte.com) and stops at a variety of popular spots.

WATER TAXIS

Beware of touts out to overcharge the unsuspecting visitor! Use only authorised motor launches bearing a yellow registration number plate inscribed with the symbol of Venice on the boarding side. It is also worth ensuring that the meter is clearly visible and that charge rates are displayed. There is a fixed starting price of €15 then a charge of €2 per minute.

A ten minute ride across the city centre will cost approximately €35 (with small additional charges for night taxis, for carrying luggage and if you have more than four passengers in your group).

If you have any queries or wish to register a complaint contact the Azienda Trasporto Persone Venezia, S. Polo, 618/a. ☎041 5210506.

The following are authorised operators

- **Coop. Bucintoro, Dorsorduro** ☎041 52 03 144
- **Coop. Ducale, S.Marco** ☎041 52 27 255
- **Coop. Motoscafi San Giorgio, S. Polo** ☎041 52 28 777
- **Coop. Motoscafi Taxi, Cannaregio, 85** ☎041 71 62 86
- **Coop. San Marco, S. Marco, 4267a** ☎041 52 35 775
- **Coop. Trasbagagli, Santa Croce, 496c** ☎041 71 37 19
- **La Fenice, S.Marco** ☎041 52 39 555

SELF DRIVE BOATS

A Venetian *topo* (open-topped motor boat), which can accommodate up to six people can be hired from two operators:

Brussa (☎041 715787, brussaisboat.it) by the Ponte delle Guglie, near the station. €20 per hour.

Cantiere Lizzio/Sport e Lavoro, 2606 Cannaregio (☎041 721 055). €120 for the day.

Beware that although this is an unusual and exciting way to explore the city, Ventian lagoons and canals are busy waterways and you really should be an experienced boat driver.

GONDOLAS

For a relaxing trip on a gondola, be prepared to put your hand in your wallet: 40min along the canals during the daytime will cost you, and up to 5 other passengers, €80 (a musical serenade is extra). Every additional 20min will be charged an extra €40.

A 40min trip by gondola at night (7pm–8am) costs €100, with an extra €50 for every further 20min.

Beware that although these are the official charges, they may also be subject to negotiation, depending on your own circumstances and where you want to go. You can decide how to reach your destination and ask the gondolier to follow the route you have chosen.

For contact details, contact the Istituzione per la Conservazione della Gondola e la Tutela del Gondoliere ☎041 52 85 075. For an official list of prices visit www.gondolavenezia.it/storia_tariffe.asp.

TRAGHETTI

You don't need to spend lots of money to ride in a gondola. Simply hop aboard a *traghetto* (gondola ferry). These operate at eight points along the Grand Canal (Ferrovia, San Marcuola, Santa Sofia, Riva del Carbon, San Tomà, San Samuele, Santa Maria del Giglio and Dogana). The relative absence of bridges across the Grand Canal (Calatrava, Scalzi, Rialto and Accademia), has given the traditional gondolier a continuing ferry role in Venice's day to day public transport system, a role that has been dramatically whittled down by the vaporettos. The Venetian custom is to remain standing up. For less steady visitors however there is no compulsion to stand during the crossing; it is better to arrive seated than to be fished out of the Grand Canal!

A *traghetto* costs a mere €0.50 (slightly higher from San Samuele during exhibitions at Palazzo Grassi). Times of operation are posted at the landing stages, though beware they finish quite early (before 8pm) and in winter services may be suspended completely.

WHAT TO SEE AND DO

Outdoor Fun

When you feel the need for a break from culture, you don't have far to go. Lido offers swimming, cycling and golf; Cavallino (6mi/10km east of Venice) boasts 9.5mi/15km of beaches and is said to be the largest open-air resort in Europe, while neighbouring Lido di Jesolo—not to be confused with Lido—is another huge beach strip with plenty of water sports on offer.

CYCLING

Cycling is not permitted in the historic centre but bikes are allowed on several of the lagoon islands (including Lido, Pellestrina, Sant'Erasmo), as well as mainland Venice (Mestre and Marghera) and Cavallino.
There are several places to hire bikes at the Lido and Cavallino.
From the Lido, try www.venicebikerental.com and www.lidoonbike.it. Hire rates are around €8–10 per day.

GOLF

The nearest chamionship golf course is Circolo Golf on The Lido (☎041 731 333 circologolfvenezia.it). Many big names have played here and Arnold Palmer holds the course record of 67.

FISHING

Ernest Hemingway once fished in the lagoon (even though he was more interested in duck shooting here!). For sport fishing call ☎041 528 5123.

MOUNTAIN SPORTS

Cortina d'Ampezzo is the adventure capital of the Dolomites catering for just about every winter and summer mountain sport.
For one-stop adventure sports call at **The Cortina Adrenaline Center** (www.adrenalincenter.it) which offers canyoning, rafting, kayaking, bob sledding), mountain biking, snow rafting, trekking with snowshoes (and sled) and wilderness training.

Rock Climbing
For climbing and trekking contact the **Gruppo Guide Alpine Scuola di Alpinismo** in Cortina d'Ampezzo (☎0436 86 85 05 www.guidecortina.com).

Skiing and other winter sports
The Dolomites and the nearby Val pusteria (Pustertal) with its Kronplatz ski area, are blessed with many world-class ski resorts with schools that cater for foreign visitors. Cortina d'Ampezzo is the most famous, most glamorous and has the widest range, but other top resorts include Vigo di Fassa, Canazei), St Ulrich/Ortisel, Selva Val Gardena, Bruneck (Dietenheim), Dobbiaco (Toblach) and San Martino di Castrozza (see pages 239–244 for details).

Lord Byron In Venice

Lord Byron, the great poet, was famous for swimming in Venice as detailed in this letter he wrote in 1821: *"In 1818 the chevalier Mengaldo (a Gentleman of Bassano) a good swimmer, wished to swim with my friend Mr. Alexander Scott and myself. As he seemed particularly anxious on the subject, we indulged him. We all three started from the island of the Lido and swam to Venice. At the entrance of the Grand Canal, Scott and I were a good deal ahead, and we saw no more of our foreign friend, which however was of no consequence, as there was a gondola to hold his clothes and pick him up. Scott swam on past the Rialto, when he got out less from fatigue than from chill, having been for hours in the water without rest of stay except what is to be obtained by floating on one's back, this being the condition of our performance. I continued my course on to Santa Chiara, comprising the whole of the Grand Canal/beside the distance from the Lido, and got out where the laguna once more opened to Farina. I had been in the water by my watch without help or rest and never touching ground or boat for four hours and twenty minutes."*

In fact Byron had covered a distance of around 4.5mi/7km!

RIDING

The best place for horseriding is in the beautiful hills of the Colli Berici just south of Vicenza. Visit www.colliberici.com (then Sport/Equitazione) for details of various ranches and schools.

WATER SPORTS

Bathing
Go to the Lido, Cavallino or Lido di Jesolo for sea bathing. On Lido the best beaches have been annexed by the big hotels and if you want access to these you will have to pay. There are free public beaches at both the northern and southern extremities of the island. The water anywhere on the Lido is not particularly clean: the quality is better at Cavallino and Lido di Jesolo

Windsurfing
Windsurfs are for hire at Cavallino and Lido di Jesolo.

Activities for Children `Kids`

In this guide, sights of interest to children are indicated with a `Kids` symbol.

Venice isn't an obvious place to take children as there are no museums or attractions geared to them and there is little room to let off steam running

Shark Bay, Aqualandia

© Aqualandia

around. Kicking or throwing a ball in the historic centre can have dire consequences with the city authorities, and feeding the pigeons was banned. However, for children of a certain age, a city with canals for main streets and boats instead of motor cars has a real fascination. Consider staying away from the centre, where younger ones will have running space. The glass blowers at **Murano**★★ and the **Natural History Museum** may captivate well-behaved youngsters, while a trip to the seaside is always a good idea. There is not so much space, and often a quieter atmosphere at Lido, but Cavallino and Lido di Jesolo are geared for families. The big attraction for kids at Jesolo is the Aqualandia **waterpark** (*open mid-May to mid-Sept daily 10am–6pm; €28, child 1m–1.4m €24; 0421 37 16 48, www.aqualandia.it*).

A little further east, at Caorle, there is another smaller water park, Parco Acquatico (*open late May to early Sept daily 10am–6pm; €17, child up to 1.3m €14; 042 181 423, www.aquafollie.it*). Caorle also has good beaches.

Calendar of Events

Here is a selection of the most important and colourful annual events:

6 JANUARY

Regata della Befana – Epiphany boat race with contestants dressed as witches racing to a giant stocking at Rialto Bridge!

10 DAYS BEFORE LENT (FEB–MAR)

Carnival – The year's most famous celebration featuring costumed revellers in masks throughout the city (*see ART and CULTURE*).

MARCH

Su e zo per i ponti – A non-competitive race through the streets of Venice.

MAUNDY THURSDAY

Benediction – Candle-lighting procession outside Basilica di San Marco.

25 APRIL

Feast day of St Mark – Men give their sweethearts a *bòcolo* (a red rose).

MAY

The **Vogalonga** – A non-competitive regatta open to foreign rowers around the islands. www.vogalonga.com.

ASCENSION DAY

The **Sensa** commemorates the Sposalizio del Mar (*see Time Line 1177*).

THIRD WEEK JUNE

The **Heineken Jammin Festival** takes place at San Giuliano Park, in Mestre on the mainland). The 2012 line up included Red Hot Chili Peppers, The Prodigy, and The Cure.

THIRD SUNDAY IN JULY

Festa del Redentore. Feast of the Redeemer, commemorating the end of the plague in 1576, culminating in a huge fireworks display over the lagoon (*see GIUDECCA*).

LATE AUGUST–EARLY SEPT

Venice Film Festival – glittering movie jamboree with top starts from all over the world jetting into the Lido (*see IL LIDO*).

SEPTEMBER

Biennale – *Even Numbered Years only. Sept–Nov (Dance in Jun; Theatre end of Jul).* International exhibitions of art and culture (*see SANT'ELENA E SAN PITERO*).

Regata Storica – *First Sun in Sept.* Historic regatta re-enactment with

© A Zane / MICHELIN

The Historic Regatta

a costumed pageant and races on
the Grand Canal.

21 NOVEMBER

Feast of the Madonna della Salute
- commemorating the end of the
plague in 1576 with a bridge of
boats across the Grand Canal to
La Salute (*see La SALUTE*).

Books

ART

Venetian Painting: a Concise History –
John Steer
(Thames and Hudson 1970)
The Stones of Venice – John Ruskin
(Da Capo Press 1985)
Palladio and Palladianism –
Robert Tavernor
(Thames and Hudson 1991)
Palladio – JS Ackerman, P Dearborn
Massar (Illustrator)
(Penguin Books 1991)
Palladio's Villas – Paul Holberton
(John Murray 1991)
Five Centuries of Music in Venice –
HC Robbins Landon, John Julius
Norwich (Thames and Hudson 1991)
Ruskin's Venice: The Stones Revisited
– Sarah Quill, Alan Windsor (Intro-
duction) (Ashgate Publ. 1999)

HISTORICAL REFERENCE

The Travels of Marco Polo –
Marco Polo, R Latham (Trans)
(Penguin Books 1965)
A History of Venice – John Julius Nor-
wich (Penguin Books 1983)
The Venetian Empire – Jan Morris (Pen-
guin Books 1990)
Venice Rediscovered – John Pemble
(Oxford University Press 1996)

LITERATURE

Italian Journey – Goethe
(Penguin Books 1970)
The Aspern Papers –
Henry James, Anthony Curtis (Ed)
(Penguin Books 1984)
The Wings of the Dove –
Henry James, J Bayley (Ed), P Crick
(Ed) (Penguin Books 1986)
The Desire and Pursuit of the Whole –
Frederick Rolfe (Da Capo Press 1986)
*Territorial Rights: Complete and
Unabridged* – Muriel Spark, Nigel
Hawthorne (Narrator) (Chivers
Audio Books 1990)
The Quest for Corvo –
AJA Symons (Quartet Books 1993)
Across the River and into the Trees –
Ernest Hemingway (Arrow 1994)
Thus was Adonis Murdered –
Sarah Caudwell (Dell Publishing
Company 1994)
A Literary Companion to Venice – Ian
Littlewood (St Martin's Press 1995)
Dead Lagoon – Michael Dibdin
(Faber and Faber 1995)

WORLD HERITAGE SITES

In 1972, the United Nations Educational, Scientific and Cultural Organisation (UNESCO) adopted a Convention for the preservation of cultural and natural sites. To date, more than 150 States Parties have signed this international agreement, which has listed over 600 sites "of outstanding universal value" on the World Heritage List. Each year, a committee of representatives from 21 countries, assisted by technical organisations (ICOMOS – International Council on Monuments and Sites; IUCN – International Union for Conservation of Nature and Natural Resources; ICCROM – International Centre for the Study of the Preservation and Restoration of Cultural Property, the Rome Centre), evaluates the proposals for new sites to be included on the list, which grows longer as more countries sign the Convention. To be considered, a site must be nominated by the country in which it is located.

The protected **cultural heritage** may be monuments (buildings, sculptures, archaeological structures etc) with unique historical, artistic or scientific features; groups of buildings (such as religious communities, ancient cities); or sites (human settlements, examples of exceptional landscapes, cultural landscapes) which are the combined works of man and nature and of exceptional beauty. **Natural sites** may relate to the earth's geological history, the development of human cultures and significant ecological processes, or may contain superlative natural phenomena or provide a habitat for threatened species.

UNESCO World Heritage Sites in Italy

- Rock Drawings, Valcamonica
- Church and Dominican Convent of Santa Maria delle Grazie, with *The Last Supper* by Leonardo da Vinci, Milan
- Historic Centre of Florence
- Venice and its Lagoon
- Piazza del Duomo, Pisa
- Historic Centre of San Gimignano
- The Sassi (troglodyte dwellings) of Matera
- City of Vicenza and the Palladian Villas of the Veneto
- Historic Centre of Siena
- Historic Centre of Naples
- Crespi d'Adda
- The Renaissance City of Ferrara and the Po Delta
- Castel del Monte
- The Trulli of Alberobello
- Early Christian Monuments of Ravenna
- Historic Centre of Pienza
- 18C Royal Palace at Caserta with the Park, the Aqueduct of Vanvitelli and San Leucio Complex
- Residences of the Royal House of Savoy, Piedmont
- Botanical Garden, Padua
- Cathedral, Torre Civica and Piazza Grande, Modena
- The Archaeological Sites of Pompeii, Herculaneum and Torre Annunziata
- Villa Romana del Casale, Piazza Armerina
- Su Nuraxi, Barumini
- Portovenere, the Cinque Terre and the Islands (Palmaria, Tino and Tinetto)
- The Amalfi Coast
- The Archaeological Site of Agrigento
- Cilento and Vallo di Diano National Park with the Archaeological Sites of Paestum and Velia and the Certosa di Padula
- The Archaeological Site and Patriarchal Basilica of Aquileia
- Historic Centre of Urbino
- Villa Adriana and Villa d'Este, Tivoli
- Verona
- The Aeolian Islands
- Assisi, the Basilica di San Francesco and other Franciscan sites
- Late Baroque Towns of the Val di Noto (southeastern Sicily)
- Rome and the Holy See

Death in Venice and Other Stories –
    Thomas Mann (Minerva 1996)
The Passion – Jeanette Winterson
    (Vintage 1996)
The Comfort of Strangers – Ian McEwan
    (Vintage 1997)
Volpone – Ben Jonson [can be found
    in *Volpone and Other Early Plays*
    – Ben Jonson, Lorna Hutson (Ed)
    (Penguin Books 1998)]
The Merchant of Venice – William
    Shakespeare, Jay L Halio (Ed)
    (Oxford Paperbacks 1998)
An Italian Journey – Jean Giono,
    J Cumming (Trans) (Northwestern
    University Press 1998)
Miss Garnet's Angel – Salley Vickers
    (HarperCollins 2001)
The City of Falling Angels– John Berendt
    (Companion Guides 1997)

OTHER GUIDES

Ghetto of Venice – Roberta Curiel,
    Bernard Dov Cooperman
    (Tauris Parke 1990)
Venice – Ian Littlewood
    (John Murray 1992)
Companion Guide to Venice – Hugh
    Honour (Companion Guides 1997)
Venice for Pleasure – JG Links
    (Pallas Athene 1999)
*The Stones of Florence and Venice
    Observed* – Mary McCarthy
    (Penguin Books 2000)
    Piazzale Roma

Films

Top Hat (1935).
    Ginger Rogers and Fred Astaire
    dancing cheek to cheek and hav-
    ing a good time in La Serenissima.
Summertime (1955)
    Romance sparks between Rossano
    Brazzi and Katharine Hepburn in
    Summertime. She falls in love and
    also into the canal (did her own
    stunt) at Campo San Barnaba!
From Russia with Love (1963)
    Sean Connery as James Bond goes
    to Murano in search of a particular
    glassmaker. An amphibious
    gondola scatters pigeons in
    St Mark's Square!

Death in Venice (1971)
    Based on the novella by Thomas
    Mann, Luchino Visconti directs
    Dirk Bogarde in the lead role;
    panoramic shots span the sultry
    lagoon and the Lido, particularly
    Hotel des Bains.
Don't Look Now (1973)
    This psychic thriller is based on
    a story by Daphne du Maurier.
    Nicholas Roeg directs Donald
    Sutherland and Julie Christie.
Casanova (1976)
    Fellini films the life and loves of the
    notorious Venetian rake.
Don Giovanni (1979)
    A beautiful adaptation of
    Mozart's opera, populated by
    masked figures stepping out of
    swirling mists from boats in the
    Brenta Valley.
*Indiana Jones and
    The Last Crusade* (1989)
    Indy jumps out of the library into
    Campo San Barnaba, in a cameo.
Blame it on the Bellboy (1992)
    Mistaken identity in this comedy
    of hotel errors set in Venice.
Carrington (1995)
    The painter, Dora Carrington
    (Emma Thompson) and the artist,
    Lytton Strachey (Jonathan Pryce)
    in WW1 England and on a visit to
    Venice.
Othello (1995)
    Directed by Oliver Parker, Laurence
    Fishburne as Othello and Kenneth
    Branagh as Iago play out their
    tragic Shakespearian roles.
Everyone Says I Love You (1996)
    Woody Allen directs and stars in
    the musical, set in New York, Venice
    (Scuola di San Rocco) and Paris.
Dangerous Beauty (1998)
    Intellectual and courtesan Victoria
    Franco in 16C Venice.
The Talented Mr. Ripley (1999)
    Anthony Minghella directs Matt
    Damon, Gwyneth Paltrow, Jude
    Law and Cate Blanchett, shot
    partly in Venice.
Pane e tulipani (Bread and Tulips)
    (2000)
    A portrait of the real Venice, inhab-
    ited by mildly eccentric characters.

The Italian Job (2003)
> This thriller begins with a bank heist in Venice, also is set in the Italian Alps.

Casino Royale (2006)
> As James Bond, Daniel Craig finds the usual mayhem including an entire palazzo demolished into the Grand Canal!

Brideshead Revisited (2008)
> Aristocratic memoirs, partly filmed in Venice, starring Emma Thompson, Michael Gambon and Greta Scacchi.

The Tourist (2010)
> The canal chase scenes are more intriguing than the lack of chemistry between Angelina Jolie and Johnny Depp.

Shun Li and the Poet (Io Sono Li) (2011)
> A delicate friendship between a Chinese immigrant and a poet fisherman, set in a bar and the silvery waters of Chioggia.

BASIC INFORMATION

Business Hours

SHOPS

Shops are generally open from 9am to 12.30/1pm and 1pm to 6pm, although many stay open during lunchtime. More shops are open in high season than in low season, and normally extend their business hours to accommodate the extra customers. Some businesses are closed on Mondays. *For bank opening times, see Money.*

MUSEUMS AND CHURCHES

The main churches in Venice are open 7am–noon and 4–6pm. Visitors should be dressed appropriately: long trousers for men; no bare shoulders or very short skirts for women. If you do not observe these conventions you may be refused entry. (Small change is useful for activating light time-switches).
Museum times and days vary considerably; some also close on Mondays.

Communications

The state telecommunication system is run by the **Compania Italiana Telecom (CIT)**. Telephone bureaux have banks of public telephones where customers pay for the line at the end of the trunk call (*Fondaco dei Tedeschi*).

Reduced rates for national calls apply after 6.30pm and between 10pm and 8am for international calls.

PUBLIC PHONES

Public telephone boxes are to be found along streets and in most bars. They may be operated by phone cards (*see below*) and by telephone credit cards. To make a call, lift the receiver, insert payment, await a dial tone, punch in the required number and wait for a reply.

PHONE CARDS

These are sold in various denominations supplied by CIT offices and post offices as well as tobacconists (*tabaccaio* sign bearing a white T on a black background).

DIALLING CODES

For calls **within Venice**, dial the correspondent's number, including the 041 prefix code for Venice.
For calls to **other towns in Italy**, dial the code for the town or district beginning with an 0, followed by the correspondent's number.
For **international calls** dial 00 followed by the country code:

+61 for Australia
+1 for Canada

+64 for New Zealand
+44 for the UK
+1 for the USA

The international code for Italy is +39, the code for Venice is 041 – note that you should no longer drop the first 0 of the area code.

INTERNET

Most good hotels (of 3-star status and above) will provide internet access to guests. There are relatively few other options, excluding occasional internet cafes around the city centre. The city has free wi-fi hot spots, which require registration (www.cittadinanzadigitale.it).

Electricity

The voltage is 220 ac, 50 cycles per second; the sockets are for two-pin plugs. It is advisable to take an adaptor for hair dryers, shavers, computers and other electrical equipment.

Emergencies

EMERGENCY NUMBERS

General Emergency Services (equivalent of UK 999, US 911): ☎112

Mail

In Italy post offices are open 8.30am–2pm (noon Sat and last day of the month). The main post offices are at the Fondaco dei Tedeschi and just off Piazza San Marco, behind the Napoleon Wing by the Correr museum. Letters sent **poste restante** (*fermo posta*) can be collected from the main post office. Stamps are sold in post offices and tobacconists (*tabaccheria*).

Money

The unit of currency is the **euro** which is issued in notes (€5, €10, €20, €50, €100, €200 and €500) and in coins (1 cent, 2 cents, 5 cents, 10 cents, 20 cents, 50 cents, €1 and €2).

BANKS

ATMs (Bancomat) are plentiful in Venice. Banks are usually open Monday to Friday, 8.30am–1.30pm and 2.30pm–4pm. Some branches open in the city centre and shopping centres on Saturday mornings, but most are closed on Saturdays, Sundays and public holidays. Some hotels will change travellers' cheques. Money can be changed in post offices, exchange bureaus and at railway stations and airports. Commission is always charged. Money withdrawn from Bancomat machines with a PIN incurs a lower commission charge than from a transaction in a bank.

CREDIT CARDS

Payment by credit card is widespread in shops, hotels and restaurants and at some petrol stations.

Pharmacies

A pharmacy (*farmacia*) is identified by a red or green and white cross. When it is closed, it will advertise the names of the nearest on-duty chemist and a list of doctors on call.

Public Holidays

Public holidays (*giorni festivi*) include Saturdays and Sundays.
- January:
  1 (New Year) and 6 (Epiphany)
- Easter: Sunday and Monday (*lunedì dell'Angelo*)
- April: 25 (St Mark's Day and liberation in 1945)
- May: 1
- August: 15 (Assumption – *Ferragosto*)
- November: 1

◆ December:
8 (Immaculate Conception),
25 and 26 (Christmas and
St Stephen's day).

A working day is a *giorno feriale*.

Reduced Rates

If you plan on visiting the interiors of
Venice's more important churches,
then it is sensible to obtain a **Chorus**
pass in advance from the **Associazione Chiese di Venezia,** San Polo, 298,
30125 Venezia, Italy (☎041 27 50 462;
www.chorusvenezia.org). This provides entry to 16 churches in Venice,
is valid for one year, and costs €10. As
admission to each individual church
administered by Chorus costs €3, you
will soon save money.

If you are a museum buff, consider
buying a **MUVE Friend Card** (€45,
valid 12 months) for entry to all Civic
Museums. For details, ☎041 427
30892; www.visitmuve.it.

Finally, if you wish to roll together
churches, museums and *all* other
sights, plus the option of transport,
then consider purchasing the **Venice
Card.** This offers discounts on a
number of tourist sights and facilities,
such as transport, public toilets, car
parks etc.

The Venice Card offers unlimited
use of public transport on land and
water, free admission to 13 museums
(including the Doges Palace), and
the 16 Chorus-group churches, plus
discounts on other admissions to
exhibitions and events. The card is
valid 7 days and costs €39.90. A Junior
Venice card, for anyone aged six to
29 costs €2.90. Another advantage of
the Venice Card is that you can bypass
queues. For further information on
ticket offices and to purchase on-line
visit www.hellovenezia.com.

Youth Discounts

For €4, young people aged 14 to 29
can purchase a **Rolling Venice** card,
which offers over 200 discounts at
participating youth hostels, campsites,
hotels, restaurants, university can-
teens, museums and shops, as well as
reduced rates for public transport and
the International Biennale of Art.
The card is available from tourist
offices and Hello Venezia outlets; visit
www.hellovenezia.com for a list.

Smoking

In line with the rest of Europe there is
a ban on smoking in all public places,
though some bars and cafes may have
areas where it is possible to smoke.

Taxes

As of 2011, as was instituted also in
Rome and Florence, even overnight
guests are now taxed, per person, per
night, which is applied for the first five
nights. Likewise, high and low seasons
have been completely redefined:
in 2013, Venice classified February
1-November 30 as high season.

Time

The time in Italy is the same as in the
rest of mainland Europe (one hour
ahead of the United Kingdom) and
changes during the last weekend
in March and October between
summer time (*ora legale*) and winter
time (*ora solare*).

Tipping

With the exception of tourist honeypots,
such as in and around the Piazza San
Marco and around the Rialto, Venice is
no more, nor any less tip-conscious than
any other European tourist-oriented city.
Restaurants often add a 12% service
charge and *coperto* (cover charge for
bread, pretzels etc) to the bill, in which
case there is no need to tip further.
Guides and taxi drivers will expect a tip
of around 10 per cent (though this is by
no means compulsory), porters, hotel
maids and toilet attendants should be
tipped a few coins.

USEFUL WORDS & PHRASES

Basic

si/no – yes/no
per favore – please
grazie – thank you
buongiorno –
    good morning
buona sera – good
    afternoon/evening
buona notte –
    goodnight
arrivederci – goodbye
scusi – excuse me
piccolo/un po' –
    small/a little
grande – large/big
meno – less
molto – much/very
più – more
basta! – enough!
quando? – when?
perché? – why?
perché – because
con/senza –
    with/without
l'aeroporto –
    the airport
la stazione –
    the station
un biglietto – a ticket
**una scheda per il
    telefono** –
    telephone card

Numbers

1	uno
2	due
3	tre
4	quattro
5	cinque
6	sei
7	sette
8	otto
9	nove
10	dieci
11	undici
12	dodici
13	tredici
14	quattordici
15	quindici
16	sedici
17	diciassette
18	diciotto
19	diciannove
20	venti
30	trenta
40	quaranta
50	cinquanta
60	sessanta
70	settanta
80	ottanta
90	novanta
100	cento
1 000	mille
2 000	duemila

Time

1.00 – l'una
1.15 – una e un quarto –
    one fifteen
1.30 – un' ora e mezzo
    – one thirty
1.45 – l'una e quaranta
    cinque – one
    forty-five
mattina – morning
pomeriggio –
    afternoon
sera – evening
ieri – yesterday
oggi – today
domani – tomorrow
una settimana – a
    week
lunedì – Monday
martedì – Tuesday
mercoledì –
    Wednesday
giovedì – Thursday
venerdì – Friday
sabato – Saturday
domenica – Sunday
inverno – winter
primavera – spring
estate – summer
autunno – autumn/fall

Food & Drink

un piatto – a plate
un coltello – a knife
una forchetta – a fork
un cucchiaio – a spoon
il cibo – food
un piatto vegetariano
    – a vegetarian dish
un bicchiere – a glass
**acqua minerale
    (gassata)** – mineral
    water (fizzy)
vino rosso – red wine
    (**bianco** – white)
una birra (alla spina) –
    a beer (draught)
carne – meat
manzo/vitello –
    beef/veal
maiale – pork
agnello – lamb
**prosciutto cotto
    (crudo)** – cooked
    ham (cured)
pollo – chicken
pesce – fish
    (**pesca** – peach)
uova – eggs
    (**uva** – grapes)
verdura –
    green vegetables
burro – butter
formaggio – cheese
un dolce – a dessert
frutta – fruit
zucchero – sugar
sale/pepe – salt/pepper
senape – mustard
olio/aceto – oil/vinegar
si puo visitare? –
    can one visit?

On the Road

il fiume – the river
un lago – a lake
un belvedere –
    a viewpoint
un bosco – a wood
l'autostrada – motorway
la patente –
    driving licence
un garage – repair garage
nel parcheggio –
    in the car park
benzina – petrol/gas
una gomma – a tyre
le luci – headlights
il parabrezza – the
    windscreen
il motore – the engine

Shopping

un negozio – a shop
la posta – a post office
francobolli – stamps
macellaio – a butcher's
farmacia – a chemist's
sciroppo per la tosse –
    cough mixture
pastiglie per la gola – throat pastilles
cerotto – sticking plaster
scottato dal sole – sunburn
mal di pancia – stomach-ache
mal di testa – headache
punture di zanzara/ape/vespa –
    mosquito bite/bee-/wasp-sting
il panificio – a baker's
pane (integrale) – bread (wholemeal)
un supermercato – a supermarket
un giornale – a newspaper
pescivendolo – a fishmonger

Sightseeing

si puo visitare? – can one visit?
chiuso/aperto – closed/open
destra/sinistra – right/left
nord/sud – north/south
est/ovest – east/west
la strada per ...? – the road for ...?
una vista – a view
al primo piano – on the first floor
tirare – pull
spingere – push
bussare – ring (the bell)
le luci – lights
le scale – stairs
l'ascensore – lift
i bagni per uomo/per donna – WC
    facilities men's/ladies'
**una camera singola/doppia/mat-
rimoniale** – a single room/with
    twin beds/double bed
con doccia/con bagno – with
    shower/bath
un giorno/una notte – one day/night

Urban Sites

la città – the town
una chiesa – a church
il duomo – the cathedral
una cappella – a chapel
il chiostro – the cloisters
la navata – the nave
il coro – the choir or chancel
il transetto – the transept
la cripta – the crypt
un palazzo – a town house or mansion

© Arcangelo Piai/Sime/
Photononstop

Cichèti, local sandwich with smoked ham

una casa – a house
un castello – a castle
un monastero/convento –
    an abbey/monastery
un cortile – a courtyard
un museo – a museum
una torre – a tower
un campanile – a belfry
una piazza – a square
un giardino – a garden
un parco – a park
una via/strada – a street/road
un ponte – a bridge
un molo – a pier or jetty
un cimitero – a cemetery
la barca – boat
il motoscafo – motor boat
la spiaggia – the beach
il mare – the sea
pericolo – danger
vietato – prohibited or forbidden

Useful Phrases

Parla inglese? – Do you speak
    English?
Entri! – Come in!
Non capisco – I do not understand
    Dov'è...? – Where's…?
Parli piano per favore – Please
    speak slowly
Dove sono i bagni? – Where are the
    toilets?
**A che ora parte il treno/l'autobus/
l'aereo...?** – At what time does
    the train/bus/plane leave?
A che ora arriva il treno...? – At
    what time does the train… arrive?
Quanto costa? – How much does
    it cost?
**Dove posso comprare un giornale
inglese?** – Where can I buy an
    English newspaper?
Dove posso cambiare i miei soldi? –
    Where can I change my money?
**Posso pagare con una carta di
credito?** – May I pay with a
    credit card?

Piazzetta San Marco and Palazzo Ducale from the lagoon
© Silvio Verrecchia / iStockphoto

NATURE

The mainland of Italy reaches out a finger towards Venice, and the gap is spanned by the Ponte della Libertà (Bridge of Liberty). Otherwise, the coast's ominous profile cast in reflection across the Venetian lagoon is that of industrial developments at Mestre and Porto Marghera. These have grown around the ageless waters of the Brenta Naviglio, which flow peacefully into the lagoon at Malcontenta. The modern Tessera Airport and the prettified Jesolo beach huts betray the affluence of tourism.

The Veneto

This area comprises mainly the vast alluvial Po Delta and its tributaries which are overlooked in the north by the Venetian Pre-Alps, and further north again in the **Cadore** district by the western massifs of the Dolomites. The highly-eroded limestone massif of the **Dolomites** extends across the Veneto and Trentino-Alto Adige. The Cadore is an agricultural region growing wheat, maize, mulberry bushes, olives, fruit trees and vines. The industrial sector includes oil refineries, smelting works and chemical plants which are concentrated in the vicinity of Venice at Mestre-Marghera, as well as a large production of hydroelectric energy in the valleys of the Pre-Alps. The latter supplies the textile industry.

The landscape is punctuated by two small volcanic groups, the **Berici Mountains** south of Vicenza and the **Euganean Hills** near Padua. The slopes of these blackish heights support vines and peach orchards, and there are several hot springs.

In the **Po Delta** and that of the Adige lie impoverished and desolate areas, subject to flooding. Following reclamation certain areas are farmed on an industrial scale for wheat and sugar beet. The coastline takes the form of lagoons (*lagune*) separated from the sea by spits of sand pierced by gaps (*porti*). It is one of these lagoons that both provides and threatens the survival of Venice.

The Venetian Lagoon

The Venetian Lagoon extends over an area of 550sq km/213sq mi, making it the largest in Italy. It was formed at the end of the Ice Age by the convergence of flooded rivers, swollen by melted snow from the Alps and Apennines.

Today it provides a natural and complex habitat to wetland flora and fauna between the Cavallino coast to the northeast and the Lido and Chioggia to the southwest. Water levels are maintained by the sea: its tides constitute both an ever-present threat to the delicate make-up of the Venetian Lagoon while also providing its regular safeguard from stagnation. The sea merges with the canals' fresh water through three channels (**bocche di porto**) by the Lido, at Chioggia and Malamocco, where dikes were installed during the 19C and 20C.

A few lagoon terms

Bacino scolante: earth that carries rain and river water into the lagoon.

Barene: sandbanks protruding from the water and immersed at high tide.

Bricole: groups of colourful wooden masts roped together which mark out canals fit for navigation.

Ghebi: tiny canals that meander their way across the sandbanks.

Punto zero: standard reference for measuring the water level in the lagoon, established by the Punta della Salute tide gauge. The levels are usually 23cm/9.3in higher than the average sea level.

Valli da pesca: diked stretches of the lagoon set aside for fishing.

Velme: small strips of land which, unlike the *barene*, can be seen only at low tide, when they appear on the surface.

AN AGE-OLD PROBLEM

In the 12C, Europe enjoyed a long period of mild weather followed by a noticeable rise in temperature; then came torrential rains that caused high tides and flooding. The **River Brenta** broke its banks and water flooded a large part of the lagoon, depositing silt, mud and detritus. Malaria broke out. The Republic of Venice tried to defend itself by placing palisades along the coast, diverting the course of the rivers and building great dikes, but the lagoon continued to pose a threat. Over the ensuing centuries (15C–17C), major drainage programmes were implemented that affected the River Brenta, River Piave, River Livenza and River Sile. In 1896 the operation aimed at diverting the waters of the Brenta was finally completed, channelling them into the mouth of the Bacchiglione. Despite these measures, as water levels continue to rise and fall, the sand deposited in the lagoon by the rivers is buffeted back inland by the sea and the wind. Thus the sandbanks are formed and strengthened. All the while, caught between marine erosion and the rebuilding action of the rivers, the fate of Venice itself is at stake: after more than 1 000 years of existence, the city is slowly sinking.

The Venetian Lagoon can be likened to a sophisticated system that has achieved a subtle balance between excessive **sedi-**

Why do tides occur?

Gravitational forces caused by the earth's rotation around the sun and its relation to the moon are responsible for tides. Being nearer the earth, the moon exerts the greater force over changes in liquid levels and the movement of the oceans and seas. The strength of this force is affected by air pressure and winds. In the case of Venice, the greatest floods have always followed major sirocco storms. When the moon passes over the meridian of an area, it causes a high tide; when it is at 90º to that meridian, it produces a low tide. When the earth, moon and sun are aligned, the tide reaches its maximum levels.

mentation (leading to the emergence of "new" land) and **erosion** (in which the deposits carried by the sea and rivers are so scarce that a stretch of lagoon can turn into a stretch of sea). This is precisely the risk currently threatening the lagoon. About one quarter of the lagoon surface is rendered unnavigable by the existence of sandbanks or **barene**. Their importance is huge: they encourage the proliferation of a great many animal and vegetal species while attracting sediments that might otherwise be scattered in the water, contributing to reducing the swell.

© Guido Alberto Rossi / Tips Images

Aerial view of the island of San Francesco del Deserto surrounded by the lagoon

About 4 000ha/15sq mi are taken up by the large inhabited islands and smaller, deserted ones, leaving another 40 000ha/155sq mi occupied by water. Anyone surprised at seeing how shallow a Venetian canal may be when drained of its water (from an average of 1–2m/3–7ft to a maximum depth of 8–10m/26–33ft) will understand why the seabed of the open lagoon is often exposed at low tide. Despite this lack of depth, which gives the lagoon its millpond appearance, a complex network of crisscrossed channels maintains currents and easy movement. Navigable areas are marked by lone wooden posts or groups of poles roped together, known as **bricole**. The deepest channels are those nearest the mouths of the ports, and as the distance from the sea increases, these rivulets become shallower and narrower (**ghebi**), dwindling across the sandbanks before disappearing into *chiari*, basins where salt water and rainwater mingle.

TIDES

Tidal changes occur every six hours, fluctuating between two high points per day. Low atmospheric pressure and the sirocco and bora winds are known to accentuate high tide, whereas high atmospheric pressure and northwesterly winds tend to bring on a low tide. In this case, some of the rivers may dry up. Sea water is thereby drawn into the lagoon through the three ports, flushing "new" water in and "old" water out, assisted by a current from the rivers on the opposite side. Parts affected by these tides are therefore known as the "living" lagoon, whereas sections little affected by this lifeline are referred to as the "dead" lagoon. These outlying parts tend towards marsh, channelled with canals, *ghebi* between fishing banks and diked lakes built by and for the fishing industry.

The health of the lagoon is totally dependent upon the influx of "new" water brought by the tides. However, the inflow of fresh water provided by the rivers that once maintained saline levels has been greatly reduced as the rivers have progressively been diverted. This diversion has also reduced the strength of current across the lagoon and allowed vast quantities of polluting material to be deposited.

In the 20C the problem was exacerbated by the growth of industrial sites around Mestre and Porto Maghera and the accommodation of petrol tankers, with obvious implications on the environment of the lagoon. The reduction in oxygenated water flowing through the canals of Venice is gradually eroding the ability of plant and marine life to survive. Only those organisms with short life cycles have had time to adapt,

Tourists walking on the raised platform to avoid the flooding on the pavement overlooking Bacino di San Marco

© Chris Kewish / World Illustrated / Photoshot

and so quantities of macroalgae (*ulva rigida*) and insects (mosquitoes and the like) have increased at a fantastic rate. The tide along the coasts can fluctuate wildly; for it to be classified as tidal flooding, its level has to reach or exceed 1.10m/3ft 6in. The last such occurrence happened on 4 November 1966 when consequences were felt way beyond the shores of Venice: the Arno overflowed in Florence, with tragic results. That year an alarming prediction said that Venice might possibly disappear. Fortunately, radical action against further subsidence, including the closure of artesian wells on the mainland (1975), has proved the prophecy false.

Similar crises of this kind are documented as far back as 589. Contemporary personal accounts are terrifying. **Paolo Diacono** (c.720–799) wrote of the first flood tide: *"non in terra neque in aqua sumus viventes"* (neither on earth nor in water were we alive). Records from 1410 state that "almost one thousand people coming from the fair at Mestre and other places drowned".

Since the 17C the water level of the Venetian Lagoon has dropped by 60cm/24in. In past centuries, once every five years, the tide would rise above the damp-proof foundations made of Istrian stone that were built to protect the houses against salt deposits. Nowadays, in the lower areas, these foundations are immersed in water more than 40 times in a single year and the buildings can do very little to stall the degradation process.

Venice, victim of the tides

On 4 November 1966 the mareograph at Punta della Salute registered an exceptionally high tide of 1.94m/6ft. Medium to high tides usually reach a level of around 70cm/28in, flooding the Piazza San Marco and, with a further 30cm/12in, even narrow alley streets would be inundated. Between December and February the city can be the scene of very low tides indeed, estimated at less than 90cm/36in. In 2012 acqua alta reached its fourth-highest level in recent history, 1.40 m.

At the end of the 18C, when the first part of the Riva degli Schiavoni promenade was completed, Venetian magistrates

ordered that the letter "C" be engraved on the city houses and their foundations. The letter was to indicate the average level of the highest-known tides. However, today it is difficult to spot these inscriptions since most of them are located under the level of the sea.

Venice in Peril

Flooding

The Centro Previsioni e Segnalazioni Maree provides warnings of impending danger and information on forecasts and tide tables. Tidal flooding tends to occur between April and December, and forecast warnings are issued about 48 hours in advance. Details are published in the *Gazzettino* and posted up on the landing stages of the vaporettos. Should the level threaten to exceed 1.10m/3ft 7in, 16 sirens sound five times for 10 seconds each time, three or four hours in advance of the high point.

Should high tide not exceed 1.20m/ 3ft 11in, the **AMAV** (Azienda Multiservizio Ambientale Venezia) sees to the laying of footbridges along prescribed routes. However, if the water level goes above this limit, then footbridges can become dangerous because they start to float. In the case of tidal flooding, the AMAV is unable to maintain its principal function (rubbish collection), because its boats are no longer able to pass

What is an insula?

In the lagoon city, an *insula* is a tiny piece of territory which is circumscribed by a river or a canal. These *insule* are therefore linked to each other by a network of bridges. A small cluster of them is said to form a *sestiere*, one of Venice's six administrative divisions.

Marine Parade

The external surface of a **bricola** seems literally corroded by crustaceans, whereas within, bivalvular molluscs called *teredini* have taken up residence. Closest to the surface and buffeted by the tides are live crustaceans (*balani*) and green algae. Below, in calmer currents, live mussels (*mitili*). The submerged part is the kingdom of the sponges: the tube-shaped *ascidie* and the *hydrozoans*.

under the bridges. It is therefore made responsible for laying down emergency footbridges. Meanwhile, the Venetian Municipality requests the population to just hang on to their household waste! In the UK, Venice in Peril (The British Committee for the Preservation of Venice) can help with forecasts and the latest news, ☎020 7736 6891, www.veniceinperil.org.

High tide, which is announced by the rather sinister sound of the sirens, floods the lowest-lying parts of the city not only by bursting the banks of St Mark's Basin and the canals and rivers of the city, but also by gushing out of the drains, cracks and manhole covers in Venice's streets and squares.

Today's concerns

In the past, land and water were clearly separated, with the lagoon acting as a link between the two, drawing on both to produce life and movement. However, the presence of factories, farms and areas inhabited by man have gradually changed the face of the *gronda*, the sloped land licking at the lagoon shores. Today, the lagoon has reached a sort of "standstill": it takes two weeks for waste material to leave the lagoon and end up in the open sea. Every year more than 1million m³/35.3million cu ft of solid matter is lost. Erosion, the sediments lost in the water, and the rising level of the sea all contribute to lowering the lagoon depths. This phenomenon is threatening the sandbanks known as **barene**, which are doomed to disappear by the year 2050 if drastic action is not taken to remedy the situation.

Water fluctuations and land subsidence

Variations in the level of the water are referred to as *eustatismo*. In the course of the last century, this phenomenon caused the waters of Venice to rise by 8cm/3.2in. This rise has led to dire consequences, aggravated by the effects of local subsidence, causing the land to drop, representing around 15cm/6.2in for the same period. Therefore, the city of Venice has "sunk" by around 23cm/9.2in since the end of the 19C.

Erosion

Erosion is the result of a number of factors: higher water levels, subsidence, digging for artificial canals, and the swell, which slowly increases while the seabed slumps and the sandbanks dwindle.

Pollution

Finally, to crown this somewhat pessimistic picture, pollution is responsible for the destruction of phanerogamic flora, invaluable sea-water plants whose roots serve to prevent erosion and stabilise the seabed. Water pollution has also killed the algae and other marine varieties which once thrived on sandbanks and mudflats and which are no longer able to attract sediments.

Tackling the problem

The risk of losing Venice through both tides and progressive de-population is so great that the Italian State has declared the salvation of the city to be a question of "pre-eminent national interest". The residents of Venice appear to be particularly concerned about high-to-medium tides, which cause flooding of the city. Consequently, a number of projects currently being examined or implemented are aimed at making these inhabited areas far safer. It is a highly delicate and complex situation: the town of Venice and the myriad islands are home to many buildings, monuments and works of art which cohabit in perfect harmony but, technically speaking, require different forms of intervention. On the San Marco and Tolentini islands, the stability of paved streets, bridges and houses was meticulously checked, as well as that of underground passages and sewage drains. In the lower sections, the paving has been raised (as is clearly visible on Campo San Zanipòlo) and the shores of the lagoon consolidated to cope more efficiently against tides below 100cm/40in (120cm/48in in Chioggia).

A project is under way to deal with exceptionally high tides by placing mobile barriers at the three entrances to the port. A prototype of this system, the MoSE (Experimental Electronic Module) comprises a huge mobile sluice-gate devised to regulate the movement of the tides. It was tested along the Canale di Treporti facing the Lido from 1988–1992. It is thought that the final project would need to provide 79 of these sluice-gates.

In the Experimental Centre for Hydraulic Models, at Voltabarozzo, near Padua, a simulated mock-up of the lagoon area allows studies to be carried out into projects for the harbour mouths, the safeguarding of the coastal region and of the jetties.

In the meantime, reconstruction of the coastal region of Cavallino and Pellestrina is being carried out. The coastal area has been consolidated with 2million m³/70.6 million cu ft of sand taken from the sea. These deposits were also used to reinforce sandbanks, which play a crucial role as they combat the swell and local winds while protecting the environment. In an attempt to increase their stability, these coastal dunes have been planted with *ammofila*, a variety of grass that thrives on sandy soil.

The north pier at Chioggia has been strengthened, 50km/31mi of canals have been dredged and the sediment obtained through this operation used to rebuild 300ha/740 acres of sandbanks. The restoration of sandbanks is achieved by fencing off a stretch of the lagoon with wooden masts. A large canvas sheet is then fixed to the poles and laid down over the sea depths. Sediments are poured into this artificial basin as well as water, which is then filtered by the canvas.

Further operations currently under way involve cleaning up the lagoon waters, gathering the macroalgae and salvaging the smaller islands such as Lazzaretto Vecchio.

The fight to save Venice

In 1966, the year in which record water levels were registered in Venice, UNESCO stressed the urgency of the fight to save this beautiful city and her lagoon. A number of organisations and committees, both public and private, were set up to salvage and restore Venice's cultural heritage, namely the **Ufficio per la Salvaguardia di Venezia**. The Head of the Monuments and Fine Arts Department is involved in the technical aspects of this undertaking and UNESCO oversees the allocation of funds raised by several private committees. Every year millions of euros are spent on rescue operations aimed at preserving the architectural, historical and artistic treasures of the city, as well as on scholarships for artisans and research. Each of these committees is directly

---

Fishing Areas

Known as **valli da pesca**, these stretches of the lagoon are used for fishing, taking into consideration the migratory movements of the fish. Because they have been diked, they are not exposed to the ebbing of the water. During the spring season, the fish (mainly eel, sea bass and gilt-head bream) congregate in the lagoon, attracted by the organic vegetation brought along by rivers and mountain waters after the thaw.

In winter, when weather conditions are especially harsh, the fish try to swim back towards the sea, but on reaching the **chiaveghe** (structures with bulkheads built to regulate the flow of the sea water) they are caught and sorted by traditional methods. Among the various nets used for fishing, two in particular stand out: the *bilancione*, a huge trawl net suspended from four tall piers, and the *cogolo*, a cylindrical net consisting of several parts, ending in a cone.

concerned with a specific project on a regular basis. Among the many foreign organisations dedicated to saving Venice, the most important are **The Venice in Peril Fund** (Great Britain, www.veniceinperil.org/), **Save Venice** (United States, www.savevenice.org, **Comité Français pour la Sauvegarde de Venise** (France, www.cfsvenise.org).

LIFE FORMS

The lagoon comprises a vast and rich habitat for fauna and flora, part of which may even be glimpsed from the vaporetto between Venice and Burano or from a car driving through the section enclosed by the Cavallino coast. The best way, however, to appreciate the extent of vegetation and animal life thriving in this "watery plain" is to explore the sandbanks by boat.

The waters of the lagoon vary in salt concentration depending on their proximity to the river outlets, where the water is almost fresh. In the middle they tend to be brackish; near the ports, where the tides inject sea water, they are far saltier. At the same time, areas around the river deltas tend to be muddy, whereas by the port mouths the lagoon bed is sandy.

Fauna

At the lower end of the food chain, different types of **molluscs** breed successfully on the wooden piles or *bricole*.

The principal category is undoubtedly that of the **fish kingdom**, which has defined the very character of the lagoon, with its distinctive collection in shoals around sandbanks, and the interaction of human beings with this environment as they seek to exploit such rich resources.

Crab and shrimp are central to the fishing industry and to Venetian cuisine. From a boat it soon becomes obvious where the fishing banks are situated as these attract various species of aquatic birds: wild duck (mallard and teal), tens of thousands of coots, herons and marsh harriers. Besides the common sparrows, swallows and blackbirds, the Venetian Lagoon is visited by special migratory birds, often with highly coloured plumage.

It is perhaps their beauty, strangeness and cleverness that is most fascinating: the black-whiskered bearded tit clings to the reeds; the reed warbler builds a floating nest between four reeds, which rises and falls with the tide; the kingfisher dives acrobatically and the moorhen nods her head in time to the rhythm of her strokes; little grebe pop out of the water only to dive quickly and silently below the surface again and emerge where least expected.

The very rich **bird life** of the lagoon also includes the cormorant, the inevitable sea-gull, the sea swallow, whose whirling wings and V-shaped tail allow it to swoop effortlessly time and again, and the little egret, recognisable by its elegant carriage and startlingly white feathers with which women adorned themselves at the beginning of the 20C. Even more beautiful is the black-winged stilt, whose sombre wings contrast with its white body and the red of its long legs; its thin, distinguished beak adds a touch of refinement.

Elegance seems to be a trait shared by all the birds of the lagoon, among which the mute swan must reign supreme.

There are numerous marsh harriers and hen harriers among the birds of prey.

Among the mammals, the rodent provides a somewhat harmful presence. The rat, the so-called *pantagena*, is at home anywhere, on the city squares as well as in rubbish dumps and attics.

Flora

The **sandbanks** are abundantly cloaked in vegetation: glasswort, sea lavender and asters turn the mounds first green, then red, then blue, then grey. Rooted in the water are various reeds

---

Sluice-gates

These ambitious structures should be placed side by side to form a floating barrier linked to the seabed, rising and falling with the movement of the waves. Each gate, 20–30m/66–98ft long, 20m/66ft wide and 3–5m/10–16ft thick, contains compressed air controlled by valves, which enables the gate to be lowered.

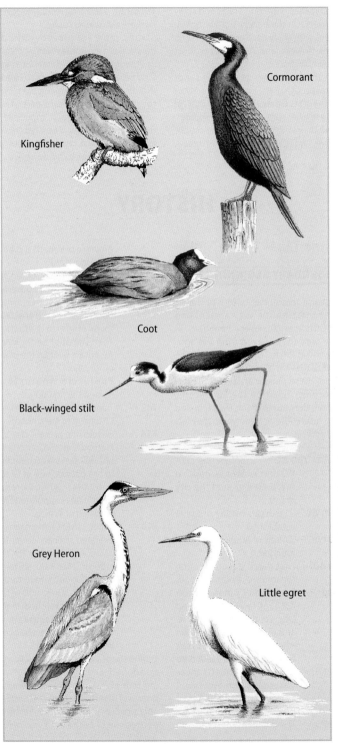

Kingfisher

Cormorant

Coot

Black-winged stilt

Grey Heron

Little egret

and rushes with long stalks and spiky flowers. On the beaches grow convolvulus with shiny dark-green leaves and pink flowers, and sea rocket with its violet blooms.

On the first dunes of shifting sands grows couch grass, a perennial member of the grass family. Farther back, tufts of coarse grass sprout among the spurges, with their long stalks of small lancet-like leaves and flowers with yellowish bracts.

Tall bushy *gramineae* (*erianthus ravennae*) are also widely found.

Shrubs and trees grow beyond the dunes: along the Romea highway, south of Chioggia, between Santa Anna and Cavanella d'Adige, is the Bosco Nordio (Nordio Wood) of evergreen oaks. Even the market gardens form part of the vegetation of the lagoon, especially in the south at Chioggia, where red chicory (*radicchio*) is grown, highly prized but not as famous as the *radicchio* of Treviso.

HISTORY

Time Line

LEGENDARY BEGINNINGS

It seems reasonable to turn to Homer when tracing the very ancient and uncertain origins of the Venetians. In the *Iliad* they arrived from Paflagonia to aid Priam. They were called the **Enetii**. Having abandoned their native land, these people arrived in the territory occupied by the Eugeneans, whom they put to flight. They founded the future Altino, from where they left for Torcello.

1000–700 BC — The Venetian civilisation known as *atestino* is founded around the city of Este.

530 BC — Etruscan colony of Spina established.

181 BC — Colony of Aquileia is founded.

42 AD — First dated documentation regarding the port of Altino.

400 — From Padua, Altino, Concordia Sagittaria, Aquileia and Oderzo, the future inhabitants of Venice visit the lagoon solely for its provisions of salt and fish. In the 6C Cassiodoro (c.490–583) requests these watermen, fishermen and salt-workers to help supply Ravenna.

568 — The Lombards descend into Italy. The Roman-Byzantine province of Venetia is gradually conquered.

639 — Oderzo, the capital of Venetia, falls. The Byzantine governor moves to Cittanova, which takes the name **Heracleia**, from Emperor Heraclius. The Church of Santa Maria Assunta is built on the island of Torcello.

697 — **Paoluccio Anafesto** is named the first doge.

742 — Transfer of the ducal seat from Cittanova to Malamocco.

775 — Olivolo, the present-day San Pietro di Castello, becomes a bishop's see. It is accountable to the patriarchate of Grado until 1451, when Lorenzo Giustinian is appointed First Patriarch of Venice.

810 — Pepin, son of Charlemagne, is defeated after an attempted invasion of Dalmatia and the lagoon. Many inhabitants of the lagoon move to the Realtine Islands, where the dogate is established. In 811 **Agnello Partecipazio** or "Particiaco" is elected doge. **Venice is born.**

During the 9C, when the dogeship was transferred, and for the three following centuries, Venice was made up of dozens of islands. The city was considerably smaller than it is today, however, because most of the land was below sea level.

VENICE THROUGH THE CENTURIES

- 7C
- to 9C
- to 11C
- to mind 12C
- to 16C

THE INDEPENDENT CITY, RULER OF THE ADRIATIC

814 — With the **Pax Nicephori (Treaty of Nicephorus)**, Charlemagne cedes his claims to the lagoon, and Venice guarantees her neutrality throughout the political struggles that were to rage in Italy during the eras of feudalism and the intercity state rivalry.

828 — The body of St Mark is stolen from Alexandria in Egypt and brought to Venice, where work begins on the construction of the first basilica the following year.

829 — In his will Doge Giustiniano Particiaco calls for the construction of **San Marco**, which was to become the ducal chapel.

840 — In the **Pactum Lotarii** (Peace of Lothar) the Byzantine ruler confirms the autonomy of Venice and assures her navy the control of the seas.

946 or 948 — Narentine Slav pirates carry out the legendary abduction of the maidens (&see SAN ZACCARIA).

976 — The Venetians rebel against the repressive **Doge Pietro Candiano IV**, who chooses to ignore the maritime power base of Venice and instead engages foreign troops to conquer territories on the mainland, in order to enhance his own political standing and reputation. This provokes a fierce popular revolt culminating in the murder of the Doge (&see box, next page). Fire damages St Mark's, the Doges' Palace and San Teodoro, destroying more than 300 houses, at the time built almost exclusively of wood.

Pietro Orseolo I is elected doge at **San Pietro di Castello**.

1000 — After defeating the Croats and the Narentines, Venice assumes her role as ruler and protector of Dalmatia with

976: an witness account

Seized with panic, the doge, his wife and their young son sought safety by heading to the entrance of St Mark's. There they were stopped by noblemen. Pietro's promises to accept any compromise were of no avail. *"Affirming that he was... deserving of death, they shouted... that there could be no salvation for him. They immediately surrounded him and cruelly ran him through with the points of their swords so that his immortal spirit abandoned his bodily prison in search of the retreat of the blessed"*. John Julius Norwich adds that, *"for what we know of Pietro Candiano IV, this happy final destination is somewhat improbable"*.

the title *dux Dalmatinorum* (Duke of Dalmatia).

1032 — The Venetians' strong spirit of independence precipitated a dislike for any government that resembled a monarchy and so, to avoid such a danger, the power of the doge is "split" between two ducal councillors, each one responsible for half of the city, with the Grand Canal as the dividing line.

11C — In the second half of the century the new Basilica of St Mark is built, modelled upon the Basilica of the Apostles at Constantinople.

1081 — Venice defends Byzantium from attack by the Norman Robert Guiscard.
The following year, the **Crisobollo** issued by the Byzantine Emperor, Alessio I Comneno, allows Venetians to trade freely throughout the empire and to open shops in Constantinople without having to pay duty on their goods.

1099 — Venice defeats the Pisans near Rhodes, where the Venetian and Pisan fleets are taking part in the Crusades. The released Pisan prisoners undertake not to haunt the waters of Byzantium.

1104 — The first nucleus of the Arsenal is created.
The following year the city is ravaged by fire.

1122–24 — Under the dogeship of **Domenico Michiel**, Venice attacks and defeats the Egyptian fleet that was besieging Jaffa, taking possession of the merchant ships and their cargo of treasure trove and spices. She then goes on to participate in the victorious siege of Tyre, and the sacking of Byzantine ports in the Aegean and the Adriatic. These shows of force were crucial in restoring the reputation and political status enjoyed by the city before the King of Hungary had affirmed his power in Dalmatia, and in persuading the current Byzantine Emperor, **Giovanni Comneno**, to accept the fundamental independence of the city, recognised by his predecessors.

1143 — The **Council of the Wise Men**, or *Consilium Sapientium*, is already in existence by this date. Thought to have consisted of 35 members presided over by the doge, this organisation was to evolve into the Great Council.

1145–53 — Istria, already protected by Venice, now finds herself totally subjugated as the doge is proclaimed *totius Istriæ dominator*.

1171 — Emergency measures are implemented by the Eastern Empire angered by the plundering of their trade ships by Venetian, Genoese and Pisan navies. The disastrous expedition of **Doge Vitale Michiel II**, whose crew was decimated by the plague, is judged very harshly by the Venetians, and leads to his murder. His successor, **Sebastiano Ziani** (1172), is elected under a system similar to that which later (1268) was sanctioned by law and lasted into the following centuries.

During the dogeship of Vitale Michiel II, the six **sestieri** are created as subdivisions of the city, thereby facilitating the collection of taxes.

1175 — Construction of a wooden Rialto Bridge.

1177 — It is in Venice that **Pope Alexander III** and **Federico Barbarossa** end the conflict between the city states and their antagonists, the Church and the Swabian Empire. According to legend, this is the occasion that saw Alexander III donate his ring in the Marriage of the Sea (🕯 see box below)

1178 — Eleven men are nominated to elect the 40 electors of the doge, including six ducal councillors – one for each sestiere.

1201–04 — **Fourth Crusade**. Doge **Enrico Dandolo**, a man of extraordinary energy despite being 90 and blind, attacks **Constantinople** (1203), which succumbs decisively to a second assault the following year. The Eastern Latin Empire is formed under an emperor nominated by six Venetians and six crusader barons. Spoils and lands are divided between the emperor, who took a quarter of the empire, the barons and the Venetians. Recognition is given to the doge's lordship

Venetian Justice

Vitale Michiel's assassin found refuge among the houses around San Zaccaria. The complicity of the Venetians in that area was severely punished: their houses were destroyed and the construction of any building in stone was prohibited. This law was eventually abolished in 1948.

over "a quarter and a half of the empire".

13C — Around 1220 the **Quarantia**, a bench of 40 magistrates with judicial powers, is formed as part of the Great Council.

1240 — Venice besieges Ferrara, thus securing commercial control of the Po Valley.

1255 — First dated documentation about the **Pregadi**, who are charged (*pregati*) with expressing opinions and fulfilling particular duties as members of the **Senate**. The Council of the Pregadi is appointed by the Great Council, to deal with questions of navigation and international politics, thus assuming both legislative and executive functions.

1257–70 — Venice enters into conflict with Genoa. The Venetians defeat the Genoese at Acre, from where they brought the **Acrean pillars** now in front and to the right of the basilica.

The Eastern Latin Empire falls when the Byzantine Emperor, **Michele Paleologo III**, an

The Marriage with the Sea

According to one version of the legend, a fisherman obtained the "wedding ring" from St Mark on the night that Satan threatened to destroy Venice with a storm. Another legend relates that on Ascension Day, the doge solemnly proclaimed from the *Bucintoro* (state barge), in Latin *"We wed you, o sea, as a sign of true and perpetual dominion"*, casting a gold ring into the sea as he spoke. The ceremony began outside St Mark's, where the procession rallied before continuing on to the fort of San Andrea near the Lido. There the ring was cast into the sea. On his return, the doge stopped at San Nicolò on the Lido to attend Mass.

Departure of the Bucentaur on Ascension Day by Francesco Guardi (Musée du Louvre)

ally of the Genoese, takes possession of Constantinople. The Genoese are subsequently bound by treaty (1270) to Louis IX of France, who needs the Genoese fleet for the Crusades.

1268 — New rules are drafted for the election of the doge. The Great Council has first to nominate the **Council of Forty**, charged with electing the next doge, by means of a 10-stage process of elections and drawing lots. The first doge appointed in this way is **Lorenzo Tiepolo**.

El Paron de la Repubblica

The **Great Council** held a quintessential position at the heart of the Venetian Republic, since it carried out all the duties of state. Not only did it pass laws, it also had the power to select the most important people in Venice. When it met in the chamber of the Doges' Palace, the doge would preside from the centre of the Tribunale or Bench of St Mark, while nobles seated upon armchairs would line the walls or fill rows of parallel benches down the length of the room.

1284 — The **gold ducat** is minted, equal in weight and gold content to the Florentine florin, which had been in circulation for 30 years (0.997g gold per 3.55g coin). The gold ducat was accepted currency until the fall of the Republic. When silver ducats were struck in 1561 the gold ducat became known as the *zecchino*.

1294–99 — Venice is once more at war with Genoa. At the **Battle of Curzola** (1298) the victorious Genoese sustain grievous losses. The treaty signed in 1299 sanctions the Genoese dominance over the Riviera and that of the Venetians over the Adriatic.

1297 — This is the year of the **Locking of the Great Council**, a reform that considerably increased the number of council members to more than 1 000, as well as tightening up the system for their selection. Current as well as former members have to conform to rigorous procedures. By 1323, nomination is standardised, membership is for life and passed down the

Lion's mouth (Palazzo Ducale)

© E. Zane / MICHELIN

Bocca di Leone

The "lions' mouths" or "mouths of truth" (*see the example opposite*) were found along the streets or in the walls of public buildings. These lion-head masks were set with fierce expressions. The mouth was carved hollow to accommodate anonymous denunciations posted to the State. These denunciations were taken into account only if two witnesses were cited.

generations. Later still, the Great Council degenerates into a corps for the Venetian nobility.

1308–13 — Venice, dissatisfied with the duty levied on all the goods travelling through the Po Valley and wishing to consolidate its power over the area, attacks Ferrara. **Pope Clement V**, keen to defend his right of sovereignty over the city, issues from Avignon an **interdict** on Venice, which lasts until 1313.

1310 — **Baiamonte Tiepolo**, a Venetian nobleman, tries to depose Doge Pietro Gradenigo. The revolt is suppressed with much bloodshed, and prompts the creation of a remarkable judicial body known as the **Council of Ten**, whose prime function is to protect constitutional institutions. Presided over by the doge, this body consisted of 10 members of the Senate and six wise men. It employed the service of secret police and informers to investigate suspicious citizens and deal with denunciations and charges of libel against the State posted in the **lions' mouths**.

1321 — The poet **Dante Alighieri** stays in Venice in his capacity as ambassador to the Lords of Ravenna.

1347–48 — A Venetian galley introduces the **plague** from Crimea, which was to decimate the densely populated city (over 100 000 inhabitants) by three-fifths.

1350–55 — The conflict with Genoa continues.

In 1350, Venice is troubled by heavy traffic that often causes serious accidents; it is established that horses should be provided with "bell-collars to warn pedestrians of their passage".

DOGESHIP OF MARINO FALIER (1354–55)

Marino Falier was 80 when he was elected doge. Irascible and resentful, he began his dogeship under the worst of omens. The day he arrived in Venice, the **bucintoro**, the grandiose dogal barge, decorated with friezes and gold carvings, could not draw alongside its mooring because of fog; secondly, on arriving on the piazza, the doge entered the palace by passing between the two columns where outlaws were executed; lastly, he was offended by insults about his wife scrawled on his chair by a young boy. Falier became even more viperish when he found out how lightly the culprit had been punished.

He decided to mete out punishment and exact his revenge by plotting murder on those members of the nobility whom he thought had betrayed him. The conspiracy was exposed in time. The doge was accused of treason and sentence passed for his execution. A black-draped portrait in the chamber of the Great Council, recording his unhappy rule, bears a defamatory but accurate inscription. (☙see *PIAZZA SAN MARCO: Palazzo Ducale*). The story of Marino Falier inspired both Byron and Swinburne (who both wrote works bearing the same title: *Marino Falier*), Donizetti (*Marin Falier*) and Delacroix.

1358 — Dalmatia or *"Schiavonia"* is ceded to Hungary.

1378–81 — A fourth offence is mounted by the Venetians against Genoa to liberate Chioggia from Genoese and then Paduan hands.

1386 — Corfu comes under Venetian rule.

1389–1420 — Venice gradually gains dominion over a vast territory corresponding, more or less, to the present areas of Veneto and Friuli.

1409 — Venice regains possession of Dalmatia.

1410 — Venice is badly hit by a high tide.

1424 — Building begins on the Ca' d'Oro.

1425–54 — During the dogeship of **Francesco Foscari**, by now head of an oligarchic system (since 1423 the formula had been dropped which had once required the popular approval of the new doge; "If it is pleasing to you"), Venice is at war with the Lombards. **Carmagnola** takes part in the battles and, suspected of treason, is condemned by the Council of Ten to be beheaded between the columns of the Piazzetta. After three decades of battle, Venetian territory stretches as far as the River Adda.

In 1428 Venice is devastated by an exceptionally high tide.

1463–79 — The capture of the Venetian Argosy by the Turks is one of several humiliations to which Venice has to succumb, including the loss of Cumae and Scutari in Albania that prompts an annual levy of 10 000 ducats. This tribute is finally abolished at the death of Mehmet II.

1472 — **Caterina Cornaro** marries Giacomo Lusignano II, King of Cyprus, after whose death Queen Caterina is toppled by a coup d'état. (☙see *RIALTO*).

1490 — The art of printing is introduced from Germany by **Aldo Manuzio**, who sets up his own printing press. It is famed for its refined italic characters and for the intellectual nature of his books, stamped with a dolphin and an anchor.

1494 — Charles VIII, King of France, arrives in Italy to conquer the Kingdom of Naples. The anti-French league, of which Venice was part, fails to defeat him in the **Battle of Fornovo** the following year.

1499 — The Turks attack Lepanto. Antonio Grimani is defeated off the coast of Sapienza: in Venice he earns the epithet *"Antonio Grimani, ruin of the Christians"*. The Turks sack Friuli. The peace treaty of 1503 sanctions the loss of Lepanto, Modone and Corone.

Paradise Replaces the Coronation of the Virgin

In 1365 the Chamber of the Great Council was decorated with the fresco by Guariento (recorded 1338–70), representing *The Coronation of the Virgin*. After the fire, it was decided to "remake Paradise as it was before". After a first competition, won by Veronese and Bassano, the work was never executed. A second competition awarded the work to Tintoretto, who with his son Domenico in 1588–1592 painted the immense *Paradise*, reputed to be the largest canvas oil painting in the world.

The De' Barbari map

1500 — The **De' Barbari map** is published, providing a strangely evocative and realistic impression of the city.

1508 — In order to split up Venetian territory, Julius II, Louis XII and Emperor Maximilian I form the **League of Cambrai**, in alliance with Spain, Hungary, the Duke of Savoy, the Duke of Ferrara and the Marquis of Mantua. After an initial defeat, Venice takes seven years to recover her possessions as far as the Adda.

1514 — The Rialto market is destroyed by fire.

1516 — The Jews are segregated in the Ghetto district.

DANGEROUS YEARS

1538 — Andrea Doria, admiral under Emperor Charles V and a Venetian ally, is defeated at Prevesa. The Turks now control the seas.

1539 — A secret service is set up by the **State Inquisitors**, the *Supreme Tribunale*, comprising three inquisitors: "the Red", a dogal councillor in a scarlet gown, and "the Blacks", two members of the Council of Ten. Working on information from informers, they take part in intrigue and counter-espionage.

1570 — The Turks land in Cyprus and conquer Nicosia.

1571 — After the siege and fall of Famagusta, **Marcantonio Bragadin**, the Venetian governor, is flayed alive by the Turks.

LEPANTO

Joined in the Holy League with the Pope and Spain, Venice confronted the Turks at Lepanto on 7 October 1571. The Christian fleet, commanded by **Sebastiano Venier**, comprised 202 galleys and six smaller ships, of which more than half were Venetian. The Turkish fleet comprised 208 galleys and a flotilla of 63 boats. The Turks were heavily defeated: 30 000 men were killed, 80 ships sunk and 140 captured. The League lost 7 600 men and 12 ships.

Among the wounded Christians was **Miguel de Cervantes**, author of *Don Quixote*, who always considered the Battle of Lepanto the most important event not only of his life, but of all history. Cervantes believed that the injury to his left hand, which was permanently crippled, was "to the greater glory of his right one".

1573 — Venice signs a treaty with the Turks that clinches control over Cyprus, which is abandoned and left to decline.

1577 — Fire damages much of the Doges' Palace. Refurbishment is undertaken by Antonio da Ponte.

1587 — The **Banco della Piazza**, the first public Venetian bank, is set up. The second, the **Banco Giro** (or Banco del Giro), is created in 1619 (🔗 *see RIALTO*).

1588 — The Rialto Bridge is rebuilt in stone.

1593 — The fortress of Palmanova is built, designed in the form of a nine-pointed star to defend the eastern borders against the Turks and Habsburgs. To commemorate the victory at the Battle of Lepanto, the foundation stone is laid down on 7 October.

1599–1604 — The **River Po**, which deposits huge quantities of sediments around Chioggia, is diverted towards Goro.

1600 — Once again, the city of Venice is flooded at high tide.

ANOTHER INTERDICT

In order to understand the relationship that existed between Venice and the Holy See, it is useful to note what the Venetians, who held themselves to be "first Venetian and then Christian", used to boldly claim: "We believe fully in St Mark, sufficiently in God and not at all in the Pope".

The Pope did not accept the right to religious freedom that Venice granted the Protestants. In 1605 the denunciation before the Council of Ten of two priests,

accused of various crimes, proved to be the last straw. The Pope maintained that the two should have been handed over to the ecclesiastical authorities. On the Venetian side was a Servite priest, **Paolo Sarpi**, whose arguments seemed heretical to Rome. When the Pope threatened an interdict and excommunicated Venice, the city responded: "Your excommunication we regard as nothing and we care not a fig about it."

The interdict lasted for a year. Although the relationship between Venice and the Vatican normalised, Paolo Sarpi was the victim of an assassination attempt in 1607. Recovered from his wounds and surveying the dagger with which he had been stabbed, he is said to have declared: "I recognise the style of the Roman Church."

1609 — **Galileo Galilei** presents the telescope to the doge.

1613–17 — After raids by the **Uskoks**, pirates from Bosnia and Turkish Dalmatia protected by the Habsburgs, Venice goes to war over Istria and Friuli, which results in the Uskoks being deported to central Croatia.

1618 — Spain instigates a complex conspiracy against Venice. The Council of Ten intervenes decisively as usual: one of the

The Battle of Lepanto by Michieli (Palazzo Ducale)

© Palazzo Ducale, Venezia / SCALA

participants is sewn into a sack and thrown into the sea; another two are hung upside down on the gallows of the Piazzetta.

1622 — **Antonio Foscarini**, the illustrious senator and ambassador to France and England, is found guilty of spying. He is condemned to death and succumbs to the usual treatment of being hung by one foot in the Piazzetta. Some time later, it is revealed that the accusations against Foscarini were false. The man who had spread these accusations is tried by the Three (🔎 *see previous pages: 1539*) and condemned to death. Venice makes public admission of her grave error. A state declaration is sent to his family and to embassies, and copies are pasted around the city.

1628–30 — Following the death of Ferdinand of Gonzaga, Mantua is claimed both by the French, led by Charles of Gonzaga-Nevers, and the Habsburgs. It is under siege from German troops when Venice intervenes: the city is nevertheless lost to the French. Mantua is savagely ransacked as the **plague** ravages the region, decimating the local population and Germans, before spreading to Venice. In little more than a year, the Serenissima loses 50 000 inhabitants. When at last the contagion subsides, construction is begun on the Church of Santa Maria della Salute in fulfilment of a vow.

THE SULTAN'S HAREM AND THE WAR OF CANDIA (CRETE)

The Knights of Malta habitually committed acts of piracy of which Venice disapproved because they were detrimental to her relationship with the East. In 1644 the Knights attacked a Turkish galleon in the Aegean and captured part of the

The Libro d'Oro

The Golden Book, first drawn up in the 16C, was the register of the civil status of Venetian nobility. Specific conditions for entry had to be fulfilled. Whoever was not high-born, and thus not inscribed, could not hold a government office.

Sultan's harem. The Sultan avenged himself not by attacking Malta, but Candia – Crete was then known by the name of its capital – convinced that the Venetians were behind this act.

The war dragged on for over 20 years, despite the Turkish fleet having suffered a naval defeat, second only to Lepanto, in 1656. Finally, Captain **Francesco Morosini**, backed by 3 600 men, signed the surrender in 1699, with which Venice lost the island.

1684–99 — Francesco Morosini, the ally of Austria and Russia, reconquers the Peloponnese peninsula, thereby acquiring the nickname "the Peloponnesian". Unfortunately, during this military operation, a Venetian mortar is fired at the Parthenon which, being used by the Turks to store their reserves of gunpowder, is severely damaged. He is elected doge in 1688. In 1699, although the former Venetian territories had not all been reclaimed, the Treaty of Carlowitz temporarily checks Turkish military campaigns.

18C AND DECLINE

Although in decline, when faced with a choice between alliance and independence, Venice once again opted for autonomy by refusing to side either with France or the Habsburgs in conflict for two centuries.

1714–18 — Venice loses the Peloponnese forever in a final battle against the Turks, sealed by the **Treaty of Passarowitz**,

The dogal "corno" (Museo Correr)

Muso Correr, Venezia/SCALA

dust which has remarkable binding qualities when mixed with water, sand and lime.

1784 — The Procurator **Andrea Tron**, nicknamed *el Paron* (the Leader) for his strong personality and political standing, which most citizens regarded as above the doge, laments that *"there are no shades of our old merchants among the citizens or subjects"* before the spread of *"weakness of character, overwhelming luxury, idle shows and presumptuous entertainment and vice"* in Venice.

1784–86 — These are the years of the final naval incursions. Admiral **Angelo Emo** wages battles against pirates along the North African coast.

signed in 1718. She maintains possession of Istria, Dalmatia, the Ionian islands and a few territories in Albania.

1744–82 — The *Murazzi* (protective wall around the lagoon) is built at Pellestrina and Sottomarina, 14m/46ft wide and 4.5m/14ft 8in higher than the average level of the tide. It is made with Istrian stone and pozzolana, a type of volcanic

A BREAK WITH TRADITION AND THE DEMISE OF THE REPUBLIC

1789 — The last doge to be elected, **Ludovico Manin**, ironically is the first not to be born of the old Venetian nobility, but of an émigré family from Friuli that had paid 100 000 ducats for inclusion in the **Golden Book** in 1651.

1792 — The opera house reopens as **La Fenice**.

Before the decline of Venice, the city still shows consideration for its fragile lagoon. It defines a series of boundaries referred to as the "lagoon perimeter", inside which it was forbidden to carry out any activity that might endanger the natural habitat of the lake.

1797 — **Napoleon** invades Venetian territory in 1796 while pursuing his Austrian enemy and successfully ejecting it from Italy – a possession he only maintains by posting troops in Verona and controlling access to the Brenner Pass. A temporary pact is made

Draining the Rivers

Local authorities routinely undertake to dry out the city rivers to cleanse the water and restore bridges. It is only then that water depths and the hollowness of the river bed are apparent. Dark and malodorous, the waters tend to collect waste as well as objects that fall in by accident.

Documents relating to this practice can be traced back to the late 13C and the early 14C. It has been established that these dredging operations have been carried out regularly since the 15C to renew the water and facilitate navigation. The main bodies in charge of implementing this work are the Magistratura del Piovego and the Savi alle Acque.

with the Austrians at Leoben (18 April 1797). This is ratified six months later on 18 October by the **Treaty of Campoformio** signed by Francis II, Emperor of Austria, and Napoleon Bonaparte. It confirms that Austria renounces her claim over Belgium and Lombardy to take possession of the Veneto as far as the Adige, Friuli, Istria, Dalmatia, the Po Valley and the islands in the Adriatic. France takes the Albanian coast and the Ionian islands. Venice is left with the former Papal States of Romagna, Ferrara and Bologna.

Venice's fate, in effect, is sealed by her resistance to ally herself to Napoleon. Not only does she show no remorse when anti-French feeling is stoked by the clergy during Easter week to the point of vicious rioting in Verona (a Venetian dominion), but she positively congratulates her officers for firing at a French patrol in the Adriatic and killing the French crew. Napoleon's exasperation is documented: *"I will have no more Inquisition, no more Senate. I shall be an Attila to the State of Venice"*.

Without the reassurance of Venice's recapitulation, the government would have to be seized and war would be inevitable. The Senate meets for the last time on 29 April. By Friday 12 May, Napoleon's demands have to be conceded and the Great Council meets for a last, very tense sitting. A provisional government is approved by an "unconstitutional" Council falling short of its quorum of 600 by 63, many members having fled to their country estates on terra firma. Laying down the *cufieta*, the bonnet worn by the doge under his crown, Ludovico Manin turned with dignity to his servant: *"Take it away, I will have no further use for this"*.

AFTER THE FALL

1805 — With the Treaty of Presburg, Napoleon formally reclaims Venice as part of the Kingdom of Italy.

1815 — The Congress of Vienna establishes that Venice, the Veneto and Lombardy should belong to Austria.

1821 — The Italians show unrest caused by the failed attempts to achieve unification. Anti-Austrian movements break out.

1839–53 — Construction of the north and south dikes at Malamocco is completed.

1841 — The railway bridge linking Venice to Mestre is built.

1844 — The patriot founders of the secret organisation Esperia, Attilio and Emilio Bandiera, together with a sympathiser, Domenico Moro, are shot at Cosenza.

1847 — The lawyer **Daniele Manin** and the writer **Niccolò Tommaseo** are awarded prizes by the 11th Congresso degli Scienziati.

1848 — Daniele Manin is nominated President of the Republic of St Mark and begins reorganising a provisional government, before leading an insurrection against the Austrians supported by Niccolò Tommaseo. Both eminent men are subsequently exiled.

1854–58 — Identical iron bridges are built near the Accademia and the station.

1866 — After the Prussian defeat of the Austrians at Sadowa, Venice votes to be part of a unified Italy by a majority of 674 426 to 69.

1895 — The **International Biennale of Art** is founded. Exhibition facilities are expanded

Distinguishing Between Canals and Rivers

Although all Venetian waterways tend to be called canals, only three real canals exist in the city: Canal Grande, Canale della Giudecca and Canale di Cannaregio. Canals, which are wider, are tributaries of the lagoon, whereas the narrow rivers (*rii*) can be compared to streets: they are not linked to the sea and wend their way across the city along a sinuous, meandering course. The only exception is the Cannaregio *sestiere*, as any plan of Venice will show.

through the 19C with the erection of various modern pavilions.

1902 — The bell-tower of St Mark's collapses.

1915–18 — Venice suffers several bomb attacks but her misfortunes are not caused only by the war: once again the city is flooded by the rising waters.

1932 — First International Film Festival.

1933 — Inauguration of the Ponte Littorio, now called the Ponte della Libertà.

1943–44 — On July 25, 1943, the Italian Fascist government fell. German troops arrived in Italy on September 8, 1943. On September 16, Giuseppe Jona, president of the Jewish community of Venice, committed suicide rather than hand over the lists of the names of the Jewish community. 204 Jews were deported from Venice by the Nazis, only 8 returned from the death camps.

1953 — Giuseppe Roncalli is appointed Patriarch of Venice before being elected **Pope John XXIII** and instigating the Second Vatican Council.

1953–69 — Architect **Frank Lloyd Wright** (1869–1959) plans a student centre, the Masieri Memorial, to be built along the Grand Canal. In 1964 **Le Corbusier** (1887–1965) proposes designs for the Civil Hospital. **Louis Kahn** (1901–74) undertakes a project for a new Congress Hall. None of these undertakings sees the light of day.

1966 — During November the high tide rises to an alarming level. The waters flood the *Murazzi* at Pellestrina and reach many of the city houses.

1969 — Albino Luciani is appointed Patriarch of Venice and elected Pope in 1978, assuming the name **John Paul I**, which he bore until his death, a month later.

THE LAGOON LIVES ON

If the glory of Venice belongs to a bygone era, its lagoon provides a continuous link with the past, preserving a quality and style of life unique to its shores, regardless of the threat of subsidence or flooding. In 1925 alone, the Piazza San Marco, the "salon of Venice", was flooded eight times. Since then it has succumbed to inundation on more than 50 occasions.

Pollution, today's worst enemy

The 20C was the era of industrialisation. Marghera was created in the 1920s and, after the Second World War, the areas taken up by industrial activity expanded quite considerably. Oil was known to seep into the canal, threatening the ecological balance of the lagoon, whose precarious state was further endangered by the draining of land to build industrial areas and Marco Polo Airport. Between 1950 and 1970, the waste turned out by refineries and by chemical and metallurgical factories at **Porto Marghera** would often end up in the lagoon. During the 1980s a number of purification plants were set up nearby and they now recycle an estimated 80% of the area's industrial refuse. Pollution, caused by excessive amounts of nitrogen and phosphates, chemical fertilisers and insecticides, and organic substances generated by industrial complexes and urban communities, destroys part of the lagoon flora and fauna, encourages the proliferation of algae and stunts that of the phanerogamic species, whose roots are extremely useful, since they prevent the onslaught of erosion.

1973 — The Italian State declares that the preservation of Venice is of "pre-eminent national interest".

1988–92 — The MoSE prototype, a huge mobile sluice-gate devised to regulate the movement of the tides, is installed in the lagoon waters on an experimental basis.

1989 — The famous rock band **Pink Floyd** are invited to play in St Mark's Square. The council's gamble on bringing modern music to the heart of Venice backfires horribly as concert goers cause mayhem and thousands of pounds of damage. The city council resigns en bloc.

1996 — The opera house **La Fenice** burns down on 29 January.

2001 — Approval is given for the completion of the mobile tide barriers designed to protect the city.

2003 — The reconstructed **La Fenice** opens to the public.

2004 — The 650ft (200m) long cruise ship *Mona Lisa* runs aground in fog in St Mark's Basin, provoking fears of a major accident in the heart of Venice.

Traffic in Venice

© Samuel Rosa / Stock.Xchng

2008 — Venice's fourth bridge across the Grand Canal, the **Ponte di Calatrava** is completed. **Pigeon feeding** in the Piazza is banned.

2011 Venice established a hotel tax for individuals.

2012 After ousting the previous director, Venice Film Festival announced a new director and streamlined its program.

The trouble with tourists...

Henry James once remarked "There are some disagreeable things in Venice, but nothing so disagreeable as the visitors". It is a sentiment that many Venetians echo in private if not public.

Birdseed sellers out of work

Venetian officials first voted to outlaw pigeon feeding in 1997 but the Piazza San Marco was exempted because of the iconic status of the birds and their feeders. However by 2008 it had become clear that to make a significant reduction in the bird population, their most obvious food supply – St. Mark's official birdseed sellers – had to go.

Sergio Lafisca, the Venice health expert responsible for the Department of Prevention, estimates that there are about 130,000 pigeons living in Venice's historic centre. Aside from human health considerations (the birds are real and potential carriers of disease) the birds' droppings, claws and beaks cause significant damage to the monuments. In fact a recent report concluded that the pigeons costs each resident around €275 a year in terms of clean up and repairs.

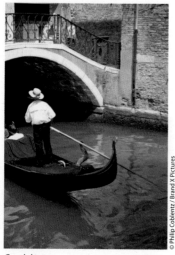

Gondola

© Philip Coblentz / Brand X Pictures

In no other functioning major city on earth is the resident population so heavily outnumbered by visitors as it is in Venice. Some 62,000 live in the historic city (Centro storico), while another 31,000 live on other islands in the lagoon. Each year they are invaded by around 20 million visitors. No one knows the real total and this in itself is a problem for managing the infrastructure.

According to the tourist board (in 2004), 6 million visitors spend one night or more in Venice every year. A further 15 million flood its streets and alleys only for the day, marching into the Piazza San Marco, perhaps paying a swift visit to the Basilica di San Marco, before heading out again. In fact It is said that around 80 percent of tourists don't even bother to visit a single monument while in Venice. Whatever the true figures, there is no doubt that day-trippers contribute little in economic terms and cause immense problems in terms of pollution and congestion. It helps to remember, like driving, stay to the right when walking. Venice of course is dependant on tourism, which accounts for 70 percent of its economy. However, on days when more than 60,000 visitors arrive, in a city where just 33,000 can be accommodated comfortably, entire systems are taxed from transport to pedestrian bridges and sidewalks. It is often said that the charm of Venice is more at risk from the tourist tidal wave than from sinking into the sea. The transport authority, ACTV, periodically experiments with new lines in response to citizens' complaints that (day-trip) tourists were cramming onto water buses, leaving residents stuck on dry land. People who live and work in Venice demand better transportation, paying a greatly reduced fare on (all) *vaporetti* than what tourists pay.

The city's approach has been to offer tourists a pass that offers significant savings when visiting over a number of days (plus it offers the privilege of jumping queues). Higher fees are paid for single trips or for a one-day pass. In June 2012 a new vaporetto line, Art Vaporetto, was launched to serve tourists with an audio guide, making stops at major points of interest.

However, as of 2011, as was instituted also in Rome and Florence, even overnight guests are now taxed, per person, per night, which is applied for the first five nights. Likewise, high and low seasons have been completely redefined: in 2013, Venice classified February 1-November 30 as high season.

Recent years have seen a tougher approach taken against misbehaving visitors. A previous mayor instituted regulations for decorum and fines for violations. Stewards patrol St Mark's Square and other historic sites and impose on-the-spot fines to tourists found picnicking, walking around bare-chested or barefooted and littering.

"...a Venetian gondola? That singular conveyance, came down unchanged from ballad times, black as nothing else on earth except a coffin – what pictures it calls up of lawless, silent adventures in the slashing night; or even more, what visions of death itself, the bier and solemn rites and last soundless voyage! And has anyone remarked that the seat in such a bark, the arm-chair lacquered in coffin-black, and dully black-upholstered, is the softest, most luxurious, most relaxing seat in the world?"

Thomas Mann – *Death in Venice*

"The bathing, on a calm day, must be the worst in Europe: water like hot saliva, cigar-ends floating into one's mouth, and shoals of jelly-fish."

Robert Byron – *The Road to Oxiana*, 1937

Unique to Venice

The inhospitable nature of the lagoon, from which Venice sprung up as if by magic, has demanded of the Venetians an extraordinary ability to adjust to a particular lifestyle implemented through a rare spirit of initiative. To combat the waters, either too high or too low, and to make their way around the myriad islands, the Venetians built the gondola and hundreds of bridges; they also planted thousands of poles.

THE GONDOLA

No one knows exactly when the gondola was invented: the word *gundula* appears as early as 1094 in a decree of Doge Vitale Falier, although the reference relates to a massive boat equipped with a large crew of rowers – a far cry from the gondola we know today.

In the 14C, small boats covered with a central canopy bore metal decorations on the prow and stern. At the end of the century the vessel began to be made longer and lighter, the prow and stern were raised and the **felze** or cabin was added, affording shelter in bad weather. Some had decorated prows. Others were painted in bright colours and decked with satin, silk and gleaming brass. On the prow and stern stood painted cherubs bearing the coat of arms of the family to which the gondola belonged. From the 16C, boats were toned down by being painted black: a colour we might judge to be rather funereal, but in Venice red, not black, is the colour of mourning. Today the gondola is about 11m/36ft long, 1.42m/4ft wide and comprises 280 pieces of wood.

Building a gondola

The shipyards where gondolas are built and repaired are called **squeri**. At one time, each of these was allocated primarily to a family from Cadore in the Dolomites, hence the reason why their wooden galleried constructions resembled alpine houses (*see ACCADEMIA: Squero di San Trovaso*).

The **ferro**, a sabre-toothed projection made of iron placed at the prow and stern, is without doubt the most crucial element of the gondola: implemented initially as a fender to safeguard against

Gondola under repair

© khr128 / iStockphoto

Gondolas and Palins in Venice

knocks, it serves as a counterweight to the gondoliere, and to align the boat around hazards in the narrowest passages. The curved fin is said to echo the dogal *corno* and to symbolise its power over the six **sestieri** represented by the six serrations. The tooth that "guards" the gondola itself is the Giudecca.

The **forcola** or rowlock, is an intricate piece of carving hewn from walnut, designed as a pivot that allows the oar maximum mobility. The oar is made of well-seasoned beech. Two bronze sea horses cleat the cords of the seats.

PALINE, DAME AND BRICOLE

Whether travelling by gondola, vaporetto or boat, there is always the risk of running aground. Navigable channels are identified by means of **bricole** – a series of large poles (*pali*) roped together – whereas the entrance to a canal or a junction is indicated by *dame*, which are smaller poles than the *bricole*. The **paline** are those thin individual poles that project from the water at odd intervals, to which private craft are tethered. They are particularly evocative if painted with coloured swirling stripes, outside some fine building to mark the landing stage of a patrician family in days gone by.

THE BRIDGES

During the tussles of *su e zo per i ponti*, "up and down the bridges" (&see *Calendar of Events, in Planning Your Trip*), there are several like the Ponte Chiodo (&see *CA' D'ORO*) without railings or parapet, where rival factions such as the Castellani and Nicolotti faced each other during "fist fights" (&see *I CARMINI*). Projects for bridges with three arches met with less success (&see *Il GHETTO*).

Canal with a bridge

ART AND CULTURE

The history of architecture, art and culture in general in Venice cannot be divorced from the physical and geographical constraints that throughout the ages the Venetians have had to overcome with mastery and ingenuity. The city still bears the stamp of the former Byzantine Empire, but over the years the streets have also succumbed to the influence of Renaissance, Classical and Baroque architecture. Artists have played a role in forging the atmosphere of the city, while remaining faithful to the Venetian spirit.

Architecture

BUILDING IN VENICE

Houses on piles

The city is not built on water, but in the water. It was built either on sandbanks above the water level, which gave rise to real islands, or on small sandy mounds which had remained at the water's surface.

In either case, great larch or oak **pali** are driven deep through the sand, mud or silt, forming an unstable lagoon floor, to the bedrock of hard clay. These 2–4m/6ft 6in–13ft piles are organised in concentric circles or spirals starting from the outer perimeter of the building to be constructed, at intervals of 60–80cm/24–32in. In this way the piles provide a base onto which a raft-like platform (*zattera*) of horizontal beams (*zatterone*) may be secured. To reinforce this wooden floor, it is lined with boulders of **Istrian stone** that provide a solid course for the brick and mortar on which it is possible to build.

The number of piles used can sometimes be considerable: 1 106 657 for the Church of Santa Maria della Salute, and 10 000 for the Rialto Bridge!

Building materials

Unfortunately, since the lagoon offers very little in terms of building materials, it is necessary to import these from other areas.

Most of the **timber** is brought from the Cadore forests and the Balkans. It is used not only for the foundation piles, but also for the frames and ceilings of the houses. Occasionally it is incorporated into masonry walls, not so much as reinforcement but rather as "shock absorbers": this procedure lends greater flexibility to the structure, which resolves some of the problems raised by the instability of the subsoil. **Marble**, used to front façades, is principally sourced from the Euganei Hills (*south of Padua*) or from Greece. **Istria limestone**, hard, white and marble-like, has the added advantage of being resistant to salt erosion; it is therefore frequently used in Venice for bridge copings and to face *palazzi*, churches, bell-towers etc. Only **brick**, which in Gothic times lent its charming pink hues to I Frari and many other quaint buildings in Venice, is made on-site from local clay.

Originality

All the houses, palaces and churches that have been erected in *La Serenissima* through the ages survive on these reinforced, drained, dried and consolidated areas reclaimed from the lagoon. It is almost as if the early Venetians made a pact with the lagoon that they would live with it rather than view it as a problem to be reckoned with. And so from the water rise mists and fogs that swirl and fade again to confer a thousand different moods on the urban landscape: one moment the millpond mirrors a perfect reflection and in another the choppy, churlish surface dissolves the shimmering profile according to whim. The lagoon intensifies the ethereal sunlight to sparkle and glitter and lend a festive air to the city, but it may also invade the landscape with a spirit of melancholy. Water consorts with the changing light and density of the air to exaggerate or deform the delicate stone lacework, the crenellated roof ornaments, the many recesses, loggias and arcades. However, poetic descriptions of atmosphere

Campo

are an insubstantial preoccupation in comparison to the physical problems posed by the lagoon: it is rather the remoteness of mainland resources and the instability of the subsoil that preoccupy the Venetian authorities. Initially, it was the cost and transport of building materials that dictated a patron's choice and influenced an architect's design of a private palace or church. Up to the 16C, local brick had been the most obvious raw material available. However, when more sophisticated and reliable forms of transport were discovered, the economic factor became considerably less important. A second major element in the equation was the risk of subsidence. To reduce this threat, houses were erected no more than two or three storeys high, except in the Ghetto, where squat buildings had low ceilings so that the total weight was proportionally less. A constant reminder of instability was the angle at which certain palaces (Palazzo Dario) and bell-towers (Santo Stefano, San Barnaba) inclined, and the regularity with which the quays (Riva degli Schiavoni) and St Mark's Square flooded. Through determination, patience and perseverance in an unpredictable environment, strengthened by a spirit of enterprise and ambitious business acumen, the Venetians learned to construct and embellish their magnificent city. Yet despite everything

that has been accomplished and all the expertise acquired, the unpropitious site for this wonderful city means that it will forever be at the mercy of natural forces: the corrosive action of salt and water, and the instability of the lagoon floor.

The Campo

The *campos*, or squares, provide points at which all roads, streets, alleys and activity converge. It is at the very heart of community life, where housewives chat and hang out their washing and where children play in the open. It is not to be confused with the **corte**, a closed public courtyard with a single entrance, or with the **cortile**, a private courtyard hidden within a patrician town house. The *campo*, sometimes dotted with a few trees, is encircled by fine patrician houses, Gothic or Renaissance in style, and blessed with its own church. At its centre, a well might occupy a choice spot. Given that the city was built on salty water and therefore had no natural drinking-water supply, rainwater had to be collected, purified and stored in cisterns that were excavated to a depth of 5–6m/16–20ft. The brick-lined tank collected water through several apertures in the *campo* floor, filtering it through fine river sand. Often the well-head, the **vera da pozzo**, would have been paid for by a patron and would therefore have been sculpted as a work of art.

Domestic architecture

Throughout Venice, with the exception of the Grand Canal, palaces rub shoulders with modest houses. Simply built in pink brick or stone, most of these houses are low in height. A few retain their openwork external staircase, double façade and "double" front entrances: one on the street and one onto the canal with its "water porch". The inner courtyard is modelled on the Roman atrium: shaded in summer and protected from the wind in winter. On the first floor or **piano nobile**, a **portego** runs perpendicular to the main front, from the street, across the internal *cortile*, through the entire width of the house to open out onto a loggia on the canal side.

The **altana** is a veranda built on a tiled roof where typical Venetian high funnel-shaped chimneys, known as *fumaioli*, project; these distinctive features were immortalised by Carpaccio in his paintings. Forever short of space, the Venetians have made clever use of their rooftops by installing these charming terraces to increase their living area. The façades are enhanced with flower-decked balconies, small carved discs, ornamental reliefs and sculpted cornices. Down the side walls, houses with *barbacani* have corbelled projections to support the timber beams of upper floors (Calle del Paradiso).

The lack of space at ground level means that there are very few gardens in Venice, and those that do exist are small, sometimes consisting of a single tree or a few flower tubs, often jealously guarded from the public eye behind high walls.

Altana

CRAFTSMANSHIP VALUED

Veneto-Byzantine

The oldest monuments found in the Venetian Lagoon are on the island of Torcello: the **Cattedrale di Santa Maria Assunta** and the complex of **Santa Fosca** bear witness to the close ties that once allied Venice with Ravenna, the Western heir to a Byzantine legacy. For several centuries Venice, through its conquests and trade links with the East, maintained a close relationship with Greece and Constantinople: the Basilica of St Mark, rebuilt in the 11C, was modelled on the 6C prototype of Byzantium churches, the Church of the Holy Apostles in Constantinople, destroyed in the 13C (the immense and sumptuous Hagia Sophia was built subsequently by the same architect along the same lines). St Mark's therefore directly transposes an expression of the Eastern Church, in terms of form, structure, volume and style, into the West.

This oriental Christianity was a major force in the fusion of an original "Veneto-Byzantine" style from the late Middle Ages onwards. The artistic iconography, strongly influenced by Byzantium, incorporates Islamic elements (decorative motifs, horseshoe arches), Palaeo-Christian features (*transennae*, capitals) and Roman details from sculpted fragments (marble blocks, column shafts, flat bricks) salvaged from villas along the Adriatic coast that had been destroyed during the barbarian invasions of the 5C and 6C.

Churches

The Byzantine-style churches like Santa Fosca, Torcello Cathedral, Santa Maria e Donato on Murano and St Mark's Basilica, best demonstrate the Eastern influence. This influence is clearly visible in the centrally planned Greek cross church or longitudinal hall church (nave and two aisles) prefixed by a narthex (covered porch which evolved into an arched portico) but independent of a free-standing baptistry (like that at Torcello). Structurally, Byzantium provided the expertise to erect domes over open spaces unencumbered by piers; it inspired the use of precious marble

© T. Zane / MICHELIN

column shafts crowned with variously shaped capitals (basket-shaped, inverted pyramid) and carved ornament (organic decoration such as foliage, symmetrically arranged animals). The practice in Ravenna (12C–13C) of applying decoration in the form of shallow relief, open fretwork, or *niello* (deeply cut engraving) and mosaic with flat gold backgrounds to both internal and external walls, was quick to be emulated by Venetian mosaicists, who copied subjects from the Old and New Testaments. Other features to be accommodated include Palaeo-Christian *transennae* (open-work window screens), *plutei* (marble tablets) and *paterae* (small carved discs) encircled within a twisted rope moulding, acanthus leaves and vine leaf tendrils, Palaeo-Christian figurative motifs (gryphons, eagles, peacocks and lions often quoted from embroideries or manuscript illuminations), marble ambos (pulpits before the chancel), and *iconostases* (screens in Greek churches separating the sanctuary from the nave).

The **Romanesque style**, which seems to appear in Venice during the 11C and 12C, is also in its own way modelled upon Byzantine art. The main forces at play were revived by the Lombard invasion from the northwest and from Ravenna in the south through which the Crusader armies would have passed.

Typical of the Venetian Romanesque style is the external appearance of high, solid, austere walls, pierced with tiny windows, relieved only by simple decoration afforded by blind arcading. The interior featured a raised nave, a vestige of Palaeo-Christian civilisation, and two aisles. Churches were planned as basilicas with a tall nave flanked by side aisles. In simple terms it is a compromise of "Western" Romanesque and "Eastern" Byzantine styles, and it is precisely from this period that Venice's oldest churches survive: San Giacomo (Rialto), San Nicolò dei Mendicoli, San Zan Degolà, San Giacomo dall'Orio and Sant'Eufemia (Giudecca). Although these churches were heavily rebuilt in the following centuries, many have retained their original massive, square, brick **campanile** or bell-tower, articulated with pilasters and blind arcading, capped with a loggia that screens the bells (San Barnaba). Only the roof, added later, differs from the original by being hexagonal, pyramidal or conical in shape. In some cases, the original church has long gone, but the Romanesque tower remains, as at San Zaccaria (*illustration: see SAN ZACCARIA*) and San Samuele. All that survives of the famous 12C Sant'Apollonia monastery is its superb cloisters, a rare vestige of Romanesque architecture.

Domestic buildings

The **Veneto-Byzantine palazzo** is no doubt the most original product of 11C–13C Venetian architecture. Known as the *casa-fondaco* (from the Arabic *funduk*, meaning depository or warehouse), this "storehouse" effectively combines the purpose of storage, commercial office and family home into one compact unit. The best preserved are the Fondaco dei Turchi, Ca' Farsetti, Palazzo Loredan and Ca' Da Mosto (*Ca'* being an abbreviation of *casa*, meaning house).

These houses further testify to the prodigiously rapid growth of the city's merchant aristocracy, empowered and enriched by maritime trade which, in turn, nurtured an interest and appreciation for Eastern Byzantine and Muslim craftsmanship.

The Foreign Merchants of Venice

Venetian trade benefited from the different cultures brought over by foreign visitors to the city. In those days, a great many nationalities were living side by side, all engaged in commercial activities: Albanians, Armenians, Dalmatians, Jews, Greeks, Persians, Germans and Turks. In this context the storehouse (*fondaco*) played an essential role, as it was used for stocking goods and was seen as the heart of the business community. In Venice, the warehouses belonging to Persian, Turkish and German merchants were particularly active.

As the need for defensive fortifications receded – on a scale seen at the first Doges' Palace – patrician town houses erected in the 11C began to conform to a set type that allowed for an easy and comfortable lifestyle. The structure would remain unchanged for several centuries to come, whereas its applied decoration would evolve according to contemporary taste. Split into three horizontal tiers, the main entrance into the storage or commercial area would have been on the canal side, through the *porta d'acqua*. On the first floor, the *piano nobile*, a continuous gallery or *loggia* would run the length of the façade between two solid walled towers, whereas at the top, a series of decorative crenellations would conceal the roofline. Only later would additional storeys sometimes be added.

Veneto-Byzantine arches have several forms: stilted round-headed arches (narrow arches with their springing line raised), horseshoe arches, Moorish ogee arches and high-pitched pointed "lancet" arches. These arches are often supported by highly prized marble shafts with decorated capitals, bearing Byzantine stylised and/or symmetrical foliage or animals. Further decoration might include Byzantine *paterae* illustrating real or mythical animals (peacocks, griffins etc) or medallions of different coloured marble, crosses or historical emblems.

Venetian Gothic

The term "Gothic", a label attributed in the 17C to the style developed by the barbarian Goths, assumes a distinctive meaning when applied to Venetian building design from the 1400s. For it is this delicate, ornamental, elegant style that has given the city its most distinctive characteristics and its architectural unity. It graces nearly all the *campi* and houses giving onto the banks of canals, styling a pointed arch or a loggia's filigree stonework. Unlike the structural changes that facilitated a new form of civil engineering in France, England and Germany, Venice merely used the Gothic style to ornament, flatter and decorate her buildings until the late 16C.

Churches

Politically, Venice was reinforcing her strength and autonomy. This prosperity allowed institutions to flourish both in the secular and religious domains, as demonstrated by the large-scale building projects undertaken by the principal monastic communities (I Frari, San Zanipòlo). With time, these were endowed by aristocratic patrons who wished to celebrate and publicise their wealth and standing (Madonna dell'Orto, Santo Stefano), entrusting to the churches their refined funerary monuments.

These were days in which the plague was rapidly spreading and they were characterised by a strong sense of urgency: poverty and charity were preached by the **Mendicant Orders**, and measures were taken to build monasteries and *scuole*, the characteristic Venetian institutions that sustained their confraternities in exchange for charity. Thus around 1245, with the benediction of **Doge Giacomo Tiepolo**, the Dominicans and Franciscans began erecting the city's most beautiful churches.

Exterior – From the 14C, designers of religious buildings began combining curved and rectilinear features in drafting their façades (San Giovanni in Bragora, I Frari, Scuola Vecchia della Misericordia). Although the structures remained austerely simple, **porches** and **windows** suddenly became encrusted with Gothic features. The severe flat-brick west front was divided into three parts: the central, nave section soared high above the flanking aisles. Plain surfaces were relieved with decorative elements in white Istrian stone: portals were framed with engaged columns and pediments, hood mouldings articulated the gables, a cornice was supported by a frieze of niches that curved around the lateral walls. Only porches made in marble or white Istrian stone carry ornamentation: crowned by recessed arches with acanthus leaf motifs as well as elegant relief decoration such as cable fluting, knot-work and foliage, they are often flanked by statuettes or engaged columns. At the east end, apses proliferated and extruded to form chevets

(I Frari, San Zanipòlo), whereas the tall square pink-brick *campanili* point skywards with a white marble open loggia (St Mark's, I Frari, Madonna dell'Orto).

Interior – The Gothic church, based on the T-shaped Latin cross to accommodate the long processions required by the liturgy down the nave, was abutted by aisles; at the east end, a wide transept could accommodate a chancel and numerous transept chapels endowed by private patrons (I Frari, San Zanipòlo). Sometimes the internal space was enclosed by a fine open timbered roof built by local shipwrights in the form of an inverted hull (Santo Stefano, San Giacomo dall'Orio) and articulated by arches painted with string-courses of acanthus leaves, or by carved wooden tie-beams.

Domestic buildings

Gothic-fronted *palazzi* enclose all the *campi* and line the secondary canals, but the most magnificent examples are to be found along the Grand Canal, which began to resemble a wonderful "triumphal waterway".

Fanciful creativity – The Venetian-Gothic **palazzo** was derived from the Byzantine model, retaining its three main characteristics: portico, loggia and decorative merlons. However, it now assumed a more noble, confident and sophisticated canon of ornamentation, which continued to be implemented until the fall of the Republic. As the patrician families stabilised their social status, they affected changes to their houses, most notably on the *piano nobile*. The simplicity of the earlier Veneto-Byzantine façades (portico and continuous loggia) was replaced by a centralised, more important arcaded loggia with cusped arches and quatrefoil motifs. In the corner section, single isolated windows interrupt the solid wall area now enhanced by the use of brick and stucco in two-tone colour combinations.

Interior layout – The *palazzo* is traditionally U-shaped in plan: a central block with perpendicular wings extended around a courtyard (*cortile*) with a well-head. Access to the *piano nobile* would have been via an open external stairway supported on Gothic arches up to a colonnaded portico with wooden architrave (Palazzo Centani). On the first floor, a broad passageway or, if enclosed, a reception hall (*portego*) ran the entire width of the house to open out onto the loggia on the canalside.

Extrovert beauty – Unlike the Florentine *palazzo*, austere, plain and impersonal, the Venetian façade may be seen as an extrovert, openly flaunting its charms to those who walk by. The windows, the eyes that open onto the outside world, are therefore natural vehicles for additional decoration.

Venice is still laden with oriental references both Christian and Muslim, and the characteristic loggias are strongly reminiscent of Palaeo-Christian stone fretwork; windows borrow from their Moorish counterparts a profile that echoes a cusped lancet and the temptation of inserting sculpted Byzantine *paterae* is still too great to resist.

By looking at the windows and their arched profiles, the various phases of Venetian Gothic may be discerned. Curvilinear arches of Moorish influence from the 14C sometimes rest on colonnettes (Corte del Million); early-15C three-cusped, four-light centred arches are often topped with a finial (Palazzo Duodo); late-15C Gothic or High Gothic arches, the most original and varied phase which might be compared with the French Flamboyant, grace the Doges' Palace. Here, one or more rows of quatrefoil oculi surmount the three-cusped arches of the loggias. The Ca' d'Oro, where **Marco d'Amadio**, a member of the **Bon** family, worked from 1421–61, is also expressive of this joyful, endearing exuberance.

Gothic sculpture

As with building, the first notable works of sculpture by known craftsmen date from this period. With **Pier Paolo** and **Jacobello dalle Masegne** (d.1403 and 1409 respectively) a style, explored by the School of Pisa, was evolved out of the static Byzantine tradition towards

Cushion capital, Torcello (9–10C)

Pluteus with peacocks
Torcello Cathedral (11C)

Composite capital, Torcello

Campanile di San Barnaba

Fretwork stone screen
San Alipio door, St Mark's

Patera with Pascal lamb

greater movement and expression, and mixed with a taste for Gothic ornament. Their work combines the use of delicate and complicated architectural elements with figurative statuary (iconostatis at St Mark's).

The Venetian School of Sculpture seemed unable truly to inspire the artistic community. *La Serenissima* was therefore forced to continue soliciting foreign artists or awarding commissions to craftsmen passing through the city.

Following in the footsteps of Pisa, Venice succumbed to the influence of Florentine art, to that of **Niccolò Lamberti** and to Sienese artists such as **Jacopo della Quercia**. **Marco Cozzi**, a remarkable woodcarver from Vicenza, created the splendid wooden chancel in the Church of the Frari, the only example of such work to survive in Venice.

Funerary monuments – The earliest 14C tombs consist of a simple sarcophagus with the recumbent figure of the deceased in front and the figures of the Madonna and Child and saints incorporated at the four corners; above, set into a recessed arch, is a lunette, painted or sometimes sculpted. Later a Gothic baldaquin of stone drapery was added, seemingly suspended in the middle from the ceiling, its drapes drawn aside by figures (angels or warriors). It is in this vein that the Dalle Masegne brothers worked from the 14C to the 15C.

Portals – Almost all the 15C portals that adorn the Venetian churches are attributed to the architect **Bartolomeo Bon** (Santo Stefano, San Zanipòlo, Madonna dell'Orto, I Frari). Each is made of stone or marble to contrast dramatically with the main fabric of the brick building, and each is decorated with a series of hood mouldings and courses of twisted rope with cusps of foliage around the pointed ogee archway; elements are further embellished with acanthus leaves, the gable is surmounted with a free-standing statue, and inside the portal shelter small niches or aedicules. Bartolomeo Bon's unquestionable masterpiece is the elegant Porta della Carta, the main entrance to the Doges' Palace, executed in Flamboyant Gothic.

Venetian Renaissance

The success and popularity of the International Gothic canon was such that it delayed the adoption of Renaissance principles in Venice. However, once introduced, the style quickly took hold and soon graced the traditional structures with a new refined magnificence. During the 1400s, under the patronage of **Doge Francesco Foscari**, *La Serenissima's* civilisation changed direction: artistic links with Tuscany and Lombardy were strengthened and, after the fall of Constantinople in 1453, ties with the Eastern Empire were severed. Humanism flourished: it drew its inspiration from Hellenistic culture and was enriched by the sagacity of Greek scholars who had fled from Constantinople. In 1495 the printer **Aldo Manuzio** began publishing the Ancient Greek classics as the city witnessed the divide between **Scuole Grandi** and **Scuole Minori** (📖 *see I CARMINI*). By the second half of the 15C, Florentine supremacy had dwindled. The new style, which originated from Tuscany, spread throughout Italy thanks to the wandering lifestyle of her artists, and gradually began to display regional characteristics – elements which Venice, in her inimitable fashion, absorbed and interpreted in her own way.

In the beginning

The earliest traces of the **Early Renaissance** are to be found in Venice's archways. The entrance to the Arsenale (1460) survives as the first full expression, complete with its Classical lions, mythological figures and Greek marble columns. Three other examples showing the same characteristics include the portal of San Giobbe, one at the Gesuiti in the Zattere quarter, and the Foscari doorway at the Doges' Palace.

In terms of sculpture, the Florentine masters Donatello and Verrocchio endowed the Serenissima with only two works, both of major importance: an evocative wooden polychrome figure of John the Baptist (1438) at I Frari, and an impressive equestrian monument in bronze of the Condottiere Bartolomeo Colleoni from Bergamo (1458) that

San Giovanni in Brágora

Four-light window of Palazzo Sagredo

I Frari belltower

Four-light window on Murano

now stands in the *campo* in front of San Zanipòlo.

Lombardo dynasty – At the turn of the 15C, the spirit of innovation that was to animate contemporary sculpture and architecture was largely due to the genius and expertise of the **Lombardo family** – from Lombardy as their name clearly implies – and in particular to **Pietro** (1435–1515) and his two sons, **Antonio** and **Tullio**. Seeking to promote a complete re-evaluation of contemporary design and the widespread implementation of the new canon, the Lombardo family fashioned the highly public façade of the Scuola San Marco dominating its prime site, the Church of Santa Maria dei Miracoli and the unusual yet noble Ca' Dario giving onto the Grand Canal. In each case structural and decorative elements (porphyry medallions, marble rosettes) interact to form a perfectly balanced ensemble governed by a harmonious system of proportions.

Stone and marble replace the brick used earlier by Gothic builders. Façades may be asymmetrical, articulated with cornices, sculpted busts, figurative statues, pilasters – fluted or with cartouches of delicate graffiti (Classical reliefs featuring masks, the attributes of the Liberal Arts and the Gods of War) – friezes of vines or festoons of foliage, animals and *putti*.

In the field of sculpture, Pietro Lombardo undertook for San Zanipòlo a series of important and distinguished funerary monuments in Istrian stone to commemorate doges (those of Pietro Mocenigo, Pasquale Malipiero and Nicolò Marcello). Tullio, meanwhile, who worked extensively with his father, is responsible for the fine reliefs set into the front of the Scuola San Marco, and for the monuments to Giovanni Mocenigo and Andrea Vendramin in San Zanipòlo.

The Lombard tradition is reflected in the formal design of such memorials, as shown in the use of the triumphal arch on several levels with superimposed niches housing allegorical statues of the Virtues, acting as a cornice over the sarcophagus. On the other hand, the fine workmanship of the figurines, along with the poise and elegance of their stance, undeniably testify to Tuscan influence.

Mauro Codussi (1440–1504) – This architect from Bergamo, a contemporary of the Lombardo brothers, seemed happier to celebrate the decorative rather than the structural function of architecture and to this end returned to the Tuscan vernacular for inspiration. Despite adhering to the guidelines pronounced by the Humanist Alberti in his treatises on architecture for a Canon of Beauty formulated according to mathematical proportion and harmony of component parts (spatial organisation, symmetrical elevations, correct application of the Classical orders – Doric, Ionic and Corinthian – the use of rustication and niches), Codussi's designs appeared to lack homogeneity. Instead, he forged a personal style

The funerary monument to Doge Pietro Mocenigo by Pietro Lombardo at San Zanipòlo

Scuola Grande di San Marco

distinguished by semicircular pediments for the fronts of churches and the Scuola San Marco, which he completed, rustication on the ground floor of his *palazzi*, engaged columns and cornices to differentiate superior storeys, and circular oculi inserted between the coupled arches of an arcade supported on coupled columns.

His early projects, which included the Clocktower and the Church of San Giovanni Grisostomo, all showed trace elements of Byzantine styling (portico decoration, Greek cross floorplan), whereas his more mature works, the sumptuous *palazzi* Corner Spinelli and Vendramin Calergi on the Grand Canal conformed to his distinctive style. This style developed into an even bolder statement at San Zaccaria and San Michele, his masterpiece, where marble or white Istrian stone were applied across all three carefully articulated sections of the elevation, both on the horizontal and vertical axes; the nave towers over the aisles linked with semicircular pediments, and friezes, shell niches and porphyry roundels provided ornamentation. Two additional designs by Codussi included Santa Maria Formosa and the beautiful Istrian stone campanile of San Pietro di Castello.

Antonio Rizzo – Antonio Rizzo (d.1499) was responsible for the internal (courtyard) façade of the Doges' Palace and the monumental Giant's Staircase faced in marble. Examples of his sculpture included the poised figures of Adam and Eve that once flanked the Foscari arch. He also varied the design of the archetypal funerary monument initiated at I Frari for Doge Nicolò Tron in 1473 by articulating it with five orders up to a semicircular pediment, and ornamenting it with several niches filled with freestanding figures.

Venetian High Renaissance

A heightened Classicism affirms itself only in the 16C, marking a distinctive, second phase of Renaissance design.

Rome, which had displaced Florence, the capital of the arts at the beginning of the previous century, as the seedbed for new ideas, was badly damaged by Charles V's Imperial army, which sacked the Holy City in 1527. From 1530, Venice established herself as the model city of Italy. For a short period, she basked in the limelight, implementing a new Classicism that soon, alas, degenerated into Mannerism.

Arcaded porticoes proliferated at ground level with ever bigger openings, supporting ordered storeys above. Imposing *palazzi* with carefully articulated lines are rusticated the entire length of the ground floor, punctuated by large centrally planned openings and ornamented with masks. For the *piano nobile*, rectangular windows, framed

Marciana Library by Sansovino

© SCALA

with fluted or coupled columns, are pedimented with circular or triangular tympana in symmetrical formation; projecting balustraded balconies add to the sculptural effect. Below the entablature, the rhythm is maintained by a series of small oval apertures.

Sansovino, master of the Classical style – The Florentine-born Jacopo Tatti, known as Sansovino (1486–1570), an accomplished sculptor and architect, was responsible for introducing to Venice a Classical canon of design. Seeking refuge in Venice after the Sack of Rome (1527), where he had been apprenticed to Bramante and Raphael, Sansovino succeeded Bartolomeo Bon as *proto* or Chief Architect to St Mark's. He was thus entrusted with the Serenissima's ambitious plans for reconstruction and embellishment, beginning with the reorganisation of the Piazza San Marco. He drafted designs for the new Library, its portico based on an archaic model, the Fabbriche Nuove in the Rialto, Palazzo Corner della Ca' Granda on the Grand Canal, the elegant loggia at the foot of St Mark's campanile (for which he also produced the bronze statues and

low-relief panels), the heavily rusticated, Tuscan-inspired Palazzo della Zecca, the imposing but incomplete Scuola Nuova della Misericordia and the Golden Staircase. Robust, but not overly austere, his initial projects (including Ca' Granda) show Sansovino completely at ease with the traditional Venetian vernacular style (buildings around the Piazza San Marco and the Piazzetta), enriching his Classical forms with original and majestic ornament; decorative detailing encrusts the portico arches and enhances the flat surfaces, whereas statuary, low-relief panels and festoons add a touch of fantasy and convey a vivid sense of movement. To affirm Sansovino's brilliance as a sculptor, one need but cite the figures of Mars and Neptune that grace the Giant's Staircase and the highly expressive John the Baptist in I Frari – they speak for themselves.

Grandiose domestic buildings – At this time, the Grand Canal assumed its claim to be a true "triumphal way" fronted by ever more elegant and ennobled patrician houses.
Veronese Sanmicheli (1484–1559), having served his apprenticeship

under Sansovino, earned recognition for his military projects (Fortress of Sant'Andrea on the Lido) and for his design of the Palazzo Corner Mocenigo in the San Polo *sestiere* and the Palazzo Grimani on the Grand Canal.

Andrea Palladio (1508–80) – Late in the 16C, the architect Andrea Palladio, a Paduan by birth, moved to Venice. He had established his reputation by designing villas in the Brenta Valley. His distinctive style, which is characterised by a balanced sense of proportion and formulated from a profound appreciation of Classical architecture, was applied to buildings that were designed to suit their purpose, their site and, most importantly, were practical to inhabit. Encouraged by the Humanist Trissino, Palladio visited Rome on several occasions to study Classical architecture in the context of theories outlined by Vitruvius (1C BC). In 1570, he published his theories based on observation in a treatise entitled *I Quattro Libri di Architettura* (*The Four Books on Architecture*). This grand opus was to have far-reaching consequences in the spreading of Classicism to the rest of Europe.

The essential principle of this "modern" Classicism is structural simplicity, achieved with the use of basic geometrical volumes of space (cube, sphere and pyramid) and symmetry. Designs for building elevations conform to the same rules, with a façade having a central portico (San Giorgio Maggiore). Palladio received commissions, in particular from the Serenissima's important and wealthy patrician families with estates in the hinterland (La Malcontenta on the Brenta). These variations on the villa design provide a new canon for informal domestic buildings that reflects both their function as country farm estates and their location: besides boasting pure Classical form and a sound knowledge of decoration as well as gardening, these houses blend in perfectly with the surrounding landscape. The scenery may therefore be enjoyed from the house and the house may be admired as a point of interest punctuating and enhancing the scenery. This consideration was later explored and developed in garden design by the 18C English exponents of Palladianism (Campbell, Burlington, Kent, Adam, Capability Brown and the like). Palladio based many of his villas on ancient pagan temples; only the domestic buildings have forsaken monumentality for utilitarian considerations.

In Venice itself, Palladio's sense of austerity and perfect harmony is reflected in his magnificent churches: San Giorgio Maggiore, Il Redentore, le Zitelle, San Francesco della Vigna. Recurring features in his architecture are long, slender engaged columns, Corinthian capitals, triangular pedimented porticoes borrowed from Roman temples, huge domes thrown into contrast by symmetrically arranged geometrical

La Malcontenta by Andrea Palladio

© SCALA

Saint Jerome by Alessandro Vittoria in Church of Santa Maria Gloriosa dei Frari

echoes that of Codussi (openings on the ground floor) although now there is a greater sense of movement and dramatic contrast, achieved in part by the use of free-standing columns that project from the façade. He was also involved in the rebuilding of the Palazzo dei Dieci Savi and the Fabbriche Vecchie in the Rialto district.

Spavento began the Classical façade onto the small Senators' courtyard of the Doges' Palace, while Guglielmo dei Grigi, better known by his epithet **il Bergamasco**, was working on the Palazzo Papadopoli and the Palazzo Camerlenghi on the Grand Canal.

High Renaissance Sculpture

Together with Palladio and Sansovino, the third important figure to import the artistic spirit of Michelangelo to Venice was **Alessandro Vittoria** (1525–1608). Famous for his austere and dignified portraits, Vittoria sculpted two lively representations of St Jerome, now at San Zanipòlo and I Frari. He demonstrated further skills in the art of applied decoration by executing the stucco ceiling of the Libreria Vecchia and the fine gilded coffered vault of the Golden Staircase in the Doges' Palace.

Other artists of note working during the 1500s include **Lorenzo Bregno**, to whom several funerary monuments are attributed (including that of Benedetto Pesaro) and the high altar at I Frari; **Girolamo Campagna** (bronze figures – I Frari and Correr Museum); **Tiziano Aspetti** (bronzes in Correr Museum, statues of Hercules and Atlantes flanking the Golden Staircase) and **Andrea Riccio** (bronzes in Correr Museum).

Venetian Baroque

Throughout the 17C the predilection for the Classical style was underpinned by the continued popularity of Palladian design. As a result, Venetian Baroque is more tempered than it ever was in Rome or elsewhere.

Baldassare Longhena (1598–1682) – This architect and sculptor is both the instigator and leading representative of Baroque art in the City of the Doges. His lasting legacy was to inspire a taste

forms; whereas inside, the enclosed space is airy and light.

After Palladio's death, Vincenzo Scamozzi saw a number of his master's projects to completion, ensuring the final effect was true to Palladio's vision, and thereby consolidating his reputation.

Vincenzo Scamozzi (1552–1616), born in Vicenza, also inherited Sansovino's projects for the redevelopment of the Piazza San Marco and erected the Procuratie Nuove (1586) modelled on the Classical example proffered by the former Library nearby. What is new however, is the interplay of decorative elements that pre-empt the advent of the Baroque. Also by Scamozzi is the Palazzo Contarini degli Scrigni on the Grand Canal.

Lo Scarpagnino completed the Fondacco dei FF and the Scuola di San Rocco initiated by Bartolomeo Bon. His style

Chiesa dei Gesuati by Domenico Rossi

for stone and a solemn architectural language which, some say, verges on the whimsical. It is essentially Classical in inspiration but with charged ornamentation, frequently copied from examples in antiquity.

His undoubted masterpiece is the Church of the Salute. It is also the most eloquent embodiment of this peculiarly Venetian strain of Baroque: it exudes confidence and an air of triumph with its vast proportions, towering dome, sense of movement conveyed by modillions featuring curved scrolls, and crowds of angels and prophets.

Charged with designing the finest Baroque *palazzi* along the Grand Canal, Longhena turned to Sansovino for inspiration. He endowed both Ca' Rezzonico and Ca' Pesaro with grand entrances, heavily rusticated ground floors, superimposed orders of tall windows deeply recessed into archways, separated by large columns and richly ornamented with masks. Particular emphasis is given to the *piano nobile,* with sharply defined architectural elements such as cornices, balustraded balconies, and dramatically sculpted *putti* or coats of arms. A similar boldness marks his high altars and commemorative monuments, of which perhaps the most exuberant is the sepulchre of Doge Giovanni Pesaro at I Frari.

After Longhena – Following the death of Longhena, the completion of his main projects was supervised by **Antonio Gaspari** (Ca' Pesaro) and **Giorgio Massari** (Ca' Rezzonico) (1687–1766), possibly Venice's greatest architect in the first half of the 18C. The remarkably exuberant ornamentation (deeply cut garlands of fruit, niches, entablatures, pediments, fluted columns, crowning statuary) is evidenced in the Church dell'Ospedalletto with its great and ponderous atlantes. The three churches designed by **Sardi**, a collaborator of Longhena, are Santa Maria del Giglio, which houses depictions of naval battles and is planned like a military fortress, Gli Scalzi and San Salvador. Two other Baroque churches are San Moisé by Tremignon (1668) and San Stae. Among the bell-towers are those of Santa Maria Formosa and All Saints.

The architect responsible for the great Church of the Gesuati (18C) is **Domenico Rossi**, who also designed its splendid white and green marble decoration imitating huge draperies falling into heavy folds. In contrast, the interior ceilings painted by **Giambattista Tiepolo** attain an unchallenged brilliance and lightness more often associated with Rococo. In sculpture, however, perhaps the main representative of the Venetian Baroque is the Flemish artist **Juste Le Court**, whose works include altar fronts, allegorical figures and panels of low relief (Santa Maria del Giglio).

Neo-Classicism

During the 18C, Venice improved her image by erecting new buildings and remodelling a number of existing ones. In counter-reaction to the Baroque, the city reverted to a pure form of Classicism that was to be labelled neo-Classicism – well before any revival had taken hold anywhere else in Europe. The emergence of rational thinking during the Age of Enlightenment had affected all disciplines, including architecture, and given birth to a novel trend dubbed neo-Classicism. One of the advocates of this new style was a Venetian Franciscan, **Carlo Lodoli**, who claimed *"only that which has a definite function or is born out of absolute necessity is worthy of existing in architecture"*; and so artists turned to Antiquity for inspiration. Simple arcading, domes and pronaoi (projecting vestibules fronted with columns and pediments) grace monumental *palazzi* and churches. The linearity of each structural element is clearly defined and elaborate schemes for interior decoration are replaced by plain, simple arrangements based on the Palladian or the Baroque model. The buildings that best illustrate this trend are the Palazzo Grassi by Massari and the Napoleon Wing enclosing the Piazza San Marco. The architects **Andrea Tirali**

(1660–1737), **Scalfarotto**, **Visentini** and **Temanza** all implemented a neo-Classical style founded on simple form and basic geometry derived from Palladio (including the use of the pronaos); a sense of grandeur was imparted from **Giovanni Battista Piranese** (1720–78), the Venetian-born architect and engraver who studied Roman civilisation and published the famous *Carceri d'Invenzione* (c.1745).

Tirali employed neo-Classical principles in designing the façade of the Church of the Tolentini, endowing it with a large pronaos and Corinthian columns, a design that was to be inspirational later for other buildings. Other neo-Classical monuments of note include the Church of San Simeone Piccolo, erected in 1720 by Scalfarotto on a circular plan, with a gigantic porch copied from that of the Tolentini, and reached up a massive staircase. Unfortunately it is somewhat overwhelmed by the gigantic green dome and **Temanza**'s Church of the Maddalena, also built on a circular plan that is crowned by a great dome, but with a foreshortened pronaos.

Perhaps the figure who dominates the artistic output of the period, however, is **Giorgio Massari** (1686–1766), from whom we have inherited such grandiose statements as the Gesuati Church on the Zattere with its Palladian façade, the Church of the Pietà, and the main door of the Accademia (1760).

Antonio Canova (1757–1822) – The last great personality in the Serenissima's illustrious history of art is Canova who, in many ways, embodies the very essence of neo-Classicism in sculpture. Highly esteemed by his patrons at home and by Napoleon, Canova left the Republic to work in Rome and Paris, where the spirit of the style was distilled into painting by Jacques-Louis David, another imperial protégé.

His work exudes great purity and sensitivity. The velvety polish imparted to the white marble – his favourite material – together with the fluid compositions and elegant forms, in which line rather than texture is emphasised, combine to suggest fragile sensuality. Venice still retains a series of low reliefs in the style

Orfeo (1775 - 1776) by Antonio Canova in Museo Correr

© Museo Correr / Fondazione Musei Civici Venezia

of the Antique and the famous group of *Daedalus and Icarus* (Correr Museum). His grandiose memorial can be visited in I Frari: it was executed by pupils and lies opposite the monument he designed for Titian.

From eclectic to modern times

The second half of the 19C was dominated by an eclectic assortment of revivalist styles in architecture: neo-Byzantine (Hotel Excelsior on the Lido, 1898–1908), neo-Romanesque, and most especially neo-Gothic (Pescheria by Rupolo, 1907, Palazzo Cavalli-Franchetti by Camillo Boito, 1895); the curious Mulino Stucky on the Guidecca (1883), remodelled in the International Gothic canon, has high walls punctuated by a spired corner tower.

Since then, no particular trend has dominated Venice: only a few isolated personalities have had interesting projects built, now well integrated into the urban landscape. These include the residential districts around Sant' Elena from the 1920s, the railway station (1954) and the Savings Bank designed by Pier Luigi Nervi and Angelo Scattolin on Campo Manin (1968). Certain projects drafted by well-known personalities never got beyond the drawing board: a student hostel by the American Frank Lloyd Wright intended to stand on the Grand Canal (1953) and a public hospital by Le Corbusier (1964).

The area that accommodates the Biennale provides space for various contemporary experimental projects. Even if the gardens where the pavilions are built are dismissed as part of the urban environment, it is worth acknowledging the more original and obsolete: Hoffman's Austrian Pavilion (1933), the Venezuelan designed by Carlo Scarpa (1954) and the Finnish by Alvar Aalto (1956).

The most famous 20C Venetian sculptor is **Arturo Martini** (1889–1947).

Art

VENETIAN PAINTING

Venice's pictorial tradition has one constant: its profound sensuality achieved

Fanciulla piena d'amore (1913) by Arturo Martini in Ca' Pesaro

© Ca' Pesaro-Galleria Internazionale d'Arte Moderna / Fondazione Musei Civici Venezia

by a predilection for colour and for light, which lends a strong poetic touch to the landscape. It is an art that mirrors the personality of the lagoon city as a watery world where everything is suffused with light: the blur of the skyline, the shimmering volumes, the haze rising above the canals that adds a bluish tinge to the scene. It is this distinctive greyish light, opaque and iridescent at the same time, that inspired the artists of the 18C.

Mosaics

The art of mosaic, inherited from the Romans, came to the lagoon long before the art of painting. In the 12C and 13C, Venice, inspired by the art of Ravenna, proceeded to arrange the mosaic murals from Torcello (*Last Judgement*), Murano and St Mark's Basilica. After the fall of Constantinople in 1204, Greek decorators and mosaic artists came to Venice to work on the great Golden Altarpiece and the mosaics in St Mark's. Consequently, the biblical iconography of the Eastern Church became markedly oriental, with Christ featuring as the central character (central apse), opening and closing a story which unfolded along walls, arches and cupolas, thus observing established biblical chronology (*see PIAZZA SAN MARCO*).

The use of mosaic continued throughout the city's history. The very last ones to grace San Marco were executed over a rather long period running from the 16C to the 19C. The assumption that early mosaics were more impressive can be

© SCALA

Depiction of Christ in mosaics, Basilica di San Marco

explained by the simple fact that artisans were unable to arrange the small pieces of glass in a regular fashion: the myriad uneven surfaces lent "flexibility" to the mural. This effect was enhanced by the light, which caught irregularities, acting as a kaleidoscope of twirling colours and reflections. If all the pieces were aligned on a perfect flat plain, the effect would be dull and lifeless.

Quattrocento Primitives

A few artists began to paint in fresco in the 13C, a process that involves applying pigment to small sections of wet lime-plaster. Paintings from this period, however, if they have survived, are all badly damaged. As regards the style of these first Venetian frescoes, they soon conformed both in design and subject matter to Byzantine iconography, drawn for the most part from portable devotional icons typical of the Eastern Church, where the Madonna and Child usually occupy pride of place.

Paolo Veneziano

This artist, also known as Paolo da Venezia (active 1333–58), emerged as the first distinctive personality in Venetian painting, his name appearing with that of his son Giovanni on a *Coronation of the Virgin* (now in the Frick Collection in New York). Working in the Byzantine tradition, his painting showed him moving away from archaic stylisation (gold backgrounds, flat and confrontational compositions, hieratic attitudes) towards greater decorative refinement and distinctive use of line. This freedom of expression and sensitive treatment of Western subject matter forestalled the evolution of the International Gothic style characterised by graceful movement and elegant form. The work of **Lorenzo Veneziano**, traced to the years 1356–72, is characterised by expressive faces, vigorous bodies and a subtle use of strong, bold colours. (Note: these painters were not actually related; the epithet *Veneziano* simply means Venetian.)

Venetian International Gothic

At the beginning of the 15C, the work of **Gentile da Fabriano** and **Pisanello** and that of the Paduan **Guariento**, who were engaged in painting a cycle of frescoes in the Doges' Palace (destroyed by fire in the 16C), marks the city's endorsement of the "International Gothic". This was a refined, bejewelled style that combined Tuscan elements already assimilated in Padua (derived from sculpted Antique decoration on the one hand and by Giotto's cycle of frescoes in the Scrovegni Chapel on the other) with a more courtly style practised in Ferrara (notably portraiture).

The stimulus provided by these two influences blended with the local, Venetian predilection for naturalism, elegant linearity, fluid movement and strong decorative appeal (even the gold-embroidered and brocade clothing is celebrated) led to a distinctive regional style akin to the International Gothic that flourished in Siena, Prague and Avignon.

Other painters worthy of note include **Nicolò di Pietro** (recorded 1394–1430), **Jacobello del Fiore** (recorded 1394–

1439), a pupil of Gentile da Fabriano who practised a detailed and intricate style, and, most especially, **Michele Giambono** (recorded 1420–62) who produced highly refined works in which Eastern oriental influence can be felt (*St Crisogono* – San Trovaso, *St Michael* – Accademia).

A new pictorial tradition

By the mid-15C, attempts at perspective are reflected in the portrayal of floors and ceilings; depth of field is suggested in the background by landscape scenes or buildings.

The first hint of the Renaissance is to be found in the works of the **Vivarini** family from Murano. The shift in emphasis comes with the break of the generations: the earlier pictures have the same quality as Gothic goldsmithery and are markedly influenced by Byzantine iconography. These pictures are by the father, **Antonio** (active 1441–50), who worked with his brother-in-law, **Giovanni d'Alemagna** (*Triptych with Madonna and Child with Saints* – Accademia; polyptychs – San Zaccaria), and his brother **Bartolomeo** (*Triptych of St Mark* – I Frari). If these are compared with works by the son **Alvise**, however, the latter's awareness of the Renaissance becomes evident (*St Anthony of Padua* – Correr Museum; *Triumph of St Ambrose* – I Frari; *Christ Carrying the Cross* – San Zanipòlo). Strangely, in the following generation, **Marco Basaiti** (1470–1530), a pupil of Alvise Vivarini, is decidedly backward-looking in his delicate treatment of landscape and use of colour (*Vocation of the Sons of Zebedee* – Accademia).

Serenity in Early Renaissance Painting

Long after the flowering of the Renaissance in Florence in the early 1400s, during the latter half of the century, Venice's artists turned their attention to defining three-dimensional space and volume, and to an improved articulation of landscape and topographical views. They also gave up the abstract use of gold background and the Gothic taste for overly decorated and complicated pictures.

Bellini family

First Jacopo, the father (d.1470), followed by his two sons, Gentile and Giovanni, managed to emancipate Venetian painting from Byzantine and Gothic influences. The actual founder of the Venetian School is probably **Giovanni Bellini** (1430–1516), also known as Giambellino, who admired Florentine painting for its pure, idealised forms, and Flemish painting for its clarity in terms of light and observed realism. He was markedly influenced by his master and brother-in-law, the Paduan-born **Andrea Mantegna** (1431–1506), who settled and worked in Venice. Mantegna was fascinated by Roman Antiquities which were commonly traded in Padua at the time, an interest acquired from his adoptive father, the painter-archaeologist Squarcione. From his study of relief carving, Mantegna forged a bold style that is completely uncompromising to the point of coldness, where perspective is almost obsessively defined, and details are drawn with scientific precision (*St Sebastian* – Accademia).

His style was, however, in some ways tempered by the example of **Antonello da Messina** who worked in Venice c.1475–76 (*Pietà* – Correr Museum) after learning to use oil paints in Flanders. Giovanni adopted this medium and developed his own deeply sensitive style that is characterised by a playful suggestion of light, a delicate and harmonious use of colour, elegant rendering of form and a strong sense of

St Anthony of Padua (1480 ca.) by Alvise Vivarini in Museo Correr

© Museo Correr / Fondazione Musei Civici Venezia

93

realism derived from Mantegna. Landscape assumes a dominant role and is used to convey the atmosphere of the picture: it provides a context in which the figures appear as pawns, set below an expanse of sky relieved by drifting clouds. These expressions of mood are worked over and over again in countless Madonnas looking tenderly down at a sleeping cherub or a Christ Child in benediction (*Madonna degli Alberetti* – Accademia), in portrayals of the Dead Christ and many *Sacre Conversazioni* (*St Vincent Ferrer Polyptych* – San Zanipòlo).

Giovanni's brother **Gentile** (1429–1507) was the first artist to be nominated Venice's official painter, a position which underpinned a brilliant career. He emerged as a talented portrait painter (Doge Giovanni Mocenigo) and applied his observational skills to portraying views of Venice, known as **vedute**, which became an influential genre in itself in the 18C. The overall objective was for painting to be true to life: *The Procession of the Relics of the True Cross in Piazza San Marco* (Accademia), for example, is a factual or documentary representation of 15C Venice, even if the painter, conscientious in every detail, was careful to align the façades and order the attendant crowds.

The advent of High Renaissance

Vittore Carpaccio (1455–1526), following in the wake of Bellini and Antonello, suffuses a lesson learned from Flemish painting with his own personal creativity to execute the cycles of paintings commissioned by the "Scuole" (see I CARMINI: The Venetian Scuole): *Miracle of the Relic of the True Cross at Rialto* for Scuola di San Giovanni Evangelista; *Legend of St Ursula* (Accademia) in which Brittany is represented as a Venetian Renaissance city; and *Legends of St George and St Jerome* for Scuola di San Giorgio degli Schiavoni, which depicts an exotic Orient. Carpaccio surpassed Bellini in sensitivity and in his inimitable talent for story-telling. His pictures are imaginatively populated with well-observed and delightful details: he even manages to reconcile his penchant for miniaturist precision with a love of broad views. In his landscapes, a key element in his paintings, are representations of a luxuriant, flowery vegetation, peopled with a host of animals (dogs, birds, rabbits, peacocks, parrots and deer). Renaissance buildings stand out, embellished with marble inlays that might have been designed by the Lombardo family, surrounded by numerous oriental motifs (palm trees, Moorish turbans). All of Carpaccio's works display the same distinctive features: boldness of line, luminosity, vivid colours, perfect sense of proportion, attention to detail and crowd scenes.

Giambattista Cima (1459–1518), known as Cima da Conegliano, drew on Giovanni Bellini for his strong, radiant light and on Carpaccio for his love of detail. His are the glorious portrayals of dignified figures, pictured in beautiful landscapes under broad open skies (*Madonna of the Orange Tree* – Accademia; *Adoration of the Shepherds* – I Carmini). By the close of the 15C, Venetian painting had reached the height of its artistic expression.

Reform

His name was Giorgio di Castelfranco but he went by the name of **Giorgione** (1475–1510). It was he who revolutionised the course of painting in the early 16C despite his short life. Giorgione is considered the first "modern" artist in the history of painting. A Renaissance man in every sense, he drew inspiration for his work from Humanist ideology, making it intellectual and sometimes shrouded in mystery, as well as open to controversial interpretation. Few works have been attributed to him with any certainty, and these are poetic in feel, almost dreamlike, but always charged with allusions to literature, music and philosophy: ephemerality and vulnerability are the subject of *The Tempest*; *La Vecchia* depicts the passage of time (both in the Accademia). His style appears more sensual than Classical. The landscape now plays an essential role in the painting; man is no longer the main subject, it is Nature itself that becomes the true protagonist – human drama is reduced to just one element in the force of Nature (such as in *The Tempest*).

St Michael
by Michele Giambono
(Accademia)

St Augustine
by Bartolomeo Vivarini
(San Zanipòlo)

St Sebastian
by Mantegna
(Ca' d'Oro)

The Madonna of the Orange Tree by Cima da Conegliano (Accademia)

The Barbarigo Alterpiece by Giovanni Bellini (San Pietro Martire, Murano)

Palma il Vecchio (1480–1528) followed in the same vein, although in later life he betrays the influence of Titian's handling of light, his juxtaposition of contrasting colour and the asymmetry of his altarpiece compositions. Palma il Vecchio specialised in *Sacre Conversazioni* (&see *SAN ZACCARIA*) and painted the portrait of Paola Priuli (Querini-Stampaglia Collection). His art does not match that of the most talented masters but its appeal is one of spontaneity and exuberant colour.

The Bergamo-born **Lorenzo Lotto** (1480–1556) is another major early-16C painter with a distinctively personal style. His pictures are disconcerting and strange, they betray the influence of Dürer's scientific treatment of detail (Dürer visited Venice in c.1495) and the painter's liking for bold contrasts (*Portrait of a Young Gentleman in his Study* – Accademia). He avoided the sensual, colourful appeal of Giorgione and Titian, preferring to employ a rather frigid, angular style modelled on the precise, slightly archaic style of Alvise Vivarini.

16C masters and their pupils

In the 16C, Venetian painting affirmed its supremacy; this was the era of the great European masters and highly skilled painters who, thanks to their respective talents, succeeded in establishing a distinctive style that was to become the hallmark of Venice and which soon earned her European recognition.

Titian

Tiziano Vecellio, known as Titian (c.1485–1576), is unquestionably the most famous artist of his time. Born in Pieve di Cadore, he remained highly active until his death, aged 90. He served his apprenticeship under Giovanni Bellini and was subsequently influenced by Giorgione (some of whose works he completed) and then Raphael. The author of large altarpieces undertaken for churches (I Frari) and Scuole (La Carità) alike, he favoured colour over form and breathed life into his canvases with a dynamic handling of paint and bold composition (*The Assumption* – I Frari; *Martyrdom of St Lawrence* – Gesuiti). His reputation far outreached the realms of the lagoon city, and led to him being commissioned to paint portraits of all the leading lights of his time at the courts of Ferrara, Mantua, Florence and Urbino; he worked for the Pope, François I and Charles V, who knighted him in 1553.

During the early part of his career, Titian's painting was fundamentally Classical in inspiration. However, between 1535 and 1545, he was seduced by Mannerism before reverting to a more dignified and serene style. At the end of his life, the melodramatic tension inherent in some compositions (*The Pietà* – Accademia) betrays the artist's mysticism at the imminence of death.

In conclusion, Titian was largely responsible for reviving interest in the large altarpiece. He succeeded in taking painting to unimagined heights of monumentality by abandoning symmetry of composition (*Pesaro Altarpiece* – I Frari), opting for large contrasting blocks of colour, displaying a sure stroke and a perfect sense of harmony.

Il Tintoretto

Contemporary with Titian, Venice harboured the genius of Jacopo Comin, known as *il Tintoretto* (1518–94), the most original and most prolific of the Venetian masters. He was born the son of a dyer (hence his name) and never left Venice (save once, maybe, to visit Rome), but he never really enjoyed success in his lifetime. Tireless and passionate about his work, an ardent admirer of Michelangelo, he preferred biblical subjects to those of Classical Antiquity (Scuola di San Rocco) and chose to portray common people instead of focusing on the excesses of the nobility. He developed a restless style: despite the interaction of rapid precise brush strokes and gentle soft touches, his work is always lyrical, a quality that is projected from his dynamic handling of paint and from the arrangement of figures in groups or alone, brought together by strong lines of composition (*Crucifixion* – Scuola di San Rocco). The use of chiaroscuro (strong contrasts of light and shade), juxtaposed complementary colours, elongated figures, daring foreshortening and a filtering light that blurs the contours of figures and architectural settings, all contribute to reinforcing the charged atmosphere of his Mannerist work.

His best pictures include the *Miracles of St Mark* painted for the Scuola di San Marco (Accademia), the *Marriage of Cana* (Santa Maria della Salute), *Paradise* (Doges' Palace, Grand Council Chamber), *The Triumph of Venice* (Doges' Palace), and *The Presentation of the Virgin in the Temple* (Madonna dell'Orto), not forgetting the 50 paintings, the largest cycle of its kind in Venice, executed for the Scuola di San Rocco, on which he worked for 23 years in collaboration with his son **Domenico Tintoretto**.

Veronese

In direct contrast with Tintoretto, **Paolo Caliari** (1528–88), born in Verona, hence his nickname *Veronese*, specialised in portraying the wealthy, opulent and carefree aristocracy of the Renaissance; in luminous colour (including the famous "Veronese green") that set off to theatrical effect the most sumptuous fabrics used for their clothing. His works in the main are endowed with optimism, fantasy and spontaneity, they seem permeated with spring light; towards the end of his life, however, Veronese's paintings change to more sombre and melancholic mood, muddied by the influence of Tintoretto's chiaroscuro and Bassano's style. Mythological scenes proliferate on the walls and ceilings of the Doges' Palace (*Apotheosis of Venice*). The subject of *The Last Supper* was reworked by Veronese several times for the refectories of Venetian monasteries, including the famous, huge canvas *Christ in the House of Levi* (Accademia), commissioned for the Dominican monastery of San Zanipòlo. This was contrived as a depiction of an entirely profane meal, while providing an excellent pretext for a work of grandiose proportions. The magnificent decoration of San Sebastiano is another masterpiece, appropriate, perhaps, given that it was his chosen ultimate resting place.

Mannerism in Venice

Whereas Tintoretto forged his style from Titian and Michelangelo, and Veronese was heir to Bellini, Giorgione and Raphael, their legacy, like that of Titian, was both powerful and influential beyond the confines of Venice, for several generations. It also naturally led to Venetian Mannerism.

Titian had many followers: **Palma il Vecchio** (1480–1528); **Pordenone** (c.1483–1539), who worked successfully in Venice from 1535–38; **Paris Bordone** (1500–71), who delighted in Venetian Renaissance architecture (*Handing the Ring to the Doge* – Accademia; *Martyrdom of St Theodore* – San Salvador) and charged his canvases with vivid colours; the prolific **Palma il Giovane** (1544–1628), the grandson of Palma il Vecchio, with an eclectic style, who provided nearly all the city's churches with large-scale paintings.

An exponent of the sensuality and silky colours explored by Giorgione and Titian, **Andrea Schiavone** (c.1510–63) moved away from realism in favour of elongated form and restless movement typical of Mannerism, in the style of Parmigianino.

Impressed by Tintoretto's painting, **Jacopo Bassano** (Jacopo da Ponte, 1512–92) paints in a provincial style marked by an exaggerated preoccupation with naturalism (*St Jerome Meditating* – Accademia), while using light effects to suggest the intensity of the scene (*Nativity* – San Giorgio Maggiore). His sons Leandro and Francesco shared this tradition of *maniera* painting, in which the pastoral and rustic element becomes the prime subject rather than the religious or profane content.

18C revival

Venetian painting, in decline during the 17C and overshadowed by the great personalities of the previous century and the Roman Baroque, enjoyed a new creative and glorious burst of energy during this period of lavish receptions in the Age of Enlightenment.

Decorative painting

Long after the taste for grandiose interior decoration had flourished in Rome and Florence during the 16C–17C, Venice revived her interest in the decorative art of Veronese found on the walls and ceilings of her churches and *palazzi* and in the Palladian villas along the Brenta. **Sebastiano Ricci** (1659–1734), the Baroque painter of rather sentimental religious pictures, reinforced his strong compositions with bright colour (*Madonna with Saints* – San Giorgio Maggiore). It was with **Giambattista Piazzetta** (1682–1754), who excelled in religious painting, that huge ceiling compositions became popular, and that figures began to be shown from below, aspiring to dizzy heights among the clouds, drawn awkwardly towards a mystical light (*Glorification of St Dominic* – San Zanipòlo). Influenced by Caravaggio, Piazzetta also painted genre pictures (featuring people from common, everyday life in mundane surroundings) with strong chiaroscuro (*The Fortune Teller* – Accademia).

Piazzetta influenced the greatest artist of the century: **Giambattista Tiepolo** (1696–1770), the pre-eminent genius of Venetian Baroque decoration and creator of huge compositions of great virtuosity full of delicate colour, golden light and infinite space. He painted vast altarpieces and covered entire ceilings with frescoes (Palazzo Labia, Scuola dei Carmini, Church of the Gesuiti, Ca' Rezzonico), turning his hand as easily to religious subjects (*Our Lady of Mount Carmel* – I Carmini) as to mythological ones, including huge Virtues set before grandiose architectural backdrops.

Portraiture and Genre

Long-established patrician families and those of an aspiring bourgeoisie altered their household arrangements to reflect changes in lifestyle. In keeping with fashions elsewhere, it became acceptable to have informal, intimate and private rooms, separate from grandiose function or occasion rooms, in which to conduct everyday business, and this trend was reflected in contemporary art. Painters were asked to provide portraits that were both flattering and informal, a genre favoured by **Rosalba Carriera** (1675–1758), who produced delicate, vibrant pastels that earned her international fame (Ca' Rezzonico, Accademia), and **Alessandro Longhi**.

Around the same time, Venetians appeared to appreciate the small-scale interior scenes painted by **Pietro Longhi** (1702–85), such as masquerades, dances and duck hunting scenes (Hemingway's future pastime in Torcello), all revealing his acute powers of observation (Ca' Rezzonico, Querini-Stampalla Collection).

Topographical painters

Besides the *maniera* and genre scenes devoid of religious, allegorical or mythological meaning, landscape for its own sake began to provide artists with a worthy subject for easel pictures. In Venice, studies of the environment focused on the city herself, and it is for these views, *vedute* in Italian, that Antonio Canal (1697–1768), known as **Canaletto**, became so famous. In his pictures, he delineates in minute detail his on-the-spot observations of the city. Although his vision is almost photographic, he exaggerates perspective and paints huge, monumental buildings. He was also known to portray festivals and regattas. Unfortunately, most of his works are now exhibited in museums outside Italy and few can be admired in Venice itself. Canaletto inspired a great many artists, namely **Bernardo Bellotto** (1720–80), one of his pupils who was also a relative.

Quite distinct from Canaletto, **Francesco Guardi** (1712–93) was bewitched by the atmosphere of the lagoon city. His vision is not photographic; instead his bold use of paint succeeds in freezing the ripples of the water and the flickering light – a preoccupation that was to fascinate the English Romantic painter Turner and the French Impressionists a century later. Besides views of the lagoon, he also painted scenes of everyday life in the manner of Pietro Longhi: *Nuns' Parlour, Interval Time in the Foyer* (Ca' Rezzonico), as did his brother **Giovianni Antonio**.

Freed from the influence of his father, after painting the Stations of the Cross in San Polo, **Giovanni Domenico (Giandomenico) Tiepolo** (1727–1804) painted 18C Venetian society on the Brenta Riviera with humour and irony,

Christ in the House of Lévi, by Véronese (Accademia)

The Fortune Teller by Giambattista Piazzetta (Accademia)

Pulchinella by Giandomenico Tiepolo (Ca' Rezzonico)

View over the Rio dei Mendicanti by Canaletto (Ca' Rezzonico)

depicting the holidaymakers as buffoons (Ca' Rezzonico: Villa Zianigo frescoes).

Modern and contemporary age

Between the 19C and the 20C Venetian painting continued on academic lines, ever faithful to the traditions set in the 18C with landscapes or urban scenes by Caffi and Ciardi, and fine portraits by Alessandro Milesi.

Motivated by mainstream developments in Europe during the early 20C, several painters produced interesting work (International Museum of Modern Art in Ca' Pesaro): **Federico Zandomeneghi** (1841–1917) who was born in Venice, worked with the Macchiaioli group before moving to Paris where he befriended Degas; **Umberto Boccioni** (1882–1916) was a founding member of the Futurist movement and painted in a style reminiscent of Signal (*The Grand Canal*); **Fragiacomo** was an Impressionist much inspired by Turner (*St Mark's Square*); **Casorati** was a Symbolist painter and portraitist.

Members of the **Burano School (Scuola di Burano)**, such as Moggioli, Gino Rossi, Sibellato and Semeghini, painted the islands of the lagoon, experimenting with techniques inspired by Van Gogh, Gauguin and Cézanne, and of the Post-Impressionists Bonnard and Vuillard.

Literature

1200–1500

The history of Venetian literature begins in 1271 when "Master **Marco Polo**, a wise and noble citizen of Venice" embarked on a journey to the Orient. Despite his tender age, the 16 year-old decided to accompany his father Niccolò and uncle Matteo, both Levantine merchants, on a very long expedition to the court of "Kublai, the Great Khan of the Mongols". Never before had such an ambitious journey to those parts been undertaken by Westerners. Unfortunately the return journey was to prove Marco's undoing, for during one of the many naval battles between the Venetians and the Genoese, the explorer

was taken prisoner by the enemy. As he languished in prison, he came to know a writer from Pisa, Rustichello, who undertook to set down on paper an account of the Venetian's experiences. So **The Book of the Wonders of the World** was born; it achieved success under the title *Il Milione*, an epithet given to Marco Polo when he described the quantities of gold he claimed to have seen. In the years that followed the death of the traveller, Venice appeared to dedicate itself less to literature than to commerce. Indeed, Venetian literary circles seem to have been affected by Humanism.

It was not until **Aldo Manuzio**, the *"ante litteram"* publisher, arrived in Venice that the situation changed. In 1499 he published the *Hypnerotomachia Poliphili*, an amusing, anonymous work written in an explosive style, using vernacular language bastardised from Venetian and Latin. Its success was modest but it seems to have heralded one of the most successful literary spells in Venice.

BEMBO TO GOLDONI: A PERIOD OF GREAT SPLENDOUR

A more conventional writer to be published by Aldo Manuzio was **Pietro Bembo**. Born into a very aristocratic family in Venice in 1470, Bembo remained the touchstone of literary developments for almost a century. His importance is largely due to *The Prose of Vulgar Language* which came out in 1528, and which contributed to the age-old debate over the use of vernacular language in literature. In it Bembo argued that he was violently opposed to the language adopted by Dante, and offered a convincing alternative that in part has influenced the evolution of Italian into the language of today.

The Paduan-born **Angelo Beolco** (1496), meanwhile, was moving in a different direction. His nickname, *il Ruzzante* (The Playful One), was derived from the peasant protagonist of his plays, whom the author often impersonated, and so the character and his creator became synonymous. The most famous play, *Il Parlamento del Ruzzante*, is a merciless portrait of peasant conditions at the time of a long and bloody war between the French and the Venetians.

Contemporary with Ruzzante was the unknown author of the **Veniexiana**, an entertaining comedy in dialect which depicted the vices and virtues (mainly the former) of the inhabitants of the lagoon city. Its significance, however, lies not so much in the amusing story it tells, full of melodramatic action, but in its marking a turning point in the cultural milieu of Venice. For between 1530 and 1540, the popular trend suddenly passed from foreign imported theatrical productions to the blossoming of "original" domestic plays.

This radical change was no doubt precipitated by the presence of **Pietro Aretino** who, as his surname suggests, was born in Arezzo. After a stay in Rome, Aretino reached Venice in 1527, just in time to publish *Il Marescalco* and *La Cortegiana*, two of the most popular and well-crafted comedies of the 16C. Their success was immediate and very well exploited by Aretino, who was astute enough to engage the new resources proffered by the printing press to increase his fame. This collaboration was, in fact, to make both the Tuscan and his publisher Marcotini a fortune. Aretino, furthermore, showed himself capable of using popular, vernacular language for literature to nothing short of tumultuous effect. His plays mocked and lampooned the authorities, attracting audiences from all walks of life, but most notably from among those in power who were anxious to know what was indeed being said. It was no surprise therefore, that he soon earned the epithet "the scourge of the princes".

Thus during the 17C, the Republic's somewhat liberal attitude must have excused the considerable freedom of thought and action enjoyed in Venice: it is difficult otherwise to explain the success of Aretino and other such lax publications that would have been prohibited elsewhere. Venice became an important publishing centre, drawing all kinds of literary characters who wished to take particular care over typographical layouts and to oversee the output of their own book. Soon hundreds of printers

> It would appear that the title of Marco Polo's book was in fact inspired by the word "Emilione", the nickname given to the family of the great navigator.

mushroomed to service hundreds of authors, dependent one upon the other.

Comedy

The theatre became a passion for citizens of all social classes. Plays proliferated, almost all written and produced on the spot. Comedies enacted in dialect enjoyed the greatest popularity; these were often based around sets of particular carnival characters identified by their traditional mask and costume, such as **Harlequin**. The needs of a growing number of theatre devotees, coupled with those of an important and thriving port, founded the beginnings of a modern news-spreading media.

Journalism

The advent of journalism in Italy could only have been feasible in a milieu like Venice. In 1760 Gasparo Gozzi launched the magazine *La Gazzetta Veneta*, which appeared twice a week for about a year. Conceived along the lines of an English periodical, features included articles on orders of the day and useful practical information on life in the city (financial announcements, public notices, advertisement listings, stock exchange reports etc). It was in *La Gazzetta* that Goldoni published his first reviews on Rusteghi.

Carlo Goldoni (1707–93)

Goldoni's father was a doctor who wished his son to follow in his footsteps but when Carlo was aged 13, he ran away from school to join a ship in Rimini that was carrying a troupe of actors to Chioggia. From there he went on to join his mother in Venice. Goldoni resumed his studies and qualified as a lawyer. Lacking the will to succeed, however, he soon turned his hand at challenging the tradition of the Commedia dell'Arte to improvise dialogue along the lines of a given plot.

Statue of Carlo Goldoni

In 1743 Goldoni wrote the script for *La donna di Garbo*. In 1750 the provocative comedy playwright impudently waged a bet with his rival Pietro Chiari that in less than a year he could write 16 new comedies: in fact he wrote 17, including the splendid *La Bottega del Caffè* (*The Coffee Shop*), set in Venice and satirising the bourgeoisie. The ingredients were simple: he used colloquial language for immediacy and formulated rounded characters based on observation of real life. He avoided political incorrectness by importing his gentrified personalities from afar, able therefore to exaggerate their airs and graces. *Arlecchino, Servitore di due Padroni* (*Servant of Two Masters*), *La Locandiera* (*The Innkeeper*) are all constructed according to the same format. Goldoni died in France.

An account of Goldoni's stay in Venice can be found in the author's memoirs (*Memorie*).

HOW THE 18C AND 19C SAW VENICE

Venice as depicted by Goldoni, full of humour and moral integrity, was a vital place that attracted the talented, the eccentric and the curious. These included **Lorenzo da Ponte**, Mozart's celebrated librettist and author of the *Marriage of Figaro*, who lingered there for "a couple of years of adventurous libertinage", and that specialist master of licentiousness **Giacomo Casanova**

(1725–98) who, between one amorous assignation and another, found time to write his interesting *Memoirs*.

Another reprobate of the same school, if the term is appropriate, the poet **Ugo Foscolo**, landed on the Riva degli Schiavoni in 1793. He stopped in the city for four years, during which he demonstrated the true colour of his personality on numerous occasions. Abandoning his regular studies, he embarked on teaching himself the Greek and Latin classics to engineer his infiltration of the very refined salon of Isabella Teorochi Albrizzi, with whom he initiated a passionate affair, he aged 16 and she 34. In the meantime, he wrote the famous *Ode to the Liberator Bonaparte*; only the "liberator", in his political intrigue, paid no heed to the revolutionary ideals of the young Foscolo, but ceded Venice to Austria to further his own hegemonic aims. The repercussions on the writer were enormous, forcing him to seek refuge in Milan, where he devoted himself to drafting *The Last Letters of Jacopo Ortis*, a prose account of the delusion he had suffered. During his sojourn in Venice, however, Foscolo also became involved with **Melchiorre Cesarotti**, an important forerunner of the early Romantic movement.

Cesarotti was a tutor in an aristocratic household whose salon Foscolo frequently attended. In 1760 Cesarotti came across a collection of poems by

Portrait of Ugo Foscolo by Fabre, Francois Xavier (1766-1837)

Ossian, a legendary bard, published by a certain MacPherson: in six months, Cesarotti had translated them into Italian verse, which he published in 1763. *Le Poesie di Ossian,* as they appeared in Italian, shot Cesarotti to fame, oblivious of the fact that these "Ossianic poems" were to be one of those most famous cases of literary fraud to be uncovered over the last 200 years. **James MacPherson** (1736–96) claimed they were a translation of a series of surviving fragments of some ancient Gaelic mythical poetry when in fact they had been fabricated, for the most part, by the Scotsman himself. Poor Cesarotti was one of the many innocents to fall for the trick.

By the end of the century, the foundations of Italian Romanticism had been laid. The Piedmontese **Silvio Pellico**, the fervent patriot and anti-Austrian agitator, was soon to write his famous and doleful *Piombi*. In *Le mie Prigioni,* Pellico narrates his whole experience from the day of his arrest (13 October 1820) to that of his release (September 1830), thereby securing a place in the heart of the nation as a hero.

Throughout the Romantic period, Venice reigned supreme. This was not so much as a result of her literary output but rather because she continued to distract so many intellectuals, such as **Lord Byron**, on their travels through Italy, happy to meet up under the shaded porticoes of the Procuratie, a custom that was to extend well into the next century.

In 1886 the Russian author **Anton Chekhov** published a collection of short stories. *Story of a Stranger* recounts his overwhelming passion for Venice, to such an extent that he feels "intoxicated with life".

20TH CENTURY

The modern history of the lagoon city rests almost exclusively in the hands of foreigners, many of whom sought refuge there from persecution at home and soon enjoyed a protected social scene. Not only were there no Venetian-born writers of note to emerge, few Italians were attracted to the decadent beauty

of *La Serenissima*. **Gabriele d'Annunzio** was a notable exception.

Marcel Proust arrived in 1900, inevitably accompanied by his mother, with whom he began translating the English writer **John Ruskin**, author of the famous *Stones of Venice*, while refining his own literary style. Proust's sojourn was a particularly happy one: reflecting in *A la recherche du temps perdu*, he writes *"However did the images of Venice give me such joy and confidence as to render me indifferent to death".*

The reflections of **Thomas Mann** are of a very different order: in *Death in Venice*, the city is portrayed as being in a state of decay. The protagonist of the novel is Gustav von Aschenbach, a German writer who, after a lifetime of rigorous discipline, feels attracted by a city described as crumbling and overrun with cholera.

In 1918 the Viennese author **Arthur Schnitzler** wrote *Casanova in Spa*, a book set in Venice and loosely based on his amorous adventures.

Among the most recent illustrious visitors to the city was **Ernest Hemingway** who set down his suitcases in the Hotel Gritti in 1948. He loved to be called "Papa" and while away the time with glasses of Montgomery, a strong Martini, at Harry's Bar. Far removed from the more rugged places associated with the writer, Hemingway once confessed to his translator Ferdinanda Pivano: *"Sitting by the Grand Canal and writing near where Mr Byron, Mr Browning and*

Ernest Hemingway in Piazza San Marco

Literary Venice

Travellers with a keen eye and a writer's pen have provided many accounts of life in the lagoon city. In his notes about Italy (1729), **Charles Louis de Montesquieu** offers a sketchy description of Venice that nonetheless lists a great many figures (six *sestieri*, seven parishes, 25 houses for monks and 36 for nuns, 500 bridges, 20 000 residents etc). **Goethe's portrayal** is infused with sentiment: *"I suddenly felt that I too reigned supreme over the Adriatic, as do all Venetians as soon as they set foot on their gondola…"*. (*Italian Journey*, 1829). In his diary about Italy (1857), **Herman Melville** presents the reader with an interesting medley of thoughts, impressions and fleeting images: *"Shimmering silver thuribles swaying softly, scattering incense over the heads of the faithful … The rich, deep complexion of the women painted by Titian is indeed close to nature …"*.

Mr D'Annunzio wrote makes Mr Papa feel he has arrived at where he is meant to be". The same year saw the publication of *Cantos* by the American poet **Ezra Pound**, who died in Venice (see *SAN ZANIPÒLO: Cemetery*) and who wrote about the city in Canto LXXVI.

In the early sixties, the Italian author **Giorgio Bassani** used the Ghetto district as a backdrop to his novel *Il Giardino dei Finzi Contini*, which was made into a famous film by **Vittorio de Sica**.

The Russian writer **Josif Brodskij**, who received the Nobel Prize for Literature in 1987, was fascinated by Venetian water and canals, a passion he recounted in *Watermark*.

GIORGIO BASSANI

IL GIARDINO DEI FINZI-CONTINI

EINAUDI

© AISA/World Illustrated / Photoshot

The first edition of Il Giardino dei Finzi Contini by Giorgio Bassani published in 1962

Another Slav author who evokes the lagoon city was Polish-born **Gustaw Herling** who, in *Portrait of Venice* (1994), evokes his "sentimental involvement with Venice".

Music

PRELUDE TO VIVALDI

Renaissance

Whereas in Rome a brilliant revival in music flourished under the auspices of **Giovanni Pierluigi da Palestrina** (1525–94), who headed a polyphonic school dedicated to sacred music, patronage in Venice was limited to more secular applications. Perhaps the turning point is marked by the Flemish **Willaert** (c.1490–1562), the choirmaster at St Mark's, who set a trend that was to be continued by his pupil Andrea Gabrieli.

Andrea Gabrieli (c.1510–86) – Organist at St Mark's, Gabrieli emerged as an important composer and influential teacher of organ and choral music in the Venetian tradition. His innovative use of the *concertato* (a small group of instruments or voices), contrasted with the *ripieno* (a larger body of musicians), forestalled the implementation of the *concerto* form developed and exploited later by Corelli. This allowed Gabrieli to experiment with harmony and dissonance by combining various "parts" for choir, or the human voice with instruments. His most lasting contribution is a large body of choral works for both sacred (motets for four to 12 voices, masses for six voices, the *Psalms of David* for six voices) and secular texts (madrigals for three to 12 voices).

Giovanni Gabrieli (c.1557–1612) – Andrea's nephew Giovanni inherited the position of organist at St Mark's and further propagated the fame of the Venetian School abroad (the Dutch master Sweelinck, Hans Leo Hassler, Heinrich Schutz, Bach's precursor and founder of German church music, were already pupils). Among his compositions, which comprised sacred, secular and instrumental pieces, the most notable are his motets, the **Sacred Symphonies**. His more avant-garde works include **sonatas** for violin, which he used to explore antiphonal effects: at the time the violin was the instrument that best sustained the popular taste for monophonic music (following a single line of notes). By adding a **basso continuo** or figured bass line, with long drawn notes, he was able to develop harmonies with the accompaniment, thereby providing sustained and textured melody. This Gabrieli applied not only to choral arrangements but to instrumental pieces for two violins and clavichord or cello.

The Baroque Period

With the 17C began another rich and fruitful period for Venetian music. Melodrama became a formal genre; formulated from accounts of contemporary historical events or legends, exaggerated stories were re-enacted to audiences in elaborately contrived stage settings. Francesco Cavalli (1602–76), a chorister at St Mark's, Marc'Antonio Cesti (1623–69) and Giovanni Legrenzi (1626–90), choirmaster at St Mark's, all collaborated at an operatic school in Venice which, in 1637, opened the first commercial opera house, San Cassiano. Here Monteverdi's operas were later performed.

The 18th Century

By the mid-1700s, Venice was renowned for the more typically Neapolitan kind of comic operas by **Baldassarre Galuppi** (see BURANO), who, together with Giovanni Platti (1700–63), contributed to the development of the sonata (literally meaning "sounded", imply-

Famous organ-builders

Gaetano Callido (1727–1813) built about 400 organs throughout the Veneto, Dalmatia and even the Holy Land: all three organs at St Mark's were restored by him in 1766. Four years later, he was appointed the official, permanent organ-maker to the city. His sons Agostino and Antonio continued to practise their father's craft until 1821.

ing music that is instrumental rather than sung) for strings and keyboard. In response to works by the Bach dynasty in Germany, they composed pieces for one (harpsichord) or two instruments (harpsichord and violin) in homophonic (several lines of notes moving in chords) and polyphonic (several lines of notes each with its own distinctive pattern) arrangements in several movements (usually three).

The harpsichord enjoyed particular favour, despite the advent of the piano, developed by Bartolomeo Cristofori (1655–1732) by substituting hammers for quills. Among the most famous players of the harpsichord, besides Galuppi and Platti, were the two **Marcello** brothers, **Benedetto** (1686–1739), who also composed sacred music and concertos for five instruments, and **Alessandro** (1684–1750), who wrote sonatas for violin and basso continuo and concertos for oboe and strings that hitherto have been attributed to Benedetto. Also active in Venice in this period was **Tomaso Albinoni** (1671–1750), who more closely followed in the German Baroque tradition and foreshadows Vivaldi in his instrumental compositions.

17C Opera

During the 17C, thanks to Claudio Monteverdi, who conducted the choir at San Marco, Venice became known as the world's leading centre for operatic art, placing herself ahead of Florence and Mantua. In those days, the lagoon city boasted a total of 17 theatres.

Venice in Music

From *The Four Seasons* by Vivaldi to traditional Venetian songs, music heard for the first time in Venice will evoke memories of its canals and piazzas. The works of classical and traditional music below embody a particularly Venetian flavour.

- Various artists, *Musiche veneziane per voce e strumenti,* Claves
- Various artists, *Music of the Tintoretto Age,* Edelweiss
- Various artists, *A Piano Recital for Venice,* Edelweiss
- Various artists, *Voice and Lute in Venice in the 16th Century,* Edelweiss
- Various artists, *Musiche veneziane per voce e strumenti* (*Teresa Berganza*), Claves
- Various artists, *Musiche veneziane per trombe e tromboni,* Claves
- Various artists, *Souvenirs de Venise: The Songmakers' Almanac,* Hyperion
- Tomaso Albinoni, *Musiche veneziane,* Claves
- Andrea and Giovanni Gabrieli, *Musica organistica,* Tactus
- Giovanni Gabrieli, *Sinfonie sacre,* Oiseau-lyre
- Baldassarre Galuppi, *Musiche veneziane: concerti e sinfonie,* Claves
- Baldassarre Galuppi, *Musiche veneziane: passatempo al cembalo,* Claves
- Baldassarre Galuppi; Antonio Vivaldi, *Musiche veneziane: Magnificat; Gloria,* Claves
- Alessandro Marcello, *Concerto in re minore per oboe, archi e organo,* Philips
- Monteverdi, Rigatti, Grandi, Cavalli, *Venetian Vespers,* Archiv
- Antonio Vivaldi, *The Four Seasons*
- Antonio Vivaldi, *Musiche veneziane: Six Concertos for Flute,* Claves
- Antonio Vivaldi, *Musiche veneziane: concerti,* Claves

Venetian music – The *Concerto in D minor for oboe, strings and organ* by Alessandro Marcello was long attributed to his brother Benedetto. This well-known piece of music accompanied the Italian film *The Anonymous Venetian*, which starred Tony Musante and Florinda Bolkan.

ANTONIO VIVALDI (1678–1741)

It is undoubtedly Vivaldi who best epitomises Venetian music: even JS Bach (1685–1750) drew openly on the compositions of the *"Prete Rosso"* (👆 *see SAN GIORGIO degli SCHIAVONI*), who was literally rediscovered in the mid-20C, after years of oblivion.

Vivaldi was a prolific composer, using a three-movement form of the concerto, *allegro-adagio-allegro,* and freeing up the *Sonata da Camera* as a series of contrasting descriptive passages as in the *Four Seasons,* the *Goldfinch* and *Night concerti.* Altogether, Vivaldi composed over 500 concertos for violin, viola d'amore, cello, mandolin, flute, oboe, bassoon, trumpet, cornet and string orchestra.

His parents

Giovanni Battista Vivaldi, father of Antonio, was a professional barber and musician: this would be surprising today, but many Venetians of the time combined both professions. Giovanni Battista, nicknamed *il Rosso* after the colour of his auburn hair, obviously a family trait, was a violin virtuoso in 17C Venice, more specifically in the area around **San Martino** where most of the city's musicians congregated at the Scuola, the *Sovvegno di Santa Cecilia,* whose patron naturally was St Cecilia.

Camilla Calicchio, the mother of Antonio, was born in the area around **San Giovanni in Bràgora** (👆 *see ARSENALE*), where Antonio was baptised a second time, having been subjected to the formalities of a blessing at home on 4 March 1678, shortly after his birth, when it appeared that he might not survive.

Il Prete Rosso

Antonio was ordained at **San Giovanni Novo,** even though he dedicated himself to the cause of music rather than to the priesthood, content to remain a secular priest or abbot. He took up residence in Fondamenta del Dose, near the Ponte del Paradiso, before abandoning the Castello *sestiere* in favour of St Mark's, where he lived on the Riva del Carbon. When he left these lodgings in 1740 it was to leave Venice completely, dying in poverty in Vienna the following year.

The Musician

Vivaldi's main musical activity is associated first and foremost with the Pietà and the Theatre of San Angelo.

The Pietà was one of the great **foundling hospitals** which, between the 17C and 18C, doubled as one of the musical conservatories of Venice, each having its own church where concerts were held. These "hospitals" functioned as charitable institutions and orphanages for girls (*ospitaliere*), who received an education and, if gifted, musical instruction to enable them to take part in the choirs and orchestras of which the establishments were so proud.

Associated as it is with the fame of Vivaldi, the Pietà became the best known of the hospital-churches. Standing on the Riva degli Schiavoni it cannot be mistaken or missed, although the present church is not the original one where Vivaldi had been music teacher and composer. The former church stood where the Metropole Hotel now stands, slightly to the right of the present church.

The San Angelo Theatre no longer exists. It was there that the violin virtuoso acted as musical director, impresario, composer and performed more secular works.

AFTER VIVALDI

The musical splendour of Venice, which regaled contemporary ears for three centuries and continues to survive today in churches and concert halls, faded with the passing of its most illustrious representative. In more recent times, one interesting composer emerges from the Venetian and German traditions and that is **Ermanno Wolf-Ferrari** (1876–1948), who was particularly impressed by Mozart's operatic works and inspired

Vivaldi – the "Prete Rosso"

© SCALA

by the theatre of Goldoni: both influences are evident in his own life's opus *Gioielli della Madonna, Le Donne Curiose, I Quattro rusteghi, Il Campiello,* etc.

Yet more recently still, the city has resumed its role as a lively and innovative artistic centre by playing host to such experimental musicians as **Bruno Maderna** (1920–73) and **Luigi Nono** (1924–90).

Venice was also the birthplace of the conductor Giuseppe Sinopoli (1946–2001), who was to become an authority on Mahler's work.

VENETIAN BY ADOPTION

Tribute should also be paid to visiting composers who died in Venice.

Claudio Monteverdi (1567–1643) was one genius who breathed personality and characterisation into opera: he lies buried at I Frari (*see I FRARI*). **Domenico Cimarosa** (1749–1801), often regarded as the Italian Mozart, died in Campo Sant' Angelo (*see La FENICE*). The apparently aloof and detached **Igor Stravinsky** (1882–1971) is buried in the cemetery of San Michele.

However, it was **Richard Wagner** (1813–83), possibly the most controversial composer in musical history, who most desired to be adopted by his beloved Venice. The maestro died on 13 February in the Palazzo Vendramin Calergi (*see Il CANAL GRANDE*) in the company of his wife, Cosima, and the gondolier Gigio Trevisan, nicknamed Ganassete.

During Wagner's peaceful stay in Venice, he would go to St Mark's Square daily where, seated at Quadri's or Florian's, he was sometimes recognised by the leader of the municipal band who would ask him to conduct: Wagner would agree, happy to direct his own compositions for the Venetians. It was here that Wagner composed the second act of *Tristan* (the English horn part having been inspired by the evening song of the gondoliers), wrote part of *Parsifal* and initiated work on the *Maestri cantori* inspired by Titian's *Assumption* that he so admired at I Frari.

Carnevale (Carnival)

During the 18C, the Venice Carnival opened at the beginning of October and ended on the Tuesday preceding Lent, with only one short interruption for Christmas festivities. In those days, masks were worn throughout the carnival but they were also used in other circumstances: during the Fiera della Sensa lasting for two weeks, on the occasion of doges' elections and their sons' weddings, and when famous personalities arrived in town.

The culmination of Carnival is 10 days before Lent (Feb–Mar) with the "volo dell'angelo" or "flight of the angel". In

Carnival attire

© N. Bosques / MICHELIN

this ceremony, an acrobat descends the bell-tower of St Mark's and glides over the piazza to the Doges' Palace by means of two ropes. In the past, the acrobat was dressed as a Turk rather than an angel. The trend now is to begin Carnival festivities earlier, in hopes of relieving the crush of the crowds in the final week. The city has even consulted with Rome and Viareggio, in particular, to upgrade their celebrations to take some of the pressure off Venice.

"BUONGIORNO, SIORA MASCARA"

A key feature of Carnival is the mask. It is said that masks were first introduced to Venice in 1204 when Doge Enrico Dandolo brought veiled Muslim women back to Venice after his conquest of Constantinople. As in Mozart's opera *Don Giovanni* (Act 2), masked people greeted each other routinely with the saying "Buongiorno Siora Mascara" during the 17C. To go about one's business dressed in the *baùta* – a mask complete with its hooded black shawl – was so normal that a formal request was lodged by the clergy for Venetians to remove their disguise at least in church.

RETURN OF THE CARNIVAL

The greater the decline of Venice, the sharper her sense of fun. Come 1797 when the French assumed power, thus ending the glory of the Venetian Republic for all time, the city continued her revelries, thriving on her taste for jokes and riddles, laughter and carnival, which was eventually revived late in the 19C. Even when this modern carnival was reinstated, with an open invitation to all to congregate in Piazza San Marco – the only time the space is truly filled by the crowds – it was a masked attendance. Whether it be with the *baùta*, the full-length cloak (*tabarro*), the three-horned hat (*tricorno*) or the long-nosed mask (*maschera a becco*) that doctors used to wear during the plague epidemics, the rule of the game is always the same: never investigate the identity of the person wearing the mask.

Carnival participants

The need to don a mask seems to come as second nature to a Venetian. Maybe because, in the words of Silvio Ceccat: *"The streets are narrow, the population is small. You meet someone at every corner. Everyone knows everyone else's business. Today there are no cars to protect anonymity as yesterday there were no coaches in which to hide … People used to and still do feel naked in Venice. So naked, indeed, that clothes are not enough and hence the need for the mask …".*

Today's festivities are organised by the city and include various colourful historic pageants and performances, The finale is the Grand Ball in the Piazza on Shrove Tuesday. As only A-list celebrities and the great and good of Venice are allowed to attend this jamboree, mere mortals have to content themselves with lesser private and public parties. There is also a huge fireworks display.

THE CITY TODAY

The Venetians

To describe the countless faces of Venice and ignore the particular personality of the citizens who live here would present a misleading picture of the city: it would sustain the unfortunate, commonly held view of the place as a museum to which a cursory visit is made. To refute this, stroll down to Campo della Pescaria, linger in a bar in Campo San Luca over a glass of wine, or idle away on a bench in Campo San Giacomo dall'Orio to eavesdrop on a nearby conversation. Shopping around Sant'Elena will provide a glimpse of the living spirit of Venice. The best impressions of Venice are gleaned away from the obvious tourist areas.

Venetians can be unpredictable characters, both charming and astute (a quality sharpened by an age-old affinity for business), with a tendency to appear effusively genial in Italian and yet suspiciously distant in their native dialect.

THE CITY'S SPLIT PERSONALITY

Every visitor must formulate his or her own opinion of Venice: it may be a highly personal response to the unique atmosphere of this enchanting city; it may be one tainted by bad weather, high prices and at the height of summer a particular stretch of a canal can sometimes smell unpleasant – but it is not common and should not deter a single visitor. To stereotype the flavour of Venice would be detrimental to the magic of the place.

Just outside the tourist mainstream, a local resident is often ready to regale visitors with tales while the long-serving employee at a magnificent *palazzo* will enjoy sharing its enthralling history with whoever gives him the chance; the parish priest, in his sacristy, is happy to unlock secret doors to hidden treasures in his custody. Theirs is "the" Venetian personality too complex to be defined but too colourful to be ignored.

VENETIAN IDIOSYNCRASY

Historically, at least, the Venetian is born with a positive outlook on life that is maintained by an imperturbable nature in which emotional involvement is tempered by a certain indifference to anything that lies beyond the lagoon. This has led them to a noticeably predisposed state of tolerance, an innate quality acquired from a knowledge of different peoples distilled over the centuries. The blend of an almost Anglo-Saxon aplomb with boundless and all-embracing curiosity renders this personality even more fascinating.

Yet perhaps the attribute that most readily springs to mind is the pleasure the Venetian derives from gossiping, a pastime that delights all the more given the subtle sense of humour with which all Venetians are naturally and happily endowed, regardless of age, intellect or social class.

Jocular chatter is always conducted in dialect to allow quips and puns to sparkle and scintillate to full effect. It fills the bars and cafés, the shops and markets, but most of all the streets and squares, exchanged in passing or during a pause, which the Venetians take pleasure in granting themselves at every opportunity. Unlike citizens of other cities, Venetians are wholly sociable creatures, revelling in the advantages of sharing their environment with like-minded people who draw the calm and philosophical conclusion that only the truly essential priorities of life are worth worrying about, thus regarding the inconveniences of existence as rela-

tive. With a clear conscience and light heart, Venetians walk with a purposeful stride: it is clear when they are on their way somewhere, moving at a sustained speed, whether empty handed or earnestly pushing awkward carts up and over the bridges, heralded by a sprightly *"Atansion!"* from behind.

It is rare to meet an ill-intentioned Venetian, partly because the very structure of the city impedes criminal designs: where would you escape to?

Yet all is far from happy in this magnificent theme park of a city. The average age of Venetians is around 45, way older than most Italian cities, and over one third of the population is over 60. Unless they are employed directly in tourism there is little reason for youngsters to stay. Property is horribly expensive, damp and difficult to maintain and commuting against the tide of visitors coming the other way each day is a nightmare.

Venetian Lexicon

The living breath of Venice is its dialect. Accents have been used to facilitate pronunciation.

COLLOQUIAL TERMS

Baùta: a carnival mask comprising a black hood and a lace shawl
Brìcola: wooden pole used for mooring boats or, if roped to others, to delineate navigable channels
Carèga: chair
Ciàcola: gossip or chatter
Fèlze: the gondola awning set up in winter to protect the main seat
Ocio!: Look out!
Ostreghèta!: Good heavens!
Pantegàna: a large rat
Putèo: a child
Tòco/tochetìn: a piece/little piece

EATING AND DRINKING

Armelìn: apricot
Bacalà mantecà: boiled salt-cod, mixed with oil, garlic and parsley

Bàcaro: a Venetian bistro, usually crowded from early morning

Bagìgi: peanuts

Baìcoli: typical dry, flat, cutlet-shaped sweet biscuits

Bìgoi: wholemeal spaghetti, generally served in *salsa* with a lightly fried mixture of anchovies and onions

Bìsi: peas

Bussolài buranèi: an S- or ring-shaped biscuit from Burano

Càpe sànte: scallops

Cichèto: Venetian tidbit (salt-cod, marinated sardine or a meatball) that accompanies a glass of wine

Dìndio: turkey

Frìtole: carnival pancakes made with raisins and pine nuts

Lugànega: a long thin sausage

Naransa: orange

Ombra, ombrèta: the traditional and much respected glass of wine taken standing at a bar

Parsùto: ham

Peòci: mussels

Pòmi: apple

Prosecco: dry sparkling wine

Rìsi e bìsi: rice and peas traditionally eaten during the Feast of St Mark

Sàrde in saòr: fried sardines, with a sweet-and-sour sauce of onions, vinegar, pine nuts and raisins

Sgropìn: lemon sorbet of vodka and *prosecco*, served usually after fish

Sprìz (Spritz): famous Venetian aperitif: white wine with a dash of bitters and soda water

Stracaganàse: dried chestnuts, literally translated as "jaw-acher"

Soprèssa: fresh salami

Tiramisù: famous dessert made of biscuits soaked in coffee, layered with full-fat *mascarpone* cream cheese blended with egg and sugar, powdered with bitter cocoa

PLACE NAMES

Altàna: a wooden roof-terrace or veranda

Assassini: a canal or street name alluding to where a murderer might have sought refuge

Beccarìe: butchers who have lent their name to streets, squares, bridges

Calli: from the Latin *callis*, most streets in Venice bear this name (variations: *calli larghe*, *callette* and *calleselle*)

Campiello: a little *campo* or square

Campo: Venetian for a square; the only *piazza* in Venice is Piazza San Marco

Fiubèra: buckle sellers who have lent their name to streets or vaulted arcades where they once set up shop

Fondamenta: a road which runs parallel to a *rio* or canal

Fòntego: a warehouse where foreign merchants lodged

Fornèr: a common name identifying where the local bread ovens were

Frezzerìa: commercial zone around St Mark's that was once the site of an arrow factory

Lista: the stretch of street in front of an ambassador's residence; diplomatic immunity is indicated by its white stone

Luganeghèr: grocery store

Megio: millet; alludes to grain (millet or wheat) warehouses storing supplies for times of hardship

Milìon: the nickname of Marco Polo's family, who lived over the Milion courtyard behind San Giovanni Grisostomo; also the title of the adventurer's travel experiences

Paradiso: this name given to a street or bridge refers to the lamps that were used on Good Friday to light the area of Santa Maria Formosa

Parrocchia: literally meaning "parish", this locality around a church serves as a subdivision of a *sestiere*

Pescarìa: a fish market

Piazzetta: little squares: the two in Venice are Piazzetta dei Leoncini and Piazzetta San Marco

Piovàn: common in Venetian topography; relating to a priest

Piscina: place where there used to be a pool or sheet of water

Pistòr: the baker who kneaded dough

Ponte: the 400 or so bridges in Venice are marked by this name

Italian coffee

Espresso – very short, dense, black and very strong
Caffè lungo/caffè americano – a short, strong espresso with added hot water
Caffè corretto – an espresso "corrected" with brandy or *grappa* (eau-de-vie)
Caffè macchiato – an espresso with a dash of milk, freddo (cold) or caldo (hot)
Cappuccino or **cappuccio** – an espresso topped with hot fluffy milk
Caffè latte – a glass of hot milk flavoured with an espresso coffee
Venice has some of its own coffee roasters (*torrefazioni*) that produce excellent coffee: Marchi; Girani; Doge; India; Venezia; and others.

Ice-cream flavours

Gelato is best at a specialist *gelateria* that is *artigianale* without additives.

Stracciatella – chocolate chip. **Gianduia** – dark or milk chocolate and hazelnut. **Fior di latte** or **panna** – plain milk or cream. **Crema** – vanilla enriched with egg. **Cioccolato** (fondente)– chocolate (bittersweet). **Nocciola** – hazelnut. **Frutta di bosco** – fruits of the forest (blueberries, blackberries etc). **Limone** – lemon sorbet. **Fragola** – strawberry. **Pistacchio** – made with bright green pistachio nuts. **Pesca** – peach. **Albicocca** – apricot. **Lampone** – raspberry.

Ramo: a side street

Rialto: from the Latin *rivoaltus*, a word that indicates the islands from which the city originated

Rio terà: a street formed by a land-filled canal

Ruga: from the French *rue*, a synonym for street, usually one devoted to a commercial activity

Salizzarda: from the word *salizo* or paving stone; denotes a paved street

San Stae: the Venetian contraction of San Eustachio – St Eustace

San Stin: another Venetian contraction of San Stefanino

San Zan Degolà: refers to San Giovanni Decollato – the beheaded John the Baptist

Scaletèr: a doughnut seller, from the word *scaleta*, a doughnut with marks like a flight of steps

Sestieri: the six divisions of Venice: **Cannaregio:** from the Latin *cannarecium* or *canaleclum*, a marshy area where cane grows; **Castello:** alluding, perhaps, to the Roman fortification at Olivolo; **Dorsoduro:** includes the Giudecca and is named after the type of hill on which it developed; **San Marco, San Polo** and **Santa Croce**

Sottopòrtego: a vaulted passageway running perpendicular to the building's façade on the ground floor; at one time lined with shops

Squèro: a boatyard where gondolas are built and repaired

Tette: slang for breasts, applied to a bridge or street where bare-breasted women of easy virtue used to lean out of windows

Zattere: the long *fondamenta* that extends to the Giudecca Canal, recalling the *zattere* or wood-laden rafts which used to stop there

VENETIAN WORDS IN THE ENGLISH LANGUAGE

Arsenal: a store for military equipment

Carpaccio: an appetizer of thinly sliced raw beef

Ghetto: a socially restricted zone

Gondola: a type of boat or a cable car

Harlequin: a comic character/buffoon/diamond pattern

Lagoon: an area of shallow water divided from the sea by sandy dunes

Lido: a fashionable beach resort/public open-air swimming pool

Regatta: a boat race

Food and Wine

Venice has traded with the world since the dawn of time; throughout its history the city has therefore been cosmopolitan in every sense of the word. A thousand different ethnic types have crowded the streets and squares just as they have populated the pictures of Titian and Veronese. They have added colour to the Venetian scene, idiom and dialect to the vernacular language and, above all, exotic spice to the indigenous cultural and culinary traditions. The perfumes and fragrances exchanged in Venice have been blended and refined through time, mixing exotic and local flavours. Nothing has been lost. The multicoloured multitude of merchants has been replaced with crowds of tourists, and so the alchemy continues.

Social history has also played its part: besides the gastronomic refinement inherited from an aristocratic past, solid peasant cooking still underpins many local dishes, even if the poorest have long since been enhanced or become luxuries in modern times.

Tourism has nurtured a demand for restaurants that alternate between luxurious and anonymous "tourist" catering, but the age-old rhythm of the city and the convivial habits of its citizens still survive and flourish: **un ombra di vin** (a "shadow" or bit of wine) accompanied by a **cichetto** (a tapas-like morsel) or three, consumed in a **bacaro,** are life's daily small luxuries for the locals.

Cichetti (the plural of cichetto) comprise all kinds of foods from sliced fried vegetables to delicious garlic meatballs (*polpette*), squid, salt-cod and prawns to mini pizzas and bruschettas.

When ordering a glass of wine "un ombra", specify "bianco" white, or for red, rosso.

SEAFOOD

Venetians are especially proud of their seafood. A traditional plate of *antipasto* offers a chance to relish a wonderful selection of local shellfish including **caparozzoli** (clams), **cozze** (mussels) **peòci** (mussels), **bòvoli** (sea snails) and **canòce** (shrimps), as well as **granseole** and **gransipori** (crab).

As a *primo* or starter, **bigoi in salsa** (thick spaghetti cords served with lightly fried onions and anchovies) is one of the most popular first courses, (beware that after this you may be too full to eat any more!). In Northern Italy rice is more popular than pasta so look for many types of risotto. These are made with meat and/or fresh vegetables (**primavera**), grown locally in market gardens, or with fish, or **'in tecia'** – with cuttlefish.

Fish from the Adriatic is often served grilled, accompanied, in spring, by **castràure** (young fried artichokes).

Fresh fish on sale in a market, Venice

© Yana Savostitskaya / Dreamstime.com

Pasta (and polenta)

Cannelloni – stuffed tubes, topped with tomato and bechamel sauce, baked in the oven

Farfalle – butterfly or bows

Fettuccine – thin tagliatelle served with various sauces

Fusilli – corkscrew pasta often served with heartier sauces

Gnocchi – dumplings made with potato and flour

Lasagne – sheets of pasta layered with meat, vegetables, or fish, with a tomato or bechamel sauce, and baked in the oven

Maccheroni – small tubes

Paglia e fieno – thin threads of egg and spinach pasta (literally meaning straw and hay)

Pappardelle – broad flat ribbons of freshly made pasta, very often served in a rich sauce (wild boar – *cinghiale*; hare – *lepre; porcini* mushrooms)

Pasta e fasòi – pasta served with Borlotti beans, typical family dish at home

Polenta – cornmeal porridge, also grilled or baked, accompanied by rich sauces.

Ravioli – cushions of freshly made egg pasta stuffed with meat, fish or spinach and cheese (*spinaci e ricotta*); delicious with butter and sage (*burro e salvia*) or meat sauce (*al ragù*)

Spaghetti – long threads of pasta, often with shellfish (*frutta di mare*) or clams (*vongole*)

Tagliatelle – egg pasta in long ribbons

Tortellini – little pouches of egg pasta stuffed with meat, vegetables, or cheese, served with a sauce or in clear broth (*in brodo*)

Eels (**anguilla**, or **bisàto** in dialect), are not so common and are served either broiled or poached. Wild fowl and game are delicacies in winter months.

Vinegar is used in all kinds of ways, notably for pickling and for preparing **sarde in saòr**, a delicious sweet-and-sour sardine dish. Also popular is **seppie al nero**, cuttlefish in its own ink, a rich-tasting dish often served as risotto, the rice darkened from soaking up the ink! Another truly typical dish is **bacalà mantecato**, salt-cod beaten to a smooth cream with oil, garlic and parsley and served with polenta. It is often served as a cichetto, on bread or perhaps a cracker. Fried softshell lagoon crabs, **moeche**, are truly a delicacy.

MEAT DISHES

One of the most traditional *secondi* or main courses is **fegato alla veneziana**, (calf's liver and onions), a combination created in Venice but now popular everywhere. The defining factor for Venetians, however, is how thinly the meat is cut, and the long gentle cooking of the onions.

However no meat is as thinly cut as another Venetian invention, **carpaccio**, slices of raw beef served with olive oil and lemon. It was invented at Harry's Bar in Venice, where it was first served to the countess Amalia Nani Mocenigo in 1950 who, on doctor's orders, had requested raw meat. It was named carpaccio by Giuseppe Cipriani, the bar's owner, after the great Venetian painter because the colours reminded him of a favorite painting!

Another meat dish is **carne in tecia** – a braised beef stew, traditionally cooked in terracotta (tecia). Look also for duck and other waterfowl.

SOUPS AND VEGATABLES

For flavoursome country cooking, try **panàda veneziana**, a wholesome soup with bread, garlic, oil, bay leaf and Parmesan cheese, or **pastissàda**, of green vegetables, cheese, sausage, pasta or polenta bound together traditionally to use up leftovers. **Zuppa di Pesce** is a wholesome and hearty soup, of the market's mixed fish. Don't miss spring artichokes from the island of Sant'Erasmo,

Sweets shop in Veneto, selling essi buranèi (right)

served raw and sliced very thinly, or the bottoms sauteed in olive oil with garlic. Also, pumpkin, beans, asparagus, chicory, and radicchio are great favourites among the locals.

DOLCI

For dessert, try the famous Veneto **tiramisu,** which combines biscuits, coffee, sweet marscapone cheese and eggs, dusted with cocoa. **St. Martin's Cake**, a sweet biscuit shaped like a man on horseback, appears in November. Another very Venetian custom is to serve **baìcoli** biscuits, to dunk in hot chocolate or dessert wine; biscuits from Burano, **bussolài**, are moulded into ring or "S" shapes, called *essi buranèi*; or the **Veneziana**, a kind of brioche covered with chopped almonds and sugar. **Creme frite**, fried cream, has a pudding consistency. Carnival treats are often fried: **frìtole** are fritters flavoured with raisins and sometimes pine nuts. **Pinsa**, a biscuit flavoured with fennel seeds, raisins, dried figs and candied peel, is a speciality baked at Epiphany.

SALUTI !

The most common drink in Venice (and the Veneto), after *un ombra* (*see page 113*), is a **spritz**, which is Prosecco with a dash of bitters and soda water; ask for *com Aperol* (an orange bitter made in Padova).

Venice's most famous cocktail is the **Bellini**, white peach juice and pulp with *Prosecco*; the **Tiziano**, substitutes strawberry grape juice; the **Mimosa**, orange juice; the **Rossini**, strawberry juice. Ernest Hemingway was a frequent visitor to **Harry's Bar**, where he would order his own special cocktail, the **Montgomery**, named after the famous general. It was made with one measure of vermouth to 15 measures of gin and is served only by that particular establishment.

Prosecco wine from the Veneto's Conegliano Valdobbiadene is made primarily from the Giera grape, most popular in its sparking version, very light and very refreshing.

The king of the Veneto reds is **Amarone della Valpolicella** , from the province of Verona, a dense wine made from partially dried Corvina, Rondinella and Marinara grapes; also delicious and made from the same grapes is Recioto della Vapolicella and **Valpolicella**, slightly lower in alcohol content and more economical. Among other intriguing Veneto wines to try for red are **Bardolino** rand reds from the Colli Berici and other areas. For whites, try **Soave**, **Tai** and **Tocai**, although many are partial to whites from **Friuli** such as Schioppettino, Friulano, and Ribolla gialla.

*Mosaics inside Basilica di San Marco
on Piazza San Marco*
© Peter Barritt / age fotostock

ACCADEMIA★★★

(⁊, DX)

VAPORETTO: ACCADEMIA OR ZATTERE

This area, named after its famous Academy of Fine Art, is permanently thronged by people on the move: locals going about their everyday business; visitors arriving on the vaporetti, drawn to the art treasures; students milling outside the nearby university, lending a bohemian atmosphere to the area. Whatever your business here it is always worth stopping for a short break at one of the bars or trattorias.

▶ **Orient Yourself:** The north side of the area is dominated by the Gallerie dell'Accademia, the south side boasts the Zattere, the long promenade that overlooks the Giudecca canal and Giudecca island. Boats depart frequently from the Zattere for the airport.

⊙ **Don't Miss:** The Accademia Gallery, of course, and the picturesque gondola dockyard, Squero di San Trovaso.

○ **Organising Your Time:** Allow 2hrs for the Academy Gallery and 1hr for the area.

○ **Also See:** Neighbouring sights: I CARMINI, La SALUTE.

Walking Tour

Ponte dell'Accademia (⁊, DX)

This famous landmark wooden bridge, one of only three that cross the Grand Canal, replaces an old iron construction built by the Austrians in 1854 to allow their "peacekeeping" forces free access to both sides of the city. As then, it links the elegant and spacious Campo di San Stefano with the Accademia, eventually leading right up to the Zattere. The bridge is a popular spot for visitors to take their photograph with the Grand Canal as a picturesque backdrop.

Gallerie dell'Accademia★★★ (⁊, DX)

○*Open 8.15am–7.15pm (2pm Mon), last admission 45min before closing. The gallery limits the number of people allowed in at any one time, so if you are visiting at a busy time of year, book ahead either online or by telephone.* ○*Closed 1 Jan, 1 May, 25 Dec.* ⚏€6.50, *more during temp exhibits.* ☎041 52 00 345. www. gallerieaccademia.org.

The **Academy of Fine Art** exhibits what is arguably the city's most important collection of artworks, encapsulating the development of Venetian painting from

Ponte dell'Accademia

© Christian Reister / age fotostock

GALLERIE DELL'ACCADEMIA

the 14C to the 18C, in a complex of buildings converted in the 19C. These structures include the Monastery of Lateran Canons, designed by Andrea Palladio (1508–80), the Church of La Carità, an atmospheric building that was redesigned by Bartolomeo Bon (recorded 1441–64), and the Scuola Santa Maria della Carità, the first Scuola Grande, which was erected in 1260 (*see I CARMINI: The Venetian Scuole*). The tour starts in the large Sala Capitolare at the top of the 18C staircase.

Room I

The Sala Capitolare (chapter house) is the place where, from the 15C, the Scuola Grande of the Santa Maria della Carità used to meet. This large room has a gilded panelled ceiling by Marco Cozzi (1484), divided into sections with a cherub in each. The figure of God in the central tondo, attributed to Alvise **Vivarini** (1445–1505), replaces that of the Madonna della Misericordia, the patron who would have occupied the section originally. The room is devoted to Venetian Gothic masters from the 14C and the first half of the 15C, including Paolo Veneziano (*Coronation of the Virgin* at the top of the stairs straight ahead) and Lorenzo Veneziano. The huge painting, *Coronation of the Virgin in Paradise*, at the end of the room, is by

Jacobello del Fiore (*right*). Note Michele Giambino's works also on display here; Giambino, who worked between 1420 and 1462, is the most important artist to work in the International Gothic style in Venice.

Room II

This room displays eight important 15C altarpieces. On the entrance wall: the *Crucifixion and Apotheosis of the Ten Thousand Martyrs of Mount Ararat* by **Vittore Carpaccio** (c.1465–c.1526) depicts the legendary massacre of the Roman soldiers betrayed by their own captains after beating the Armenian rebels (*right*). On the wall to the right hang the famous *Virgin and Child with Saints*, also known as the *Pala di San Giobbe*, by **Giovanni Bellini** (c.1470–1516) taken from the Church of San Giobbe; the *Agony in the Garden* by Marco Basaiti (c.1470–c.1530) (*right*) and the *Presentation of Christ in the Temple* by Vittorio Carpaccio (*left*).

On the end wall: the *Madonna of the Orange Tree* by Cima da Conegliano (1459–1517) (*right*) hangs alongside his *Incredulity of St Thomas and the Great Bishop* in which the three figures are silhouetted against the sky with a village in the distance (*left*).

The *Calling of the Sons of Zebedee*, by Marco Basaiti, is a particularly beautiful and engaging treatment of the subject of Christ recruiting his Apostles, the

variety of scenery with the focus on the water and the magical quality of the colour (*centre*).

On the wall to the left: the *Mourning of the Dead Christ* by Giovanni Bellini and assistants (*right*) and the *Madonna with Child Enthroned* by Cima da Conegliano (*left*).

Room III

This room contains works by Sebastiano del Piombo, Cima da Conegliano and Giovanni Bellini.

▶ *Cross to the far end for access to the small adjoining Rooms IV and V, among the most important rooms in the gallery.*

Room IV

St George by **Andrea Mantegna** (1431–1506) hangs on the wall to the left, one of only two paintings by the master who so influenced Bellini and consequently the evolution of Venetian painting. The painting has a Tuscan feel about it: the knight, a synthesis of Humanism, is reminiscent of Donatello.

On the wall to the right, Giovanni Bellini's *Madonna with Child between St Catherine and Mary Magdalene* depicts four figures thrown into relief by a strong transverse light that lifts them out of the darkness; note, however, the suggestion of serene beauty and tender spirituality so typical of Bellini. In contrast, on the right, is

Apparition of the Crucified of Mount Ararat in the Church of Sant' Antonio di Castello, Carpaccio, c.1512, Gallerie dell' Accademia

© Tipsimages

the *Portrait of a Young Man* by the Dutch artist Hans Memling (c.1435-94) with its sharp delineation of features and characterisation; lost in tranquil meditation, the young man's face is embued with inner calm.

Room V

The Tempest by **Giorgione** (c.1467–1510) is the crystallisation of a state of mind rather than the representation of a specific moment in time, an attempt at capturing the essence of a poetic narrative taken from literature. The protagonists of this "fantasy picture" are the three figures, the ruins, the water and the village dramatically caught in an iridescent green light by a flash of lightning.

Another famous work by Giorgione hangs on the left. *The Old Woman* is a compelling portrait, appealing yet uncompromising. Self-explanatory, it has been described as a "hymn to fleeing youth," touched with the inevitable sadness of realised awareness, highlighted by the inscription in the cartouche *col tempo* ("with time"). The picture is especially charged with meaning if one considers how Giorgione's untimely death in 1510 from the plague cut short a life full of promise. To the right of the door are the *Allegories* by Giovanni Bellini, particularly exquisite small paintings intended as decorative panels to set into a piece of furniture or mirror.

On the wall in front of the exit hang the *Madonna and the Seraphim* and the *Madonna under the Trees* by Giovanni Bellini. The title of the latter refers to the trees that serve as foreground to the landscape, channelling perspective across the countryside to distant snow-capped peaks.

Room VI

This long room houses works by Tintoretto (1518–94) and Veronese (1528–88).

Room VII

This little room is home to the famous 1524 *Portait of a Young Gentleman in his Study* by **Lorenzo Lotto** (c.1480–1577), in which the sitter's concentration seems to have been interrupted by a thought or a memory; distracted from his reading, his long delicate fingers idly flick through the pages as he muses perhaps upon the passing of time, staring into the distance, his pale, chiselled face contrasting with his black coat.

Admire works by Vasari, Palma il Vecchio and Titian in **Room VIII**; then proceed to Room X.

Room X

The *Madonna with Child Enthroned* by Veronese (*left of the entrance*) recalls the Pesaro altarpiece in the Frari (*see I FRARI*). The *Pietà* by Titian (1490–1576) (*right of the entrance, in the middle*) was intended by the artist for his own tomb at the Frari but remained unfinished on his death. Note on the right, at the Sibyl's feet, the hand raised in supplication.

On the wall with the doorway into the next room hangs Veronese's *Betrothal of St Catherine* (*left*).

Opposite the entrance hang Tintoretto's canvases depicting the life of St Mark. From left to right: *St Mark's Dream* (in fact the dream of St Mark's son, Dominic), *St Mark Saves a Saracen, St Mark Liberates a Slave* – the oblique lighting effects heighten the drama of the scene with St Mark falling head first; the *Theft of the Body of St Mark* (the final panel in the series, the *Finding of the Body of St Mark* is now in the Brera Collection in Milan). Note how the figures in the foreground appear thrown into relief by the use of chiaroscuro, where forms, picked out by strong light, are contrasted against another recessed into shadow; here phantom-like figures fade into the darkness, sloping off in search of safety in the palace.

The whole of the right wall is taken by Veronese's controversial *Christ in the House of Levi*, conceived as a *Last Supper* (1573) for the refectory of Santi Giovanni e Paolo (*see SAN ZANIPÒLO*). Shortly after the painting was unveiled, Veronese was summoned before a tribunal of the Inquisition on a charge of heresy for not adhering to the description of the event as related in the Gospels. Veronese defended himself on the grounds of artistic licence. He promptly changed the painting's title to suit a more secular subject that might also justify the painter's predilection for such opulent textures as brocade, glass and gold.

Rooms XI to XIX

This room accommodates works by **Giambattista Tiepolo** (1696–1770) including the frieze that depicts the *Castigation of the Serpents* and the fresco pendentives from the Scalzi Church (destroyed in 1915). *Dinner in the House of Simon* by **Bernardo Strozzi** (1581–1644) is particularly vibrant, notably animated by the expressive face of the figure filling the chalice. The *Crucifixion of St Peter* composed around its strong diagonal axes by Luca Giordano (1643–1705) is also here.

On the left wall hangs the masterpiece by Bonifacio de' Pitati (c.1487–1553). The *Rich Man Epulone* projects a tranquil scene, rich with incidental detail and contrasting personality, populated with musicians, a beggar, huntsmen and lovers converging in a wood, as a fire rages on the right.

Room XII is dedicated to landscape painting from the late 17C and early 18C, including works by Marco Ricci, Giuseppe Zais and Francesco Zuccarelli. Access to the two side rooms, **Rooms XIII** (in which hang several works by Tintoretto, including his portrait of the Procurator Jacopo Soranzo) and **XIV**, which show works from the 16C and 17C, is through Room XII. The corridor then becomes **Room XV** which leads to side rooms on the left **(Room XVII)** full of the most typical Venetian paintings: **Canaletto** (1697–1768) – although a prolific Venetian painter, all save a handful of his works hang in collections abroad,

having been sold to foreign gentlemen on the Grand Tour or requisitioned by Napoleon; Bernardo Bellotto (1721–80); Francesco **Guardi** (1712–93); Giambattista Piazzetta (1683–1754); Rosalba Carriera (1675–1758), whose series of informal pastel portraits are provocative studies of personality; Pietro Longhi (1702–85) (the famous *Dancing Lesson*). **Room XVIa** accommodates works from the 18C, including the *Fortune Teller* by Giambattista Piazzetta.

Room XVIII serves as a passageway into **Room XXIII**, the old Church of La Carità, which now contains works from the 15C/16C Venetian School.

The *Annunciation* by Antonello de Saliba (active 1497–1535), displayed in **Room XIX**, is, in fact, a copy of a work bearing the same title in the Galleria Nazionale di Palermo in Sicily, executed by Antonello da Messina, Da Saliba's uncle.

▶ *Access to Room XX is through Room XIX.*

Room XX

This room contains the famous collection of paintings illustrating the story of the *Miracles of the Relic of the True Cross*, executed by various artists between the 15C and 16C, for the Scuola di San Giovanni Evangelista.

The *Procession in St Mark's Square* by Gentile Bellini (1429–1507) covers the wall facing the entrance. The work is an important representation of the square in the mid-15C (👁 *see PIAZZA SAN MARCO*). Other paintings by Gentile Bellini on the right wall include (*from left to right*) the *Healing of Pietro de' Ludovici* and the *Miracle of the Cross on the Ponte di San Lorenzo* in which Andrea Vendramin is shown retrieving the Reliquary of the True Cross from the canal. Note that Caterina Cornaro (👁 *see RIALTO: Ca' Corer della Regina*) is just visible on the left-hand side of the latter work. On the same wall hangs a work by Giovanni Mansueti (active in Venice from 1485 to c.1526): the *Healing of Benvegnudo's Daughter of San Polo* sets the scene in a beautiful Renaissance interior (*right*). Carpaccio's *Miracle of the Relic of the True Cross at Rialto* can be seen on the

The English Ambassadors Taking their Leave (detail) by Carpaccio (Accademia)

© Accademia, Venezia / SCALA

entrance wall. Interestingly, the subject of the painting – the miraculous healing of a madman taking place on the first-floor loggia on the left – seems secondary to the profusion of topographical detail showing Venice at the end of the 15C: the wooden Rialto Bridge, the Fondaco dei Tedeschi on the right as it was before the events of 1505 (⚲*see La FENICE*), the Ca' da Mosto (⚲*see Il CANAL GRANDE*) and the bell-towers of San Giovanni Grisostomo and the Church of All Saints (⚲*see RIALTO*).

Room XXI

This room contains the colourful and magical series of canvases by **Carpaccio** that retell the *Story of St Ursula* (1491–98).

▸ *Start with the wall facing the entrance (left) and proceed clockwise.*

The first panel, *Arrival of the English Ambassadors,* shows the ambassadors arriving at the (Catholic) court in Brittany bearing a proposal of marriage from their English (pagan) prince, Hereus. Ursula (*to the right*) is shown dictating her conditions of marriage (including his baptism and promise to undertake a pilgrimage accompanied by Ursula and a large number of virgins), in the presence of her wet nurse seated on the steps. The next scene shows *The English Ambassadors Taking their Leave,* in which the king hands over the reply: it may well be that it is being written up by the scribe who is concentrating on his task. In the *Return of the Ambassadors* the cortège bringing the reply to the king is followed by a crowd to the edge of the lagoon, the towers suggestive of the Arsenale. Certain details of the painting are particularly noteworthy: the central scene is almost theatrical, the eye caught by the handsome youth turning away as if affronted; the figure sitting on the bank is the "Steward," whose duty it is to herald the arrival of the ambassadors, invited by the doge, with music, while a monkey on the right watches a guinea fowl.

The *Meeting of Ursula and Hereus and the Departure of the Pilgrims* is a composite scene, divided by the pennant, showing the prince taking his leave; Hereus and Ursula bid farewell to the rulers of Brittany before departing for Rome. Note the sharp contrast between the harsh, darkened representation of the English capital on the left and the colourful Breton town on the right, represented according to Humanist ideals.

In *Ursula's Dream* the scene is more compact, set in Ursula's room where the light reveals more domestic details: reminiscent of *St Augustine in his Studio* (⚲*see SAN GIORGIO degli SCHIAVONI*), the angel reaches out for the palm of martyrdom. The *Meeting of the Pilgrims with Pope Cyriac under the Walls of Rome* takes place against the background of the Castel Sant'Angelo, between two groups of virgin pilgrims (Ursula's companions) to the left and the prelates to the right. In the centre, the betrothed are waiting to be crowned. Note Carpaccio's delight in using strong and contrasting colours, notably red and white.

The *Arrival in Cologne* depicts how, on their arrival in the city, Ursula and her father, who has joined the pilgrims, learn that the city is in the hands of the Huns.

Ursula's eventful life on earth concludes with the *Martyrdom of the Pilgrims and Ursula's Funeral,* in which the two scenes are separated by the column. In the centre the warrior is removing blood from his sword. The final panel in the cycle, however, showing the *Apotheosis of St Ursula and her Companions*, is perhaps the saddest.

Room XXIV, on the way out, is the former Sala dell'Albergo. It houses one of the collection's highlights: Titian's *Presentation of the Virgin to the Temple* (1530s).

▸ *To reach San Trovaso, walk southwest of the Accademia, and cross the Rio di San Trovaso.*

Chiesa San Trovaso (**7**, DX)

Entrance on the canal side. The church is dedicated to two saints (Gervasius and Protasius, the protomartyrs of Milan) whose names have been contracted to "Trovaso." Built in the 9C, the original church was totally remodelled by architects of the Palladian School between the 16C and 17C. Built in the plan of a Latin cross, it has a single nave with side chapels. In the presbytery, a chapel off to the right, hangs *Christ Crucified between the Two Marys,* by Jacopo Tintoretto's son Domenico (c.1560–1635) and *St Chrysogonus on Horseback* by Michele Giambono (active 1420–62). Other paintings by the Tintorettos as well as works by Palma il Giovane (1548–1628) and Andrea Vicentino (end 15C–early 16C) grace the church.

▶ *Farther along the Rio di San Trovaso between the church and the Zattere lies a quaint boatyard.*

Squero di San Trovaso (**7**, DX)

This is one of the few *squeri* still in operation in Venice and is certainly the most famous, not least because of its unusual building. In a city of elegantly refined Byzantine *palazzi,* this seems idiosyncratic. Built of wood, with its geraniums tumbling from the balcony in summertime, it looks more like an alpine chalet. This little boatyard is much more than merely picturesque however - it continues to function as a dockyard where gondolas are built and repaired, often in the open air, in full view of intrigued onlookers on the opposite side of the canal.

▶ *To reach the Church of the Gesuati, proceed eastward along the Zattere.*

Gesuati (**7**, DY)

🕐 Open Mon–Sat 10am–5pm. 🕐 Closed 1 Jan, Easter, 15 Aug, 25 Dec. ☞ €3. ☎041 27 50 462. www.chorusvenezia.org.

The Church of Santa Maria del Rosario ai Gesuati is a famous landmark on the Zattere from the water. It is dedicated to the Madonna of the Rosary, honoured by a 14C order of laymen, the Clerici apostolici S Hieronymi, quite distinct from the Jesuit brotherhood. Shortly after the order was dissolved by Pope Clement IX in 1668, the incumbent order of Dominicans commissioned the architect Giorgio Massari (c.1686–1766) to remodel the building. For the new façade he borrowed elements from the Church of San Giorgio Maggiore. Highlights of the luminous interior include the *Crucifixion* by Tintoretto, *Three Saints* by Piazzetta (1683–1754) and a *Madonna* by **Giambattista Tiepolo**.

Chiesa della Visitazione (**7**, DXY)

Near the Gesuati, the Church of the Visitation was built in its present form between the 15C and the beginning of the 16C. It boast two fine ceiling paintings by **Giambattista Tiepolo**.

ARSENALE★

(**10**, HX)

VAPORETTO: ARSENALE OR RIVA DEGLI SCHIAVONI

Renowned for its historical shipyard with its landmark towers, this area is steeped in the city's past naval prowess. It was thanks to her ships more than anything else that Venice flourished as a maritime power.

▶ **Orient Yourself:** Part of the Castello neighbourhood, the Arsenale district lies in a relatively quiet and secluded part of Venice, east of the Piazza San Marco.

🌣 **Don't Miss:** The sculpture-heavy entrance of the Arsenale; note especially the large ground-level lion sculptures.

🕐 **Organising Your Time:** The suggested itinerary below takes about 3hrs.

Kids **Especially for Kids:** The Naval Museum, with its dozens of watercraft.

🌣 **Also See:** SAN GIORGIO degli SCHIAVONI, SANT'ELENA e SAN PIETRO, SAN ZACCARIA.

Walking Tour

Arsenale

⊶*Closed to the public.* A naval base, depository for arms, and maintenance shop, the Arsenal served as the main shipyard, the heart of the Venetian State. Enclosed within medieval walls, it has two main entrances along the Rio dell'Arsenale: the **land entrance**, a grand Renaissance triumphal arch, constitutes the most important gateway, dating to c.1460, and presided over by the lions from Ancient Greece (Athens and Piraeus) brought over by Francesco Morosini after his victory over Morea in 1687. The **water entrance** (**10**, **HX**), through which the vaporetto passes, is marked by two towers rebuilt in 1686.

A Bit of History

The first recorded dockyard in Venice, the **Arsenale Vecchio**, dates to about 1104 when the demands of the Crusades stimulated shipbuilding. At one time, there were 24 active boatyards. In the 14C, the Arsenal was extended towards the southeast (**Arsenale Nuovo**). Altogether 16 000 *marangoni*, men apprenticed as joiners and trained as shipwrights, were employed. The boat-building techniques were highly advanced, and the Venetians were already implementing production lines. During the second half of the 15C, the **Arsenale Nuovissimo** was extended to the north of the area – on the Galeazzi Canal (1564). Destroyed during the French occupation of 1797, the Arsenal was rebuilt by the Austrians between 1814 and 1830. After the Venetians attacked it in 1848, the area was abandoned during the third Austrian occupation (1849–66). Restructuring work began in the late 19C, and continued to 1914.

The Buildings

The street names serve as a reminder of the various trades and activities: Calle della Pegola (fish), Calle dei Bombardieri (cannon-ball foundries), Calle del Piombo (lead), and Calle delle Ancore (anchors). Mills churned out hemp rope; other structures included sail lofts, artillery warehouses and slipways.

Along the canal lies the **Scalo del Bucintoro** (*second on the right after the towers*), designed by **Sanmicheli** (1484–1559). This dock was home to **Bucintoro**, a magnificent state barge built for the Doge (*see PIAZZA SAN MARCO: Museo Correr*) by the **arsenalotti**, special artisans who worked in teams.

Entrance to the Arsenale

© Ignatius Wooster / Fotolia

On entering the **Galeazzi Canal** the first building on the right is the **Complesso degli Squadratori**. Skeletons of the ships were squared here.

▶ *Walk south toward Campo San Biagio to reach the Museo Storico Navale.*

Museo Storico Navale★ (**10**, HX) `Kids`

🕑 Open Mon–Sat 8.45am–1.30pm (1pm Sat). 🕑Closed holidays. ✆€1.55. ☎041 24 41 399 or 041 52 00 276. www.marina. difesa.it/venezia.

This vast naval museum will delight any boat enthusiast and prove a veritable treasure trove to anyone intrigued by Venice's shipbuilding industry. The museum comprises five floors and houses a large collection of artifacts: a torpedo, taffrail lights, mortars, cannons, firearms and sabres and scale models of the city and her fortresses.

As you enter, the **ground floor** holds cannons, various weaponry and a room with models. Note the large lanterns from Venetian flagships.

On the **first floor** are displays of wooden sculptures that decorated the galleys, coats of arms, naval weaponry, nautical instruments (including compasses and octants), parchment *portolani* (pilots' charts and navigation material specifying details of coastal areas, harbours, anchorages and dangerous waters), engravings, models of ships, fine examples of galleys' broadsides, the supposed remains of Lazzarro Mocenigo's flagship which disappeared in the Dardanelles in 1657 and a model of the state barge, the *Bucintoro* (🔥*see PIAZZA SAN MARCO: Museo Correr*).

The **second floor** is dedicated to naval history during the 19C and 20C and includes scale models and naval uniforms.

The **third floor** displays an extensive collection of ex-votos (offerings given by mariners to a church in thanks or commemoration of an event), a luxury vessel from the 18C, gondolas (including Peggy Guggenheim's) and a model of a working boatyard, the Squero di San Trovaso (🔥*see ACCADEMIA*). One room is devoted to models of Asian giunca and sampans.

On the **fourth floor** there is a shell collection, plus sections on Vikings and the Swedish navy and its relationship with Venice. The rescue expedition of the airship *Italia* is also remembered here.

▶ *On leaving the main building, rest on the benches outside to the left; then follow the Rio dell'Arsenale to the second section of the museum on the right.*

Even though the vessels are not displayed in their full glory in this setting, the pavilions house some interesting craft: a 1932 hydrofoil used for racing, a torpedo-launch (1942), an 1890 diving vessel and the remains of the steam ship **Elettra**.

▶ *Cross the Arsenale bridge, which leads into the Campo dell'Arsenale.*

Along the Fondamenta di Fronte zone of quiet alleyways and peaceful squares. A short walk leads to the Church of San Francesco della Vigna.

▶ *Proceed along the Fondamenta di Fronte into Campo San Martino. Cross the bridge at the Fondamenta Penini and turn left into Calle delle Muneghette. In Campiello Due Pozzi, take Calle del Mandolin on the left. Turn right into Calle degli Scudi, which leads directly to Campo di San Francesco della Vigna.*

Coming from the south is particularly interesting as the route passes between the columns of an unusual 19C portico, of a delicate pinkish-brown colour, which links the naval headquarters with the Renaissance Palazzo Gritti, otherwise known as *La Nunziatura* (the Nunciature). Originally owned by **Doge Andrea Gritti** (1523–38), it was ceded by the Republic to Pope Pius IV (1559–65), who allowed it to be used by Apostolic delegates.

San Francesco della Vigna★ (**10**, HU)

The name comes from the fact that there were vineyards here when the Franciscans first erected the church, begun in 1534. The main façade features a crowning pediment by **Palladio**.

The *campanile* is one of the highest in Venice. Works of note include the *Four Evangelists* by **Giovanni Battista Tiepolo**, a *Virgin with Child* by **Veronese** and a *Madonna with Child and Saints* by **Giovanni Bellini**.

The church also accommodates the tomb of **Doge Marc'Antonio Trevisan** (1553–54). Its masterpiece is **Madonna and Child Enthroned**★ painted in 1450 by the monk **Antonio da Negroponte**.

▷ *From Campo San Francesco della Vigna take Calle San Francesco and then, to the left, Calle de Te Deum. Continue south, crossing the canal for the first time to reach the Fondamenta San Giorgio degli Schiavoni. Take the next bridge and continue to the Scuola di San Giorgio degli Schiavoni (see SAN GIORGIO degli SCHIAVONI).*

The Fondamenta dei Furlani leads southwards to the **Church of San Antonin**, which was founded in the 7C and rebuilt by Baldassare Longhena (1598–1682).

Salizzada San Antonin enters **Campo Bandiera e Moro** (⬛, **HX**). The square opens onto the back of Riva degli Schiavoni. The heroes of the Risorgimento, Attilio and Emilio Bandiera, were born here and remembered in the name of the square, alongside Domenico Moro, another patriot who died with them.

San Giovanni in Bràgora★ (⬛, HX)

The interior of this late 15C church comprises a nave with a trussed ceiling and two aisles. In the left aisle, near the font, a copy of deed confirming the baptism of Antonio Vivaldi is displayed. The highlight is the **Baptism of Christ**★★ by Cima da Conegliano (c.1459–c.1517). Also on view are works by **Alvise Vivarini**, Palma il Giovane (1544–1628) and Paris Bordone (1500–71). A stylised, truly Gothic *Madonna and Child with St John and St Andrew*★ (1478) by Alvise's uncle, Bartolomeo Vivarini (1432–c.1491) and *St Andrew with St Martin and St Jerome*, the work of Francesco Bissolo (c.1470–1554), are also featured.

CA' D'ORO★★★

(⬛, ET)

VAPORETTO: CA' D'ORO, SAN ALVISE OR MADONNA DELL'ORTO.

The much photographed Ca' d'Oro is the jewel in the crown of the tranquil *sestiere* of **Cannaregio**. Its arches are as symbolic of the city's style and identity as its gondolas, and a visit here, gazing down across the river onto the Rialto fish market, is a quintessential part of the Venetian experience.

▷ **Orient Yourself:** Cannaregio dominates the northwest side of the Grand Canal and stretches eastwards from the Santa Lucia train station, in the vicinity of the Ponta della Libertà, to include the Strada Nuova and the Ca' d'Oro.

☺ **Don't Miss:** *St Sebastian* by Mantegna in the Ca' d'Oro's gallery.

🕐 **Organising Your Time:** Allow half a day to explore this neighbourhood.

♿ **Also See:** Neighbouring sights Il GHETTO; SAN ZANIPOLO.

A Bit of History

When Marino Contarini commissioned the construction of his *domus magna* at the beginning of the 15C, the French artist Jean Charlier, known as Zuane de Franza di Sant'Aponal, painted the façade in blue, black, white and around the architectural carving it was gilded, hence the name given to the *palazzo*, "House of Gold". The original gold may have long gone but the Ca' d'Oro remains the city's gold standard in Venetian Gothic domestic architecture. Several Lombard masters, followers of Matteo Raverti (active 1385–1436),

Façade of Ca' d'Oro

were involved in the construction of the Ca' d'Oro and under the leadership of Giovanni (c.1360–1442) and Bartolomeo Bon (active 1441–64) the Venetian masters took over. The well-head at the centre of the courtyard is attributable to Bartolomeo Bon, the son of Giovanni. The figures represent the three theological virtues of Fortitude, Justice and Charity.

Nowadays it is the façade and its reflection in the Grand Canal which most captivates the visitor. After a long period of restoration, the subdued colours have regained their magical intensity and the delicate marble tracery and crenellation are complete. The façade is harmonious in its asymmetry, despite possible plans for a left wing.

The original structure commissioned by the Contarini was subject to various alterations requested by numerous owners who lived there over the course of the centuries. Restoration work started in the 19C, when Prince Troubetskoy bought the Ca' d'Oro as a present for the ballerina Maria Taglioni.

The restoration was not faithful to the original construction. At the end of the 19C, more accurate restoration work was undertaken by **Baron Giorgio Franchetti**, who was responsible for the implementation of the gallery that now houses a varied collection of paintings, Renaissance bronze sculpture and medals spanning seven centuries from the 11C to the 18C.

Visit

♿ ⏰*Open 8.15am–7.15pm (2pm Mon); last admission 30min before closing.* ⏰*Closed 1 Jan, 1 May, 25 Dec.* ⊘€6. *Venice Card (* ☎ *see p45).* ☎*041 52 00 345. www.cadoro.org.*

Take a few moments to enjoy the handsome courtyard with its exquisite marble flooring and statuary. The staircase and well-head are original features. Both were ripped out of the *palazzo*, but reinstated by subsequent owners.

Galleria Franchetti

The first floor is devoted to Veneto-Byzantine art from the 11C to the 13C. Notable for its luminosity is the central panel of the polyptych dedicated to the *Passion* by **Antonio Vivarini** (c.1420–84), which depicts the Crucifixion. Another significant work is the English 15C *Scenes from the Passion of St Catherine*.

The highlight of the gallery is **Andrea Mantegna**'s uncompleted *St Sebastian*★★, set in a niche at the end of the corridor on the right. Note the *memento mori* attached to the candle stating *Nihil nisi divinum stabile est – Coetera fumus* (*Nothing if not divine is eternal – all the rest is smoke*) and the fact that the candle has just been blown out by the wind which ruffles St Sebastian's hair. The surge in popularity of St Sebastian during the early Renaissance is thought to be associated with his martyrdom by multiple arrow wounds, a fate involving the similar searing pain endured by those afflicted with the plague. The other was an opportunity for a painter to prove his worth by depicting the nude torso of the young man modelled upon Classical sculpture. The other saint invoked by the plague-stricken is the pilgrim **San Rocco**, who was believed to have protected Venice from the epidemic. The saint seems to indicate where the bubonic swellings have appeared by the position of his arms.

Among the bronzes, the work of **Pier Giacomo Bonaccolsi** (c.1460–1528) stands out. The official sculptor at the Gonzaga court at Mantua, he was better known for his emulation of sculptures in the Antique style – note the *Apollo* on display in one of the small showcases). Note also the *Annunciation* which appears to be set in Venice itself and the *Death of the Virgin,* painted by **Vittore Carpaccio** (c.1465–1526) and his studio, for the Scuola degli Albanesi.

The *Flagellation* by **Luca Signorelli** (c.1445–1523) is to be found on the same floor, along with the vibrant sequence from the *Life of Lucretia* in two paintings by Biagio d'Antonio (active to 1508). The latter depicts the departure of Sextus Tarquin from the Roman camp at Ardea, the rape of Lucretia, her suicide and funeral. The *Virgin with Child and St John*, a tondo by Jacopo del Sellaio (1442–93), is also on display here.

Exhibits on the floor above include the *Portrait of the Procurator Nicolò Priuli* by **Tintoretto**; Flemish tapestries from the second half of the 16C; *Venus with a Mirror* by **Titian** (1490–1576), which is incomplete on the right-hand side; *Portrait of a Gentleman* by **Sir Anthony van Dyck** (1599–1641) and *Venus Asleep with her Lover,* by **Paris Bordone** (1500–71). Two specifically Venetian scenes are by **Francesco Guardi** (1712–93): *St Mark's Square,* and the *View of the Wharf towards the Basilica of Santa Maria della Salute.*

Of great importance despite being very damaged are frescoes painted by **Giorgione** (c.1476–1510) and Titian for the façades of the **Fondaco dei Tedeschi**. All that remains of Giorgione's work is the *Nude*. Titian's work is still discernible in the frieze with the *Justice* and the great coat of arms.

Other interesting works include: paintings by Flemish artists, notable for their domestic interiors and landscapes; *The Crucifixion* by a follower of Van Eyck, remarkable for topographical detail, particularly with regard to the fortified city that emerges from the background.

The Franchetti collection of ceramics is displayed in the adjoining Palazzo Duodo.

▶ *On leaving the Galleria Franchetti, turn left on Calle di Ca' d'Oro, then left onto Strada Nuova.*

Walking Tour

Strada Nuova (◳, EFT)

This bustling thoroughfare runs almost parallel to the Grand Canal. It is part of the throbbing artery that starts at the Santa Lucia Station, snakes through the Cannaregio *sestiere* and eventually leads to the Rialto. Opened in 1871, the street is vibrant with the uninterrupted flow of people as visitors shuttle to and from the station and the Rialto, and locals do their shopping. It is lined with all sorts of shops, particularly the stretch of Rio Terrà San Leonardo near the station and around the lively market. Fish stalls run the length of the Fondamenta della Pescaria, alongside the Cannaregio Canal. Stop for a treat in a bakery, or take a break at an outdoor cafe – this is a great location to watch Venetians and visitors go by.

▶ *Continue left to the Fondamenta San Felice off the campo of the same name.*

Once past the **Church of San Felice**, which houses *St Demetrius with his Follower* by Tintoretto (1518–94), the canal follows the *fondamenta* and emerges in a corner of the city that is rarely frequented by tourists. Time seems to stand still in this peaceful district, which is a world apart from the noise and crowds of the Strada Nuova.

▶ *Turn right at Campo San Fosca.*

Campo San Fosca is dominated by a church of the same name and a monument to the remarkable **Paolo Sarpi** (1552–1623), a Venetian monk and scientist. He was a fierce defender of the Republic and stood against Rome when Pope Paul V claimed rights in the reli-

gious courts. His arguments were so well founded that the Pope finally conceded to Venice. An attempt to assassinate him took place soon afterwards. Fra Sarpi is also credited with discovering the dilation of the iris and making the first map of the moon.

▶ *Cross the first bridge, then the second to reach San Marziale church.*

The austere exterior of the **Chiesa di San Marziale** (🗺, **ET**) contrasts sharply with its rich Baroque interior. The ceiling decoration is the work of Sebastiano Ricci (1659–1734).

▶ *Continue to Fondamente della Misericordia. Turn right and follow it to the end.*

Here stands the **Scuola Nuova della Misericordia**, a building designed by Sansovino in 1534 as the "new" seat of the Order and built in brick, but never completed.

▶ *Turn left along the water and cross the bridge.*

Campo dell'Abbazia (🗺, FT)

The centre of this square, paved in brick in a herringbone pattern, is marked by a fine well-head. Bordering on the Rio della Sensa and the Misericordia Canal, the *campo* is hemmed in by the **Church of Santa Maria della Misericordia** (🗺, **FT**), otherwise known as Santa Maria Valverde after the island on which it was built in the 10C, and by the **Scuola Vecchia della Misericordia** (🗺, **FT**). The Baroque façade of the church, the work of Clemente Moli (1651–59), contrasts sharply with the Gothic brick façade of the Scuola of 1451.

▶ *Head west along the Rio della Sensa. Turn right on Corte Vecchia.*

Corte Vecchia leads to a viewpoint overlooking the **Sacca della Misericordia** (🗺, **FST**), a cove buffeted by the wind, from where the view stretches into the distance, punctuated only by the Island of San Michele, the tranquil cemetery on the water.

© Gwen Cannon / MICHELIN

One of the "Moors"

© Renaud Visage/age fotostock

Madonna dell'Orto

▶ *Retrace your steps, turn right and cross the bridge over Rio dei Muri. Pass* **Casa del Tintoretto** *at no 3399, the house where the artist died in 1594 (a plaque marks the exterior). Turn right onto Campo dei Mori.*

Campo dei Mori (🄳, ES)

The square's name alludes to the three-Mastelli brothers, a family of merchants from Morea in the Peloponnese who settled in Venice in 1112. The name Mastelli was coined after the thousands of *mastelli* (buckets) of gold *zecchini* or Venetian sequins they were meant to own. Their intriguing 13C statues lean against the houses: the fourth figure is of Sior Antonio Rioba, thought to be their servant. His original stone nose has been replaced by a rather unflattering pointed piece of metal and the figure is now used as an object of satire to lampoon local politicians and visiting dignitaries.

Along the Rio della Madonna dell'Orto stands the brothers' **Palazzo Mastelli del Cammello** (🄳, ES), notable for its Gothic detailing, corner column and low relief featuring a man pulling a camel.

▶ *Continue over the bridge to Fondamenta Gasparo Contarini.*

Madonna dell'Orto★ (🄳, ES)

🕙*Open Mon–Sat 10am–5pm.* 🕙*Closed 1 Jan, Easter, 15 Aug, 25 Dec.* ✺€3. ☎041 27 50 462. www.chorusvenezia.org.

This is known as the Tintoretto Church, as it was the parish church of the Tintoretto family. The richly ornamented brick façade betrays the various stages of construction from its foundation in the 14C, through early Gothic and Renaissance periods. Patronage was entrusted to the miracle-working Madonna dell'Orto (Our Lady of the Garden) when a statue of the Madonna and Child was found in a sculptor's garden. The spacious interior accommodates important works of art: *John the Baptist* by Cima da Conegliano (1459–1517); *St Vincent* by Jacopo Palma il Vecchio (c.1480-1528); *Martyrdom of St Lawrence* by Daniel van den Dyck (1614-63). Over the entrance to the Mauro Chapel is the *Presentation of the Virgin in the Temple* (1551) by **Tintoretto** (1518–94), whose burial place is marked by a slab in a chapel on the right. Other works by the master, as well as by his son Domenico and by Palma il Giovane, adorn the church.

Next to the church stands the **Scuola dei Mercanti** (🄳, ES), seat of the Guild of Merchants since 1570, when it transferred itself there from the Frari. Palladio participated in its renovation (1571–72) and is responsible for the portal which overlooks the *fondamenta*.

▶ *Return to Campo dei Mori and turn right onto Fondamenta della Sensa. To reach the Church of Sant' Alvise, turn right on Calle del Capitello.*

Sant'Alvise★ (, DS)

◷Open Mon–Sat 10am–5pm. ◷Closed 1 Jan, Easter, 15 Aug, 25 Dec. ◷€3. ◷041 27 50 462. www.chorusvenezia.org.

The simple brick façade is pierced by a rose window and a portal. Originally Gothic in style, the façade was greatly modified during the 16C. The statue in the lunette is of St Louis of Anjou, who lived towards the end of the 13C and was named Alvise by the Venetians.

The 17C frescoes by Antonio Torri and Pietro Ricchi lend an evocative three-dimensional effect to the flat ceiling. The entrance area is overlooked by the *barco*, the choir stalls used by the nuns, supported by columns with 15C capitals and Gothic buttresses. Above the columns stand 15C statues of *Christ the Redeemer* and *John the Baptist*. As you enter, note the 15C **tempera panel paintings** on the left, by a pupil of Lazzaro Bastiani (active 1449–1512). On the right wall are Tiepolo's *Flagellation* and *Crown of Thorns* (1740); his *Christ's Way to Calvary* (1749) is in the presbytery. The 16C wooden polychrome statue of Sant'Alvise shows the saint dressed in a Franciscan habit with a splendid crown.

▶ *Retrace your steps, heading towards the Grand Canal.*

IL CANAL GRANDE★★★

Arguably the most famous, the most beautiful, and certainly the most unusual High Street in the world, the Grand Canal bisects the island of Venice in the form of an inverted S. It is only 3km/2mi long though packs so much in that it feels much bigger. Other vital statistics are that it is between 30m/98ft and 70m/229ft wide and on average it is 5.5m/18ft deep). When he was living in Palazzo Mocenigo, Lord Byron was in the habit of swimming across the Grand Canal. Mark Twain described the appearance of the canal in moonlight as magical; Goethe felt himself to be "Lord of the Adriatic" here; and Dickens, convinced the ghost of Shylock roamed the bridges of the city, felt the spirit of Shakespeare strongly in Venice. A short journey along the canal will undoubtedly leave as magical an impression on modern-day travellers as it did on its illustrious visitors of the past.

▶ **Orient Yourself**: To best experience the Grand Canal, take the vaporetto from the railway station (Santa Lucia) to Piazza San Marco. Sit at the back in the open air for the best views. If you can't get a seat at the back, wait for the next boat – it won't be long.

▣ **Don't Miss:** There are so many great landmarks to pick out, but the Rialto Bridge is the most famous.

◷ **Organising Your Time:** It takes around 35–40min non-stop by vaporetto from Santa Lucia (Ferrovia Scalzi) to Piazza San Marco, but you could easily spend a full day (and longer) hopping on or off at places of interest.

A Bit of History

The origins of the Grand Canal, which may once have been a branch of the River Medoacus (◷see *VILLAS OF THE BRENTA*), are lost in time. The *traghetti* (gondolas which cross the river) have provided a ferry service between the banks of the canal since the year 1000: some of the existing landing stages have been in place since the 13C, many either serving mills that were operated by the

The Fourth Bridge

Venice acquired a new bridge in 2008 to much fanfare – its fourth across the Grand Canal was the first in more than 70 years. It was designed by Santiago Calatrava, the Spanish engineer and designer famous for his grandiose modernist works in Valencia. The exquisitely modern arched truss bridge, a single sleek span between the Santa Lucia railway station and Piazzale Roma, shows no visible means of support. To integrate it somewhat with the vernacular architecture it is partly built of local Istrian marble, Venice's most important raw material.

Controversy dogged the project. Many questioned whether this was the best location to build a new bridge, the contrast of its bold modern design, it was way over the original budget, there were safety issues, it was behind schedule, and, incomprehensibly it was not accessible to wheelchairs. The span is approached by illuminated glass steps and, belatedly, provision was made for disabled users.

The **Ponte della Costituzione (Constitution Bridge)**, informally called **Ponte di Calatrava**, was named for its opening date, which was the 60th anniversary of the Italian constitution.

tides or *squeri* where the gondolas were built; then there were the workshops for the Guild of Wool Weavers and Cloth-makers, which employed the poor to card, finish, dye and press the textiles. It is along the canal especially that the beauty of the city unfolds: façades of vibrant colours, resplendent with gilding, exude the festive spirit and optimism of the Venetians, who have never known the threat of oppression, not even in the Middle Ages, when the rest of the world had to build fortresses to defend themselves. The *palazzi* that flank the Grand Canal are the Venetian nobility's expression of pride and self-satisfaction: they were the only people who could vouchsafe a piece of this water garden (see *Il GHETTO: Palazzo Labia*). Commercial, banking and state enterprises have been in operation along the canal since the Renaissance; churches and *palazzi* were being built right up until the Republic breathed its last breath.

Left Bank

Stazione di Santa Lucia (🗉, CT)
Described by Gustav von Aschenbach, the main character in *Death in Venice*, as the "tradesmen's entrance" to the city, the station has served as the gateway to the city since 1860 when the first station was built. The present building was erected in 1954.

Gli Scalzi (🗉, CT)
This Baroque church was designed by Longhena (1598–1682). Its most distinctive features are the niches in the façade (1672–78), which are adorned with statues and framed with paired columns (see *Il GHETTO*).

Ponte degli Scalzi (🗉, CT)
Originally built in 1858, the bridge, named after the "discalced" (meaning unshod and pertaining to religious orders, such as the Carmelites and Franciscans), was designed by the same civil engineer, Neville, as the first Accademia Bridge. It was rebuilt in 1934.

San Geremia (🗉, CDT)
From the water, all that can be seen of this church is the Chapel of Santa Lucia, which houses the remains of the Sicilian martyr (see *Il GHETTO*).

Palazzo Labia★★ (🗉, CDT)
This elegant 18C residence on the corner of the Cannaregio Canal is slightly set back from the Grand Canal. The ground floor is rusticated, with Ionic and Corinthian pilasters on the two floors above: the large windows open out onto balconies. The eagles which protrude from under the roof refer to the heraldry of the Labia family (see *Il GHETTO*).

★★ PALAZZO LABIA

★ Palazzo Vendramin Calergi

S. Marcuola

① ㊖ S. Marcuola

S. Geremia

CANAL GRANDE ★★★

Gli Scalzi

Riva de Biasio

①

Fondaco dei Turchi

Fondaco del Megio

S. Lucia

Ferrovia

① ㊖

P.te degli Scalzi

S. Simeon Piccolo

VALLARESSO

P. ROMA

CANAL

Palazzo Pisani Moretta

① ㊖

S. Toma'

Palazzo Balbi

CANAL

Palazzi Mocenigo

Ca' Foscari

Palazzo Grassi ★

★★ CA' REZZONICO

Ca'Rezzonico

①

S. Samuele

㊖

Palazzo Moro

Palazzo Loredan dell'Ambasciatore

Palazzo Cavalli Franchetti

CANAL

Accademia

① ㊖

Ponte dell'Accademia

ACCADEMIA ★★★

CANALE

DELLA

GIUDECCA

CANAL GRANDE

S. Stae ①
S. Stae
Ca' Pesaro ★
Ca' Corner
della Regina
CA' D'ORO ★★★
Ca' d'Oro ①
Pescheria
Ca' da Mosto
Fabbriche
Nuove
Fabbriche
Vecchie
Palazzo dei
Camerlenghi
Fondaco
d. Tedeschi
P^TE DI RIALTO ★★
Rialto
① ㉒
Palazzo
Bernardo
S. Silvestro
①
Palazzo Loredan
GRANDE ★★★
S. Angelo ①
Palazzo Lando
Corner Spinelli
★★★ PIAZZA
S. MARCO
★★ P^ta dei
Sospiri
Palazzo Corner
della Ca' Granda
① ㉒
Vallaresso
LIDO
BACINO
① Giglio
Palazzo
Barbarigo
★ Ca'
Dario
GRANDE ★★★
Salute ①
DI
S. MARCO
Pal. Venier
dei Leoni
(★★ COLL. P.
GUGGENHEIM)
Palazzo
Salviati
S. MARIA
D. SALUTE ★★
Dogana da Mar

Illustration: R. Corbel

⚓ Gondola route

① Vaporetto number
Salute   and stop

0   100 m

© Guido Alberto Rossi / Tips Images

Aerial view of the Canal Grande

San Marcuola (🗟, DT)

This church is quite distinctive from others overlooking the Grand Canal: the roughly-bricked façade remains incomplete. Interestingly, this façade is actually the side of the church. Although its present appearance is Baroque in style, the church is altogether much older (🖝*see IL GHETTO*).

Palazzo Vendramin Calergi★ (🖪, ET)

This Renaissance palace, commissioned by the noble family of Loredan al Codussi, who worked in the city between 1502 and 1504, is a magnificent synthesis of Byzantine and Gothic architectural features. From 1844 it was home to the Duchesse de Berry, the daughter-in-law of Charles X of France. **Richard Wagner** lived here, composing the second act of *Tristan and Isolde* between 1858 and 1859. Although the composer died in the Palazzo Vendramin, where he had also worked on *Parsifal*, his memory is enshrined in the **Sala Richard Wagner** (🕙*open by appointment only; ☎041 52 32 544; www.vendramincalergi.com*). The *palazzo* currently serves as the winter headquarters of the municipal casino.

Ca' d'Oro★★★ (🖪, ET)

The *palazzo's* façade, in the ornate Gothic style, presents a colonnade lapped by

the water's edge and, on the upper floors, two enclosed loggias with arched windows, interlaced with intersecting tracery and quatrefoils. Oddly, this decorative feature is not centred in the façade. The right section consists of a blank wall between single-arched windows. Cordons of marble accentuate the corners (🖝*see CA' D'ORO*).

Ca' da Mosto (🖪, FU)

Erected in the 13C, this Veneto-Byzantine *palazzo* was the birthplace of Alvise da Mosto (1432–88), the great navigator who explored the western coast of Africa. The portico betrays the building's dual function as house and warehouse. Note the first-floor ceiling decorated with circular coffering or patera. Between the 16C and 18C, the *palazzo* served as the city's finest hotel, the **Leon Bianco**.

Fondaco dei Tedeschi (🖪, FU)

This 13C *palazzo* served as the headquarters of German traders and as a warehouse for their goods. Devastated by fire (1505–08), it was rebuilt by Giorgio Spavento (in Venice between the 15C and 16C) and by Scarpagnino (in Venice between 1505 and 1549). The façade that overlooks the Grand Canal, and which was at one time frescoed by Giorgione (c.1476–1510) and Titian

(1490–1576), has a portico on the ground floor, as befitted a *fondaco* (warehouse). Nowadays the building houses the main post office (&*see La FENICE*).

Ponte di Rialto★★ (4, FU)
The **Rialto Bridge** is the most important crossing point between the two banks of the Grand Canal. Although today's bridge is the sixth version – the original was built in 1175 – this is the first stone-built construction. The work of Antonio da Ponte, it was opened in 1591. The shops which are housed in the symmetrical arcades were originally used by money changers, bankers and moneylenders, in close proximity to the first Zecca (Mint – &*see RIALTO*).

Palazzo Loredan (4, EFV)
Also a *fondaco* (warehouse), this Veneto-Byzantine *palazzo* retains some original features: part of the portico and windows opening out onto the loggia, interlaced with pateras, run the length of the *piano nobile* (first floor). Palazzo Loredan and the nearby Palazzo Farsetti now house municipal offices.

Palazzo Lando Corner Spinelli (4, EV)
Erected in 1490, this Renaissance *palazzo* was most probably designed by Mauro Codussi. The façade in Istrian stone is heavily rusticated. The upper storeys are punctuated with typical two-light windows, and a Renaissance frieze of festoons runs below the attic windows. It resembles the Palazzo Vendramin Calergi.

Right Bank

San Simeon Piccolo (3, CT)
This is the first eye-catching landmark after the station. Distinctive features include a Corinthian *pronaos* (front portico) up a flight of steps and a green dome. The church was designed by Scalfarotto (c.1700–64) in the tradition set by Palladio and Longhena.

Ponte degli Scalzi (3, CT)
(&*see Left Bank, over page*).

Fondaco dei Turchi (3, DT)
Dating to the 13C, this Veneto-Byzantine *fondaco* was built as a private house and turned into commercial premises in 1621. Its current appearance is largely due to its restoration in the late-19C. With the side towers framing the façade, the portico and the floor above are laced with arches. Between 1621 and 1838 the warehouse was used by Turks, hence its name. The building houses the Natural History Museum (&*see I FRARI*).

Fondaco del Megio (3, DT)
This distinctive building, with walls of roughly hewn brick and tiny windows, dates to the 15C. Note the lion below the ornate crenellation. The structure was used as a grain store, notably for millet (*miglio = megio* – hence the name).

San Stae (4, ET)
&*Open Mon–Sat 10am–5pm.* &*Closed 1 Jan, Easter, 15 Aug, 25 Dec.* &€3. ℡041 27 50 462. www.chorusvenezia.org.
Dedicated to St Eustace, this church was completely renovated during the 17C. The elaborate Baroque façade (1709), dominated by a pedimented bay set between two roughcast wings, is attributed to Domenico Rossi (1678–1742). Its broken tympanum, crowned with statues over the entrance, is original. Inside a single nave are works by Piazzetta (1683–1754), Ricci (1659–1734) and Tiepolo (1696–1770) that forestall a shift in style towards the Rococo. Doge Alvise Mocenigo is buried here.

Ca' Pesaro★ (4, ET)
At the death of Baldassare Longhena (1682), completion of the building was assigned to Antonio Gaspari (c.1670–c.1730). Unusual is its diamond-pointed rustication of the ground floor and row of lions' heads. On the second and third floors, great arched windows with single columns grace an open loggia. Today, the building is home to the Museum of Oriental Art and the International Gallery of Modern Art (&*see RIALTO*).

Ca' Corner della Regina (4, ET)
Designed by Domenico Rossi (1678–1742), the heavily rusticated ground floor gives way to plainer upper storeys punctuated

by balconies and windows framed with columns. Currently the home of the National Archives of Contemporary Art (*see RIALTO*).

Pescheria (4, ET)
The portico of this neo-Gothic building, which dates back to the beginning of the 20C, now holds the famous fish market, hence the name (*see RIALTO*).

Fabbriche Nuove (4, FU)
This rather plain building on the bend of the Grand Canal was designed by **Sansovino**. Its rusticated ground floor at one time would have consisted of *magazzini* (small shops) and warehousing. The first floor was occupied by magistrates' courts (*see RIALTO*).

Fabbriche Vecchie (4, FU)
Destroyed by fire, the warehouses were rebuilt by Scarpagnino (active in Venice between 1505 and 1549). Even the "old workshops" boast their own columned portico (*see RIALTO*).

Palazzo dei Camerlenghi (4, FU)
Situated in the lee of the bridge, this Renaissance palace was designed by Guglielmo dei Grigi, known as Bergamasco (active in Venice between c.1515–30), for the Camerlenghi, who were government officials responsible for the State's financial affairs. The pentagonal building has large windows aligned below a frieze of festoons.

Ponte di Rialto★★ (4, FU)
(*see Left Bank, opposite*).

Palazzo Bernardo (4, EV)
Gothic in style (1442), the building boasts splendid five-arched windows, pointed on the first floor, and quatrefoils on the second floor.

Palazzo Pisani Moretta (7, DV)
Also late Gothic, the Palazzo Pisani Moretta dates from the second half of the 15C. Like Palazzo Bernardo, the windows have five lights and intersecting tracery that enclose quatrefoils on the upper floors.

Palazzo Balbi (7, DX)
The façade of this *palazzo*, which is attributed to Alessandro Vittoria (1525–c.1600), is divided into three sections. Above a rusticated ground floor, the central bay is pierced by an arrangement of three arched windows.

Left Bank

Palazzo Mocenigo (7, DX)
This building comprises four adjacent *palazzi*. The first dates back to 1579, when it was rebuilt according to the designs of Alessandro Vittoria. The second and third buildings, which are identical, are from the end of the 16C; the last, the so-called "Casa Vecchia," a Gothic construction, was remodelled during the first half of the 17C.
The Romantic poet **Lord Byron** (1788–1824) started work on his *Don Juan* while he lived here. This English "Don Giovanni" often swam home from a day at San Lazzaro (*see SAN LAZZARO degli ARMENI*) or an evening at the Lido, a habit that instituted a swimming race that was held until 1949 and rewarded by the Byron Cup.

Palazzo Grassi★ (7, DX)
Erected in 1749 by Giorgio Massari, this last Venetian palace to be built before the fall of the Republic is designed with all the majesty of neo-Classical domestic architecture. Inside, the courtyard has a fine colonnade and a grand staircase frescoed by Alessandro Longhi populated with masked figures. Other rooms are frescoed by Jacopo Guarana (1720–1808) and Fabio Canal (1703–67). Today the building is used for prestigious temporary exhibitions (*open during exhibitions only; ☎041 52 31 680; www.palazzograssi.it*) and is also home to a very good cafe and bookshop.

Ponte dell'Accademia (7, DX)
Venice had to wait until 1854 for its second crossing of the Grand Canal after the Rialto Bridge. The original iron construction, restricted in height, hindered the passage of the vaporettos; the bridge was therefore replaced in 1932, this time built of wood because of lack of funds. The present bridge is a

Ca' Rezzonico

© Ca' Rezzonico / Fondazione Musei Civici Venezia

copy of its wooden predecessor (☞*see ACCADEMIA*).

Palazzo Cavalli Franchetti (**7**, DX)

The splendid façade of this late-15C *palazzo*, complete with delicate tracery work, five-arched windows with intersecting tracery and quatrefoil motifs, casts its intricate reflection across the Grand Canal. It was rebuilt towards the end of the 19C.

Palazzo Corner della Ca' Granda (**8**, EX)

Nowadays this Renaissance palace is used as the police headquarters (*Prefettura*). It was built for the nephew of Caterina Cornaro by Sansovino (1486–1570). The rusticated ground floor has a three-arch portico; elegantly aligned arched windows on the upper floors alternate with paired columns.

Next door, the little red house was used by **Canova** as his studio (1770s) and during the First World War by the controversial, poet, novelist and Fascist politician, **Gabriele d'Annunzio**.

Right Bank

Ca' Foscari (**7**, DX)

The glorious façade of this *palazzo* rises above the Grand Canal at the junction with the Rio Foscari. Perfect symmetry aligns the three orders of arched windows that alternate with single light openings and stonework. The original 14C building was rebuilt closer to the water's edge after 1550. Nowadays it is part of the university (☞*see I CARMINI*).

Ca' Rezzonico★★ (**7**, DX)

This house was the last palace designed by Longhena, who lived to see only the completion of the first floor, before Massari took over. Note the extensive embellishment of the *piano nobile* and the fine configuration of balconies. It presently contains the Museo del '700 veneziano, or Museum of 18C Venice (☞*see I CARMINI*) and collections of Venetian finery related to the Carnival.

Palazzo Moro (**7**, DX)

Situated just beyond the Ca' Rezzonico vaporetto stop, this 16C *palazzo* is aus-

Portrait of a Young Gentleman in his Study by Lotto, Accademia

tere in its simplicity. It was here that the Moro family resided, one of whom suffered the tragic marriage that was to inspire **Shakespeare** (1564–1616) to write *Othello*, and portray the famous "Moor of Venice".

Palazzo Loredan dell'Ambasciatore (**7**, DX)
Otherwise known as "The Ambassador's House," the late-Gothic Palazzo Loredan has splendid arched windows.

Accademia★★★(**7**, DX)
The Academy of Fine Arts has been housed here since the beginning of the 19C. The adjoining church, rebuilt between 1441 and 1452, has been subject to considerable restoration through the ages, most famously by Palladio (1508–80) (*see ACCADEMIA*).

Ponte dell'Accademia (**7**, DX)
(*see Left Bank*).

Palazzo Barbarigo (**8**, EX)
The mosaics that decorate the façade depict Charles V in Titian's studio and Henry III of France on Murano. These were installed by the glass-blowers and mosaic-makers responsible for the reconstruction of the 16C palace in the late-19C. This building provided **Henry James** with inspiration for his novel *The Wings of the Dove*. In 2007 it opened its doors as a splendid art-deco-inspired luxury hotel.

Palazzo Venier dei Leoni (**8**, EX)
It requires some imagination to picture how this palace was intended to look by its designer Lorenzo Boschetti in 1749, (there is a scale model of it in the Correr Museum). Financial problems forced the Venier family to stop work on the building and all that survives of the original is its rusticated ground floor.

It is "guarded" by a large stone lion, a link to a story that the Venier family once kept a pet lion in the garden!

The building currently houses the world-famous **Peggy Guggenheim Collection** of modern art (*see La SALUTE, Collezione Peggy Guggenheim*).

Ca' Dario★ (**8**, EX)
This small, late-15C *palazzo* is most distinctively embellished with polychrome marble decoration. It was built by the Lombardo family for Giovanni Dario, the secretary to the Senate of the Republic at the Sultan's court.

Palazzo Salviati (**8**, EX)
Like Palazzo Barbarigo, the 19C Palazzo Salviati was owned by glass-makers who provided its fine mosaics.

Santa Maria della Salute★★ (**8**, FX)
The massive white structure with its distinctive spiral volutes (the so-called *orecchioni*, or big ears) is visible from afar. Designed by Longhena, it was erected upon the wishes of the doge as a gesture of supplication to end the plague of 1630, a story recounted in the Italian novel by Alessandro Manzoni, *I Promessi Sposi* (*see La SALUTE*).

Dogana da Mar (**8**, FX)
It was here on this extension of the Dorsoduro district that goods used to be unloaded and duty on them levied. The present construction, dominated by a tower on which two Atlantes support the weight of the World and the figure of Fortune, dates to the second half of the 17C (*see La SALUTE*).

© Accademia, Venezia / SCALA

I CARMINI ★

(7, CX)

This stretch of the **Dorsoduro** district includes a lively mix of university life with the daily markets in the Campo Santa Margherita and along the Rio di San Barnaba. Here waterborne greengrocers sell the freshest produce, including delicate artichokes from Sant'Erasmo. It is not difficult to find an eatery catering to students and tourists, or indeed a quintessentially Italian bar. There are plenty of shops catering for locals rather than just visitors and also the odd authentic *bottega*, particularly between San Barnaba and Campo di Santa Margherita, selling wood carvings and masks.

▶ **Orient Yourself:** South of the Grand Canal, the Dorsoduro neighbourhood sweeps west from La Salute to the Canale Scomenzera, encompassing the Zattere promenade along the Guidecca canal.
- **Don't Miss:** Ca'Rezzonico, an outstanding palazzo, exquisitely furnished. If you have time to see only one palazzo, this is the one.
- **Organising Your Time:** About half a day, plus 2hrs for Ca'Rezzonico.
- **Especially for Kids:** Children will enjoy watching the constant parade of all manner of watercraft on the Guidecca canal, including massive cruise ships.
- **Also See:** ACCADEMIA, SAN ROCCO.

Walking Tour

Campo Santa Margherita (7, CX)

The distinctive features of this large square are the Scuola dei Varoteri (Confraternity of Tanners) and the stunted campanile of the former Church of Santa Margherita. Cafés, shops and market stalls add a buzz. Its relatively humble appearance derives largely from its position alongside the Rio della Scoazzera (meaning sewage channel), now running underground, which dissuaded the nobility from building patrician *palazzi* in its vicinity.

Scuola Grande dei Carmini★ (7, CX)

⏱ *Open daily 11am–4pm.* ⏹ *Closed 1 Jan, 25 Dec.* €5. ☎ *041 52 89 420.*
The narrowest end of the Campo di Santa Margherita houses the Scuola dei Carmini (Guild of Dyers), devotees of the Virgin of Carmelo, borne out by the central picture on the ceiling of the Salone, *The Virgin in Glory Appearing to the Blessed Simon Stock, Consigning to him the Scapular* (a simple arrangement of two squares of white cloth tied together with strings over the shoulder, a standard part of the

Order's costume). This panel and eight others were executed by **Giovanni Battista Tiepolo**. The **Sala dell'Archivio** is decorated with 18C wall hangings. On the wall next to the entrance to the **Sala dell'Albergo** is *Judith and Holofernes* by Piazzetta (1683–1754).

I Carmini (7, CX)

The simple Renaissance façade of this church and its 14C porch, decorated

Ceiling of Scuola Grande dei Carmini

© Th. Jonglez / MICHELIN

The Venetian Scuole

Instituted during the Middle Ages, the Venetian Scuole (literally meaning "school") were lay confraternities or guilds drawn from the merchant classes active in all aspects of everyday life, until the fall of the Republic. Patricians subscribed to the most prestigious Scuole, which excluded the poor, those engaged in morally dubious activities, and women, unless they were part of a member's family.

Each Scuola had its own patron saint and **Mariegola**, a rule book and constitution of the guild. The Scuola di San Giorgio degli Schiavoni and the Scuola degli Albanesi were dedicated to assisting foreign workers financially and spiritually. Others were formed of artisans sharing a common trade. Those of a religious nature were known as the **Scuole di Battuti**, reflecting their penitential practices.

From the 15C, the Scuole were divided into *Scuole Grandi* and *Scuole Minori*, as resolved by the Council of Ten. At the time, some 400 Scuole were in existence: the buildings that housed the most important guilds were magnificent palaces, with their interiors decorated by famous artists.

with Veneto-Byzantine pateras framing the portal on the left side, are in stark contrast to the rich decoration of the interior. At first sight, the red columns dividing the three aisles, the dark 17C and 18C paintings and the heavy black and gold of the statues lend a lugubrious atmosphere; yet the brightness of the internal space, the woodwork decoration so typical of such 14C churches, and its many paintings, soften the initial impression.

Dedicated to Santa Maria del Carmelo, the church contains some interesting works of art: among them are (*left aisle, near the entrance*) Padovanino's *San Liberale Saves Two Men Condemned to Death* and *St Nicholas between John the Baptist and Saint Lucy with Angels* by Lorenzo Lotto; (*right wall*) *Feeding of the Five Thousand* by Palma il Giovane; (*above the fourth altar, right aisle*) *Presentation of Christ in the Temple* by Tintoretto. Many of the paintings were restored by funds from the American Committee to Rescue Italian Art.

▶ *Cross the bridge, turn immediately left and proceed to the end of the fondamenta which runs alongside the canal. The Church of San Nicolò dei Mendicoli stands on the right.*

San Nicolò dei Mendicoli (🖸, BX)

The dedication of the church to the *Mendicoli* alludes to the beggars who used to live in the area, notably the *pinzochere* (impoverished religious women) who

sheltered in the portico. Indications are that the church was founded in the 7C, although this building dates for the most part from the 12C, as does the massive bell-tower. The central bay of the façade and its portico echo those of the Church of San Giacomo di Rialto. Inside, the wooden statuary dates to the 16C, when the iconostasis was given its present appearance. The paintings by followers of Veronese (1528–88) depict *Episodes from the Life of Christ*.

▶ *Return along the fondamenta and cross the canal by the second bridge.*

Beyond the **Church of Angelo Raffaele** (🖸, BX), which contains the *Stories of Tobias and the Angel* purportedly by Gian'Antonio Guardi (1699–1760) on the parapet of the organ, Calle Nave branches off to the left towards the Church of St Sebastian.

San Sebastiano★★ (🗗, CX)

🕐*Open Mon–Sat 10am–5pm.* 🕐*Closed 1 Jan, Easter, 15 Aug, 25 Dec.* ✎€3. ☎041 27 50 462; www.chorusvenezia.org.

The true beauty of this church lies in its rich internal decoration: Vasari described Veronese's paintings as "joyous, beautiful and well-conceived". It is worth scanning the individual masterpieces before allowing time to absorb the overall effect.

Along the right side in the first side chapel hangs *St Nicholas* by **Titian** (c.1490–1576); in the third is a *Crucifix-*

ion by Veronese (1528–88); the *Tomb of Livio Podacattaro*, Bishop of Candia (Cyprus), is by Sansovino (1486–1570); opposite, next to the organ, stands the **bust of Veronese** that marks the burial site of the master painter who so celebrated the beauty of the world with depictions of luxurious silk and velvet, buxom women in flesh and stone, surrounded by gold, glass and silver. It is the opulent quality of his art that renders the Church of St Sebastian unique; it was with this cycle of frescoes that the painter was preoccupied for the most significant part of his life.

St Sebastian recurs as the subject of many of the frescoes: above Podacattaro's tomb and behind the statue (*right*), the saint is shown pierced by arrows from archers on the wall opposite. His martyrdom is also depicted.

▶ *Take the long calle that links the churches of San Sebastiano and San Barnaba.*

The water-borne vegetable stalls, or verduriere

Calle Lunga S Barnaba boasts few monuments or important sights but remains a particularly typical part of local Venice, lined with friendly eating places, paint shops and a model-maker's shop selling intricate miniatures.

Campo San Barnaba (**7**, CX)

The buzz of this popular square is generated by a healthy mix of tourists and locals alike. It is confined by the simple white façade of the titular church, small shops, cafes and the food stalls along the Rio di San Barnaba near the Ponte dei Pugni.

▶ *Cross the canal, either by the Ponte dei Pugni or another bridge immediately to the left of the façade of the church, and walk towards the Grand Canal.*

Ca' Rezzonico★★ (**7**, DX)

The last *palazzo* to be designed by **Baldassare Longhena** was, in fact, completed by **Giorgio Massari** (c.1686–1766). It is markedly the product of two very distinctive masters who, despite their differences of opinion, worked towards the same end. **Henry James** (1843–1916) considered the Ca' Rezzonico to be such a majestic piece of architecture as to be almost mythological; Ruskin (1819–1900), who detested the Baroque style, likened the pilasters to "piles of cheeses."

Originally commissioned for the Bon family, ownership was transferred incomplete to a family from Lake Como; one of its progeny was to become Pope Clement XIII (1758).

Ca' Rezzonico was once owned by **Robert Browning** (1812–89) and his wife, the poet Elizabeth Barrett (1806–61), before passing to their son Robert (1849–1913). He was better known as "Pen", coined as an abbreviation of *penini*, which in Venetian dialect means small feet. Robert Browning junior was forced to sell the *palazzo* in 1906 when his divorce obliged him to return a large dowry.

Ca' Rezzonico now houses the **Museo del Settecento Veneziano** (Museum of 18C Venice).

Museo del Settecento Veneziano

♿ ⏱ *Open Apr 1–Oct 31 Wed–Mon 10am–6pm (5pm early Nov 1–Mar 31). Last admission one hour before closing.*

🕐 *Closed 1 Jan, 1 May, 25 Dec.* 👓 *€8.*
📞 *041 24 10 100. http://carezzonico.vis-itmuve.it.*

The visit begins with an enormous staircase, designed, as with the other state rooms on the *piano nobile,* to impress guests and host elaborate Carnival fancy-dress parties. The **Salone da Ballo** (ballroom) is dominated by the great coat of arms of the Rezzonico family and frescoed by the master of *trompe l'oeil,* **Giambattista Crosato** (c.1685–1758). On the ceiling, *Apollo's Chariot* is flanked by the *Four Parts of the World.* Early-18C Venetian pieces include the ebony figurines and delicate chairs that once belonged to the Venier family. In spring, classical **musical concerts** are staged here.

The ceiling of the **Sala dell'Allegoria Nuziale** was frescoed by Tiepolo in 1757 for the society wedding of Ludovico, one of the members of the Rezzonico family,

Housed in the **Sala dei Pastelli** (Pastel Room) are portraits by **Rosalba Carriera** (1675–1757), including one of *Cecilia Guardi Tiepolo,* the wife of Giambattista Crosato and mother of the artist Lorenzo Tiepolo. The furniture is Rococo, delicate and ornamentally fanciful and over-decorative.

The **Sala degli Arazzi** (Tapestry Room) is hung with Flemish tapestries from the end of the late-17C that tell the story of Solomon and the Queen of Sheba. The furniture here is also Rococo. The frescoed ceiling from c.1756 is the work of Jacopo Guarana (1720–1808). Note the yellow lacquer door with chinoiserie decoration, very fashionable at the time.

The **Sala del Trono** (Throne Room) derives its name from the majestic golden throne adorned with nymphs, sea horses and *putti* that was used by Pope Pius VI on his visit to Venice in 1782. It is worth noticing Bernardino Castelli's particularly impressive portrait of *Pietro Barbarigo* (c.1780) set in its grandiose frame decorated with allegorical figures. The ceiling panel depicting *Merit* (crowned with laurel and attended by Nobility and Virtue) *Ascending to the Temple of Glory* was painted by **Tiepolo**.

Continue into the **portego**, where a golden sedan chair covered in red silk is kept. The doorway onto the stairs, is ornamented with two sculptures by Alessandro Vittoria (1525–1608).

In the **Sala del Tiepolo** (Tiepolo Room) the ceiling depicts *Virtue and Nobility Bringing Down Perfidy.* The four *Heads* on either side of the chimney are attributed to the sons of the great artist, Giandomenico (1727–1804) and Lorenzo Tiepolo (1736–76). Other notable works hung here include the *Portrait of the Architect Bartolomeo Ferracina* by Alessandro Longhi (1733–1813) The *bureau* in walnut is 18C; the games table with carved legs dates back to the late 17C/early 18C; the 17C cabinet was used as a strongbox.

The next room is the **library**, furnished with gilded leather chairs and a clock made in London.

Despite its name, the **Sala del Lazzarini** houses only one work by this artist, *Orpheus Massacred by the Bacchants* (1698), displayed on the left as you enter the room.

In the **Sala del Brustolon**, the flower-stand table is decorated with an *Allegory of Strength*, personified by Hector. The 18C Murano chandelier is the best example of its kind to have survived intact from this period.

▶ *Return to the portego for access to the second floor.*

Upstairs in the *portego* are topographical works by **Canaletto**: *View over the Rio dei Mendicanti* and *View of the Grand Canal from Ca' Balbi to the Rialto Bridge.* Other works include those by Guardi, Piazzetta, Pellegrini and Strozzi.

Giandomenico's frescoes, which depict a crowd of peasants turned away from the viewer, once graced the Tiepolo Villa at Zianigo, near Mirano. They are now housed in a room at the end of the *portego*, on the right.

The **Sala del Clavicembalo** accommodates an early-18C harpsichord that gives the room its name. Works on display in the small corridor include *View of the Castel Cogolo* by Francesco Guardi (1712–39) in poor condition, *A Pastoral*

Scene by Francesco Zuccarelli (1702–88) and *Teaching the Art of the Coroneri* (the *coroneri* being makers of crowns, rosaries and buttons) by Francesco Guardi. The **Sala del Parlatorio** (Parlour Room) contains paintings by Pietro Longhi and two well-known pieces by Francesco Guardi: the *Parlour of the Nuns of San Zaccharia* and a miniature of *Palazzo Dandolo to San Moisé.*

▸ *Access to the Sala del Longhi (Longhi Room) is back through the portego.*

Among the 29 paintings by **Pietro Longhi**, note particularly his *Portrait of Francesco Guardi.* Longhi has been compared to England's William Hogarth as a social commentator of his times, although the depictions of quiet Venetian patrician domesticity are more benign than those of his English counterpart. The ceiling panel of *Zephyr and Flora* is by Tiepolo.

Chinoiserie predominates in the **Sala delle Lacche Verdi** (Green Lacquer Room). The *Triumph of Diana,* on the ceiling, is by Gian Antonio Guardi. Note the particularly evocative painting of the *Frozen Lagoon* (1788), by a follower of Francesco Battaglia.

The three frescoes in the **Sala del Guardi** (Guardi Room) are by **Giovanni Antonio**: *Venus and Love, Apollo* and *Minerva.* Little biographical detail exists about the Guardi brothers, Francesco (1712–93) and Giovanni Antonio (1699–1760), other than the fact that they relied on the tourist market for most of their trade. Francesco, the "Veduta" painter, uses paint freely to capture sparkling light in his topographical landscapes (a quality later admired and taken up by the Impressionists), whereas the elder brother animated his scenes with figures in a way that was to influence 18C British watercolour painting.

The **Alcova** (Alcove) is a reconstruction of a bedroom and boudoir; the pastel *Madonna* is by **Rosalba Carriera.** The 17C silver toilette service is the work of Augsburg silversmiths. Giandomenico Tiepolo is responsible for the ceiling of the wardrobe; the stucco decoration

La lettera del moro (1751) by Pietro Falca detto Longhi, Ca' Rezzonico

and the frescoes in the boudoir are by Jacopo Guarana.

▸ *Access to the third floor is via the portego.*

The spacious **Pinacoteca Egidio Martini** houses a collection of paintings from the Venetian School dating from the 15C–20C. The visit of 18C Venice concludes with a reconstruction of the **"Ai Do San Marchi"** pharmacy.

▸ *Retrace your steps along the Fondamenta Rezzonico and turn right into Calle delle Botteghe, take Calle della Malvasia on the right and then Calle del Cappeller on the left. Follow to Ca' Foscari.*

Ca' Foscari (**7**, DX)

A famous example of the Gothic style, Ca' Foscari was built in 1452 for the Doge Francesco Foscari. Today it accommodates the headquarters of the **University of Venice**. The approach from Calle Foscari is not ideal as the view of the *palazzo* is restricted by the crenellated wall that surrounds the courtyard. Bustling with student activity, the Ca' Foscari is best seen from the Grand Canal which, in turn, may be glimpsed from the salone on the ground floor, which hosts occasionl exhibitions (*see Il CANAL GRANDE*).

LA FENICE ★

(B, EX)

VAPORETTO: S. MARCO, S. MARIA DEL GIGLIO, S. SAMUELE, S. ANGELO OR RIALTO

Occupying the loop of the Grand Canal this is a very lively part of Venice. As well as the city's famous theatre the area has plenty of good shops; for books try the Campo San Luca and for masks, look between Campo Manin and Campo Sant'Angelo. The route between St Mark's and Campo Santo Stefano boasts many elegant shops and hotels, and around the Church of San Moisé are art, glass and bookbinding workshops.

▶ **Orient Yourself:** The area in the immediate vicinity of the theatre is known as the "seven campi between the bridges," a reference to the Campi di San Bartolomeo, San Salvador, San Luca, Manin, Sant'Angelo, Santo Stefano and San Vidal, situated between the Rialto Bridge and Accademia Bridge. Although the theatre occupies a fairly quiet setting, it is edged by a bustling commercial hub of restaurants and shops.

⊙ **Don't Miss:** The designer boutiques and street entertainers along the Calle Larga 22 Marzo.

🕓 **Organising Your Time:** Allow 2hrs for the itinerary and another 1hr for a guided tour of the theatre.

⌚ **Also See:** PIAZZA SAN MARCO, RIALTO.

Walking Tour

Gran Teatro La Fenice ★ (B, EX)

🕓 *Guided tours (45min) daily 9.30am–6pm unless the theatre is being used for other purposes.* ⊙*Closed 1 Jan, 1 May, 25 Dec.* ⊙€8.50. ☎041 78 66 75; tours ☎041 24 24. www.teatrolafenice.it or www.festfenice.com.

Situated in a secluded and picturesque little square of Campo San Fantin, the opera house and music-theatre was inaugurated in 1792 after its predecessor (1673) burned down in 1774. Construction was initiated by **Giannantonio Selva** (1751–1819), a friend of Canova, who won the commission in a competition. Almost completely destroyed by fire in 1836, it was rebuilt and renamed La Fenice (The Phoenix) in honour of its emergence from the ashes. Neo-Classical in style, La Fenice had two façades and two entrances, including one overlooking the canal. It is not difficult to imagine the difficulties posed by the spatial requirements of the auditorium, which was much bigger than the apparently narrow façade, a problem overcome by means of an ingenious series of stairways.

This "jewel box of a theatre" (Isaac Sterne) burned down again on 29 January 1996 when it was closed for restoration. Damage was exacerbated by the fact that fire services were unable to reach the scene along normal routes as neighbouring canals had been drained for cleaning. John Berendt gives a fascinating account of the event in his book *The City of Falling Angels* (⌚*see Further Reading in Planning Your Trip*). Special funds were set up by the Italian government, the Venice in Peril Fund and the American Save Venice Committee. Reconstructed to architect **Aldo Rossi's** plan, the theatre reopened on 14 December 2003.

Campo San Fantin (B, EX)

The Renaissance church **Chiesa San Fantin** was begun by Scarpagnino (active in Venice between 1505 and 1549) and completed by Sansovino. Inside are two works by Palma il Giovane (1544–1628).

On the other side of the campo is the the **Ateneo Veneto** (⊙*open Mon–Fri, 10am–1pm & 3–6.30pm, library 9.30am–5.30pm;* ⊙*closed holidays, Aug, 21 Nov, 23 Dec–6 Jan;* ☎041 52 24 459, www. ateneoveneto.org), formerly home to

Façade of Gran Teatro La Fenice

the **Scuola di San Fantin**. The Scuola belonged to the Guild of San Girolamo for *picai* (hangmen), who escorted the condemned to the site of their execution and oversaw their burial. The front (c.1580) was designed by Alessandro Vittoria. Today, the building accommodates the **Ateneo Veneto** (🖫, **EX**). The Aula Magna on the ground floor has a fine wooden panelled ceiling decorated by Palma il Giovane; the Aula Tommaseo houses works by Antonio Zanchi (1631–1722) (*ceiling and, on entering, the right wall*) and Francesco Fontebasso (1709–69) (*opposite*). The Sala di Lettura (Reading Room) is decorated by Veronese (1528–88).

▶ *Follow Calle delle Veste off Campo San Fantin to Calle Larga XXII Marzo, which is closed off on the left by the sumptuous façade of the Church of San Moisé.*

(🖫 In the other direction, Calle del Fruttarol leads to a bridge with a view of the *palazzo* on the canal where **Mozart** stayed during the Carnival in 1771, marked by a commemorative wall plaque.)

San Moisé (🖫, **FX**)

Undoubtedly, the most striking feature of this church is its façade: built by Longhena's pupil **Alessandro Tremignon**

in the 17C with the help of the Flemish artist Meyring, a disciple of Bernini, it is the epitome of excess. Divided into three sections both horizontally and vertically, the edifice features every sort of adornment on the front. The lower tier is designed as a triumphal arch, dominated by memorials to members of the Fini family. The interior is also Baroque. Its sense of dramatic gesture is conveyed in Tintoretto's *Christ Washing his Disciples' Feet* (*in the chapel*).

At the other end of Calle Larga XXII Marzo is **Campo Santa Maria Zobenigo**, situated in front of the **church** of the same name (🕙 *open Mon–Sat 10am–5pm;* 🕙 *closed 1 Jan, Easter, 15 Aug, 25 Dec;* ⌨€3; ☎041 27 50 462, *www.chorusvenezia.org*). The magnificent façade by Giuseppe Sardi is reminiscent of that of the Church of San Moisé: in this case, the dedication is to a naval

---

Famous Premieres

Celebrated works that have been performed for the first time in the Fenice include *Tancredi* (1813), *Sigismondo* (1814) and *Semiramide* (1823) by **Gioachino Rossini**, and *Ernani* (1844), *Attila* (1846), *Rigoletto* (1851), *La Traviata* (1853) and *Simon Boccanegra* (1857) by **Giuseppe Verdi**.

captain. Its incompleted 18C bell-tower remains a box covered with a small roof. On the inside wall of the façade, note the small 15C Lombard-style relief of St Jerome. Inside hangs Tintoretto's *Four Evangelists* (*behind the high altar, under the organ*).

▶ *Continue straight on (west) for Campo San Maurizio and Campo Santo Stefano.*

Campo San Maurizio (8, EX)

The peace of this square is usually only broken by the busy 3-day antiques market which descends here four times a year (consult the official tourist board website, under "events" for dates). To the right of the church is a view of the campanile of Santo Stefano. The former **Scuola degli Albanesi**, with its Renaissance reliefs, sits on the left. Previous residents of the *palazzo* opposite include the novelist Alessandro Manzoni (1785–1873) and Giorgio Baffo (1694–1768), who wrote salacious poetry in Venetian dialect.

Campo Santo Stefano (8, EX)

This *campo* is one of the most elegant squares in the city. Dominated by a church in which concerts are regularly given, this lively meeting place is animated by busy outdoor cafes and people making their way to and from the Accademia Bridge. It's a perfect venue for an early evening stroll or *passeggiata*. Towering over the square is a monument (1882) to **Niccolò Tommaseo** (1802–74, journalist and essayist).

Overlooking the square is the **Palazzo Loredan** (8, EV), now home to the Venetian Institute of Science, Arts and Letters and its prestigious library (◷ *open Mon–Fri 9am–12.45pm, 1.30–5pm;* ☎041 24 07 711; *www.istitutoveneto.it*). In 1536 the Loredan family commissioned Scarpagnino (active in Venice between 1505 and 1549) to rebuild the palace recently acquired from the Mocenigo family. Note its Palladian northern façade.

Straight ahead is the **Palazzo Pisani** (8, **EX**), one of the largest private palaces in the city, on the square of the same name. Having been acquired by a noble family between the 17C and 18C,

Girolamo Frigimelica (1653–1732) was commissioned to remodel the building. The *palazzo* is now the home of the **Benedetto Marcello Music Conservatory**.

Palazzo Morosini (8, EX), which dates to the 14C and was restored at the end of the 17C by Antonio Gaspari. Former residents include Francesco Morosini, Doge between 1688 and 1694. The *palazzo* is now the home of the New Consortium of Venice, a group of 40 companies set up in 2005 with a remit to save the city from the encroaching sea.

Santo Stefano★ (8, EX)

◷ *Open Mon–Sat 10am–5pm.* ◷ *Closed 1 Jan, Easter, 15 Aug, 25 Dec.* ☞€3. ☎041 27 50 462. www.chorusvenezia.org.

Gothic in style, the church comprises a central vaulted nave flanked by lower side bays. Construction of St Stephen's and the adjacent convent was begun in the latter half of the 13C; the church, however, was modified in the 15C. The campanile (60m/196ft 10in high) is one of the most famous in Venice. Building on the lower section was resumed in 1544; when it collapsed in 1585, it was the new masonry that crumbled, hit by lightning so violent that the bells melted. Further damage incurred by subsidence between the 17C and 18C has left the tower leaning at an angle, as do all the other bell-towers in Venice. Like other churches in Venice, St Stephen's is a pantheon to the glory of the city: it contains the tombs of **Giovanni Gabrieli** (composer and organist) and of **Francesco Morosini** (doge 1688–94), as well as Baldassare Longhena's monument to Capt. Bartolomeo d'Alviano. In the sacristy hang works by Tintoretto: in the *Last Supper*, the dog and cat allude to the dispute raging between the Catholic and Protestant Churches over belief in the mystery of the Eucharist.

Campo Sant'Angelo (8, EX)

This rather austere square en route between St Mark's and the Accademia, is bordered by some handsome *palazzi* overlooking the canal.

The **Oratorio dell'Annunciata** (Oratory of the Annunziata) has replaced the church that gave the square its name,

The Renaissance Palazzo

Based on Roman originals, the Italian *palazzo* was designed to fulfil commercial and residential demands. Arranged around a central courtyard, it most often comprises three storeys. The ground floor was used for storage or shops (*magazzini*) that opened out onto the street; this level tends to be heavily rusticated. The first floor, or *piano nobile*, was used by the occupying family as living quarters: externally lighter in texture, the interior had high ceilings and large windows providing ample light and ventilation. The top storey, below the roof and much lower in proportion, served as quarters for servants and children.

formerly associated with the Scuola dei Zoti, the guild for disabled sailors. The plaque on the wall of **Palazzo Duodo** commemorates the composer, Domenico Cimarosa (1749–1801), who died here.

The Gothic portal on the bridge leads into the cloisters of St Stephen (now the headquarters of the Regional Accountancy Board).

▶ *Rio Terrà della Mandola branches left off Calle dello Spezièr and leads to the Palazzo Fortuny.*

Palazzo Fortuny (🗟, EV)

Dating to the 15C, the building boasts two mullioned windows with five arches. The Palazzo Pesaro degli Orfei was acquired by the painter, photographer, stage designer and textile designer, **Mariano Fortuny y Madrazo** (1871–1949), in 1899. Formerly a music school, it is now the **Museo Fortuny** (♿🕙*open Wed–Mon 10am–6pm, open only during exhibits;* 🕙*closed 1 Jan, 25 Dec;* ⬤€10; ☎041 52 00 995, http://fortuny.visitmuve.it/) devoted to the artist's work.

The *calle* that leads from Campo Sant'Angelo to Campo Manin is always busy with people coming and going, usually distracted by the many shops along the way.

▶ *The bridge over the Rio di San Luca leads into the modern Campo Manin.*

Campo Manin (🗟, EV)

Few features distinguish this square other than the monument to **Daniele Manin** (1875), the shops down along

one side and the **Cassa di Risparmio di Venezia**, designed by **Pierluigi Nervi** (1891–1979) and Angelo Scattolin, which provides an idea of modern Venetian architecture.

▶ *Take the calle on the right.*

Scala del Bovolo★ (🗟, EFX)

⊶*closed until 2010 for restoration.* ☎041 53 22 920. www.scalabovolo.org.

The delicate spiral **Bovolo Staircase** is all the more impressive, situated as it is off a tiny, peaceful courtyard overlooked by private houses. The staircase (*bovolo* in Venetian dialect), which seems to harmonise with a composite style drawn from both Gothic and Renaissance

© Laea Pessina / MICHELIN

The Bovolo Staircase

styles, is attributed to Giovanni Candi, who died in 1506. Encased in a tower, it provides access to the *palazzo*'s loggias. From the top extends a lovely, if somewhat disorientating **view**★★ over the Venetian rooftops.

▶ *To get to Campo San Luca pass either to the left or the right of the Cassa di Risparmio; to reach the church of the same name, continue along the Salizzada.*

Campo San Luca (8, FV)

This lively *campo* is one of the most popular meeting places in Venice. It is lined with cafés, well-known stores, bookshops, travel agencies, fast-food outlets and a host of shops in the immediate vicinity. The **Church of St Luke** (San Luca) contains the *Virgin in Glory Appearing to St Luke While Writing the Gospel* by Veronese (1528–88). When the floor was repaved at the beginning of the 20C, the gravestones of those buried there, including the writer Aretino, were not relaid.

Calle Goldoni leads from the Campo San Luca back to Piazza San Marco via the **Bacino Orseolo**, where you can admire several of the city's gleaming black gondolas at rest in a dock.

Also off the Campo, on the opposite side, is Calle del Teatro. The theatre in question is the **Teatro Goldoni** (8, FV), named in honour of Italy's famed playwright, Carlo Goldoni. At one time, there were many theatres in Venice: today, La Fenice, the Goldoni and the Teatro Màlibran among the few active theatres.

San Salvador (8, FV)

The 7C Church of San Salvador was consecrated by Pope Alexander III during his visit to Venice to meet Barbarossa in 1177. Despite having been subjected to various phases of rebuilding, the 17C façade survives with a cannon ball embedded in the masonry since 1849. The main layout was designed by Spavento, who combines an assured use of Classical structural elements with refined sculptural ornament, a style that foreshadows Mannerism and the bold Classicism of Palladio.

Inside, three square bays are aligned to form a nave, each cubic space rising to a semicircular dome. A number of significant paintings include the main altarpiece, *The Transfiguration* by **Titian** (c.1490–1576) and, in the last bay on the right before the transept, his *Annunciation*. To the right of the main chapel hangs *The Martyrdom of St Theodoric* by Paris Bordone (1500–71). In the Santissimo Chapel on the left of the main altar is *The Disciples at Emmaus* by **Giovanni Bellini** (c.1432–1516); the organ doors (*by the side door*) are painted by Titian's brother, Francesco Vecellio (1475–1560).

Telecom Italia Future Centre

🕐*Open daily, 10am–6pm.* 🕐*Closed 1 Jan, 25 Dec.* ☎*041 52 13 200. www. telecomfuturecentre.it.*

Housed in the beautifully restored cloister of the **San Salvador convent** adjacent to the San Salvador church, is a showcase of Telecom Italia, Italy's leading telephone company.

Campo San Bartolomeo (4, FU)

This *campo* is a busy crossroads between St Mark's, the Rialto, the Accademia and the Strada Nuova. Bars and tourist shops surround the square, which is dominated by a spirited late-19C **statue of Goldoni** (👉*see pages 101–102*).

Fondaco dei Tedeschi (4, FU)

What once served an association of German traders – the most powerful trading group in the city from the 13C onwards – now houses the main post office headquarters. Destroyed in a fire in 1505, the Fondaco (warehouse) was rebuilt by Giorgio Spavento and Scarpagnino, who conceived the idea of a square courtyard. The frescoes that adorn the façade facing the Grand Canal are the work of **Giorgione** and the earliest-known works by Titian. One of the reasons why the two artists received the frescos commission was because they had helped the firefighters to put out the flames. More of the frescoes, subsequently removed from the Fondaco, can be seen in the Ca' d'Oro (👉*see page 129*).

I FRARI ★★★

(🅱, DV)

VAPORETTO: S. TOMÀ, STAZIONE, RIVA DI BIASIO, S. STAE

By contrast with the much visited Frari the remainder of this part of the San Polo *sestiere* is a residential quarter devoid of great monuments and lacking mainstream visitor attractions and tourist-related fripperies found elsewhere in the city. Instead, keep your eyes peeled for the more mundane details which provide a small insight into the daily life of modern-day Venetians.

▸ **Orient Yourself:** Located on the west side of the Grand Canal, within the first loop of the river, in the San Polo *sestiere*.

🗙 **Don't Miss:** Titian's masterpiece, *Assumption of the Virgin,* in the Maggiore Chapel within the Frari Church.

🕘 **Organising Your Time:** The suggested itinerary takes about half a day.

🧒 **Especially for Kids:** The Natural History Museum.

👍 **Also See:** Neighbouring sights: I CARMINI, SAN ROCCO.

Visit

🕘*Open daily, 9am (1pm Sun)–6pm (last admission 5.45pm).* 🕘*Closed 1 Jan, Easter, 15 Aug, 25 Dec.* ♿€3. ☎041 27 50 462. www.chorusvenezia.org.

This great church, Santa Maria Gloriosa dei Frari, is known simply as the Frari, which is derived from the abbreviation of Fra(*ti Mino*)ri. It frequently draws comparison with the Church of Santi Giovanni e Paolo (👍*see page 207*) because of its sheer scale and style. Monumental in stature, flanked by the second tallest campanile (70m/229ft 6in) after St Mark's, this building is strikingly magnificent, massive yet articulated with fine architectural detail, conforming to Franciscan archetypes, yet quite original. It impresses from every angle. The best view of the apses, the oldest part, is to be had from the Scuola di San Rocco (opposite); if contemplated from the bridge built by the monks in 1428, it appears just as breathtaking, its late-Gothic tripartite façade a masterpiece of design.

Exterior

The doorway is surmounted by a *Risen Christ* by Alessandro Vittoria (1581), flanked slightly below by the *Virgin with Child* and *St Francis* by Bartolomeo Bon (active 1441–64), supported on two finely crafted engaged columns. High above, inserted into the plain brick-work, are four circular window openings edged in white Istrian stone.

Over the side door into St Mark's or the Corner Chapel (*at the end on the left*) the Madonna is shown restraining the Christ child from struggling to break free.

Interior

The church is constructed in the form of a Latin cross. The nave is divided from the aisles by 12 huge cylindrical piers that soar up to the criss-cross of transverse and longitudinal timber beams underpinning the quadripartite vaults. The red and white floor tiles are from Verona.

© Stefano Brozzi/age fotostock

Santa Maria Gloriosa dei Frari

I FRARI

which houses the *Triptych of St Mark* by Bartolomeo Vivarini (c.1432–91). High up on the wall opposite is *Christ's Descent into Limbo* by Jacopo Palma il Giovane. The marble baptismal font with John the Baptist is by Sansovino.

Next comes the Milanese Chapel with its *Sant'Ambrogio* altarpiece by Alvise Vivarini and Marco Basaiti.

The **Maggiore Chapel** is the focal point of the magnificent perspective of the Frari Church. All points converge on Titian's **Assumption of the Virgin**, which was commissioned by the Franciscans in 1516. This major work, the first religious subject undertaken by the painter, caused the friars some consternation because of its unorthodox iconography. Instead of Mary's restful contemplation, the crowded painting shows the Apostles disturbed by the mystery of this supernatural event; *putti* and winged angels, singing and playing music, emphasise the upward movement of the composition, as the (nervous) Virgin looking ever upwards towards God the Father is received in the Kingdom of Heaven in a triumph of light and colour. The brilliance of heaven is exaggerated by the careful portrayal of light from the realms of shadow and darkness on earth, via the more shaded zone occupied by angels, up to the explosion of bright light pushing the figure of the Virgin into bold perspective. Against the presbytery walls are two important monuments, one commemorating **Doge Nicolò Tron** by Antonio Rizzo – probably the most important Renaissance sculptural group in Venice (*left*) – and the other, from the 15C, to **Doge Francesco Foscari**, attributed to Nicolò di Giovanni Fiorentino.

In the right arm of the transept, the jewel of the Chapel of John the Baptist is the only Venetian work by **Donatello**, his *John the Baptist* depicted with the index finger of his right hand raised against Herod as a sign of admonition (unfortunately the finger is missing).

The first noteworthy monument (*left aisle*) is neo-Classical and dedicated to **Canova** (1757–1822) (**1**). It was designed by the sculptor to commemorate Titian but was never completed. The allegorical figures before the pyramid represent Sorrow (portrait of Canova) with Venice (*left*), in the company of Sculpture (heavily veiled), Painting and Architecture.

Beyond the Baroque monument to **Doge Giovanni Pesaro** is the famous **Madonna di Ca'Pesaro Chapel**, dominated by Titian's altarpiece. Some commentators believe this represents the artist's wife.

Serving as a glorious harbinger to the Maggiore Chapel and Titian's *Assumption* are the 15C **choir stalls**, comprising 124 decorated stalls. The two organs on the right are signed Gaetano Callido (1794) and Giovanni Piaggia (1732) respectively. Beyond, early-17C paintings by Andrea Micheli, known as Vicentino, illustrate the Works of Corporeal Mercy (*left*) alongside his *Creation of the World*, the *Brazen Serpent*, a *Last Judgement* and the *Glory of Paradise* (*right*).

In the left transept, the first chapel on the left is the St Mark's or Corner Chapel,

Beyond the former Santissimo Chapel, now dedicated to Maximilian Kolbe, comes the Bernardo Chapel containing a *Polyptych* by Bartolomeo Vivarini (1482). *Before going into the sacristy note:*

◆ the equestrian monument to **Paolo Savelli** (d.1405) (**2**) who fought for Venice against the Carraresi;

◆ on the door to the sacristy, the 16C monument to **Benedetto Pesaro** (**3**) by Giovambattista Bregno. Between the columns that frame the doorway, note the Lion of St Mark's holding the closed Gospel: during periods of political conflict, Venice, unable to listen to the biblical teachings of peace, would "close" the Gospel and leave it under the lion's paw;

◆ the terracotta monument to the **Blessed Peacemaker of the Frari** (**4**) with the 15C portrayal of the Baptism of Christ in the lunette;

◆ to the right of the transept, the monument to **Jacopo Marcello** (**5**), the captain of the Venetian fleet who died in 1488 during the conquest of the city of Gallipoli. The work is by Pietro Lombardo.

The **sacristy** houses a splendid **Triptych** by **Giovanni Bellini**. Opposite is a lunette (1339) by Paolo Veneziano that was designed to be set above the Byzantine sarcophagus of **Doge Francesco Dandolo** (1329–39) in the adjacent Sala del Capitolo (⊙⃥ *closed to the public*); the Capitolo was used for the periodic assembly of religious orders.

The **Chapel of St Catherine of Alexandria** (**6**) is decorated with an altarpiece by Palma il Giovane, illustrating the saint's salvation from the torture of the wheel. In the next bay is the unusual statue of *St Jerome* (1504) (**7**) by Alessandro Vittoria, which recalls the style of Michelangelo. The **altar of Purification** (**8**) is ornamented with a painting by Salviati.

Titian's Mausoleum (**9**), hewn in marble from Carrara, was executed during the decade 1842–52. Titian, who died of the plague in 1576, was buried in the Frari in accord with his wishes, but by the end of the 16C all traces of his body had disappeared.

The Assumption of the Virgin by Titian

© S Maria Gloriosa dei Frari, Venezia / SCALA

Directly opposite the marble pyramid with mourners is **Canova's Mausoleum,** built in 1827 by his pupils to a design Canova had made for Titian's tomb.

Beside this is the **monument to Doge Giovanni Pésaro** (died 1669), complete with giant ragged-trousered Moors and decomposing bodies. The original work was by Longhena but the more graphic pieces are later additions by the German, Melchiorre Barthel. It has been called the most grotesque monument in the city – it is certainly one of the most bombastic.

Walking Tour

▶ *Cross the canal in front of the church and turn left to Campo San Stin. Then take Calle del Tabacco and Calle dell'Olio as far as Campiello della Scuola.*

Scuola Grande di San Giovanni Evangelista (⊞, DU)

🕐*Open periodically when not hosting meetings, 9.30am-5pm by appointment only.* ⊚€5. ☎041 71 82 34. *www.scuola sangiovanni.it.*

The courtyard outside the Scuola of St John the Evangelist has been described as *"a little masterpiece of Venetian Renaissance architecture."*

The Scuola was the second of the **Scuole Grandi** (👓*see I CARMINI: The Venetian Scuole*) to be founded in 1201, and honoured by a confraternity of flagellants who attended religious processions stripped to the waist and whipping themselves with scourges. They are represented in the relief carvings dated 1349 at the front, which itself dates from 1454, when the large ogee windows were inserted.

The double stairway inside, lit with large arched windows, was built by Codussi. On the first floor, the oval windows were added by Giorgio Massari (1727), who raised the height of the **salone**. Various craftsmen are responsible for the decoration on the ceiling and the walls, including Domenico Tintoretto and Pietro Longhi.

The salone adjoins the Oratory of the Cross built to house Carpaccio's cycle of the *Miracles of the Relic of the True Cross*, now on display in the Accademia.

▸ *Continue straight on as far as the Grand Canal, to come out opposite Santa Lucia Station. Turn right along the water's edge.*

San Simeon Piccolo –
See Il CANAL GRANDE.

▸ *At Ponte degli Scalzi, turn right and then left into Calle Bergami.*

San Simeon Grando (🖪, CT)

So-called to distinguish it from the Church of San Simeon Piccolo, the church is also known as San Simeon Profeta. Although its origins go back as far as 967, the building has undergone considerable remodelling, particularly in the 18C. The neo-Classical white façade dates from 1861.

The internal space is divided into nave and aisles by a series of columns crowned with Byzantine capitals and shrouded in heavy red damask drapes. Although the ornamentation is generally heavy, there is an exquisite *Last Supper* by Tintoretto on the left of the entrance.

▸ *Calle Larga dei Barbi, behind the church, leads into Campo Nazario Sauro. From here continue on to Campo San Giacomo dall'Orio and down Ruga Bella or the parallel*

Ruga Vecchia, which comes out directly in front of another church.

San Giacomo dall'Orio★ (🖪, DT)

🕐 Open year-round Mon–Sat 10am–5pm. 🚫Closed Sun, 1 Jan, Easter, 15 Aug, 25 Dec. ⊚€3. ☏041 27 50 462. www.chorusvenezia.org.

The church was founded in 976 but most of its present fabric dates from 1225. The centre of the main façade features a Veneto-Byzantine patera with a statue in Istrian stone of the Apostle St James the Great standing above the portal. The bell-tower, erected in the 12C or 13C, is reminiscent of that on the island of Torcello. The three apses date back to different periods. The transept frontage dates from the 14C.

The Gothic lacunar **ceiling**, shaped like an inverted ship's hull, is striking. The nave is divided from its aisles by five baseless columns. Beside the entrance, David is depicted with excerpts from Psalm 150. The unusual stoop for the holy water is made of cipolin (onion) marble from Anatolia. Of the paintings in the choir stalls attributed to Schiavone *The Apostles in the Boat* is the most likely to be by him. The organ was built by Gaetano Callido. It is likely that the Ionic column of ancient green marble, which was brought to Venice from Byzantium has been in the church since the 13C.

In the **New Sacristy** are Palma il Giovane's *Crucifixion with the Virgin and St John* and a version of *The Marriage at Cana* also thought to be by him. The **Santissimo Chapel**, is dedicated to faith in the Eucharist.

The **Old Sacristy** (*apply to the custodian*), besides its fine wood panelling, is decorated with a cycle of paintings by Palma il Giovane.

▸ *To get to Campo San Giovanni Decollato and the church of the same name (Zan Degolà in Venetian), take Calle Larga and branch left down Calle dello Spezier.*

San Zan Degolà (🖪, DT)

Dedicated to the beheaded John the Baptist, this church can trace its origins back to 1007, when the first parish church was built on the site. The terra-

The Council of Trent

Established in 1545 and dissolved in 1563, the Council of Trent aimed to encapsulate Catholic ideals in dogma and to structure its ministry by disciplinary reform. This ecclesiastical body confirmed the Church's sole right to interpret the Bible and underlined the role of the clergy as the only intercessors between man and God. The value of the seven sacraments was reaffirmed, and the practices of baptism and confirmation were ratified. The acknowledged existence of Purgatory, the invocation of saints, the veneration of relics, and the granting of indulgences were also endorsed and rationalised. Those opposed to the rationalisation of the Roman Church went on to precipitate the Counter-Reformation and found the Protestant faction.

cotta façade is early 18C. A rose window is the main feature of the central section of the three-tier facade, framed by pilasters supporting a triangular tympanum. The relief on the right wall retells the story of John's decapitation.

As with the façade, a harmonious simplicity pervades the interior. The ceiling takes the form of an inverted ship's hull. The intense silence enhances the air of contemplation inspired by the frescoed chapels at the end of the side aisles.

▶ *Follow the calle behind the church as far as the Grand Canal. At the end, directly opposite the plain façade of the Church of San Marcuola sits the elegant palazzo that was the residence of the Turkish merchants (⌖see Il CANAL GRANDE).*

Fondaco dei Turchi/Museo di Storia Naturale (🗲, DT) 🗗 Kids

&. ⓘ*Open Tue–Fri 9am–1pm, Sat–Sun 10am–4pm; last admission 30min before closing.* ⓘ*Note that several rooms/exhibits are closed while long-term restoration is taking place.* ⓘ*Closed 1 Jan, 1 May, 25 Dec.* ☏*041 27 50 206. http://msn.visitmuve.it.*

This 12–13C palace and former Turks' Warehouse now houses the Natural History Museum. Abandoned from 1838 to 1865, the municipal authority later renovated it and transformed it into the Museo Correr. The building's present use was proposed in 1922. A major renovation was completed in 2010. Vast, visually lively and varied, it is a perfect family outing. Displays are arranged by theme: palaeontology; natural collec-

Museo di Storia Naturale

tions, both as Curiosity Rooms as well as for study; and form and function in living things. The ground floor has an aquarium dedicated to regional coastal species (and out of view, the taxidermists' laboratories). The first floor has a display on the Venetian Lagoon. The second floor traces the path of life; fossils from Bolca near Verona illustrate the evolution of vertebrates, on to dinosaurs including the 12 ft/3.6m high Ouranosaurus skeleton and a giant crocodile skull. The theme then turns to collecting; a 16C-style Curiosity Room shows off specimens that were collected for their natural beauty and to amaze; other collections are grouped according to scientific classifications.

IL GHETTO ★★

(🖪, DT)

VAPORETTO: FERROVIA, PONTE DELLE GUGLIE, SAN MARCUOLA

This is the original Ghetto, being the first Jewish quarter to be differentiated as such in Western Europe. The term was probably coined from the word geto in Venetian dialect, meaning mortar foundry: the letter g, normally pronounced soft (as in George), was hardened by the first Jews who came from Germany. The busy shops and market around Fondamenta della Pescaria and Rio Terrà San Leonardo contrast with the tranquillity of the squares and the calli with their distinctive yellow signs and elegant Hebrew characters.

▶ **Orient Yourself:** The Ghetto occupies a corner of the Cannaregio sestiere northeast of the train station near the Cannaregio Canal. The heart of the Ghetto is Campo di Ghetto Nuovo.

🔎 **Don't Miss:** The monumental Palazzo Labia and its attractive square.

🕐 **Organising Your Time:** Allow 3 to 4hrs for a leisurely visit.

Kids Especially for Kids: The playground at Parco Savorgnan.

👣 **Also See:** Neighbouring sights: CA' D'ORO.

A Bit of History

Although signs in the Ghetto refer to *Vecchio* (old) and *Nuovo* (new) these should not be interpreted in any chronological sense to the area as a whole: they are merely references to the old and new foundries. In fact, the Jews were first confined to the Ghetto Nuovo – then a practically impenetrable fortified island. At the time, the houses were rather squat and low-lying; the area was subjected to a form of curfew at nightfall, after which time the drawbridge was raised and the area sealed off. It was only in 1866 that access to the Ghetto was freed up and Jews were granted the same rights as other Venetian citizens. As long as the Jews were obliged to stay there, however, they were at least protected. Indeed, it was precisely because their community was confined to this small area that their houses climbed ever taller. It seems ironic, now, to think that Jews were prohibited from undertaking any kind of building work, be it on their houses, their five synagogues, or their *scuole*. Instead, they became *strazzaroli* (dealers in secondhand clothes and goods), doctors, and bankers involved in moneylending activities: the colours of their stalls were red (*no. 2912*), green and black.

Sign of the Times

An 18C notice in the Old Ghetto warns Jews converted to Christianity not to frequent the ghetto, nor the houses of other Jews, on pain of "hanging, prison, hard labour, flogging, pillory." The means by which the Serenissima authorities were to be informed was secret denunciation via the infamous holes in the wall known as **bocca di leone**. These tablets also advertise the dues to be expected by the accuser, paid in recompense from the property of the accused.

Visit

The approach to Campo di Ghetto Nuovo from Calle Farnese might suggest that the area is fortified. From the bridge before the *sottoportego* the view is particularly evocative: unusually tall houses seem to tower out of the canal, tenuously strung together by a crisscross of washing lines that seem permanently weighted with laundry.

Museo Ebraico (🖪, DT)

🕐*Open year-round Sun–Fri 10am–6pm (Jun–Sept 7pm).* 🚶*Guided tours of the synagogues, Sun–Fri hourly from*

10.30am; last tour Jun–Sept 5.30pm, Oct–May 3.30pm. Guided tours to the ancient Jewish Cemetery, by reservation. ○*Closed 1 Jan, 1 May, 25 Dec and Jewish festivals. Full tour ⊙€8.50; entrance to museum only €3.* ☎*041 71 53 59. www. museoebraico.it.*

The **Jewish Museum** (which also includes the Ghetto synagogues) has assembled together many precious artifacts relating to Judaism including many decorative objects and ornaments connected with the sacred scrolls (⌂*see Box below*). Of all the Toràh covers in the collection, the one featuring the Jews encamped, the manna and the hand of Moses issuing forth water from the rock is particularly precious.

Synagogues★★

Occupying the upper floors of various buildings, the five windows and the lanterns peeping out from under the roofs indicate the presence of a place of prayer.

All five synagogues in Venice (the Italiana, Levantina, Spagnola, Canton and the oldest, Tedesca) share the same bifocal layout in which the pulpit (*bimà*) and the cupboard that contains the scrolls (*aròn*) are placed, one in front of the other, along the smaller side of the room, with the women's gallery above. The Spagnola and Levantina Synagogues are situated in the Ghetto Vecchio, which was assigned to the Jews in 1541.

The **Spagnola Synagogue** (🖪, **DT**), the largest, was rebuilt by Longhena in the 17C. Longhena and his followers were probably responsible also for the res-

The Sacred Scrolls

For the Jews, the Law (*Toràh*, literally "teaching") comes in the form of the Pentateuch: the five Books of Moses, comprising Genesis, Exodus, Leviticus, Numbers and Deuteronomy. Transcribed onto parchment, the scrolls are wound around two batons that are unfurled during readings. The scrolls are stored in a rigid container or rolled up in a mantle.

The rolls are stored in the Holy Ark. Given their sacredness, they can be neither exposed nor touched: a silver holder is used during readings.

toration of the Levantina Synagogue, which is used during the summer months. The Tedesca (Ashkenazi), Canton and Italiana Synagogues are situated in Campo di Ghetto Nuovo.

The **Canton Synagogue** (🖪, **DT**), named either after the banker who commissioned its construction in the 16C or the Venetian term *canton* which refers to its corner position, is renowned for its series of rare illustrations along the upper section of the walls. Strict observation of the second commandment prohibits the representation of any creature in the sky, on land or in water, of God or of man; even a suggestion of landscape inside a synagogue could be considered a distraction from prayer. However, the most important moments of Jewish history are recounted here. These include: *the Sending of Manna from Heaven, the Parting of the Red Sea* (interestingly, a

Rio di San Girolamo in the Ghetto

© B. Juge / MICHELIN

hand can be seen protruding from the water, a detail that might indicate that the artist was Egyptian), *Moses Bringing Forth Water from the Rock, the Ark of the Covenant, the Symbol of the Jewish People who Crossed the River Jordan*.

Campo di Ghetto Nuovo (🖪, DS)

This square recalls the most tragic moments in the more recent history of the Jews in Venice: reminders include a relief (1979) by the Lithuanian artist Blatas and a *Monument to the Deportees* (1993) referring to the 204 Jews who were deported from Venice by the Nazis; only 8 returned from the death camps. At the same time, the square projects a picture of everyday tranquility where ancient Jewish traditions live on: workshops manufacture objects relating to the Jewish faith, and glass ornaments and cards bear images of rabbis for those who seek inspiration to devotion, or who just want to buy a memento of this special corner of Venice.

Walking Tour

Approaching the Ghetto from Santa Lucia Station, there are several distractions: window shopping in **Rio Terrà Lista di Spagna**; observing the fish stalls along the Fondamenta della Pescheria or the market in Rio Terrà San Leonardo; exploring the churches of Scalzi and San Geremia, and Palazzo Labia.

The Throw-Away High Society

It is said that at the end of a banquet the Labia family would hurl their gold dinner plates and cutlery out of the window and into the canal, ostentatiously proclaiming their indifference to their wealth. The infamous family was more astute, however, than they might have appeared, for they had already placed fishing nets at the bottom of the canal, and so were able to retrieve their precious treasure later for use another day!

Gli Scalzi (🖪, CT)

Literally the Church of "the Discalced," its name refers to the Carmelite Order, whose members, like the Franciscans, were obliged to go about their duties barefoot (today they wear sandals). Designed by Longhena, the church features a Baroque façade faced with Carrara marble. The rather sombre interior shelters the tomb of the last doge, **Ludovico Manin**. Prior to its destruction during World War I, the ceiling was decorated with a fresco by Tiepolo: the current painting dates from 1934. Fortunately, Tiepolo's frescoes – in the vaults of the first chapel off the left aisle, and second chapel of the right aisle – survive.

▸ *Follow Rio Terrà Lista di Spagna, lined with numerous workshops, which eventually leads to Campo San Geremia.*

San Geremia e Santa Lucia (🖪, CDT)

Bathed in light, the interior of this 18C church is similar in plan to the Church of La Salute. It is here that the body of Santa Lucia lies. A Sicilian martyred under the persecution of Diocletian, she is the patron saint of the blind. Also of note is a painting by Palma il Giovane, *The Virgin Attending the Coronation in Venice*. The brick campanile, alongside, dates from the 13C.

Palazzo Labia★★ (🖪, CDT)

🕐*The ballroom and some of the state rooms are occasionally open to the public.* ✆*Enquire at the tourist office.*

The construction of this *palazzo*, built of Istrian stone, was commissioned in the late-17C by a wealthy family of Spanish merchants, to whom the building owes its name. The three façades, adorned with eagles – the family emblem – overlook Campo San Geremia, the Cannaregio Canal and a small square next to the Grand Canal. It was the exclusive prerogative of the Venetian nobility to have a residence overlooking the canal. The Labia family, who had paid to be listed in the **Libro d'Oro** (🔖*see History: 1789*) had to settle for a residence with a view of the Grand Canal, without actually overlooking it.

In honour of Maria Labia's marriage in the 18C, **Giambattista Tiepolo** was commissioned to fresco the Salone delle Festa (Banqueting Hall); it would appear that the depiction of Cleopatra was inspired by her beauty. After the fall of the Republic, the family abandoned the *palazzo*, and when Napoleon handed it over to the Austrians, a long period of neglect began. In 1948 the palace was acquired by a wealthy Mexican oil magnate who organised a sumptuous ball in 18C costume to which the international jet set were invited. Abandoned again, restoration was postponed until the 1960s when it was bought by the Veneto arm of RAI, Italy's national television network, then put up for sale again in 2008, the city binding the sale to cultural use. Apartments arranged around the *salone*, or main room, and the courtyard, include the Stanza degli Specchi (Hall of Mirrors), with *trompe l'oeil* walls; the Stanza del Mappamondo (Map of the World) and chapel adjacent; a corridor decorated with Cordoba leather; the Stanza dei Stucchi, hung with portraits of the Labia family; and a room with a lively 18C representation of the *Signs of the Zodiac*.

▶ *Take the narrow alley leading to Parco Savorgnan.*

Parco Savorgnan (**8**, CT)　Kids

This relatively large, tree-shaded expanse off Campo San Geremia offers rest and relaxation to the district. Its playground is popular with children, especially little ones. A grassy field – a rare find in Venice – provides plenty of space to run around.

▶ *Leave the park on its east side and turn left at the Cannaregio Canal.*

The Cannaregio Canal is crossed by two bridges: the Ponte delle Guglie and the Ponte dei Tre Archi (♨ *see sidebar over page*), farther along the canal.

▶ *Follow Fondamenta Venier, which runs along the canal, to the Ponte dei Tre Archi. Turn left onto the calle which leads to the San Giobbe.*

San Giobbe (**8**, CT)

This church is dedicated to the Old Testament figure of Job. Antonio Gambello began construction in the late-15C and it was completed by Pietro Lombardo. The plain façade is broken by a Renaissance portal. St Francis and Job appear in the low relief enclosed in the lunette.

Reliefs by Blatas on the Campo di Ghetto Nuovo

© AGE / Photononstop

Bridge with Three Arches

Although the three-arched structure of Venetian bridges is welcomed by pedestrians who do not have to cope with a single steep ramp, they are much less popular with canal traffic, which is forced to slow down and proceed with caution. Once a regular city feature, the last surviving three arched bridge is the **Ponte dei Tre Archi** on the Cannaregio Canal, built at the end of the 17C.

Interior features include the coat of arms of **Doge Cristoforo Moro** (1462–71), who is buried in the presbytery.

▸ *Retrace your steps, following Fondamenta Venier to the Ponte delle Guglie.*

Ponte delle Guglie (◩, DT)

Passing over the Ponte delle Guglie (1580) is practically obligatory, given that it is the bridge linking the railway station to the Strada Nuova. It takes its name, Bridge of the Gargoyles, from the architectural features that adorn the balustrade.

▸ *Cross the bridge and walk along Rio Terrà San Leonardo as far as Rio Terrà del Cristo on the right.*

San Marcuola (◩, DT)

The name is a rather puzzling contraction of two saints' names: Ermagora and Fortunato, though how this came to make up Marcuola is lost in the mists of time or perhaps Venetian dialect.

The original construction dates back to around the 10C, but the church was subsequently restructured during the course of the 18C. The façade of the square, which is a landmark overlooking the Grand Canal, was never completed. Inside, the altars are the work of Giovanni Morlaiter (1699–1781), who sculpted the high altar in the famous Church of La Salute. There is also a *Last Supper* by Tintoretto on the left wall of the chancel.

LA GIUDECCA

(◩, ◩, ◩, BGYZ)

VAPORETTO: ZITELLE, REDENTORE, GIUDECCA, S. EUFEMIA

Once the island of Giudecca was dotted with the villas of wealthy Venetian nobles; today exclusive hotels are the only reminders of the luxurious living of the past. Not far from the Fortuny textile factory showrooms, the Molino Stucky flour mill was converted into a hotel, while another waterfront palazzo houses the local youth hostel. Here one of the churches took in girls without dowry to learn sewing and lacemaking skills. The origin of the area's name is either a reference to the Jews (giudei) who lived here, or perhaps an allusion to the 11C zudegà (judgement) that guaranteed land to noble families who had been exiled from elsewhere. Nowadays Giudecca island has a relaxed and peaceful atmosphere.

▸ **Orient Yourself:** Laid out in the shape of a fishbone, the eight islands that make up Giudecca justify its original name: Spinalonga (long spine).

⊜ **Don't Miss:** A long meander along the *fondamenta* following the canals that divide the island into its eight parts, from Mulino Stucky (now the Hilton hotel) east towards the Church of San Giorgio Maggiore.

◔ **Organising Your Time:** Allow 30–45min for the walk and visit of Redentore. Then stop in the Hotel Cipriani for lunch or afternoon tea; it's advisable to make advance reservations (⌕ *see Where to Stay in Your Stay in the City*).

⚲ **Also See:** SAN GIORGIO MAGGIORE.

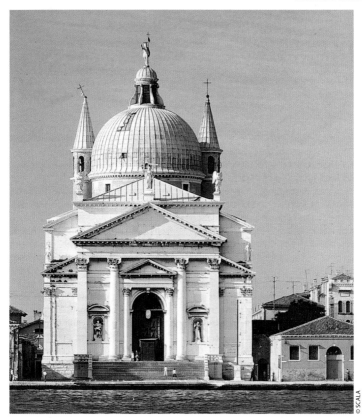

Il Redentore

Walking Tour

Molino Stucky (**7**, BY)

This prepossessing but rather awkward construction, which would perhaps be more at home in Dickens' London, is the work of late-19C German architects. It takes its name from the Swiss entrepreneur who commissioned it and for decades was an empty landmark on the Venetian skyline.

The former flour mill now houses the luxurious **Hilton Molino Stucky Venice** hotel, boasting Venice's first rooftop hotel pool and a large spa.

▶ *Follow Fondamenta S. Biagio eastwards.*

Sant'Eufemia (**7**, CY)

This is the oldest church on the island, its origins dating back to the 9C. Still graced with 11C Veneto-Byzantine capitals, the interior houses the colourful *San Rocco and the Angel* by **Bartolomeo Vivarini** (c.1432–91) (*first altar, right aisle*); the frescoed ceiling is by Giambattista Canal (1745–1825) and exalts the life of the saint to which the church is dedicated.

Il Redentore★ (**8**, EY)

ⓞ*Open Mon–Sat, 10am–5pm.* ⓞ*Closed 1 Jan, Easter, 15 Aug, 25 Dec.* ✑*€3.* ☎*041 27 50 462. www.chorusvenezia.org.*

In 1576 Venice had been decimated by the plague, which had been raging for more than a year. **Doge Alvise Mocenigo** proposed that a new church be dedicated to the Redeemer, and every year thereafter honoured by a solemn procession.

Palladio was commissioned to design the church and sought to make it fulfil its votive function above all else. Its

The Feast of the Redeemer

The Feast of the Redeemer is held on the third Sunday in July, perpetuating the tradition started by Doge Alvise Mocenigo. A bridge of boats across the Giudecca Canal is assembled to enable the procession to reach the island and allow free access to the faithful. In the evening of the preceding Saturday, a fireworks display illuminates the sky and the lagoon.

longitudinal axis was necessary for the long procession of clergy and dignitaries. The flat, rigorously Classical façade, set back from a flight of steps inspired by biblical descriptions of the Temple in Jerusalem, embodies an idealised view of the Catholic Church accommodating a modern, classically ordered building. Flooded with light, the unified interior is contained in a single nave lined with side chapels.

As with the architecture, the paintings (by Bassano, Tintoretto and others) are arranged in such a way as to reveal their significance and unfurl the mystery of life as the procession progresses. In the **sacristy** hang a *Baptism of Christ* by Veronese and a *Madonna with Child and Angels* by Alvise Vivarini.

Le Zitelle (8, FY)

The **Church of Santa Maria della Presentazione** was also designed by **Palladio**. The name *Zitelle* was coined from a reference to the girls without dowry, who were taught sewing and lacemaking in hopes they would not turn to lives of prostitution; they were accommodated in the adjoining hospice that forms part of the façade. Characteristic features of the main front include the dominant triangular tympanum, flanked by bell-turrets, over a semicircular window.

PIAZZA SAN MARCO

(8, FGX)

VAPORETTO: S. MARCO

"The finest drawing room in Europe" according to Napoleon, **St Mark's Square** is the daily destination for tens of thousands of visitors. Beyond the columns of St Mark and St Theodore, the gondolas and vaporettos come and go, noisy crowds gather around the souvenir stalls and musicians play to the habitués of the legendary cafes. Tourists follow their tour guide's raised umbrella into the basilica or loiter under the porticoes, bewitched by windows of sparkling jewellery and glass. Since time immemorial, the passing of the hours has been ceremoniously sounded by the Moors on the clock tower and the mighty bells of the campanile.

▶ **Orient Yourself:** The square is the heart of the city. All central streets lead to here and it houses the two must-visit sights of the Basilica di San Marco, with its landmark Campanile, and the Palazzo Ducale (Doges' Palace).

☺ **Don't Miss:** The piazza when an orchestra is playing outdoors near Caffè Florian: a thoroughly romantic, magical experience.

🕐 **Organising Your Time:** For a tour of the basilica, the Doges' Palace and the museums allow at least a half day. Avoid the square in summer and on special occasions such as the Carnival. The early hours of the morning and evening and spring and autumn, when the colours and the sounds are crisp and clear, are infinitely preferable.

Kids **Especially for Kids:** The view from the campanile across the rooftops and the lagoon, or boarding a gondolier from in front of the Doges Palace.

⚲ **Also See:** La FENICE, RIALTO, SAN ZACCARIA.

Basilica di San Marco on Piazza San Marco

© Brian Hamilton / World Pictures / Photoshot

A Bit of History

A canal once ran in front of the basilica but by covering it over in 1160, the length of the piazza was tripled. The columns of St Mark and St Theodore (&see below) were erected in the piazzetta, and the entire architectural complex, as adapted, became the setting before which Pope Alexander III met with the German king Frederick Barbarossa (1177).

The great Florentine sculptor and architect Jacopo Sansovino (1486–1570) redesigned the piazza, linking it to the piazzetta. He is also responsible for the **Library**. Towards the close of the 16C, attention was turned to the redevelopment of the south side of the piazza and old buildings were removed to make way for the **Procuratie Nuove**.

The present trachyte paving was designed by Andrea Tirali (c.1657–1737), who also resurfaced the area known as the **Piazzetta dei Leoncini**, named after the two lions by Giovanni Bonazza (1654–1736). Tirali then conceived the idea of accenting lines of perspective in the piazza by inlaying four "fasciae" in Carrara marble in concentric geometrical formation. Two such bands converge

The only *piazza* in Venice

St Mark's Square is the only square in all Venice to bear the more distinguished title of *piazza*. Every other Venetian square is a mere *campo*!

on the Basilica; the other two running oblique to the first pair are aligned with the columns of St Mark and St Theodore. At their speculative point of intersection stands the square base of the campanile (this is best appreciated from above).

It remained little changed until the spectacular collapse of the campanile on 14 July 1902. Miraculously, the only damage incurred was to Sansovino's Loggetta and to a small part of the Biblioteca Marciana. By 1911, the new campanile, which is an exact reproduction of the old one had restored the square's traditional appearance.

The vast trapezoidal space (176m/577ft in length, 82m/269ft maximum width) is enclosed on the north side by the **Procuratie Vecchie** and by the later 16C Procuratie Nuove opposite. In between, the neo-Classical Napoleon Wing or **Ala nuovissimo** was built in

BASILICA DI S. MARCO

accordance with the wishes of Emperor Bonaparte after the demolition in the early 1800s of the 16C Sansovino Church of San Geminiano.

Basilica di San Marco★★★
(Saint Mark's Basilica) (8, FGX)

"Peace unto you, Mark, my Evangelist. Here rests your body," the angel said to St Mark near the Rialto, as the Evangelist was journeying from Aquileia to Rome. Almost another 800 years were to

elapse before the legendary prophecy was fulfilled: the symbol of St Mark has been synonymous with the Venetian flag ever since.

According to legend...

In Egypt, around the year 800, two merchants set out for Alexandria with the intention of stealing the saint's body as it was felt that the relics would bestow upon Venice the prestige needed to "compete" with Rome or, at least, would affirm its politico-religious independence from the capital. The body was taken in a chest aboard a Venetian vessel. On arrival in Venice, the precious relic was placed in the chapel of a castle belonging to Doge Giustiniano Parte-cipazio, and subsequently consecrated in 832 as the first church dedicated to St Mark.

History of the church

As a result of the arrival of the relics of San Marco, the first patron saint of Ven-ice, San Teodoro (*Todaro* in dialect), was demoted, if not forgotten.

After the fire of 976, which seriously damaged the church, St. Mark's body was lost. But, on the occasion of the consecration of the third church to be erected on this site (25 June 1094), a part of a pilaster in the right transept crumbled to reveal a human arm. The sacred relic was removed to the crypt and later buried below the high altar.

The 11C basilica is modelled upon the Church of the Holy Apostles in Con-stantinople. It came to be the pride of the Venetians: **Doge Domenico Selvo** (1071–84) would ask merchants travel-ling to the East to bring back marble and other stone pieces (alabaster, jasper, porphyry, serpentine) for its embellish-ment. Indeed this was how the mosaics in the domes and the vaults came about.

Exterior

Silhouetted against the sky are the Basil-ica's five 13C Byzantine domes which culminate in a cross over the lantern. The lateral façades face onto Piazzetta dei Leoncini and Piazzetta San Marco.

West front

The façade is articulated horizontally by a terrace and balustrade that extends down the lateral walls; vertically, the width is divided into five bays, pierced at both levels by arches, opening at ground level into porches.

The iconography of the 17C mosaics from the left arch is as follows:

1st arch: *Transportation of the Body of St Mark into the Church* (1260–70), the only complete mosaic to survive from the façade's original decoration;

2nd arch: *St Mark Venerated by Venetian Magistrates*, based on a cartoon by Sebastiano Ricci (1659–1734);

3rd arch: (main, central archway) the 19C replacement mosaics, *Christ in Glory* and *The Last Judgement*, are enclosed in an arch populated with figures among foliage; below the mosaics, the three archivolts (inner arches) are illustrated with Roman-esque-Byzantine carvings repre-senting *the Three Kingdoms: Land, Ocean and Animal*, *the Labours of the Months* and *the Signs of the Zodiac, the Virtues and Beatitudes*. Running along the intrados of the main arch (underside) are depictions of the typical Venetian trades: note the man on the left with the crutches, thought to allude to the architect of St Mark's, gnawing his hand, preoccupied by the imperfection of his work.

4th arch: *The Body of St Mark Welcomed by the Venetians*;

5th arch: *The Theft of the Relic of St Mark*.

Modern copies now replace the four bronze horses on the balcony; the origi-nals are conserved in the museum. On the upper level, the arches terminate in Gothic cusps. The 17C mosaics depict (from left to right): *The Deposition, The Descent into Limbo, The Resurrection* and *The Ascension*.

Left side

Walk down the left flank, overlooking Piazzetta dei Leoncini, to admire the Porta

Detail, Basilica di San Marco

The Tetrarchs

© P. de Franqueville / MICHELIN

(Nov–Easter 4pm). ☙*Basilica free. Pala d'Oro €2. Treasury €5.* ⚠*Clothes must be appropriate for a place of worship; no large bags (leave these in the Ateneo San Basso (Piazzetta dei Leoncini); no photography or video cameras.* ☎*041 27 08 31. www.basilicasanmarco.it.*

Enter the basilica through the large atrium that would have been reserved for the unbaptised and new converts. Decked with mosaics that relate stories from the Old Testament, these herald others inside the church that illustrate incidents from the New Testament.

Atrium

☙*Guided tours (1hr) of the mosaics, Apr–Oct Mon–Sat 11am.* ⓘ*No tours holidays.*

At the end of the Fourth Crusade (1201–04), Venice entered a phase of self-esteem on the wave of victory after the conquest of Constantinople. Romanesque and early Christian iconography in these early mosaics are borrowed from 5C–6C illuminated manuscripts that appear to have reached Venice with the Fourth Crusade.

▶ *Start with the right dome, and follow towards the left:*

The Creation according to Genesis (3)

These are the oldest mosaics in the atrium: in three concentric circles, in an anticlockwise direction, they tell the story of Genesis, beginning with the dove, the smallest mosaic, to the east. In synthesis with the tradition of the Eastern Church, based upon the Gospel of St John (*The word was God…*), the figure of the Creator is that of Christ, beardless, to signify the period before the Incarnation. Each stage of the Creation is attended by the angels which gradually increase in numbers as the days go by. Note, on the day of the creation of the animals, the lions before God that symbolise Venice's atmosphere of pride and self-congratulation; on the day on which the Creator blesses the seventh angel – the day of rest and the day that Adam and Eve were chased from the Garden of Paradise – how they are depicted dressed in clothes. On the eighth day,

dei Fiori (4th arch, on the corner) with its Romanesque relief of *The Nativity.*

Right side

The south side abuts the Doges' Palace on the piazzetta. The first arch is framed by two columns surmounted with Romanesque griffins; the second arch contains the door to the Baptistry, framed with the **Acrean pillars (1)**. Syrian in origin, two of the 6C columns have white marble shafts; the one nearest the piazzetta is of porphyry. This porphyry column is also known as the **pietra del bando**, the proclamation stone from where laws would be announced. In 1902, when the campanile collapsed, this pedestal was damaged while protecting the corner of the Basilica.

On the corner nearest the Palace stand the famous 4C **Tetrarchs**★ **(2)** or Moors sometimes upheld to allude to the Emperors Diocletian, Maximilian, Valerian and Constantine. They are otherwise said to be Saracens who, according to legend, were turned to stone when trying to steal the treasure of St Mark.

St Mark's Interior

ⓘ*Open year-round Mon–Sat 9.45am–5pm (Nov–Easter Pala d'Oro and Treasury close 4pm. Sun and hols 2–5pm*

Christ is born, heralding the beginning of a new Creation.

The *Arch of Noah* (**4**) depicts the story of Noah and the Flood: notice the ark's little window during the deluge.

Continuing with the iconographic theme initiated in the entrance, the mosaics of the *Arch of Paradise* (**5**), designed in part by Tintoretto (1518–94) and Aliense (1556–1629), exalt the mission of the Church as the Salvation of Man by means of the Cross, Paradise and Hell; represented as symbols that break with the narrative of the Old Testament stories illustrated previously. Before passing through the doorway, it is worth looking up at the vault, where St Mark in Ecstasy is based on a cartoon by **Titian** (1490–1576).

In the niches on either side of the doorway stand the Madonna, Apostles and Evangelists; the ornamentation is Byzantine.

The story of Noah continues in the next arch with a particularly beautiful depiction of the *Tower of Babel* (**6**), marking a prelude to the division of the human race.

Story of Abraham (7)

The mosaics in the second dome comprise one cycle, dedicated to the life of Abraham. Between the various scenes are lunettes which illustrate God's promises to Abraham. In the next arch, Abraham is depicted with the confirmation in writing, as the prefiguration of Christ.

Story of Joseph (8)

The last dome on the left and the next two in the left arm illustrate the story of Joseph. In order to portray a person who is dreaming – in this case the Pharaoh – the mosaic artists resorted to a sort of bubble that unfurls. The second and third dome of this series postdate the first by about 20 years, which explains why the images and landscapes appear richer and more vibrant.

Story of Moses (9)

In the last dome of the atrium, this part of the biblical cycle concludes with the life of Moses.

Above the door, the Madonna presents her Son, flanked by St John and St Mark. This concludes the Old Testament cycle and serves as a link to the New Testament by encouraging the visitor to carry on "reading" inside the Basilica.

▸ *A steep flight of stairs leads to the Galleria and the Museo di San Marco.*

Museo di San Marco

🕐 *Open year-round daily 9.45am–4.45pm.* ▦ €4. ☎ *041 27 08 311. www.museosanmarco.it.*

Access to the Marciano Museum is via the Gallery, from where there is a marvellous view of the mosaics and an opportunity to look out over the piazza from the balcony. The museum houses tapestries, mosaics and some interesting documents relating to the history of the Basilica. The greatest draw for visitors must be the **gilded bronze horses**★★. They arrived in Venice as part of the booty from the Fourth Crusade but undoubtedly date back to a much earlier period, although opinion on their origin is divided as to whether they are 4C–3C BC Greek or 4C Roman works.

Given pride of place on the balcony, these wonderful equestrian statues were taken to Paris by Napoleon after his crushing Italian campaign, but returned in 1815. In 1974 they were removed from their original position for restoration and replaced with copies.

Mosaics★★★

⊙*Visitors are advised to view the mosaics inside St Mark's when the basilica is illuminated: Mon–Fri, 11.30am–12.30pm; Sat–Sun and holidays, all day.*

As a general orientation, the lower part of the walls depict the saints, the middle section is reserved for the Apostles and the domes are dedicated to the Creator. The key to each story is held in the dome of the apse from where the story unfolds chronologically. Christ as Pantocrator towers over the four patrons of Venice: St Nicholas, St Peter, St Mark and St Ermagora, with the area above the atrium given over to the Last Judgement. These last mosaics are also the most recent, dating as they do from the 16C.

The entrance door depicts the *Deesis*, the Saviour in benediction between the Virgin and St Mark.

The **Arch of the Apocalypse** (**10**) illustrates the visions described in the Gospel of St John; the seven candelabra symbolise the seven churches.

The dome nearest the doorway is dedicated to the *Pentecost* (**11**). Between the windows, the populace listens to the preaching of St Peter in Jerusalem; to correspond with the angels, the Four Evangelists are illustrated in the pendentives.

Approaching the central dome, the **West Arch** (**12**) presents a synthesis of the *Passion* and *Death of Christ*. Worthy of note are the cartouches in the hand of the Judeans, bearing Pilate and Christ. In the right transept, illuminated by a Gothic rose window, the **Dome of St Leonard** (**13**) or the Saints of the Sacrament, is decorated with 13C mosaics representing St Nicholas, St Clement, St Blaise and St Leonard. The **South Arch** (**14**) has Byzantine mosaics which depict the *Temptations of Christ* and *His Entry into Jerusalem*, the *Last Supper* and the *Washing of the Feet*.

In the centre is the **Dome of the Ascension** (**15**). This encapsulates the most important moments in the story of the Salvation. Witnesses to the *Ascension* include the Apostles, the Madonna and,

between the windows, the Virtues and some of the Beatitudes. Christ in benediction dominates the scene. Beneath the pendentives which depict the Four Evangelists are the Four Rivers of the Earth.

The **Presbytery Dome** is dedicated to the Season of Advent, dominated by Emmanuel in the company of Prophets, with the Virgin in the middle. The decoration of this dome dates back to the beginning of 1100. Symbols of the Evangelists adorn the pendentives.

The mosaics on the **North Arch** (**16**) designed by Tintoretto show *St Michael with Sword Drawn* with the *Last Supper* on the left and the *Marriage at Cana* on the right. In the centre, the *Healing of the Leper* is taken from a cartoon by Veronese (1528–88), the *Healing of the Bleeding Woman* and the *Resurrection of Naim's Widow's Son* are based on cartoons by Salviati (1520/25–75). The *Christ in Glory* is a 19C reconstruction.

The **Dome of St John the Evangelist** (**17**) is in the left arm of the transept. The 13C mosaics reproduce a Greek cross with biblical verses on the *Sermon on the Mount* and episodes from the Life of St John the Evangelist.

▷ *Continue along the left aisle.*

In the north aisle is the **Capital of the Crucifixion** (**18**), a white and black marble structure with a pyramidal roof surmounted by an agate. The crucifix contained therein, coming from Constantinople, would have been the cause of much bloodshed.

The mosaic panels (c.1230) opposite the side aisles depict *Christ Blessing the Prophets* – Hosea, Joel, Micah and Jeremiah (*in the left aisle*) and Ezekiel, Solomon, the Madonna in prayer, David and Isaiah (*in the right aisle*).

Pala d'Oro★★★

The **Golden Altarpiece** is preceded by a ciborium on **columns of alabaster**★★ inscribed with reliefs inspired by the Gospels and the Apocrypha. The exact date and provenance of these reliefs remain uncertain, but are usually classified as 5C–6C Greek (from Ravenna), Syrian, Egyptian or Coptic. Contained

Detail of the Golden Altarpiece

within the high altar rest the remains of St Mark and, beyond, towers the great altarpiece.

Commissioned and made in Constantinople in the 10C, the Golden Altarpiece is a masterpiece of the goldsmith's craft. Gleaming with precious stones set among enamelled panels, it continued to be embellished with new and valuable sections until the 14C.

The top section is dominated by the figure of the Archangel Michael in the centre, framed between scenes (starting from the left) of the *Entry into Jerusalem*, the *Resurrection*, the *Crucifixion*, the *Ascension*, the *Pentecost* and the *Death of the Virgin*. The focal point of the lower section is Christ Pantocrator (the Ruler of the Universe) flanked by the figures of the Evangelists. Below, the Virgin appears between the Empress Irene and the Emperor Giovanni Commeno, Prophets, Apostles and Angels. On either side, the iconographic cycle continues with episodes from the lives of Christ and St Mark.

In the apse, the doors to the tabernacle and to the sacristy are by Sansovino.

Chapels

Grouped around the presbytery it is worth stopping to look at the **iconostasis** (openwork screen) in polychrome marble. Eight columns support an architrave bearing figures of the **Apostles**, the **Madonna** and **John the Baptist** by Dalle Masegne (14C–15C). This great line is broken in the middle by a bronze and silver **Crucifix**. At either end, the iconostasis terminates with a pulpit, each reconstructed in the 14C. The **Double Pulpit** on the left comprises two sections from which lessons are read from the Gospels (*upper tier*) and the Epistles (*lower tier*). To honour the Word of God, it is crowned with a fine golden cupola which is decidedly oriental in style. The pulpit on the right, the **Pulpit of the Reliquary**, was where the relics would be displayed and where the newly elected doge would make his first appearance.

Both chapels dedicated to **St Clement** (*right apse*) and **St Peter** (*left apse*) are screened off by their own iconostasis; the one for St Clement, complete with

statues, is by Dalle Masegne. Outside each chapel, the wall is covered with mosaics (12C) illustrating episodes from the lives of St Mark and St Peter respectively; inside the domed vault of each are representations of the saints to whom each chapel is dedicated (St Peter is 13C).

The window on the right wall of the Chapel of St Clement enabled the doge to follow functions and services being held in church without leaving the comfortable confines of his palace apartments.

In the **Chapel of the Madonna Nicopeia** is a particularly venerated image of the Madonna and Child, called *Nicopeia* (meaning the Bringer of Victory or Leader), because she served as the standard of the Byzantine army. Coming from Constantinople, the figure may have been brought to Venice as booty from the Fourth Crusade.

The **Chapel of St Isidore** is off the transept, whose end wall bears *Mary's Genealogical Tree*, which dates back to the end of the 12C.

The next chapel, the **Mascoli Chapel**, is dedicated to the members of the confraternity of male worshippers. The mosaics are the work of Giambono (active 1420–62), Andrea del Castagno (c.1421–57), Jacopo Bellini (c.1396–c.1470) and **Andrea Mantegna** (1431–1506).

Treasury★

This priceless collection of religious objects, reliquaries and ornaments, which came into Venice's possession after the conquest of Constantinople in 1204, includes one particularly notable exhibit, the *Artophoron,* an 11C container for the Bread of the Eucharist, in the shape of a church, crowned with oriental-style domes.

Baptistery

Open for prayer only.

The baptistery is divided into three interconnecting areas; 14C mosaics recount the life of John the Baptist and the Infant Jesus. The most famous panel shows *Salome Dancing before Herod*. The baptismal font is by Sansovino (1486–1570), who is buried here, before the altar. The mosaics in the **Cappella Zen (19)**, the funeral chapel of Cardinal Zen who died in 1501, date from the 13C.

Il Campanile★★ (🅱, FX)

♿🕐 *Open Jul–Sept 9am–9pm; April/ Easter–Jun and Oct, 9am–7pm; rest of the year 9.30am–3.45pm.* ✦€8. ☎ 041 27 08 311. www.basilicasanmarco.it.

Although the present bell-tower was erected at the beginning of the 20C (ℓ *see A Bit of History*), it was rebuilt according to its predecessor's early-16C designs by Bartolomeo Bon in brick. The tower stands 96m/315ft high, culminating in a golden angel weather-vane that turns in the wind.

The campanile is articulated as if by a gigantic order of pilasters, up to an arched white marble section, pierced by a four-light loggia where the bells hang. Above a balustraded section, the four sides rise cleanly to a pyramid.

At the top, from where **Galileo Galilei** once extended his telescope (1609), a magnificent **view**★★ stretches from the Giudecca Canal to the Grand Canal across roofs and chimneytops to the islands in the lagoon.

Loggetta Sansoviniana

At the base of the tower, and facing St Mark's, the richly decorated Sansovino Loggetta comprises three arches supported on columns reminiscent of a triumphal arch; columns also frame the niches that accommodate the figures of Minerva, Apollo, Mercury and Peace. The reliefs above depict (*from left to right*), the Island of Candia, Venice as an allegory of Justice, and the island of Cyprus. The terrace at the front is enclosed by a balustrade, broken in the middle by a bronze gate designed by Antonio Gai (1686–1769).

The present *loggetta* was first built during the early part of the 16C by **Jacopo Tatti Sansovino** and rebuilt after the collapse of the campanile.

🕐On the right side of the basilica, near the Porta della Carta, stand the remains of a tower decorated with low-relief sculptures; as they are not directly at eye level, they tend to elude the attention of visitors. However, if you bend down a little, you will notice one in particular that is located under the Tetrarchs, just on the right. It represents two putti escaping from the jaws of two dragons. They are pictured framing a 13C inscription, believed to be one of the very first texts written in Venetian dialect.

Palazzo Ducale★★★ (Doges' Palace) (🅹, GX)

♿🕐 *Open year-round daily 9am–7pm (5pm Nov–Easter); last admission 1hr before closing.* 🕐 *Closed 1 Jan and 25 Dec.* ✦€16. Museums of St Mark's

Palazzo Ducale

© SCALA

Square ticket, also gives entry to the Clock Tower, Museo Correr, Museo Archeologico Nazionale, Monumental Rooms of Biblioteca Marciana; Museum Pass €24.50 includes other city museums. Itinerari Segreti (Secret itinerary) tickets book online (€20). ☎041 27 15 911. http://palazzoducale.visitmuve.it.

The origins of this Byzantine, Gothic and Renaissance palace go back almost as far as those of Venice itself. In 810 **Doge Agnello Partecipazio** decided that the seat of his public offices should be located on the site of the present Doges' Palace. At the time, the buildings, which included the Church of St Mark, were more of a citadel than a government office. The need for a fortified residence gradually gave way towards one with an institutional role, with loggias and porticoes on the outside, and a host of offices inside where various affairs of State could be conducted by the doge's staff.

Exterior

The harmony of the structural whole is striking: the "hollow" spaces of the portico and the loggia contrast with blocks of "solid" masonry in the upper section of the building. The effect is mitigated, however, by the rose-coloured tint of the upper floor and the darkness of the multi-arched lower floors.

The narrative function of the mosaics inside the basilica is transposed here onto the sculptural iconography that

PALAZZO DUCALE

Second floor

Scala d'Oro
Sala d. Consiglio dei Dieci
Sala della Bussola
1st floor
Sala del Senato
Armeria
Sala del Collegio
Sala dell'Anticollegio
Sala delle Quattro Porte
BASILICA DI S. MARCO

First floor

Rio di Palazzo
Scala d'Oro
Ponte dei Sospiri ★★
APPARTAMENTO DUCALE
8
9
4
5
6
2
3
7
1
to the Ponte dei Sospiri (Bridge of Sighs)
Molo
Sala del Maggior Consiglio
BASILICA DI S. MARCO
Sala dello Scrutinio
N
Piazzetta S. Marco
0   20 m

1 Liagò	4 Sala del Magistrato alle Leggi
2 Sala della Quarantia Civil Vecchia	5 Sala dei Cuoi
3 Sala dell' Armamento	6 Sala della Quarantia Criminal

APPARTAMENTO DUCALE
7 Sala degli Scarlatti
8 Sala dello Scudo
9 Sala degli Scudieri

adorns the capitals, the corners of the *palazzo* and its pillars. Decorating the palace are allegorical figures representing the Vices and Virtues, the Ages of Man and Signs of the Zodiac, all charged with moral example.

The façade onto the piazzetta rises from an arcade of 18 pointed arches along the ground floor, supported on baseless columns. The first-floor loggia also runs continuously along the façade, the horizontal emphasis accentuated by the balustrade and sequence of 34 roundels between the ogive, cusped arches, punctured with quatrefoil cutouts. From between the two red marble columns, public announcements of capital sentences were made, later to be carried out between the columns of St Mark and St Theodore in the square below.

The two upper storeys, which together are as tall as the two lower floors, seem lost in solid wall. From a distance, the building appears a distinctively soft shade of pinky-rose, with surface relief at closer proximity, provided by the interplay of terra-cotta and white bricks disposed in diamond patterns. Its massiveness is further offset by the delicate line of gables along the top.

On the first floor, the central balcony overlooking the piazzetta is 16C (artists unknown). The portrait above it is of **Doge Andrea Gritti** (1523–38) and

The Drunkenness of Noah

at each corner is a sculptural group: that projecting into the square shows the *Judgement of Solomon,* an allegory of Wisdom, thought to be by Bartolomeo Bon (active 1441–64), beyond which stands the Porta della Carta.

Porta della Carta★★

The **"Paper Doorway"** is the entrance to the palace per se. Flamboyant Gothic in style, it was constructed by Giovanni and Bartolomeo Bon between 1438 and 1442. Explanations for the name have been attributed to the many scribes who used the entrance, which also served the archives (*cartarum*). The superimposed niches are occupied by the four Cardinal Virtues sculpted by Antonio Bregno (c.1418–c.1503). Above the doorway, kneeling before the winged lion, is the Doge Francesco Foscari, who was in power when the portal was constructed. Above the window, in the roundel, is St Mark, overlooked by Justice on the pinnacle.

▶ *To reach the canal quayside from the Piazzetta San Marco, walk round the full length of both sides of the palace.*

The façade overlooking the Basin stretches between the corner sculpture groups of (*left*) *Adam, Eve and the Serpent* (late 14C) – an allegory of Sin – surmounted by the figures of Tobias and the Angel Raphael (late 14C) and *The Drunkenness of Noah* (14C–15C), a symbol of the virtue of compassion (*near the Paglia Bridge*).

The second capital from the left, known as the Capital of the Sages (*dei Sapienti*), is inscribed with the date 1344, the year in which this wing was constructed. The central balcony on the second floor was inserted in the early 15C, designed by Dalle Masegne.

The last two, more decorative, windows appear out of alignment with the others because of the internal room arrangement.

To the right, the Ponte della Paglia (literally translated as the Bridge of Straw) precedes that second and much more famous bridge across the canal.

Ponte dei Sospiri★★ (⑨, GX)

Universally known, the Bridge of Sighs owes its name to Romantic literary notions: overwhelmed by the enchanting view from the windows of this bridge, it was across here that prisoners would be led to the courtroom to learn of their fate.

The bridge, constructed in Istrian stone, links the palace with the Prigioni Nuove (New Prisons). It was built during the dogeship of **Marino Grimani** (1595–1605) and bears his coat of arms. Inside, the bridge is divided into two passages through which visitors pass on their tour of the Doges' Palace. ⓐGiven the number of rooms and the length of the tour, it is easy to lose one's bearings and to cross the bridge without realising it, so beware!

Palace Entrance

The entrance to the Palazzo is to the right of the Porta della Carta (through which visitors pass on their way out). The courtyard is graced with a fine mid-16C well-head, the mid-15C **Porticato Foscari** leading through to the **Foscari Arch**, and the **Scala dei Giganti** directly opposite. The Giants' Staircase, constructed at the end of the 15C, was designed by Antonio Rizzo (c.1440–99) and is dominated by two magnificent statues of Mars and Neptune (the gods of War and Sea) by Sansovino (1486–1570). It was at the top of these stairs that the doges used to be crowned. The well-heads in the courtyard date to the mid-16C; the east end façade, designed by Rizzo, is early Renaissance in style.

Interior

From the portico, take the **Scala d'Oro** or Golden Staircase up to the second floor. Sansovino initiated work on the staircase during the reign of **Doge Andrea Gritti** (1523–38), although work was not to be completed by Scarpagnino (recorded in Venice 1505–49) until after the appointment of Lorenzo Priuli (1556–59): note the coats of arms of the two doges on the large arch. Its Baroque-sounding name comes from reference to the rich stucco decoration in white and gold around Giovan Battista Franco's

The Bridge of Sighs

© R. Mattes / MICHELIN

(1498–1561) frescoes depicting *The Glorification of the Defence of Cyprus and Crete* and *The Virtues Necessary for Good Government*. The portrait in the atrium of Doge Gerolamo Priuli was painted by Tintoretto.

L'Appartamento Ducale

Follow the signs through to the Ducal Appartment, where a *Pietà* by Giovanni Bellini and the famous *Lion* by Vittore Carpaccio are displayed.

Sala delle Quattro Porte

Ambassadors would wait for their audience with the doge in this first room, the Chamber of the Four Doors. The decoration postdates 1574, following one of the many fires caused by the use of wood and candles. Propped up on the easel is *Venice Receiving the Homage of Neptune*, a famous canvas by Tiepolo. The frescoed ceiling is by Tintoretto and the four doorways by Palladio. The paintings on the walls depict allegorical scenes or historical subjects. Among these, *Doge Antonio Grimani in Adoration before the Faith and St Mark in Glory* was started by Titian and finished by his nephew. The painting, commemorating a visit made by Henry III, King of France, in 1574, depicts the Triumphal Arch designed by Palladio that would have been made of papier mâché, a material commonly used to create temporary stage sets for special occasions.

Sala dell'Anticollegio

An antechamber for diplomatic delegations, the room houses the *Return of Jacob with Family* by Jacopo Bassano (c.1517–92) and the *Rape of Europa* by Veronese (*facing the windows*). The paintings on either side of the doors are by Tintoretto. The fresco on the ceiling is by Veronese.

Sala del Collegio

Here in the College Chamber the doge, his throne raised on the wooden platform, presided over meetings. The "Full College" dealt with legal matters that were subsequently presented to the Senate, and political relationships between Venice and foreign courts on diplomatic missions. The stalls date to 1575. The paintings decorating the gilded wooden ceiling exalt the city; above the throne, the great panel depicting Doge Sebastiano Venier is also by Veronese. The paintings on the wall with the clock set in black Belgian marble are by Tintoretto: left of the clock, *Alvise Mocenigo Thanking the Redeemer* commemorates the votive plea for an end to the plague of 1576. Tintoretto's painting on the door continues in the same spirit of celebration.

Sala del Senato

Here in the Senate Chamber, or "Pregadi Chamber," members of the Senate were asked (*pregati*) to submit written request to participate in the meetings. The assembly presided here over all matters of State. The decor, refurbished after the fire of 1574, is peopled with doges and patron saints, in audience before the Redeemer or the Virgin. In the central panel of the ceiling Tintoretto depicted *The Triumph of Venice*. Behind the throne hangs a work of Palma il Giovane. In the painter's *Allegory of Victory over the League of Cambrai*, Venice appears as a young warrior on the attack, preceded by the lion. The pulpit was used by those taking part in the debates.

Sala del Consiglio dei Dieci

The powerful and notorious council, whose origins go back as far as 1310, used to meet in this Chamber of the Council of Ten. On the ceiling preside allegories of good government and the power of the Republic: most notable is Veronese's *Juno Offering the Doge's Corno*; the central painting of Jove is a copy after Veronese: the original, "stolen" by Napoleon, is now in the Louvre in Paris. On the walls two important historical events are depicted: *The Peace of Bologna between Pope Clement VII and Emperor Charles V* by Marco Vecellio (1545–1611), a cousin of Titian (*left*), and *Pope Alexander III Blesses Doge Sebastiano Ziani after the Battle of Salvore* by Francesco da Ponte, also known as Bassano (1549–92), and his brother Leandro (1557–1622) (*right*).

Sala della Bussola

The Ballot Chamber was also the waiting room for those who were to be interrogated by the heads (*capi*) of the Council of Ten. To the left of the ballot box is a painting by Marco Vecellio. Beside the exit door is the wooden hatch that allowed the secret denunciations to be removed from the **bocca di leone** or lion's mouth outside. Ceiling paintings are largely by followers of Veronese, although the central painting of St Mark is a copy; the original is in the Louvre.

Armeria

The various rooms making up the Armoury house objects such as trophies, relics of war, and the suit of armour of the infamous *condottiere* Gattamelata identified by the badge with a cat on the knee, and instruments of torture. The room dedicated to Francesco Morosini is marked with the sign CX, the Council of Ten's monogram.

Sala del Maggior Consiglio

The enormous Grand Council Chamber is perhaps the highlight of the tour. Here and in the nearby Sala dello Scrutinio, the new doge was elected. Except for the undamaged 14C Guariente fresco the *Coronation of the Virgin*, now in the Sala del Armamento, the paintings destroyed by the fire of 1577 were swiftly replaced

Sala del Maggior Consiglio

with more magnificent decoration. The subject of the long wall overlooking the Basin is the Fourth Crusade. Other notable paintings are those by Carlo Saraceni and Jean Le Clerc, Palma il Giovane, Domenico Tintoretto, Andrea Micheli (also known as Vicentino) and Federico Zuccari. The vast painting behind the throne was executed by Tintoretto, his son and followers.

Below the ceiling are portraits of the 76 doges who governed Venice between 804 and 1554, almost all by Domenico Tintoretto. **Marino Falier** who, in the 14C, conspired against the State and was beheaded, is remembered rather unfavourably. Portraits of the last 39 doges, spanning the years 1556–1797, are in the Scrutinio.The trussed wooden ceiling is dominated by Veronese's *Apotheosis of Venice* (1582). Other paintings on the ceiling celebrate Venice's victory in battle.

Sala dello Scrutinio

Here the *scrutinio* (counting) of the votes took place. The series of portraits of the governors of Venice concludes with the last doge, **Ludovico Manin** (1789–97), who ceded to Napoleon, which marked the subjugation of the Serenissima.The decoration of this room celebrates grandiose events in Venice's history. The ceiling comprises five large paintings, the most noteworthy being

The Naval Victory of the Venetians over the Pisans at Rodi by Vicentino and *The Venetian Victory over the Genoese at Trapani* by Giovanni Bellini. The partition wall dividing this room from the **Sala della Quarantia Civil Nuova** bears Palma il Giovane's *Last Judgement*, which replaced Tintoretto's painting destroyed during the fire.

Just before the prisons, the **Sala del Magistrato alle Leggi** preserves *The Mocking of Christ* by the Flemish master Quentin Metsys (1466–1530) and the only works by Hieronymus Bosch (c.1450–1516) in Italy.

Prigioni Nuove

Steps lead up to the Bridge of Sighs and beyond to the New Prisons on the other side of the canal. These prisons also served as the seat of the magistrature of the **Signori di Notte al Criminal**, a sort of vice squad. Note the graffiti inscribed on the stone walls.

▶ *Cross the bridge to the palace.*

Sala dei Censori

Lined with wooden seats, this chamber, known as the Censors' Chamber, accommodated a judiciary body. The paintings, mostly by Domenico Tintoretto, consist of formal portraits of magistrating censors.

Sala dell'Avogaria

The last room of the tour, the Avogaria Chamber, was the seat of another part of the former magistrature, whose members, the *avogadori*, consisted of lawyers appointed by the State. Their duty was to ensure that the law was obeyed. It is unusual for such portraits to have been presented in this way, a practice that hitherto was reserved for religious subjects.

The tour concludes with the **Sala dello Scrigno** and the **Sala della Milizia da Mar**.

The Palace Corridors (Itinerari Segreti/Secret Itinerary)

Guided morning tours. Reservations strongly encouraged. €20. Book online, http://palazzoducale. visitmuve.it.

The various magistratures that had seats in the palace operated in an environment that was anything but ostentatious. Many of the activities, most of which were secret, took place in very restricted surroundings just off the grand chambers. Linked by a maze of hidden stairs and passageways, these still exude an air of mystery.

The **Cancelleria segreta** (Secret Chancellery), which resembles a ship's deck, is ornamented with the chancellor's coats of arms.

The impressive **Sala delle Torture** (Torture Room) betrays the more intolerant, if not more characteristic face of the Republic (see Box, left). The prison cells located in the Palace were referred to as the **Pozzi e Piombi** (Wells and Leads): the *pozzi* were the deep, damp dungeons for hardened criminals; the *piombi*, so-called because they were

roofed in lead, were for those imprisoned for a couple of months. Life in the cells was not necessarily that severe: prisoners were allowed to bring some furniture and a little money with them. Punishment was intended to induce remorse by exerted psychological pressure rather than by inflicting physical suffering.

It was from the *piombi* that **Giacomo Casanova** (1725–98) made his daring escape, emerging onto the roof above the Grand Council Chamber. From here one can picture the view over Venice in former times when it was almost entirely built of wood.

After the fire of 1577, Antonio da Ponte was given only 16 months to complete the Palace's reconstruction. He drew upon the skills of the *arsenalotti* who were capable of assembling a ship in one day.

In the **Sala dei Tre Capi del Consiglio dei Dieci**, the magistrates (*capi*) who had been elected from the Council of Ten to preside over court cases would meet. Of particular interest on the ceiling are *Virtue Driving Away Vice* (*centre*) by Zelotti, and two paintings in the corner panels by Veronese.

In the **Sala dei Tre Inquisatori** (Inquisitors' Chamber) officials would pass judgement on crimes against the State. The ceiling features paintings by Tintoretto.

The Procuratie (⑧, FX)

Procuratie Nuove

Replacing the Orseolo hospice, the second seat of the Procurators was planned by Scamozzi and completed by Longhena during the first half of the 17C.

Law and Order Venetian Style

After Florence, Venice was the second state in the world to abolish torture and the first to abolish slavery. However, treatment of prisoners was guided more by diplomatic and political acumen than piety. The "law of the repentent" *ante litteram* applied to informers, whereby anyone with a relation accused of a minor crime could ensure their release from prison if they revealed valuable information that led to the capture and conviction of an assassin. Murder, religious theft, crimes against children, criminal offences against the State, return from exile or causing pollution, however, resulted in capital punishment.

Under Napoleon, the Procuratie Nuove became the **Palazzo Reale**.

▶ *To get to the Museo Correr, go through the Ala Napoleonica.*

Museo Correr★★

&♿🕐♿🐭*Same admission times, charges and contact details as Palazzo Ducale.*

This museum takes its name from **Teodoro Correr** (1750–1830), a Venetian gentleman who bequeathed his rich collection of artifacts relating to the history and art of the Serenissima to the city. The tour proceeds up the magnificent 19C staircase, through the neo-Classical **Sale Canoviane** (Canova Rooms) and on to the **History, Arts, Crafts** and **Games** Departments (*first floor*). Among its historical maps, the Museo Correr boasts one of the famous **De' Barbari** maps (c.1445–1515). Important paintings include the vivid, typically Venetian works of the German artist, Joseph Heintz the Younger (c.1600–78), most notably *Bull Baiting in Campo San Polo*. Among the sculptures by **Antonio Canova** (1757–1822) are his *Orpheus and Eurydice* and the celebrated *Daedalus and Icarus*. Other works, by Francesco Hayez (1791–1882) betray Canova's influence.

Beyond the dining room, with its particularly neo-Classical decoration, objects testify to the nobility and rich symbolism of the city's history: exhibits include doges' *corni* (caps), staffs of command, and *manine* (modelled hands used, along with the ballot urn, for counting votes in the lengthy procedure in electing a doge).

More paintings include works by Vicentino, Vassillachi, and Longhi. The *Lion of St Mark's* attributed to Michele Giambono represents Venice in one of its most typical allegories.

The **Libreria dei Teatini**, complete with 17C furnishings, accommodates books from the Teatini Convent. The **Sale dei Costumi** (Costume Rooms) contain official 17C and 18C garments worn by senators and procurators.

The **Collezione Numismatica** (Numismatic Collection) comprises coinage minted by the Republic, including the famous *zecchino* and a painting by Tintoretto.

A whole room is dedicated to the **Bucintoro**, the doge's ship aboard which the ceremony of **The Marriage with the Sea** took place. Measuring 35m/115ft long and 7m/23ft wide and propelled by 168 rowers, the ship was so tall and threfore so unstable

View of the grand staircase, Museo Correr

© Museo Correr / Fondazione Musei Civici di Venezia

that it could sail safely only in the calmest conditions.

Exhibits relevant to the Arsenale include a map, engravings and banners.

The section "Venice and the Sea" is followed by one dedicated to war, which includes the weaponry and armour from the Correr and Morosini Armouries.

From here, ascend to the second floor, and on to the **Quadreria** (Paintings Section), which presents a synthesis of the Venetian School of painting up to the early 16C.

Among Veneto-Byzantine examples is perhaps the earliest Venetian painting on wood, the lid of a wooden chest.

The following rooms are dedicated to **Paolo Veneziano** (c.1290–1362) and **Lorenzo Veneziano** (1356–72) and **Jacobello dalle Masegne**. Among the other Gothic artists represented here is **Stefano Veneziano**. In Venice **International Gothic** arrived at the beginning of the 15C. Examples include the paintings of Michele Giambono (active

1420–62) and Jacobello del Fiore (c.1370–1439).

The suggestive *Pietà*a, marked by brittle form and metallic colour, is the work of **Cosmè Tura** (c.1430–1495), who came from Ferrara. *Portrait of a Young Man*, characterised by strong contrasting colours, is attributed to another 15C artist from Ferrara, Antonio da Crevalcore.

The next room is dedicated to **Bartolomeo Vivarini** from Murano. His works betray the strong influence of Mantegna. His use of gold-leaf background, however, is more archaic and Byzantine in style.

Particularly worthy of note from the 15C Flemish School is an *Adoration of the Magi* by **Brueghel the Younger** (1564–1638), a Holy scene set in a Northern landscape blanketed with snow. The influence of Northern oil paintings on Italian art is suggested in a *Pietà*★★, the only work here by **Antonello da Messina** (c.1430–79), who visited Venice in 1475/6. The two other Flemish works in the room are by Hugo van der Goes and Dieric Bouts. One painting from the later 15C and 16C **Flemish School** is the *Temptations of St Anthony* by a follower of Hieronymus Bosch; its complex symbolism adds a disquieting, nightmarish dimension to the subject.

The **Bellinis** are gathered together in one room: they include the *Crucifixion* by **Jacopo** (1400–c.70), the *Portrait of Doge Giovanni Mocenigo* by Gentile (1429–1507) and four works by **Giovanni** (1430–1516).

Alvise Vivarini and Venetian painters from the late 15C forestall the works of **Vittore Carpaccio**, one of Venice's most acclaimed artists. His enigmatic *Two Venetian Ladies* are apparently animated by a private joke, their slightly dismissive expressions giving rise to various explanations.

The *Gentleman in the Red Cap*★★ is presently attributed to a painter from Ferrara/Bologna, although in the past it was thought to have been executed by Lotto (c.1480–1556), Giovanni Bellini or Carpaccio.

The evolution of art through the **High Renaissance** continues with **Lorenzo Lotto** (*Madonna with the Christ Child at her Breast*), before being interrupted by displays of works by 16C and 17C Greek *Madonneri* (painters depicting the Madonna in the traditional manner) and 15C and 16C majolica extending to the room beyond the Manin Library.

Museo del Risorgimento

Housed on the same floor, this museum documents the years that do not strictly belong to the story of Venice whose end came in 1797 when, after 1 000 years of glory, the Republic surrendered. Themes explored tend toward social history touching upon freemasonry, the temporary Municipality (the Government which, on the arrival of the French, pursued the abdication of Ludovico Manin), the rule of Napoleon and the Austrians. Returning to the first floor of the Museo Correr, one room displays Renaissance bronzes and another section is dedicated to **Arts and Crafts** (*Arti e Mestieri*). The **Giochi** (Games) collection includes exhibits on human pyramids that were

Two Venetian Ladies (c.1495) by Vittore Carpaccio

© Museo Correr / Fondazione Musei Civici di Venezia

"built" on wooden platforms on the Thursday before Lent and bull-baiting.

Procuratie Vecchie (🖪, FX)

The original residence of the Procurators in the 12C, these ancient loggias were initially Veneto-Byzantine in style before being rebuilt up to the first floor probably by Scarpagnino or possibly by **Mauro Codussi**. Still incomplete, they were damaged by fire in 1512, after which first Bartolomeo Bon (active c.1463–1529) then Guglielmo Grigi (active c.1515–30) added their mark, before Sansovino (1486–1570) completed work in 1532.

La Piazzetta (🖪, FGX)

This extension of St Mark's Square, between the Doges' Palace and the Biblioteca Nazionale Marciana, overlooks the sea through a magnificent portal framed by the two **Colonne di Marco e Todaro**. These two column shafts used as pedestals for St Mark and St Theodore were brought back from the East in 1172, although their specific provenance remains uncertain. The second one is a copy, the original being in the courtyard in the Doges' Palace. The lion, which the Venetians identify with their Evangelist-Saint, could be a chimera.

Famous Bars

In the arcaded portico of the Procuratie Vecchie is the **Caffè Quadri** (⬛, **FX** Y), which was founded by Giorgio Quadri in 1775 to serve Turkish coffee.

Opposite, on the other side of the piazza, is the older **Caffè Florian** (⬛ **FX** Z), also named after its first proprietor, Floriano Francesconi, which was opened in 1720. Its most renowned previous habitués have included the playwright **Carlo Goldoni** (1707–93) and the neo-Classical sculptor **Antonio Canova** (1757–1822).

West of the Procuratie Nuove, on Calle Vallaresso, sits famed **Harry's Bar**, haunt of the glitterati and most famously patronised by Ernest Hemingway.

Beware that the price of a drink in all of these places is extremely high. However think of it more as an entrance ticket to a theatrical entertainment rather than the price of a mere refreshment!

Biblioteca Nazionale Marciana★ (⬛, FX)

♿🕐🚼📷 *Same admission times, charges and contact details as Palazzo Ducale.*

As the first example of Classical architecture in Venice, this prestigious seat of Venetian culture is almost as glorious as its neighbour, the Doges' Palace. Over the Doric portico runs the loggia, its windows framed by Ionic columns, true to the Classical architectural canon of orders. **Sansovino** worked on the library from 1537. On his death, the project was completed by Scamozzi.

The Biblioteca's sculptural decoration draws on Classical mythology: the keystones of the arches are marked by leonine and mythological heads, and statues in various expressive poses overlook the piazzetta from the balustrade.

Inside, the Reading Room is located off the **Zecca** (Mint) courtyard.

With its two flights, the **staircase** is reminiscent of the Scala d'Oro (🕮 *see Palazzo Ducale*). The vaulted ceiling and cupola stucco decoration are by **Alessandro Vittoria**, the frescoes are by **Battista Franco** (*first flight*) and Battista del Moro (*second flight*). The thematic iconography is defined by a neo-Platonic concept of Man, who, influenced by cosmic forces (*first flight*) and fashioned by the Virtues (*second flight*) finally arrives at Universal Knowledge, symbolised by the book and the circle.

First floor

An important exhibit is the famous map of Venice by **Jacopo De' Barbari**, executed in 1500, the other version being in the Museo Correr. Nearby is the *Mappamondo* (1457–59) by Fra Mauro, the Camaldolite monk from San Michele in Isola. His planisphere is painted in colour and gold on parchment stuck down on wood.

Vestibule

Sansovino intended the Vestibule as a salon for Humanist lectures. Instead, it was turned into the Republic's Sculpture Museum when the Patriarch of Aquileia, Giovanni Grimani, donated his collection of sculpture and statuary to Venice; some pieces have overflowed into the Archaeological Museum (🕮 *see below*). On the ceiling, *Wisdom*, painted by Titian, has been inserted into a *trompe l'oeil* perspective by Cristoforo and Stefano Rosa, executed around 1559.

Salone Sansoviniano

At the heart of the original Library, the Sansovino Room houses the codices and manuscripts bequeathed to the Republic by **Cardinale Bessarione** (1403–72), the famous Greek Humanist. The grotesque ceiling decoration, the work of Battista Franco, is completed with 21 tondos illustrating mythological subjects, virtues and disciplines against a gold background.

The artists responsible for this ultimate "manifestation of Mannerism in Venice" are Giovanni De Mio, author of the first trio (🕮 *best viewed walking backwards away from the entrance); Giuseppe Porta*, known as Salviati (second trio); Battista Franco, (third trio); Giulio Licinio, whose third tondo, in poor condition, was replaced with one by Bernardo Strozzi depicting Sculpture; Giambattista Zelotti, whose third painting was also replaced, this time by a panel representing the *Nile, Atlas, Geometry* and *Astrology* by Padovanino, Veronese and Andrea Schiavone. Portraits of philosophers line the walls, including two by Veronese (*door side*); four by Tintoretto (*left*), then two by Schiavone, and another two by Tintoretto, although the attribution of the one on the right is uncertain (*end wall*). One by Salviati, one by Franco and one by Lambert Sustris adorn the right wall.

Museo Archeologico (⑧, FX)

🕐 *Open year-round daily 10am–7pm (5pm Nov–Mar).* 🕐 *Closed 1 Jan, 25 Dec.* ⬤€4. ☎041 52 25 978. www.polomuse-ale.venezia.beniculturali.it.

The Archaeological Museum is housed in the **Procuratie Nuove**, two doors away from the Biblioteca Marciana. It holds Greek sculpture, Egyptian and Roman fragments and a collection of coins and medals.

Start in the loggia containing the Greek inscriptions and pass through the coins and medals section before reaching the most ancient Archaic pieces, such as the famous **Grimani** Greek statues (5C–4C BC); sculpture from the 5C–4C BC including the Classical and Hellenistic phases; small sculptures from the times of Alexander the Great to the 1C BC;

Assyrian-Babylonian and Egyptian antiquities; Cypriot and Mycenaen vases; early Venetian ceramics and Etruscan *buccheri* (clay drinking vessels).

▶ *From the quayside, the view of the piazzetta is punctuated by the clock tower.*

Torre dell'Orologio (⑧, FX)

🕐 *Visit by guided tours only (book in advance). In English, Mon–Wed 10am, 11am, 1pm; Thu–Sun 2pm, 3pm.* ⬤€12.50 *Museums of St Mark's Square ticket (♿Palazzo Ducale)* ☎041 52 09 070, *or book online at www.vivaticket.it.*

Designed by Codussi, the clock tower was erected between 1496 and 1499, and constitutes the main entrance to the **Mercerie**, Venice's principal shopping street (♿*see RIALTO*).

The building's striking astronomical clock probably attracts less attention than the two Moors who sound the hour on a big bell at the top of the tower. Below it stands the lion passant of St Mark, set against a starry background. Below this tier comes a Virgin and Child before whom, on Ascension Day, appear mechanical figurines of the Three Kings. To the left, the Roman numerals tell the hour while the minutes are marked out at intervals of five to the right.

Torre dell'Orologio

One of the Moorish bellstrikers in action

A tour of the Renaissance Tower enables visitors to get a close view of the clock mechanism (😊 cover your ears if you are there on the hour!); it ends on terraces which afford a magnificent view of St. Mark's Square and the whole city.

Additional Sights

Piazzetta dei Leoncini (🖳, FX 126)

This small area tucked between the Basilica, the Palazzo Patriarcale and the side of the former Church of San Basso was designed by Longhena. Its name is derived from the red marble lions from Verona, sculpted by Giovanni Bonazza (1722).

▸ *Follow Calle della Canonica and cross the canal: the Diocesan Museum of Religious Art is on Fondamenta Sant'Apollonia on the right.*

Museo Diocesano di Arte Sacra (🖳, GX)

Call for hours and charges. ☎ 041 241 3817; www.veneziaupt.org.

Romanesque in style, the building was once part of the Benedictine Convent of Sant'Apollonia (12C–13C); its cloisters so inspired D'Annunzio that he described it in his work *Il Fuoco* (The Fire). Its arches have double-arched lintels supported along the longer sides by paired columns. The well-head in the centre is 13C. Fragments of Roman, Byzantine and Veneto-Byzantine (9C–11C) stonework line the walls.

Originally conceived by the Patriarch of Venice, **Albino Luciani** (1912–78), and Pope Giovanni Paolo, whose reign lasted just one month, the museum of religious art houses paintings and sculptures, sacred objects and congregational banners from deconsecrated churches. Its collection boasts works by artists such as Antonio Zanchi, Palma il Giovane and Jacopo Guarana.

The Moors of Venice

Although the two bronze moors have been striking the clock tower bell for half a millennium they have still only put a slight dent in it. An ancient superstition has it that stroking their exposed nether regions confers sexual potency. It is said that in the 19C a workman was knocked clean off the tower by one of the Moors hammers – whether he had "provoked" the Moors by touching them is not recorded!

RIALTO★★

(⬚, FU)

VAPORETTO: RIALTO, SAN MARCO

Situated in the heart of the commercial area, the Rialto Bridge crosses the Grand Canal and continues the long line of shops that snakes its way from St Mark's Square, along the Mercerie, as far as the side stalls and market in the **San Polo** district. Given the overwhelming hustle and bustle of the small workshops and local bars, it is easy to forget the long history of the Rialto, and the fact that it was once the seat of government in Venice.

▶ **Orient Yourself:** Signposts all over the city centre point visitors towards the Rialto and in summer, at least, there is a near continual procession of tourists making their way between the Rialto and St Mark's Square.

Don't Miss: Walking over the famous Rialto Bridge, with its colourful shops.

Organising Your Time: To follow the prescribed routes, allow about 3hrs, more time if you wish to do some shopping along the Mercerie.

Also See: La FENICE, PIAZZA SAN MARCO, SAN ZACCARIA, SAN ZANIPÒLO.

Rialto Bridge and the Mercerie

Ponte di Rialto★★ (⬚, FU)

Built c.1175, the first bridge over the Grand Canal was a significant factor in the commercial development of the area. The wooden bridge had to be replaced several times following its deliberate destruction during the uprisings led by Baiamonte Tiepolo, and twice more when it collapsed. Its design was ever more complicated by the requirements of the boatmen and the shopkeepers already established here.

Palladio proposed a cumbersome Roman-style design with three arches, but this was dismissed on the grounds that it might hinder canal traffic. Some 80 years later, this consideration became less of an issue as restrictions were imposed upon larger ships using the Grand Canal.

The new construction, designed by **Antonio da Ponte** (1512–97), was simplified to a single span, thereby ensuring ease of use by boats and barges as well as safeguarding a flow of water that prevented stagnation and maintained the delicate equilibrium of the lagoon.

© Cosmo Condina / Tips Images

Ponte di Rialto over Canal Grande at dusk

The present bridge consists of a single stone archway, 28m/92ft long and 7.5m/25ft high, which supports a central graduated alley lined with commercial units, flanked on either side by a narrower parallel passageway. Access from one aisle of shops to another is from either end of the bridge or via transverse arches in the middle. The whole complex is sheltered by a sloping roof. The Rialto was to remain the only means of crossing from one bank of the Grand Canal to the other until the mid-19C, when the Accademia Bridge and the Scalzi Bridge were built, and in 2008 the fourth bridge 'Calatrava' was erected.

Mercerie★

The large number of shops selling a variety of goods gives rise to the name of this historic commercial street. The *mercerie* (traditionally these were haberdashers selling cloth, ribbons and other merchandise, but the name is now a catch-all term) provide access between St Mark's and the Rialto. In the past, this was the route chosen by nobles intending to make a triumphal entry into the Piazza San Marco.

The Mercerie are as busy today as they were in the Middle Ages, and fall into three main sections, starting from the clock tower: **Merceria dell'Orologio** (4, FV 121), **Merceria di San Zulian** (4, FV 124) and **Merceria di San Salvador** (4, FV).

Note at Merceria dell'Orologio 149, a relief recording the event that spread panic among the rebels led by Baiamonte Tiepolo, who disbanded when a stone mortar was dropped on a standard-bearer.

San Zulian (4, FV)

Founded in the 9C but now cramped by adjacent buildings, the façade is nonetheless richly ornamented. Above the portal, Tommaso Rangone, the benefactor of the church, is portrayed by Sansovino. Note also the columns that frame the cartouches and the windows below the pediments. Under the main tympanum is a typically Venetian feature, a *serliana* consisting of a window with three openings, named after **Sebastiano Serlio**. The church was remodelled during the late Renaissance by Sansovino and Alessandro Vittoria.

The square internal space extends to a presbytery with two side chapels. The paintings by Palma il Giovane and Veronese are notable.

San Salvador (8, FV) –
♿ *See La FENICE.*

Walking Tours

There are three options from Campo San Bartolomeo (♿ *see La FENICE*): southwest towards the Accademia (♿ *see ACCADEMIA*), north towards the Strada Nuova or across the Rialto Bridge.

Towards Strada Nuova

This busy but attractive urban route between the Accademia and the Mercerie makes its way past all kinds of shops.

Fondaco dei Tedeschi (4, FU)
– ♿ *See La FENICE.*

San Giovanni Grisostomo (4, FU)

Shoehorned between the houses into a narrow passageway is the simple yet remarkable reddish façade of the **Church of St John Chrysostom**. Founded in 1080, the church was given its current appearance by **Mauro Codussi** and his son Domenico, who completed the project after his father's death. The compact and well-proportioned interior, dominated by a dome resting on four piers, is in the form of a Greek cross. In the first chapel on the right is a painting by **Giovanni Bellini**; the second chapel is dedicated to St Joseph, with an altarpiece by Johann Karl Loth. The presbytery is literally plastered with 17C scenes from the life of the church's patron saint, coupled with episodes from the life of Christ. The central section, by Sebastiano del Piombo, depicts the saints John Chrysostom, Paul, John the Baptist, Liberale, Mary Magdelene, Cecilia and Catherine. In the left transept, the marble *Coronation of the Virgin* is by Tullio Lombardo.

Not Just Pedestrian Traffic

In the Middle Ages, the main means of transport in Venice was on horseback; movement through the streets became impossible given the number of horses. In 1291, it was decreed that horsemen should dismount their charges in Campo San Salvador before continuing on foot and that, in any event, horses should not be allowed into the Piazza. Instead, they had to be left by the clock tower, where (as hard as it might be to imagine) stood a copse of elder.

▶ *Continue straight on to the large but crowded Campo Santi Apostoli.*

Campo Santi Apostoli (🅰, FT)

This square is the start of the Strada Nuova, and as such it serves as a busy thoroughfare, with shops and bars in almost all the nearby *calli*.

Only one side of the rectangular **Church of All Saints** (*dei Santi Apostoli*), rebuilt in the 16C and restored in the 18C, opens onto the square. Its tall campanile is detached from the church.

Inside, the 15C **Corner Chapel**, attributed to Codussi, contains the *Communion of St Lucy* by Tiepolo. On the left wall of the presbytery is a depiction drafted by Veronese (1528–88) and executed by Heredes Pauli; in the chapel on the right are a series of early-14C Byzantine-style frescoes.

On the far side of the canal stands the 13C **Palazzo Falier** (🅰, FTU), named after its most eminent resident, **Doge Marino Falier**. At ground level, the portico shelters shops and restaurants; the two superior levels are decorated with pateras and arcaded windows.

Beyond the Rialto Bridge

San Giacomo di Rialto (🅰, FU)

Partially hidden by the stalls and the market in Campo San Giacomo di Rialto, this church is best viewed when approaching the Rialto from the San Polo *sestiere*.

San Giacomo di Rialto is considered to be the oldest church in Venice: according to one document (albeit of dubious authenticity) the city was born on 25 March 421 when three consuls arrived from Padua to establish a commercial seat at the Rialto. This church was built to celebrate the event. Its present appearance dates from the 11C, when it was rebuilt to accommodate local residents drawn to the market in the square. The façade boasts some striking features, namely the clock (despite being a 1938 reproduction), the campanile, which houses the clock and the bells, and the 14C portico.

The interior is planned as a Greek cross. Its original Greek marble columns survive, complete with 11C Veneto-Byzantine capitals carved with organic decoration. On the left is an altar by Scamozzi and bronzes by Gerolamo Campagna, who was responsible for the altar in the famous lagoon Church of San Giorgio Maggiore. On the right is an *Annunciation* by Marco Vecellio (a cousin of Titian). The main altar is by Alessandro Vittoria.

The **Banco Giro**, Venice's first public bank, was founded in 1619, just off the

Daily business in the Rialto market

© N Bosques / MICHELIN

square. The building is now occupied by the Bancogiro restaurant.

In addition to being home to banks and the magistrature, the Rialto has always been a commercial area, as the names of the *fondamenta*, *campi* and *calli* , such as *olio* (oil), *pesce* (fish), *vino* (wine), *spezie* (spices), *polli* (chicken), *beccarie* (meat) and (*luganegher*) sausage, testify to this day.

▶ *Farther along the canal, stretching down as far as the Pescaria, are the Fabbriche Vecchie and Fabbriche Nuove, a group of buildings, simple and functional in structure, that once served as commercial offices.*

Fabbriche Vecchie (🖪, FU)

This building, set back from the Fabbriche Nuove, was designed by Scarpagnino, as was much of the surrounding area, which was destroyed by fire in 1514. The ground floor is rusticated, broken by an open colonnade; the upper floors, punctuated by simple windows, seem lightweight and less imposing.

Fabbriche Nuove (🖪, FU)

These premises, directly overlooking the bend of the Grand Canal, were designed by Sansovino. As the rusticated ground floor is interrupted by its portico, so the upper storeys are articulated by windows framed with pilasters and surmounted with pediments.

▶ *After crossing the bridge, turn immediately left into Ruga Vecchia S. Giovanni. Continue for a few metres to the Church of San Giovanni Elemosinario, partially hidden behind railings on the left.*

San Giovanni Elemosinario (🖪, EFU)

🕐*Open Mon–Sat 10am–5pm.* 🕐*Closed 1 Jan, Easter, 15 Aug, 25 Dec.* 👁️*€3.* ☎️*041 27 50 462. www.chorusvenezia.org.*

The origins of this ancient church, built in the shape of a Greek cross, date back to 1071, although the original building was destroyed by fire in 1514. The church was rebuilt, possibly by Lo Scarpagnino, and completed in 1531. It now houses works by Jacopo Palma il Giovane and Il Pordenone (c.1484–1539) – also responsible for the frescoes in the dome, – as well as an altarpiece by Titian on the high altar.

Campo della Pescaria (🖪, EFU)

Under the porticoes of an impressive building (in fact it is of modern construction, dating from 1907) the Rialto's famous fish market takes place daily (except Sundays and holidays).

A vivacious atmosphere generally pervades the **Campo delle Beccarie** (🖪, **EU**) which, at one time, housed the public abattoir, and now shelters a traditional Venetian *bacaro* (wine bar) and various market stalls.

▶ *Follow the crowd streaming their way from the Rialto to Campo San Cassiano nearby – the route is almost unavoidable: left along Calli dei Botteri to the other side of the canal, then right into Calle Corpus Domini Christi.*

San Cassiano (🖪, EU)

Although the origins of this church are rooted in the 9C, it has been subjected to attempts at restoration and its present appearance is largely the result of

---

The Hunchback

Opposite San Giacomo di Rialto is the 16C **"gobbo di Rialto,"** a hunchback stooped beneath his burden. From here government decrees were proclaimed. This was also the finishing point for a punishment for minor crimes whereby the guilty party would be forced to run naked the gauntlet of citizens lining the streets from here to Piazza San Marco.

The gobbo di Rialto lending an ear to a cat

© A Zane / MICHELIN

17C remodelling. The overall impression of the interior can be overbearing: the three aisles are separated by columns hung with red and grey damask drapes. The right chapel off the apse houses three works by Leandro Bassano and one by Palma il Giovane. In the presbytery are three works by Tintoretto.

▷ *Cross the canal and follow Calle della Regina off to the right.*

Ca' Corner della Regina (◪, ET)

It was here, in the house of her brother, that **Caterina Cornaro**, Queen of Cyprus, resided after her fall from grace. The *palazzo* was then fashioned in the Gothic style. The present building, dating from the 18C, is decorated with frescoes, in the style of Tiepolo, that recount the unhappy events of her life.

▷ *Return to Calle della Regina and turn right into Campo Santa Maria Materdomini.*

Santa Maria Materdomini (◪, ET)

With its distinctive five-arched window, the church is set slightly back from the square and the 14C–15C Palazzo Zane. Influenced by the Tuscan style, it is an expression of Renaissance design: the simple Istrian stone façade, hemmed in between the houses, has been attributed to Sansovino, although the overall project may owe more to **Pietro Lombardo** and **Codussi**.

The ordered, simple marble-faced interior comprises three aisles and a domed apse. The most striking paintings are the large-scale dramatic renderings by **Tintoretto** in the left transept and a *Last Supper (opposite)* attributed to Bonifacio de' Pitati. The exquisite altarpiece in the second bay on the right is also worthy of note. Painted by **Vincenzo Catena,** a close associate of Giorgione and Bellini, the scene shows *St Christina of Bolsena* emerging from Lake Bolsena on the millstone that was meant to have drowned her. The fine terracotta *Madonna* by the main altar is 15C by Nicolò di Pietro Paradisi. The more subtle early-16C marble altarpieces (*right of the entrance and left of the main altar*) are carved by Lorenzo

Capitals in the Rialto inspired by the sea

Bregna. In the presbytery is a delicate relief by the Lombardo brothers.

▷ *Proceed towards the Grand Canal to Ca' Pesaro and the International Gallery of Modern Art.*

Ca' Pesaro★ (◪, ET)

This *palazzo* was commissioned by the Pesaro family. Initiated by Longhena, it was completed by Francesco Antonio Gaspari and now houses an important collection of oriental art and a museum of modern art (*see II CANAL GRANDE*).

Museo d'Arte Orientale

♿ ⊙*Open year-round Tue–Sun 10am–6pm (Nov–Mar 5pm). Last admission 1hr before closing.* ⊙*Closed 1 Jan, 1 May, 25 Dec.* ⊞€8.50; 3 ticket includes entrance to Galleria Internazionale di Arte

Ponte delle Tette and Fondamenta delle Tette

Venetian toponymy is full of surprises. In this case, the focus is on an area located between Campo San Cassiano and Campo San Polo, where in the 16C, Venetian prostitutes would hang out of the window, baring their *tette* – slang for breasts. Surprisingly, this kind of display was not only accepted by the religious authorities but positively encouraged, as they saw the practice as a way of reducing the risk of homosexuality, so prevalent among sailors!

Moderna). ☎*041 52 41 173. http://cape saro.visitmuve.it.*

The Museum of Oriental Art is housed on the upper floor of the *palazzo* and contains Japanese armour from the Edo Period (1615–1868), swords, lacquerwork, puppets, musical instruments and Chinese porcelain.

Galleria Internazionale di Arte Moderna

🕐*Open year-round Tue–Sun 10am–6pm; (Nov–Easter 5pm); last admission 1hr before closing.* 🕐*Closed 1 Jan, 1 May, 25 Dec.* ◌*same as Museo d'Arte Orientale (* 🕯*above).* ☎*041 72 11 27. http:// capesaro.visitmuve.it.*

This gallery hosts important modern art from the end of the 19C onwards, notably from the Futurist movement. On display are works by **Klinger** (1857–1920), **Chagall** (1877–1985), **Klimt** (1862–1918), **Bonnard** (1867–1947), **Matisse** (1869–1954), **Kandinsky** (1866–1944), **Klee** (1879–1940), Tan-

guy (1900–55), **Henry Moore** (1898–1986), **Miró** (1893–1983), **Ernst** (1891–1976), Boccioni (1882–1916), Rosso (1858–1928), De Pisis (1896–1956), **Morandi** (1890–1964), **De Chirico** (1888–1978), Casorati (1883–1963), **Carrà** (1881–1966), **Sironi** (1885–1961) and **Pizzinato** (1910–).

There is also a permanent exhibition featuring works by Guglielmo Ciardi (1842–1917), who perpetuated the Venetian landscape tradition. Works from the latter half of the 19C include Venetian pieces by Luigi Nono (1850–1918), Alessandro Milesi (1856–1945) and Giacomo Favretto (1849–87).

Museo di Palazzo Mocenigo (🏛, ET)

🕐*Open year-round Tue–Sun 10am–5pm (Nov–Mar 4pm).* 🕐*Closed 1 Jan, 1 May, 25 Dec.* ◌*€4 (more during temp exhibits).* ☎*041 72 17 98. http://mocenigo. visitmuve.it.*

The Palazzo Mocenigo was the residence from the 17C onwards of the San Stae branch of the Mocenigo family, one of the most important families of the Venetian patriciate, seven members of which became doges between 1414 and 1778. Their portraits hang in the entrance. It is a large building of gothic origin extensively rebuilt at the beginning of the 17C, when it attained its present appearance.

This museum provides an idea of Venetian life among the noble classes in the 17C and 18C. Today the interiors are used to display fabrics and costumes belonging to the **Centro Studi di Storia del Tessuto e del Costume**, a foundation dedicated to the study and conservation of fabrics and costumes. On show are a range of woven materials and textiles dating back as far as the early days of the Republic.

© Ca' Pesaro - Galleria Internazionale d'Arte Moderna / Fondazione Musei Civici di Venezia

Detail of Giuditta II (Salomé), (1909) by Gustav Klimt

LA SALUTE ★★

(8, FX)

VAPORETTTO: SALUTE, ACCADEMIA

Despite the hordes of tourists visiting the landmark church of Santa Maria della Salute and the famous Guggenheim Collection of modern art, this corner of the **Dorsoduro** district is otherwise very peaceful. It is mostly residential, with not many shops, cafes and wine bars (to be found in the adjacent San Trovaso and San Barnaba districts). Foreign artists' workshops and the nearby Anglican Church, along with the numerous American and British tourists, give these streets an Anglo-American flavour; some of the street directions are even given in English.

▸ **Orient Yourself:** Edging the south side of the Grand Canal and extending eastward towards St Mark's Basin, the Salute area faces the portion of the San Marco *sestiere* centred on the Gritti Palace. To the south, it encompasses the Zattere, the long walkway that borders the Guidecca Canal.
⊘ **Don't Miss:** Sitting on the broad steps of La Salute for a moment, to take in the sights and sounds of the Grand Canal, as well as strolling along the Zattere.
◷ **Organising Your Time:** Allow about 3hrs for the walking tour, plus another hour for the Guggenheim Collection.
⌕ **Also See:** ACCADEMIA.

Walking Tour

Santa Maria della Salute ★★ (8, FX)

◷ *Open daily 9am–noon and 3–5:30pm.* ☎ *041 24 11 018. www.seminario venezia.it.*

The Basilica of Santa Maria della Salute is one of the most important and obvious points of reference on the skyline of Venice. It is also very dear to the Venetians: in 1630, when their city was racked by plague, they pledged a solemn vow to erect a church should the epidemic subside. Their prayers were answered and, in 1631, **Baldassare Longhena**, the pre-eminent Venetian Baroque architect of the day, was commissioned to develop the project.

This impressive basilica is rendered all the more majestic by its magnificent flight of steps up to the entrance. Dominated by the towering central dome, the great round volume emerges from an

Santa Maria della Salute

© imagebroker / hemis.fr

The Feast of the Madonna della Salute

Venice has been celebrating the end of the plague of 1630 for over 370 years. On 21 November, a bridge is made of boats stretching across the canal to La Salute to allow devotees and pilgrims to reach the basilica with ease. Celebrations for the Feast of the Madonna of La Salute – which have a certain parochial air about them – last all day. Venetians remember the day with the lighting of a candle.

octagonal base: a geometric shape that radiates to eight façades presided over by a figure flanked by two angels over each pediment. Like Palladio before him, Longhena uses Classical architectural forms to build bold outlines and articulate every subsidiary part of his design: he employs figurative sculpture to punctuate profiles, to relieve flat planes and to reiterate the human dimension. The proliferation of statues at every level is a reminder that Longhena was born into a family of stonecarvers. Akin to a freestanding sculpture, the church occupies a prominent position from every viewing angle.

At the apex is a figure of the Madonna clutching the baton of the *Capitano da Mar* (Captain-General of the Sea), poised above the balustraded lantern. Note also the figure of the patron presiding over the main pediment of the façade.

On the smaller dome stands St Mark, flanked by the weathervanes of the two *campanili* beyond, marking the far end of the church. At the drum level, great concentric volutes, also known as *orecchioni* (big ears), link the lower level of the outer section with the dome.

The interior is dictated by the main cupola, with the central area opening out into six chapels. The polychrome marble floor converges on a central circle of five roses which, together with the other roses of the wider circle, suggest the idea of a rosary. The central inscription in Latin states that it is from here that the health (*salute*) and salvation accorded to Venice emanates: tradition has it that the city was born on the Feast of the Annunciation (25 March 421) to signify the protection accorded to Venice by the Virgin.

On the left side, the last bay before the high altar is ornamented with the *Descent of the Holy Spirit,* painted by **Titian** (1490–1576) in 1555.

At the high altar is a 12C icon, the *Madonna della Salute*, also referred to as *Mesopanditissa* because it came from a place of the same name in Candia (Crete). The sculptural group above (1670–74) represents Venice, liberated from the plague, at the Virgin's feet: it is the work of the Flemish artist Juste Le Court (1627–79). The Plague is depicted, being chased away by the angel.

The sacristy boasts a wealth of treasures, the most eye-catching being the *Wedding at Cana* by **Tintoretto** (1518–94), in which the artist has included himself (as the first Apostle on the left), his friends and their wives.

The various depictions of the *Madonna in Prayer* are by **Sassoferrato**.

On leaving the sacristy, in the corridor before the chapels (*right*), are three notable altarpieces by **Luca Giordano**.

▶ *Walk east along Fondamenta Dogana.*

La Dogana (⑧, FX)

Dating to the 15C, the Dogana da Mar originally served as the customs point for goods arriving by sea. Fashioned to resemble a ship's hull, the building's present appearance dates from the 17C. A statue of *Fortune* towers over a golden globe, representing the world, supported by two Atlantes.

Punta della Dogana

🕐*Open year-round Wed–Mon 10am–7pm.* 🕐*Closed Tue, 24-25 Dec.* 💳*€15 (€20 inc Palazzo Grassi).* ☎*041 27 19 039. http://www.palazzograssi.it.* Opened in 2009, this museum houses contemporary art from the François Pinault Collection. Dogana Café serves breakfast, snacks, and drinks.

▶ *Walk around the Dogana and then turn southwest, along the Giudecca Canal.*

Le Zattere★ (**7**, **8**, CFXY)

A walk along these *fondamente* provides exactly the kind of thrilling view that might be expected from a long balcony with a perfect prospect over the Giudecca Canal to the island of Giudecca itself on the other side.

The name Zattere was coined from the transportation of wood on rafts or *zattere* along here in the 17C.

The buildings evoke a past that involved both hard physical work and profound religious faith: the former **Magazzini del Sale**, a 14C warehouse used to store salt (*sale*) produced in Venice; the former Convent and **Church of the Spirito Santo**, from where the bridge of boats stretched across the water for the Feast of the Redentore; the **Ospedale degli Incurabili** (Hospital for Incurables), which later served as a home for abandoned children and as a musical conservatory.

The route is dotted with cafes which, in spring and summer, set tables outside on wooden platforms over the water.

▶ *To the right of Spirito Santo, take Calle della Scuola and walk straight*

on to the Palazzo Dario (♿see Il CANAL GRANDE). At its entrance, turn left towards the Guggenheim Collection.

Collezione Peggy Guggenheim★★ (**8**, EX)

♿ 🕐 *Open year-round Wed–Mon 10am–6pm.* 🕐*Closed 25 Dec.* 🎫€14. ☎ 041 24 05 411. www.guggenheim-venice.it.

The Peggy Guggenheim Collection is housed in the incomplete **Palazzo Venier dei Leoni** (1749), which was designed by Lorenzo Boschetti, the architect of the Church of St Barnabas (♿see Il CANAL GRANDE). The entrance is through a peaceful garden, in whose surrounding wall are two stones that mark the final resting places of the owner and her beloved dogs. Peggy was the niece of American industrialist, Solomon R Guggenheim, who instigated the museum of the same name in the famous spiral building by Frank Lloyd Wright in New York. She began assembling her Venice collection in 1938, acquired the *palazzo* after the Second World War and lived there adding to it until her death in 1979, when, according to her express wishes, both the *palazzo* and the collection it housed were

---

Peggy Guggenheim (1898–1979)

Born in New York, educated in Paris, worked in London and died in Venice: this colourful personality has done much to popularise modern art. In 1939 she decided to open a museum for contemporary art in London, but during the period leading up to the Second World War, when she resolved to "buy a picture a day," it became obvious that it was safer to return home. In October 1942, when she opened her gallery "Art of This Century" in New York with a collection of Cubist, Abstract and Surrealist art, she wrote "I wore one of my Tanguy earrings and one made by Calder, in order to show my impartiality between Surrealist and Abstract art." She was briefly married to Max Ernst, the Dadaist and Surrealist.

© The Solomon R. Guggenheim Foundation, Photo Archivio CameraphotoEpoche, Gift of Cassa di Risparmio di Venezia, 2005

Peggy Guggenheim with the earrings designed for her by Alexander Calder

Surrealism

The *First Surrealist Manifesto* was published in Paris in 1924 by André Breton, promoting ideas drawn from the latest psycho-analytical theories on the unconscious and subconscious. The manifesto challenged the traditional views on art and life and encouraged artistic expression inspired by dreams, drug-induced hallucinations and other suspended states of mind. Breton defined the essence of Surrealism as "pure psychic automatism, by which it is intended to express verbally, in writing, or in any other way, the true process of thought. It is the dictation of thought, free from the excise of reason, and every aesthetic or moral preoccupation."

Pictorially, Surrealism emerged from various movements: Cubism (refracted form), Futurism (movement and automation) and Dada (humour and absurdity), pioneered by Picasso, Ernst, Klee, Dali, Mirò, Magritte and others.

handed over to the Solomon Guggenheim Foundation.

The museum is arranged thematically, displaying parallel collections of Abstract and Surrealist works by the same artists.

Particularly strong in Surrealist art , the gallery contains works by **Braque** (1882–1963); **Picasso** (1881–1973); Mondrian (1872–1944); Boccioni (1882–1916); **Brancusi** (1876–1957); **Kandinsky** (1866–1944); **Chagall** (1887–1985) – including *The Rain*; Balla (1871–1958) – including *Abstract Speed+Noise*; Severini (1883–1966) – including *Sea = Ballerina*; **Mirò** (1893–1983); De Chirico (1888–1978) – including *The Red Tower*; **Max Ernst** (1891–1976); Klee (1879–1940); Magritte (1898–1967) – including *Empire of Light*; Dali (1904–89); **Pollock** (1912–

56); **Calder** (1898–1976) – including *Mobile*; Vasarely (1908–90) and **Moore** (1898–1986). Look out for the 23 sculptures designed by Picasso and executed by Egidio Costantini (1964), positioned in the window to maximize their transparency against the dark water of the Grand Canal beyond.

The Guggenheim also holds the **Mattioli Collection**, which includes 26 masterpieces by the Futurist painters Carrà (1881–1966) – including *La Galleria di Milano*; Severini – including *Ballerina in Blu*; Boccioni; and other important masters such as Morandi (1890–1964); Sironi (1885–1961); and Modigliani (1884–1920).

Outside, *The Angel of the City,* a sculpture by Marino Marini (1901–80), stands guard over the Grand Canal.

Collezione Peggy Guggenheim

SANT'ELENA E SAN PIETRO★

(▦, KLXY)

VAPORETTO: S. ELENA, GIARDINI BIENNALE

The Sant'Elena and San Pietro districts of the Castello *sestiere* are both peaceful and yet often vibrant too, as their green spaces – a novelty in Venice – attract crowds of locals. The view from the public gardens and the Park of Remembrance over the lagoon and St Mark's Basin is magnificent. Movement and activity pervade the area around the Rio di Santa Anna with its floating market, and extend to the bustling commercial activities of the only street (*via*) in Venice, to be named as such, Via Garibaldi.

▶ **Orient Yourself:** In the Castello Gardens stand the Biennale pavilions. This area is the extremity of the Castello *sestiere,* separated from the rest of the lagoon by the green space of the Park of Remembrance. Sant'Elena is quiet and, unusually for Venice, devoid of canals. The small island of San Pietro lies just north.

🌀 **Don't Miss:** Viale Garibaldi, a long pathway through a tree-shaded expanse lined with charming homes.

🕐 **Organising Your Time:** Allow 3hrs for a leisurely visit.

Kids Especially for Kids: The playground within the leafy grounds near the public garden.

🍴 **Also See:** Neighbouring sights: ARSENALE.

Isola de Sant'Elena (▦, KLXY)

Up until the 11C, the island was known as *cavana* (refuge), as it provided sheltered anchorages to boatmen and fishermen. Its present name is derived from St Helen (c.257–336), mother of the Emperor Constantine, whose relics are housed in the church (first chapel on the right) and were brought to Venice in 1211, after the Fourth Crusade.

The small monastery, established in 1060, was built by Benedictine monks from Tuscany in 1407. Subsequent rebuilding was undertaken between 1439 and 1515.

As happened to other religious institutions during Napoleon's rule, the monastery was disbanded and its assets sold and dispersed; the church was used as a warehouse and troops were billeted in the convent buildings. During the late-19C and early 20C, the area around the church and monastery was extended and urbanised. Today, the church and convent accommodate Servite monks. This quarter is one of the cheapest parts of the city to dine out; places for a pizza

or a particularly inexpensive *menu a prezzo fisso* (set price meal) proliferate.

Church (▦, LY)

On the far side of the Rio di S. Elena rises the Church of Sant'Elena, flanked by a stadium and military base. The Gothic façade is dominated by its portal (1467). The sculptural group above, by Antonio Rizzo, shows the Capitano da Mar (Sea Captain-General), **Vittore Cappello**, kneeling before St Helen. Through the gate to the left extend the cloisters. Erected in 1956, the campanile does not conform with the essentially Gothic structure of the church.

Inside the luminous interior, a single nave terminates in an apse pierced with tall windows. The chapels radiate off the apse on the right.

Parco delle Rimembranze (▦, KY)   Kids

This Park of Remembrance is dedicated to the memory of soldiers who lost their lives in World War II. Children's play areas, plenty of green space and a skating rink make it a popular place for families on a sunny day.

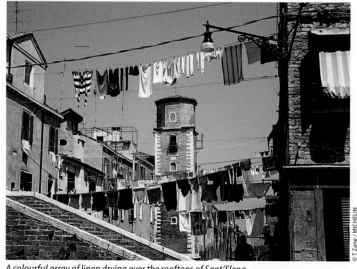

A colourful array of linen drying over the rooftops of Sant'Elena

Biennale (⬛, KY)

The 100-year plus history of this international exhibition of contemporary art (Esposizione Internazionale d'Arte della Citta di Venezia) is long and controversial. Even at its beginnings in 1895, it caused an outcry by exhibiting a painting called *Il Supremo Convegno* by **Giacomo Grosso**; It was described as "A casket with a cadaveric face coming out, while five naked young women surrounded him in despairing and lusty posing". Over a century later, at almost every Blennale, the same charges have been levelled over and over again. In fact it is often said that the Biennale thrives on conflict and controversy and its position in the eye of the storm ensures a restlessness that guarantees its vitality. No doubt it would be deemed a failure if it had not insulted or outraged a particular party for that year!

The exhibition has always been held in the Giardini Publicci, where the pavilions of the various countries which elect to exhibit here have been erected.

It is held every odd-numbered year between June and November. For more information visit www.labiennale.org.

Chiesa San Giuseppe (⬛, JX)

Beyond Viale Trento in a little square is the 16C church of San Giuseppe. In the first bay on the right is *St Michael and*

Lucifer Fighting over the Soul of Michele Bon by Jacopo (1518–94) and Domenico (c.1560–1635) Tintoretto.

▶ *Cross the bridge just left of the square and follow Calle Correra to Fondamenta Sant'Anna. Turn right, cross the bridge on the left, and continue straight up Calle Larga San Pietro to the Church of San Pietro di Castello.*

Isola di San Pietro di Castello (⬛, KX)

This island was inhabited before the city of Venice was founded. Originally known as **Olivolo**, perhaps after its olive groves, the *sestiere* commemorates a castle (hence the name Castello) that was either built or found there by the earliest Venetians. Since time immemorial, it has been the religious symbol of the city. Not only the seat of Bishop Castellano, and a dependent of the Patriarch of Grado, it still shelters the body of the first Patriarch of Venice, Lorenzo Giustiniani, who resided there in the 15C. The basilica stands in an open, grassy area, the venue for lively celebrations during the Feast of San Pietro di Castello.

Venetian Football

From September to June, Sant'Elena's stadium, Stadio Penza, comes alive on weekends with afternoon Italian-league soccer. Attendance is an opportunity for visitors to imbibe some local colour, as avid supporters stream onto the grounds and root for their team, Unione Venezia. Tickets can be purchased at the gate on game day (*games are at 2.30 or 3pm: prices begin at €10. ☎041 23 80 711; www. fbcunionevenezia.com*). The team plays in Series E.

San Pietro di Castello★ (🔢, KX)

🕐*Open Mon–Sat 10am–5pm.* 🕐*Closed 1 Jan, Easter, 15 Aug, 25 Dec.* ⬤*€3.* ☎*041 27 50 462. www.chorusveneiza.org.*

Despite the fact that its fame has always been usurped by St Mark's, the Church of St Peter at Castello was regarded as the official cathedral of Venice until 1807, when St Mark's was merely considered to be the doge's chapel. It was erected in the 8C on the foundations of a church that dates to 650. The façade conforms to Palladian design. On the right is the former late-16C Patriarchal Palace. The nearby campanile, which leans to one side, was rebuilt by Mauro Codussi (c.1440–1504).

The 17C interior comprises a Latin cross with three aisles and a large dome. Above the main portal are represented *The Feast of the Jewish Passover* by Malombra and Vassillachi (16C–17C) (*right*) and *The Feast in the House of Simon* by Jacopo Beltrame (16C) (*left*).

In the left aisle note the painting on canvas by **Veronese** (1528–88) and in the left transept in the Gothic **Lando Chapel**, the mosaic altarpiece based on a cartoon attributed to Tintoretto. The antependium (altar front) comprises a 9C Veneto-Byzantine marble transenna (openwork screen) inlaid at the base with 2C mosaic. The **Vendramin Chapel** alongside is by Longhena: the *Madonna and Child with the Damned* is by Luca Giordano (1634–1705).

Returning down the right side, the marble seat known as **St Peter's Cathedra** is from Antioch: note the unusual back adapted from an Arab-Muslim funerary stele, decorated with inscriptions from the Koran in Cufic script.

Inside San Pietro di Castello

SAN GIORGIO MAGGIORE★★

(▣, GHXY)

VAPORETTO: S. GIORGIO

The island of San Giorgio Maggiore is not only thoroughly Venetian but provides first-rate views over the city. It does not detain visitors for long however as there are no bars nor restaurants here. For this reason alone, it is a "must" for anyone searching for a unique view of Venice and for those attracted to the serenity of monastic life, albeit only for an hour or so. It is also a must for Palladio fans.

▶ **Orient Yourself:** Sitting in St. Mark's Basin near the entrance to the Guidecca Canal and facing Piazza San Marco, this small island is prime real estate in terms of exposure: its glorious church of the same name is generally the first head-turner for travellers arriving in the city by water.

🐸 **Don't Miss:** The best possible view of Venice, from the church's bell-tower.

🐸 **Good to know:** Take a bottle of water as there are no refreshment facilities. Accommodation is available in the monastery, call ☎041 52 27 827.

🕐 **Organising Your Time:** The proposed tour takes about 2hrs.

🕯 **Also See:** Neighbouring sights: La GIUDECCA.

A Bit of History

The island's name relates to a church erected here in 790; the term *maggiore* is used to distinguish it from another island, San Giorgio in Alga. Since 982, the year a Benedictine monastery was founded here, the island's history has been associated with this monastic order. It became especially favoured by doges, who on 26 December would come and attend Mass in celebration of the Feast of St Stephen. However the island's moment of glory came with the arrival of **Andrea Palladio**, commissioned to redesign the church, which had already been rebuilt between 1400 and 1500.

The island's decline, coinciding with that of the Republic of Venice, was protracted into the 1850s. After both Napoleon and the Austrians had defiled the artistic beauty of the island, its finest buildings continued to be devastated by various armies passing through, including the Italian army using the dormitory as military stores during the Second World War.

The restoration of the island to its former beauty is largely due to the Cini Foundation and to the Benedictines, who, for more than 1 000 years, have faithfully

San Giorgio Maggiore

© Ivan Vdovin/age fotostock

preserved the original liturgical tradition and Gregorian chants of San Giorgio, assisted by the Salesians, who are active in all fields of education and guidance. No one lives on the Island of San Giorgio besides these dedicated people. It is a place of retreat, of profound learning and deepest religious faith. Other than the monastery, there is nowhere to stay, nor anywhere to eat nor drink.

Walking Tour

San Giorgio Maggiore★ (🗺, GY)

🕑*Open May–Sept 9.30am–12.30pm and 2.30pm–6.30pm (5pm rest of the year and Sun; Sun morning open 8.30am–11am, 11am Mass in Gregorian Chant).* ☞*church free, campanile €5.* ☎*041 52 27 827.*

The rebuilding of the church, to designs by Palladio, began in 1566. The front is dominated by a great triangular pediment supported by four columns: a feature borrowed from a Classical temple. The bright interior enhances the ample Latin cross space enclosed within its vaulted ceiling and apsed transepts. In the third chapel, *The Martyrdom of SS Cosmas and Damian* was painted by **Jacopo Tintoretto**, who also did the two large paintings in the presbytery. The main altar is ornamented with late-16C sculptures by Gerolamo and Giuseppe Campagna. The door to the right leads into the chapel (*open for Sunday services only*) decorated with Tintoretto's last work, his *Deposition from the Cross*. The doorway in the left wall provides access to the **campanile**, given its present form by Scalfarotto in 1726. It offers the classic **view**★★★ over Venice.

Fondazione Giorgio Cini (🗺, GY)

Housed in a beautifully restored Benedictine monastery, this private institution is responsible for restoration work undertaken on many of Venice's monuments. It also stages important international conventions.

The foundation was founded by **Vittorio Cini** (1885–1977), a man who showed great courage and philanthropy during his life as a financier and government minister.

Library★

The entrance to the library is off the first cloisters and up the main staircase on the right. ♿☞ *Guided tour (1hr) Sat–Sun 10am–4.30pm.* ☞*€12.* ☎*041 52 89 900; www.cini.it.*

The library (1641–53) was designed by Longhena. It is decked with shelving and ornamented with carved wooden figures: the ceiling was decorated in the 17C Mannerist style.

Antique furnishing and objets d'art on the first piano nobile recreate the building's original character. Alongside thirty paintings of the Tuscan school are some fine pieces of applied arts: ceramics, porcelain (including a complete 275-piece 18C set by Cozzi), ivory caskets and badges, enamels, gold-work, candlesticks and chandeliers made in Murano, terracotta sculptures and furniture, including dressers, chests, bookcases, a rare Sienese marriage-chest of the mid-14th-century and an 18th-century Neapolitan sedan-chair.

Cloisters

This ancient monastery has two cloisters. The first, the **Chiostro dei Cipressi** (Cypress chloister) was designed by Palladio with paired columns and windows below curved and triangular pediments. This leads into the **Teatro Verde**, an open-air theatre with marble seats used during the summer. The second cloisters, which are older, were originally known as the **Chiostro degli Allori** (Laurel Chloister). Palladio worked with Veronese on the **Refectory** (*Refettorio*). For the end wall, Veronese painted a *Wedding at Cana,* a panel Napoleon had sent back to Paris, and which now hangs in the Louvre. Its replacement, representing *The Marriage of the Virgin,* is from the school of Tintoretto.

Dormitorio

The dormitory building is impressive for its sheer size (128m/420ft long) and lightness. Known as the *manica lunga,* meaning the long sleeve, it was conceived by Giovanni Buora at the end of the 15C. There are fine views from here towards the Riva degli Schiavoni.

On the outside is a 16C relief depicting *St George and the Dragon.*

SAN GIORGIO DEGLI SCHIAVONI★★★

(🅗, HV)

VAPORETTO: S. ZACCARIA, RIVA DEGLI SCHIAVONI

Tucked away behind the bustling Riva degli Schiavoni waterfront, this quiet atmospheric part of the Castello *sestiere* is a good contrast to the frenetic activity of St Mark's Square, just a few minutes walk away. The name Schiavoni means both Slavs from Schiavonia (equivalent to today's Dalmatia) and also slaves, a reminder of the darker historic aspects of the Republic.

▶ **Orient Yourself:** This is the heart of the Castello district and lies east of St Mark's square. It is bisected by the wide Rio di San Agostini.

☺ **Don't Miss:** Carpaccio's series of *St. George* paintings in the Scuola.

🕐 **Organising Your Time:** Allow 2hr 30min to visit the sights.

Ⓒ **Also See:** ARSENALE, SAN ZACCARIA.

Scuola di San Giorgio degli Schiavoni★★★

The original 15C buildings were remodelled by Giovanni de Zan in 1551, but the layout of the interior was retained. The *scuola* was founded by the Confraternity of the Schiavoni who, for the most part, traded with the Levant from here. Their patron saints were the three protectors of their homeland, St George, St Tryphon and St Jerome. In 1502 **Vittore Carpaccio** started working on his cycle of paintings, intended for the upper hall.

The Legend of St George

Little is known about this early martyr's life, though his cult became particularly important in the 6C. The legend of St George Slaying the Dragon seems to emerge late in the 12C, when it was popularised in the **Golden Legend**: a story possibly founded on the myth of Perseus killing the sea monster at Arsuf or Joppa. Today both the Eastern Orthodox and Western churches venerate the saint as a soldier, a tradition that originated in Palestine and was embraced by the crusaders.

The saint's slaying of the dragon and saving the virtuous princess are symbolic parables about the Church being saved from the devil.

The *Cycle of St George*★★★ took the artist five years to complete. It was moved downstairs in the 16C, to the intimate well-lit ground-floor gallery, which with its fine wooden ceiling, provided an ideal location to best show off the paintings' warm colours.

Interior

♿🕐*Open year-round Mon 2.45–6pm, Tue–Sun 9.15am–1pm and 2.45–6pm (Closed afternoon Sun and hols).* ⊚€5. ☎041 52 28 828.

☺ *It is best to read the panels from the left wall even if this does not follow the chronological order of execution. (In fact Carpaccio started painting episodes from the Life of St Jerome).*

St George and the Dragon catches the very moment when the knight attacks the dragon: the event is narrated pictorially with all the romance of heroic chivalry. The noble bearing of the saint and his steed, the dignified composure of the emotional princess and the architectural precision of the composition are true to the idealised legend, but contrast sharply with the macabre portrayal of skulls and hideously mutilated bodies.

The Triumph of St George dramatically depicts the saint on the point of killing the wounded dragon: the exotic figures are set against a background of Renaissance architecture, although the centrally planned temple is not positioned in the actual centre as this would have

St Augustine in his Study by Carpaccio (Scuola di San Giorgio degli Schiavoni)

© SCALA

disturbed the harmony of the composition.

In the next scene, *St George Baptising the Heathen King and Queen*, the group of musicians previously seen are present again as witnesses to the solemnity of the occasion; the picture is tempered only by the timorous hesitant pose of the saint. The pre-eminent significance given to the chivalry of St George may be due to the financial support given to the Scuola by the Knights of Rhodes, who considered the saint to embody all the ideals of the perfect knight.

St Tryphon Exorcising the Daughter of the Emperor Gordianus is a rare representation of the saint. Painted by Carpaccio and his assistants, the master's touch is recognisable in the architectural details and the distinctive personalities of the figures.

The two small paintings, the *Agony in the Garden* and the *Vocation of St Matthew*, are exceptions to the cycles dedicated to the lives of the Scuola's three patron saints, and serve as a prelude to episodes in the life of St Jerome.

The first canvas, *St Jerome leading his Lion into a Monastery*, offers a humorous depiction of the monks as they flee from the beast, which is more concerned with obediently following St Jerome. The building in the background is the Scuola di San Rocco.

By contrast there is no such animation or humour in the *Funeral of St Jerome*, only solemn tragedy. Set in the peaceful, ordered precinct of a monastery, the composition centres on the saint laid out on the floor, attended by monks. A basic, yet serene, sense of inevitability pervades the scene, suggested by the animals in

St Jerome (c.342–420)

Born in Dalmatia, Eusebius Hieronymus (later corrupted to Jerome) was a biblical scholar and a great traveller. After studying rhetoric in Rome, he journeyed through Gaul, Palestine, Syria, Antioch, Constantinople and Egypt. He settled into monastic life in Bethlehem and devoted his mature years to study, translating the Gospels and Old Testament into vulgar Latin, in direct opposition to Rome.

In art he is often depicted as holding a stone as a symbol of his ascetic life, as wearing a red cardinal's hat and as being in the company of the lion from whose paw he is said to have removed a thorn. Renaissance Humanist patrons popularised his portrayal as a scribe surrounded by books, while depictions of the aesthete in the desert hearken to John the Baptist in the New Testament.

the courtyard that represent the continuous natural rhythm of life and death.

St Augustine in his Study also alludes to the legend of St Jerome: the Venetian version of the story tells of St Augustine wishing to address a letter on a matter of theology to St Jerome, who had already died. His divine presence appeared in St Augustine's study admonishing him for his presumption (a Venetian edition of the letter was published in 1485). The study is flooded with natural light that highlights every detail including the dog's bemusement. The quality of rendering and exquisite attention to the furnishings, especially the open door into a second room, are reminiscent of Flemish domestic interior painting. The facial traits of St Augustine are, in fact, those of Cardinal Bessarione (1402–72), a scholar of Greek Humanism.

A variety of works in silver are displayed in the sacristy and in the upper hall.

Additional Sights

La Pietà (🏛, GX)

Edging Riva degli Schiavoni, Santa Maria della Visitazione is better known as "La Pietà" (the merciful one) after its hospice for abandoned children, dedicated in the 14C.

From afar, the church's white façade with its broad pediment supported on columns, finally added in 1906, is its distinguishing feature. Initially the church would have been integrated within the institutional complex, but in the 18C, when it was all to be remodelled by Giorgio Massari, it was decided that the church should be designed as a concert hall, given that the orphans' education was oriented towards music, at one time under the leadership of **Antonio Vivaldi**.

The internal structure is vaulted to optimise the acoustics. The orchestra and the choir are positioned along the side walls. Music is the theme of the superb frescoes on the ceiling and concerts are often staged here.

San Giorgio dei Greci (🏛, GV)

🕐*Open Mon & Wed–Sat 9am–12.30pm and 2.30–4.30pm.Closed Tue.* ☎ 041 52 39 569.

A closed complex designed by Longhena and a gently leaning tower comprise a 16C church and college buildings reserved for its Greek Orthodox community, and an icon museum. Founded originally by a colony of Greeks, a confraternity evolved to form the **Scuola di San Niccolò**. After the fall of Constantinople in 1453, its numbers increased greatly.

The long narrow façade with its prominent pediment owes much to the influence of Sansovino. The cupola was added in 1571.

Inside, the great rectangular space is sealed by a magnificent **iconostasis**★ embellished with holy figures against a gold background that screens off the apsed area. Beyond here is reserved for the clergy. The walls are lined with wooden stalls for use by the congregation during the long Orthodox rituals.

Museo di Icone Bizantine-postbizantine

♿ 🕐*Open daily 9am–5pm.* 🕐*Closed 1 Jan, 25 Dec.* ⊜€4. ☎ 041 52 26 581. www.istitutoellenico.org.

The museum houses a rich collection of Byzantine and post-Byzantine icons and paintings portraying various religious subjects, exquisite illuminated manuscripts and religious artifacts.

Return along Salizzada dei Greci past **San Antonin** (🏛, HV), a church which dates back to the 7C but which was rebuilt by Longhena. The mid-17C campanile rises to an Eastern-style cupola. Continue onto Campo Bandiera e Moro with its church, **San Giovanni in Bràgora**★ (⌖ *see ARSENALE*), where Vivaldi was baptised, before turning back towards Riva degli Schiavoni.

SAN ROCCO ★★★

(🄴, CDV)
VAPORETTO: S. TOMÀ

San Rocco is an ideal district for a stroll, providing interesting monuments and splashes of local colour. Quiet bars and cafes are situated near the main points of interest, allowing visitors to rest between sightseeing.

▸ **Orient Yourself:** San Rocco sits behind I Frari.
🕐 **Organising Your Time:** Allow at least 2hr 30min.
👓 **Also See:** I CARMINI, I FRARI and RIALTO.

A Bit of History

Little is known of **San Rocco** (c.1295–1327), protector of the plague-stricken, other than he was born in Montpellier in southwest France. According to his Venetian biographer, Francesco Diedo, Roch travelled to Italy, where he miraculously cured plague victims (in Aquapendente, Cesena, Mantua, Modena, Parma…) with the sign of the cross until he, too, succumbed to the disease in Piacenza but recovered enough to return home. On his return to Montpellier, he was mistaken for a spy in Angers and incarcerated. He died there in prison.

San Rocco was particularly venerated in Venice, which as an important port was influential in spreading plague epidemics.

The Scuole di San Rocco was formed in 1478 and its prestige was enhanced (to Grande Scuole) in 1485 when the saint's relics were transferred to its care. The present headquarters was initiated in 1516 by Bartolomeo Bon, who was dismissed in 1524 after a major disagreement with the leaders of the Scuola. The project was then entrusted to Scarpagnino, who worked on the building until his death.

The magnificence of the Scuola resides in its interior decoration, which has an interesting history of its own. In 1564, a competition was launched for the decoration of the Salla dell'Albergo (*a small room on the first floor where the Chapter met*). Several illustrious artists, including Paolo Veronese, Andrea Schiavone, and Federico Zuccari, submitted their drawings, but **Tintoretto** quickly completed a painted panel for the ceiling and promptly donated his work as a gesture of devotion. In such circumstances, the work could not be refused, and so Tintoretto went on to furnish the entire Scuola with his paintings.

Spared from Napoleon's edicts, the Confraternity of St Roch is still active today. On 16 August each year, Venice celebrates the saint with traditional pomp and circumstance.

Scuola Grande di San Rocco

Despite displaying a certain homogeneity, the façade draws together a variety of styles, most evident in the windows: those on the ground floor are early Venetian Renaissance and those above are Mannerist in design.

The rear façade, facing onto the canal, is simpler in format with a portico and finely carved details (note the heads on the pilasters on the first floor).

Interior★★★

🕐Open 28 Mar–2 Nov 9.30am–5.30pm. 🕐 Closed 1 Jan, 25 Dec. ✍€ 8; no charge 16 Aug (St Rocco's feast day). ☎ 041 52 34 864. www.scuolagrande-sanrocco.it.

Start upstairs by taking either of the two flights that feed into the single, grand staircase. Above, Scarpagnino's barrel-vaulted ceiling is painted with *St Roch Presenting the Sick to Charity, who Bears the Torch of Religion* by Giannantonio Pellegrini; the walls show *Venice with St Mark, St Roch and St Sebastian in*

Supplication for an End to the Plague by Pietro Negri (1673) (*on the left*) – note the inclusion of the Church of La Salute, which was erected as a votive gesture at the end of the plague in 1630; and (*on the right*) *The Virgin Appearing to the Plague-stricken* (1666) by Antonio Zanchi.

Sala dell'Albergo

The most striking work of art in the Albergo Room is the huge and dramatic *Crucifixion* immediately opposite the door.

In the left section of the entrance wall, the intensity of the scene in *Christ Appearing before Pilate* is concentrated by light focusing on the figure of Christ. In the middle section *Ecce Homo* is depicted, and to its left, *Christ Bearing the Cross*, a realistic rendering of the tragic journey, which Tintoretto populates with a weary cortège of figures moving in the opposite direction.

The *Three Apples* on the bench, reminiscent of Cézanne, is a fragment from the ceiling discovered above the door behind one of the capitals after four centuries.

Despite some controversy, the easel picture of *Christ Bearing the Cross* has been attributed to Giorgione and that of *Christ in Pietà* to his followers.

Sala Capitolare

In the large chapter house, subjects are based on the Old Testament (*ceiling*) and the New (*walls*).

The central ceiling panel depicts *The Brazen Serpent*, framed by two square panels depicting *Moses Striking the Rock* and *Manna Sent from Heaven*. The two large oval panels illustrate *Ezekial's Vision* and the *Fall of Man*. The other eight panels painted in green chiaroscuro conclude the Old Testament cycle.

On the side of the corridor is depicted *The Ascension*, followed by *The Pool of Bethesda*. *The Temptation of Christ* boasts a splendid Lucifer that echoes images of Eve tempting Adam.

On the wall opposite, the *Adoration of the Shepherds* is followed by the *Baptism*; in the central section opposite *The Ascension*, *The Resurrection of Christ* shows Christ seemingly bursting from the tomb as the two Marys walk in the morning light beyond; in *The Agony in the Garden*, the hour of the day imbues the scene with a faint reddish light. The focal point of perspective in *The Last Supper* is the bright halo hovering over the little figure of the Saviour.

The room also accommodates a large altarpiece, depicting the *Vision of St Roch* painted largely by Tintoretto, assisted by his son and studio; a *Self-Portrait* showing Tintoretto in a religious pose and

The Crucifixion by Tintoretto

© Scuola Grande di S Rocco, Venezia / SCALA

one of his versions of *The Visitation. The Annunciation* however is by Titian, the two other easel canvases by Tiepolo.

Sala Terrena

On the ground floor hang Tintoretto's last canvases, dedicated to Mary. *The Annunciation* – a more "popular" version if compared to the aristocratic rendering by Titian – preceding *The Adoration of the Magi, The Flight into Egypt, The Massacre of the Innocent* (imbued some might say with a sharp sense of realism and desperate tragedy by a Tintoretto overwhelmed with grief at the death of his son), and a *Mary Magdalene.*

All Tintoretto's canvases conform to the aesthetic principles outlined by the Council of Trent, scorning all artifice and intellectual iconography in favour of a direct appeal to the common people.

Walking Tour

San Rocco (🔊, CDV)

The present façade of the church (🕐*open daily 9.30am–5:30pm (1 Jan, 25 Dec –12.30pm)*). Built in the mid-1720s and remodelled in the late-18C. The statues of the *Saints* and the *Blessed* are by Marchiori and the Austrian-born Gianmaria Morlaiter. The portal, rose window and a few of the original Renaissance features survive on the side overlooking the *scuola.*

Above the entrance door, the **old organ door panels** painted by Tintoretto depict *The Annunciation* and *The Presentation of St Roch to the Pope.*

In the first side chapel of the left aisle, the altarpiece is by Sebastiano Ricci; the two tall panels by Pordenone show *St Martin* and *St Christopher,* and the panel below, *Christ Chasing the Moneychangers from the Temple,* is by Fumiani. Over the second altar is an *Annunciation and Angels* by Solimena. Four canvases by **Tintoretto** are to be found in the presbytery. On the other side of the church, towards the exit, the first altarpiece on the left is dedicated to *The Miracle of St Anthony* by Trevisani (1656–1746). In the middle, between the two altars, hang two more canvases by **Tintoretto**. The last altar is decorated with an altarpiece by Sebastiano Ricci.

▶ *Cross the canal behind the Scuola and take Calle San Pantalon, which leads to a square.*

San Pantalon (🔊, CV)

Despite its unfinished façade (1668–86), this church recalls others in Venice such as San Marcuola and San Lorenzo.

Its main interest is its interior ornamented with an undisputed masterpiece by Fumiani comprising 60 canvas ceiling panels illustrating *The Martyrdom and Glory of St Pantaleon*a, executed between 1684 and 1704, and restored in 1970. The work is a tour de force of perspective, projecting the nave high into the sky.

The presbytery decoration is by the same artist, often referred to as *fumoso* (meaning smoky) owing to his predilection for dark colours, so characteristic of a period tormented by ever-present death. To the left of the high altar, the small chapel, dedicated to a relic of the True Cross, houses *Paradise* (1444) by Antonio Vivarini. In the third chapel on the right is a work by **Veronese**.

▶ *Return to San Rocco to take Salizzada San Rocco and Calle Larga Prima to Campo San Tomà.*

Campo San Tomà (🔊, DV)

This lovely square with its simple, now deconsecrated church dates back to the 10C; it was remodelled in 1742. Straight ahead is the **Scuola dei Calegheri**, the guild of cobblers, which acquired the building in the 15C.

▶ *To reach Goldoni's house, keep to the left side of the church and cross the bridge over Rio San Tomà.*

Casa di Goldoni (🔊, DV)

♿🕐*Open year-round Thu–Tue 10am–5pm (4pm Nov–Mar).* 🕐*Closed 1 Jan, 1 May, 25 Dec.* 💶€5 or Museum Pass. ☎*041 27 59 325 or 848 08 20 00. http://carlogoldoni.visitmuve.it.*

It was in this *palazzo*, its small courtyard complete with a well and staircase, that the famous playwright **Carlo Goldoni**

St Pantaleon

One of the patron saints of the city, Pantaleon (or Pantalon) was born to a pagan father and Christian mother. According to legend, he was reconciled to Christianity while employed as a physician at the court of Emperor Galerius at Nicodemia and denounced during the persecutions prescribed by Diocletian in 303. His cult was popularised in the Eastern Church, notably during the Middle Ages, when he was honoured as one of the patron saints of physicians.

was born. The house is now home to the International Institute for Theatrical Research; one room serves as a small puppet theatre, housing works by Goldoni and Pietro Longhi.

▷ *To continue to Campo San Polo, follow the flow of people. Cross the bridge over Rio di San Polo and follow along the right side of the church.*

Campo San Polo (🖥, DU)

This splendid amphitheatre-like piazza provides a venue for many cultural and tourist events, maintaining a long historical tradition of ceremonies and entertainment. Overlooking the square are three notable *palazzi*: the Gothic-style **Palazzo Soranzo** (*no's 2169 and 2170*), and nearby, the Baroque **Palazzo Tiepolo Maffetti**, with its distinctive head of Hercules over the portal. At the opposite corner is Sanmicheli's 16C **Palazzo Corner Mocenigo**, now the seat of the Guardia di Finanza.

San Polo (🖥, DUV)

🕐*Open Mon–Sat 10am–5pm.* 🕐*Closed 1 Jan, Easter, 15 Aug, 25 Dec.* ⊜ €3. ☏*041 27 50 462. www.chorusvenezia.org.*
The façade of this ancient church (with 9C origins) was rebuilt between the 14C and 15C. Now hemmed in by houses, the church preserves its main rose window and an ornate side door decorated with carving from the turn of the 14C. Subsequent restoration in the 19C has destroyed the harmony of the original. The interior, vaulted with a ship's keel roof, accommodates (over the first altar on the right) an *Assumption of the Virgin*, and to its left a *Last Supper* by **Tintoretto.** The latter is an intimate scene full of domestic details portraying a simple way of life.

Over the second altar on the left, the *Virgin Appearing to St John of Nepomuk* is by Giambattista Tiepolo; the *Fourteen Stations of the Cross* in the Oratory of the Crucifix are by his son Giandomenico. The chapel on the left preserves the *Betrothal of the Virgin and Angels* by Veronese.

SAN ZACCARIA ★★

(🖥, GX)
VAPORETTO: S. ZACCARIA

San Zaccaria is a stone's throw from St Mark's and as a result there are numerous restaurants, pizzerias, souvenir and *passemenerie* (trimming) shops in the area. As the distance from the church increases, so the numbers of tourists thin out and the district becomes quieter and more frequented by locals. At its heart lies the attractive and atmospheric Campo Santa Maria Formosa and its busy market. Dotted with shops specialising in typical Venetian goods, this area is perfect for a leisurely stroll.

▷ **Orient Yourself:** Situated due east of St. Mark's, the area, dominated by the church of the same name, is surrounded by canals on three sides, and by the Riva degli Schiavoni waterfront quay on the fourth.
🕐 **Organising Your Time:** Allow about 2hr 30min.
🕐 **Also See:** ARSENALE, PIAZZA SAN MARCO, RIALTO.

The façade of San Zaccaria

Walking Tour

San Zaccaria★★ (⑨, GX)

⏱*Open Mon–Sat 10am–noon and 4pm–6pm. Sun 4pm–6pm. ☎041 52 21 257.*

The original church, founded in the 9C, has been partly incorporated into the new church: the right aisle was created from the left aisle of the old church. The present church, dating from the 15C, was built by Gambello and completed, on his death, by Codussi.

The splendid white façade incorporates three tiers of round-headed windows, niches and semicircular pediment. Contrived from a variety of architectural styles, its tall Gothic proportions are cloaked in Renaissance detail. At ground level the lower section is set with square polychrome panels that run horizontally. Above this, a continuous frieze of shell-headed flat niches introduce a vertical element that is then carried through the upper sections, accented first with three windows, then two and finally by a single central oculus. The Gothic configuration of tall nave and side aisles cede to Codussi's more Classical idiom: projecting piers give way to free-standing paired columns that extend up to

a cornice, crowned with free-standing figures – far removed from the statue of *St Zaccarias* by Alessandro Vittorio above the main door.

The stunning interior is covered in paintings, the most important of which is Giovanni Bellini's *Sacra Conversazione* (1505) over the second altar on the left. On the lower left wall are two panels (1500) by Palma il Giovane.

The church is dedicated to Zacharias, the father of St John the Baptist and legend has it that his body lies beneath the right aisle.

The **Cappella del Coro** is hung with works by Tintoretto, Tiepolo and Palma il Vecchio; a pair of organ panels painted by Palma il Giovane; a *Crucifixion* attributed to Van Dyck and a *Resurrection* by Domenico Tintoretto.

In the **Cappella d'Oro**, also known as the Chapel of St Tarasius, the vault is frescoed by Andrea del Castagno and Francesco da Faenza, and the three Gothic polyptychs are by Antonio Vivarini and his collaborator. At the foot of the altar are the remains of the mosaic from the apse of the 12C Romanesque-Byzantine chapel. A little farther back (*protected by glass*) are mosaics from the 9C church. Stairs

The Abduction of the Maidens

According to Venetian custom, on the Feast of the Marias, at Candlemas, two girls from each *sestiere* would be married and each would be given a coffer in which to store their dowry. Around 946, the festival was raided by Slav pirates who kidnapped the girls and held them to ransom. They were eventually rescued by the **Casselleri**, the artisans who made the bridal chests for the brides. From then on, the doge would visit the Casselleri at Santa Maria Formosa at Candlemas, where he would be presented with a straw hat and wine. The hat presented to the last doge to officiate at the ceremony can still be seen today in the Museu Correr (*see page 177*).

descend into the very atmospheric crypt, which is between 1 000 and 1 200 years old. It is almost permanently submerged in water and holds the watery graves of several early doges.

▶ *Follow Salizzada San Provolo and proceed straight to the canal; turn left for the Diocesan Museum of Religious Art. Alternatively, return to Campo Santi Filippo e Giacomo and take Calle della Chiesa, turn left before the canal and follow the water's edge through Campiello Querini and onto Campo Santa Maria Formosa.*

Campo Santa Maria Formosa (⑤, GU)

This busy square is a main thoroughfare situated between the tourist honeypots of St Mark's Square and the Church of Santi Giovanni e Paolo.

Santa Maria Formosa (⑤, GUV)

🕑*Open Mon–Sat 10am–5pm.* 🕑*Closed 1 Jan, Easter, 15 Aug, 25 Dec.* ⊛*€3.* ☎*041 27 50 462. www.chorusvenezia.org.*
The original 7C church built here was dedicated, according to legend, to St Magnus, to whom the Madonna appeared in the form of a shapely buxom (*formosa*) woman. It was rebuilt by Codussi between 1492 and 1504 and embellished with a new façade in 1604 and a new canal frontage in 1542, financed by a noble Venetian family, the Cappellos. The 17C campanile retains, above the entrance, a grimacing mask and its original pinnacle.
On passing through the main entrance, note on the left the *Madonna di Lepanto*

(1571), which once graced the naval ship commanded by Sebastiano Venier.
The interior, in the form of a Latin cross, includes two chapels: the Chapel of the Scuola dei Bombardieri (mortar foundries), which contains a *San Barnaba and Saints* by Palma il Vecchio (c.1480–1528), and a *Madonna of the Misericordia* by Bartolomeo Vivarini; and the Chapel of the Scuola dei Casselleri (trunks and chest makers).

Fondazione Querini Stampalia Onlus★ (⑤, GV)

♿🕑*Open year-round Tue–Sun 10am–6pm.* ⊛*€10.* ☎*041 27 11 411. www.querinistampalia.it.*
Housed in a modern building, this museum, which contains a library and occasionally hosts temporary exhibitions, is of interest to visitors seeking to imbibe the atmosphere of a Venice long disappeared, when life in the city was synonymous with art.
Works of art on display here include paintings by Palma il Giovane, Luca Giordano, Tiepolo, plus a clay model for a sculpture of *Letizia Ramolino Bonaparte* by Antonio Canova.
Particularly noteworthy are the **series of panels**★★ by Pietro Longhi, predominantly devoted to the sacraments and hunting; the *Scenes of Public Life in Venice*★★ by Gabriele Bella and the evocative *Presentation of Jesus in the Temple* by Giovanni Bellini.
Everyday Venetian life of the period is well depicted in the paintings *The Boxing Match* after Antonio Stom and *The Frozen Lagoon by the Fondamenta Nuove* by an anonymous 18C Venetian painter.

SAN ZANIPÒLO★★

SS GIOVANNI E PAOLO

VAPORETTO: FONDAMENTA NUOVE, CIMITERO

This area is striking not only for its majestic architecture but also for the broad range of activity in the district, from the busy commerce of the *calli* between Campo di Santi Giovanni e Paolo and Campo Santi Apostoli to the tranquillity of Campo dei Gesuiti and the Fondamente Nuove. From here, the view extends over the choppy waters of the lagoon to the cemetery of San Michele, disturbed only by the passing of the water-buses.

▷ **Orient Yourself:** Neighbouring a large hospital in the northern section of the Castello *sestiere*, the San Zanipòlo district is bounded by the Rio dei Mendicanti and the Fondamente Nuove. The walking tour below leads into the Cannaregio *sestiere,* and is followed by a tour of the island of San Michele.

✍ **Don't Miss:** The powerful equestrian statue of Bartolomeo Colleoni.

🕐 **Organising Your Time:** Allow half a day to enjoy this area.

👣 **Also See:** Neighbouring sights: CA' D'ORO; RIALTO.

Sights

Campo di Santi Giovanni e Paolo (🖬, GU).

The name *Zanipòlo* is a contraction of the names John and Paul in dialect, the two saints to whom the square is dedicated.

Equestrian monument to Bartolomeo Colleoni★★

The proud gait of Colleoni – a mercenary soldier – his face set with a wilful expression, contrasts powerfully with the restless disposition of the horse.

The commission for such a major monument was awarded to **Verrocchio** by competition. As the master died before it had been cast, Alessandro Leopardi oversaw the project and added the base. Inspiration came from the *Gattamelata* by Donatello in Padua, which, is ranked among the highest of its genre.

The decorative **well-head** is attributed to Sansovino, who was also responsible for the side of the Scuola di San Marco that faces onto the canal.

Basilica dei Santi Giovanni e Paolo★★ (🖬, GU)

🕐Open 9am–6pm Mon–Sat (Sun, hol noon–6pm; 23 Dec, Easter morning only). ☞€2.50 contrib requested. ☏041 52 35 913.

One of the largest churches in Venice, San Zanipòlo was founded by Dominican friars late in the 13C, but not consecrated until 1430.

Front

The incomplete façade comprises at ground level a central pointed arch flanked by three blind arches; above, the width is divided vertically by plain piers rising up to niches on the roof line with statues of the Dominican Saints.

On either side of the main portal, designed by Bartolomeo Bon, are the two sarcophagi of the Doges Jacopo and Lorenzo Tiepolo.

© N. Bosques / MICHELIN

Detail of the well in Campo di Santi Giovanni e Paolo

207

Campo di Santi Giovanni e Paolo and Basilica dei Santi Giovanni e Paolo

Interior

The well-lit lofty nave leads to an apse pierced by slender double lancet Gothic windows. In the form of a Latin cross, the church has three aisles and five apses. Huge columns carry great beams that support arches and the cross vaults.

The internal façade commemorates the **Mocenigo Doges**: (*centre*) Alvise I (**1**); (*left*) Pietro – (**2**) monument by Pietro Lombardo; (*right*) Giovanni – (**3**) monument by Tullio Lombardo.

Along the left aisle is the altar to St Jerome (**4**), its statue a work by Alessandro Vittoria; the pyramid nearby is in memory of the Bandiera brothers (**5**), supporters of Mazzini's *Young Italy*, who were gunned down in 1844.

At the altar to St Peter Martyr (altarpiece after Titian) is the monument to **Doge Niccolò Marcello** (**6**) by Pietro Lombardo; that to **Doge Tommaso Mocenigo** (**7**) with its great baldaquin, is the work (1423) of Niccolò Lamberti and Giovanni di Martino.

Flanking the double arch are two statues by Antonio Lombardo. Before the sacristy is the Renaissance monument to **Doge Pasquale Malipiero** (**8**) by Pietro Lombardo.

The **sacristy** is full of ornate decoration. Before turning into the transept are three panels of a *Polyptych* (**9**) by Bartolomeo Vivarini.

In the left transept, above the entrance to the Chapel of the

S. ZANIPÒLO

Cappella di S. Pio V
Cappella d. Maddalena
Cappella del Rosario
CENTRAL APSE
Cappella d. SS. Trinità
Cappella del Crocifisso
TRANSEPT
Sacristy
Cappella di S. Domenico
Cappella d. Madonna d. Pace
Cappella del Beato G. Salomoni
NAVE
SCUOLA GRANDE DI S. MARCO
Campo S.S. Giovanni e Paolo
N
0   20 m

Rosary but below the great clock, is a monument to **Doge Antonio Venier**. The **Cappella del Rosario** (Chapel of the Rosary or Lepanto Chapel) was built as a mark of gratitude for the great victory over the Turks.

On the walls are depictions by Padovanino and Benedetto Caliari. Opposite the altar, Veronese has painted himself in the guise of the man standing beyond the column. Beyond the apsed chapels on the left, the central apse is replete with other **funerary monuments**.

Immediately on the left is that of **Doge Marco Corner** (**10**) by Nino Pisano, followed by the sepulchre of **Doge Andrea Vendramin** (**11**), a majestic work by Tullio Lombardo.

On the right is the funerary monument to **Doge Michele Morosini** (1382) (**12**) from the workshops of Dalle Masegne. Here also is that of **Doge Leonardo Loredan**.

The first apsidal chapel on the right is dedicated to **Mary Magdalene**. The *Four Evangelists* are frescoed by Palma il Giovane; on the right wall is the monument to the **Sea-Captain Vittor Pisani** (1324–80); on the left is a particularly haunting piece known as *Vanity* or *The Conceited Woman* (17C), depicting a young girl looking at her reflection in a mirror and seeing Death.

In the adjacent **Cappella del Crocifisso** (Chapel of the Crucifix), the *Grieving Virgin* and *John the Baptist* are by Alessandro Vittoria.

In the right arm of the transept, the **stained glass** (**14**) evidences intense colour.

The **Cappella di San Domenico** (Chapel of St Dominic), in the right aisle, houses the *Glory of St Dominic* by Piazzetta (1683–1754).

Before the **Cappella della Madonna della Pace** (Chapel of the Madonna of Peace) stands the **Valier monument** (1705–08), the largest of the Doge monuments. The chapel houses a Byzantine icon and works by Leandro Bassano (*left wall*), Aliense (*right wall*) and Palma il Giovane (*vault*).

In front of the Baroque **Cappella del Beato Giacomo Salomoni** is the tomb-stone of Ludovico Diedo who died in 1466, a fine example of *niello* engraving. Over the next altar sits an early *Polyptych* (**15**) by Giovanni Bellini.

The final monument comprises an urn said to contain the skin of Captain Marcantonio Bragadin, who was flayed alive by the Turks in 1571 after the surrender of Famagusta.

Behind the basilica, along Barbaria delle Tole, stands the **Chiesa dell'Ospedaletto**, whose Sala della Musica is open to the public , also for occasional concerts. (*Thu–Sat; 3.30–6.30pm; €3; 041 26 01 974 or 041 92 49 33, www.scalabovolo.org*).

Scuola Grande di San Marco★ (**5**, GTU)

The building provides a facade for Venice's hospital (Ospedaletto; first and foremost this is a hospital, so entrance may be limited and discretion is advised) but it is possible to visit the library daily, 8.30am–2pm (except Sat–Sun and public hols). Follow the signs for Biblioteca di San Marco at the far end of the first room, turn right, go upstairs and ring the bell. 041 52 94 323.

This ancient **Scuola**, founded in 1260, was transferred here from its original seat in Santa Croce in 1438. Destroyed in the fire of 1485, it was reconstructed by Lombardo, and his sons Antonio and Tullio, before being completed by Lombardo's arch rival, Mauro Codussi. It has reverted to the purpose for which it was founded; at the beginning of the 19C, the building was transformed into

The Condottiere

Bartolomeo Colleoni (1400–76) was one of many mercenary soldiers (*condottieri*) engaged by the Venetian Republic to defend and acquire her territories. A native of Bergamo, Colleoni served Venice for a long time, with considerable success. He also served Francesco Sforza. Returning to the Republic of Venice, he was relegated to Malpaga Castle, where he died. His tomb is housed in the Colleoni Chapel in Bergamo.

a hospital, first for military and now general civic use.

At ground level, the **façade** boasts an effective series of *trompe l'oeil* panels; two bold lions guard the left entrance and, to their right, two groups of figures crowd around St Mark healing and baptising Anianus, a cobbler from Alexandria.

Interior

The **Sala dell'Albergo** now accommodates the medical library and several large pictures, one by Palma il Vecchio and one by Jacopo and Domenico Tintoretto.

Before leaving the room, note the lion with the closed Gospel, a conceit alluding to whether Venice, at the time, was at war or at peace.

The **Sala Capitolare**, also known as the Sala San Marco, has a blue and gold ceiling bearing the symbols of the Scuole. The lion in the centre holds an open Gospel. The large panel behind the altar is the work of Palma il Giovane. Those to each side are by Jacopo and Domenico Tintoretto, as is the painting on the opposite wall.

In addition to the antique medical instruments, there are also some valuable 16C texts on display in the Sala Capitolare, some of which were illustrated by Titian.

▶ *Follow Calle Larga Gallina to Campo Santa Maria Nova, from where the rear of the Church of Santa Maria dei Miracoli may be contemplated.*

Walking Tour

Santa Maria dei Miracoli★ (4, FU)

🕐*Open Mon–Sat 10am–5pm.* 🕐*Closed 1 Jan, Easter, 15 Aug, 25 Dec.* €3. ☎ 041 27 50 462. www.chorusvenezia.org.

This exquisite Renaissance church, positioned on the edge of a canal overlooking the small Campo dei Miracoli, recalls the distinctive nature of 14C Tuscan design both in terms of its crisply carved architectural ornament and its marble detailing. The church is the work of Lombardo (🔆*see above*), erected to house a miracle-working image of the Madonna by Nicolò di Pietro (1409). In 1489, it was dedicated to the *Immacolata* (the Virgin), the doctrine of the Immaculate Conception having been proclaimed 12 years before this.

The **interior**, especially the barrel vault, resembles a casket. Prophets and patriarchs are depicted in the 50 compartments of the coffered ceiling (🔆*best appreciated with the mirror provided for this purpose*).

▶ *Cross the bridge into Campiello Santa Maria Nova, pass before San Cancian and proceed straight on. Take Calle del Manganer in Campiello Cason, which leads to the back of the Church of Santi Apostoli.*

Campo Santi Apostoli –
🔆*See RIALTO.*

▶ *Behind the church, take Rio Terà dei Santi Apostoli and carry straight on.*

The walk to the vast Campo dei Gesuiti will reveal secluded corners of Venice that are typical of the Cannaregio *sestiere*.

Gesuiti★ (4, FT)

The Jesuit church stands in a peaceful square. It is all the more striking for its white marble Baroque façade, decorated

A Renaissance jewel – Santa Maria dei Miracoli

© Gwen Cannon / MICHELIN

with numerous statues, which include one of the *Virgin*, to which it is dedicated, over the pediment. The present building was erected between 1715 and 1729 on the site of the ancient Church of Santa Maria dei Crociferi (1150).

The sumptuous interior is enhanced by the white and gold stucco ceiling, the two central sections of which are by Francesco Fontebasso. Over the first altar on the left sits *The Martyrdom of St Lawrence* by Titian; in the left transept is the *Assumption of the Virgin* by Tintoretto. In the sacristy is a cycle of paintings by Palma il Giovane which, among other things, narrates stories from the Bible and of the True Cross.

Oratorio dei Crociferi★ (🄳, FT)

🕐 *Temporarily closed to the public.* 🎟 €2. ☎ 041 53 22 920. www.scalabo volo.org.

Adjoining the Church of the Jesuits, the Oratory of the Crossbearers dates from the 13C. It was run by the Crutched Friars (*Fratres Cruciferi*), an Order of mendicant friars that was eventually suppressed in 1656. The hospital also served as a refuge for those who had fought in the Crusades. In 1414, it was transformed into a hospice for 12 destitute old ladies. Much of its decoration, on the history of the Crutched Friars, was undertaken between 1583 and 1592 by Palma il Giovane. Included in the painting on the end wall is **Doge Renier Zen**, a principal benefactor of the hospital of Santa Maria dei Crociferi.

On either side of the altar, two paintings depict the foundation of the Order. The three canvases on the left wall illustrate scenes from the life of **Pasquale Cicogna**, Procurator of St Mark's and Doge. Above the doors are represented *The Flagellation* and *The Dead Christ*. In homage to the Virgin, to whom the chapel is dedicated, the ceiling has been decorated with the *Assumption*.

▷ *Continue towards the lagoon.*

Fondamenta Nuove (🄳, 🄴, FHT)

The Fondamenta Nuove, which runs alongside the lagoon, was constructed at the end of the 16C. Today water-buses (vaporettos) depart from here for the islands of San Michele, Murano, Burano and Torcello. Venice's main theatre, the **Teatro Fondamenta Nuove**, is to be found near the Sacca della Misericordia.

▷ *Take the vaporetto for the island of San Michele.*

San Michele in Isola (🄴, HS)

Venetians and many famous visitors have chosen to be buried here.

This great white church – the first Renaissance church in Venice – was designed by Codussi. The façade includes a fine doorway, topped with a pediment and a statue of the *Madonna*. Two arched windows frame the central bay with its rose window. Note the shells in the lateral niches and how the radiating ribs disappear into the shell.

The interior extends down to a full set of choir stalls, presided over by *St Jerome* carved by the Flemish artist, Juste Le Court. The whole is enclosed beneath a sumptuous coffered ceiling. The sacristy ceiling, however, is later in date, painted by Romualdo Mauro. The **Emiliani Chapel**, on the left flank, is decorated by Guglielmo de' Grigi, known as "il Bergamasco" (the man from Bergamo).

Cimitero (Cemetery) (🄴, GHS)

Ask for a map at the entrance. 🕐 *Open year-round daily 7.30am–6pm (Oct–Mar, 4pm). 7.30am–noon 1 Jan, Easter, 25 Dec.*

Here lie **Ezra Pound** (1885–1972), **Igor Stravinsky** (1882–1971), **Sergei Pavlovich Diaghilev** (1872–1929) and **Josif Brodskij** (1940–96), a Russian poet and Nobel Prize winner (1987), who drew on Venice for his work entitled *Fundamentals for the Incurable*:

Condemned for his anti-American propaganda, **Ezra Pound**, the author of the *Cantos*, was first interned in a concentration camp and then in an asylum, before spending his last years in Italy. He is buried in the Evangelical section to the left on entering. **Igor Stravinsky**, the Russian composer, along with his associate **Sergei Diaghilev**, the émigré founder of the Russian Ballet, are buried in the Greek section, at the end. Also in San Michele Cemetery lie the musician Luigi Nono (1924–90) and the great Goldoni actor **Cesco Baseggio** (1897–1971).

Basilica dei SS Maria e Donato, Murano
© John Kirk / iStockphoto.com

BURANO★★

Burano is the most colourful of the lagoon islands. At the doors and windows of the houses, painted in the brightest colours of the rainbow, a few women still work on their lace pillows while the men attend to their fishing nets and boats. Visitors may be hailed with friendly "invitations" from the locals selling *passementerie* (articles bordered in lace) displayed by the "lace-houses".

▶ **Orient Yourself:** Burano lies about 5mi/8km northeast of Venice just south of the island of Torcello. It takes about 45min to get from Fondamenta Nuove (line 12) to Burano. The last stretch of the journey is along the Mazzorbo Canal, which separates Burano from the island of Mazzorbo. The two islands are linked by a wooden bridge.

✎ **Don't Miss:** Demonstrations by the lacemakers at the lacemakers museum.

🕐 **Organising Your Time:** Allow a couple of hours.

🍴 **Also See:** Neighbouring sights: SAN FRANCESCO del DESERTO, TORCELLO.

A Bit of History

Venice has been known for lace-making since the 16C. The practice was first established in the palaces as a domestic activity, to be supervised by the noble ladies, before spreading to the hospitals and women's institutions where residents were obliged to take up the occupation.

Traditional production depended on the combined use of the needle and bobbin, and proliferated until the second half of the 17C, when demand was threatened by competition from France, which ironically had instituted an industry employing Venetian lacemakers. During the 18C the Venetian authorities were forced to take measures to halt the exodus of lacemakers; certain manufacturers such as

The most colourful of the lagoon islands

© R. Mattes / MICHELIN

Raniere e Gabrieli were granted preferential privileges and traditional methods were compromised, allowing for a simpler, bobbin-only technique to be used. Between the 18C and 19C, however, demand dwindled until eventually the production of lace for clothing was discontinued.

By the second decade of the 19C there were just two lace factories left, one in Venice and one on Burano, and needlepoint continued as a private, domestic pastime. To safeguard designs and practices, a school was set up in 1872 and charged with the organisation and education of the lacemakers, and their production.

Today very little lace is made in the traditional way as it is so labour intensive – it is said that it takes three years for ten women to make a single medium-sized tablecloth. It is therefore very expensive and (buyer beware) any lace that is sold cheaply is almost certainly imported from China.

▶ *From the vaporetto landing, follow Via Galuppi into the square dominated by a statue of the renowned musician from Burano, Baldassarre Galuppi.*

Sights

Piazza Baldassarre Galuppi

The square is dominated by the austere façade of the 16C Church of San Martino and its 18C campanile, built by Andrea Tirali, which leans 1.85m/6ft 1in.

Inside is a *Crucifixion* by **Tiepolo** (*left aisle*) and, on the left of the presbytery, a great sarcophagus around which a miracle is said to have happened. It is explained in a painting, the *Miracle of the Children and the Urn,* attributed to **Alessandro Zanchi**.

The inhabitants of Burano also attribute the fact that they were spared from the plague in 1630 to the divine intervention of their patrons (the island of Torcello was also saved). The skeletons of the three saints today lie in the altar below the sarcophagus.

Island of Artists

Not surprisingly Burano has long been a magnet for artists and a school of painting evolved here before the First World War. Like the houses, one of the characteristics of the Burano School is a strong use of colour. Pay a visit to the Restaurant Da Romano, a sponsor of the artists since 1947, to see examples of their work. The beautiful pastel coloured shades of the houses attract not only visiting tourists, French designer Philippe Starck owns several Burano houses.

Museo del Merletto di Burano

Off the piazza on via Baldassare Galuppi opposite the Galuppi restaurant is Burano's most **colourful house**, known after the owner as Bepe's.

Museo del Merletto (Lace Museum)

🕐 *Open year-round Wed–Mon 10am–6pm (Nov–Mar 5pm).* 🕐 *Closed 1 Jan, 1 May, 25 Dec.* ◉ *€5.* ☎ *041 73 00 34.* *http://museomerletto.visitmuve.it.*

Important collection of collars, napkins, parasols, bedspreads, centrepieces, handkerchiefs and lace edgings are on display in this recently restored museum. Practical demonstrations by experts illustrate just how painstaking the traditional Burano methods are.

CHIOGGIA

Although there is a Venetian quality about this lagoon fishing port – most notable in its canals and double-arched windows and other architectural detail – the atmosphere is very different. The traffic on pavements, roads and water is constant. Chioggia is one of Italy's busiest fishing ports and there's a frenetic urgency with which all local matters of marine and fishing business are dealt with in this working-class town.

▫ **Information:** Lungomare Adriatico, Sottomarina. ☎041 40 10 68. www.chioggiatourism.it.

⊙ **Don't Miss:** The Mercanto Ittico (Fish Market) in early morning.

▶ **Orient Yourself:** Chioggia is not strictly a lagoon island, as it rests on two parallel islands, linked to terra firma by a long bridge. 12mi/19km south of Venice (as the crow flies), along the Adriatic Sea, and north of the Brenta Valley. From the Brenta villas, take the SS 309, which has beautiful views over the Venetian Lagoon. Bus service operates every 30min from Piazzale Roma to Chioggia-Sottomarina taking around 1hr. Or bicycle south from the Lido.

🕐 **Organising Your Time:** For a leisurely walk around Chioggia allow a couple of hours. The Mercato Ippico (Fish Market) opens to the trade at 4am and to the public 6-8am, 4-6:45pm (closed Sat afternoon, Sun-Mon). Near the port night owls can watch fishermen returning, from midnight to 3 or 4am.

🕯 **Also See:** BRENTA VALLEY.

A Bit of History

One of the channels of the Brenta Delta was, in Antiquity, called *Fossa Clodia*, from which **Clodia**, Chioggia's former name, derives. In the 1C BC the Romans transformed it into a commercial harbour. The problems began in the 9C, following destruction from Charlemagne's son Pepin. Between the 11C and 12C, the saltpans constituted a major source of income for Chioggia. Between 1378 and 1381 it became the field of battle between the rival factions Genoa and Venice. The Serenissima was victorious, but Chioggia was annihilated.

Rebuilding began and continued over the ensuing century. Venice intended that Chioggia should be reinforced as a defence post for the lagoon.

The town of Chioggia grew up as close to the sea as possible, configured from these early times around Corso del Popolo and the Canale della Vena. Economic development was then halted: when the Brenta was diverted, the harbour gradually silted up, excluding large vessels. The canal that was dug separating the islet from the mainland served to consolidate defences. From the 16C fishing began to supersede the saltpans as the main industry. In the 19C Chioggia's isolation was in part breached by the building of the bridge carrying the Romea road. On the water, if you look carefully in some spots you can still see a trabucco, a traditional spindly wooden fishing pier, seen also in the 2011 film, *Io Sono Li* (*Shun Li and the Poet*).

Sights

Corso del Popolo

The main street, *Corso del Popolo,* runs parallel to the Canale della Vena – the Fossa Clodia of Ancient times – rendered more colourful and lively by its excellent **fish market**, (open every early morning except Sun–Mon, holidays, entrance at Via G. Poli 1) to end in Piazzetta Vigo. The column bearing a winged lion marks the end of the Fossa Clodia. To cross the

> ## Fish Restaurants
>
> Not surprisingly the town is renowned for its fish and seafood restaurants with bight-eyed produce fresh off the boat at prices well below those of Venice. The only thing missing is the starched tablecloths.

canal, walk over the stone bridge, the Ponte Vigo, built in 1685.

The *Corso* is dotted with the Duomo and several of the Chioggia churches and (no. 932) the family house of painter Rosalba Carriera (1675-1757) where Goldino later lived for a few years. The Church of **San Andrea** has an 11C Romanesque campanile rising from a square base. **San Giacomo** was rebuilt in the 18C; **San Francesco delle Muneghette** was founded in the 15C but rebuilt in the 18C.

Duomo

The island's principal church, dedicated to Santa Maria Assunta, was founded in the 11C. Razed to the ground by fire, it was rebuilt in 1633 by Baldassare Longhena and retains its 14C square bell-tower.

Isola di San Domenico

At the far end of Chioggia, this promontory is reached by following Calle di San Croce, beyond Ponte Vigo. The church has a 13C campanile and a painting of *Saint Paul* by Carpaccio.

Museums

At the other end of the island to the bus stop are two small museums; the **Museo Diocesano d'Arte Sacra**, Sacred Art Museum (*open Thu 9am–noon, Fri & Sun 3–5pm; €3; 041 55 07 477*. Close by is the **Museo della Laguna Sud** (*open Tue–Wed 9am–1pm, Thu–Sun 9am–1pm & 7–11pm; €3.50; 041 55 00 911*). Other museums include Clock, Zoological, and Art (Pinacoteca). *www.turismovenezia.it/Chioggia*.

IL LIDO � ☱ ☱

The Lido is Venice's seaside resort. Once sophisticated but now slightly decadent, for many visitors it is forever associated with the legacy of Luchino Visconti's *Death in Venice*, which was filmed at the Hotel des Bains, and haunted by the disconcerting yet majestic Hotel Excelsior, so reminiscent in style and sheer boldness of Ludwig of Bavaria's castle in Neuschwanstein. The Lido plays host to the glittering Venice International Film Festival every late August/September, when film directors, actors and critics meet, accompanied by their inevitable jet-setting entourage and crowds of curious onlookers.

- **Information:** 6/a Gran Viale S.M.Elisabetta. ☎041 5298711. www.turismovenezia.
- ▶ **Orient Yourself:** Extending roughly north-south to the east of Venice, the Lido resembles a long, thin leg of land (7.5mi/9km long and around half a mile/0.8km wide), fronting the Adriatic Sea. The sandy stretch serves as a barrier island for the Venetian lagoon and a beach for Venetian residents. It is easy to get to the Lido: hop onto vaporetto line **1**, **82** or **N** from Piazza San Marco and half an hour later you will arrive at Santa Maria Elisabetta.
- 🖐 **Don't Miss:** The beach in summer, though beware that the best stretches are privately owned.
- 🕐 **Organising Your Time:** Allow a couple of hours soaking in the sights and sounds.
- Kids **Especially for Kids:** Biking around the island and the beach.

Venice International Film Festival

The first of its kind, the film festival was inaugurated in 1932 at the Hotel Excelsior, on the initiative of Conte Volpi di Misurata and Luciano De Feo, Secretary General of the International Institute of Cinematographic Art. At that time, the **Festival of International Cinematographic Art** was more of an exhibition of the art of cinematography, organised to complement the Biennale. The festival's top prize is the Golden Lion (Leone d'Oro) award. Many of the films that have won this in the past are small-budget arthouse productions that have remained anonymous to the film-going public at large. A reorganization took place in 2012 with a new director and streamlined program. Recent exceptions however are the two Ang Lee movies *Brokeback Mountain* (2005) and *Lust, Caution* (2007) and Sophie Coppola's *Somewhere* (2011). *www.labiennale.org*.

Sights

Gran Viale Santa Maria Elisabetta and the Beach

Gran Viale is the Lido's main thoroughfare; from the vaporetto stop, it stretches to the Piazzale Bucintoro (*accessible by bus*), which leads to Lungomare Gug-

Lido beach

© Juliet Coombe / Lonely Planet Images

lielmo Marconi. In recent years some of the Lido's best hotels have been converted for private use. Colourful beach huts line the seafront. The Casino, a golf club, bike rental, and an airport are also located here.

Jewish Cemetery
🕐 *Opening times call ☎ 041 71 53 59. www.museoebraico.it.*
At the north end of the island, the old Jewish Cemetery, which dates from 1389, can be seen at San Nicolò.

MURANO★★

From the water, Murano appears to be walled-in by its long line of furnaces. As you step off the vaporetto, you will be urged, even cajoled, to visit the glassworks. While the commercial aspect of the "invitation" can be irritating, it is well worth watching the various stages and processes. Murano is also an island of art in other senses too. Don't get so distracted by the tantalising glass shops that you forget to visit the island's two fine churches.

▸ **Orient Yourself:** Murano sits less than a mile to the northeast of Venice and is broken up by several wide canals. To get to Murano, board vaporetto line 12, 13, 41 or 42 at Fondamenta Nuove.

Don't Miss: The Museum of Glass and the Church of Santa Maria e San Donato, especially its mosaic floor.

🕐 **Organising Your Time:** Allow about 2hr 30min.

Also See: Neighbouring sights: SAN ZANIPÒLO.

A Bit of History

By the end of the 13C, glassmaking was so widespread in Venice that the threat of fire ravaging the city was ever constant. Countless small fires frequently broke out as a result of the widespread use of wood and candles; had these incidents not been contained, it would not have taken much for fire to spread quickly, with disastrous consequences. Finally, three nervous centuries later, the Grand Council decided to move the glassworks away from the city to Murano. This had the bonus that it would also help protect the secrets of the glassmaking process.

The most likely theory to explain the origins of glass is rooted in the ancient Orient where potters learned how glass was formed from silicon sand when glazing their ceramics by firing them in a kiln. The process was already in widespread use by the time the books of Job and Proverbs were written, as recorded in the Bible, and commonly practised in Egypt by the 4th millenium BC, as small objects found in datable tombs would imply. The colours blue and green were created by the addition of copper and cobalt oxide. The technique for blowing glass, however, as favoured by the Romans, came later. Before its arrival in Venice, glass was produced in Greece and Turkey. In 1203, fol-

The island of Murano in the lagoon

© Luke Daniek / iStockphoto.com

lowing the occupation of Constantinople, Venice secured the "exclusive" collabora-

Murano glass lamps

tion of immigrant potters in exchange for preferential treatment from the Republic. However, the terms of agreement were ruthless; if the glassmakers refused to return to the city, they were hunted down and killed. Partly as a result of this the city's supremacy in glassmaking remained uncontested until the end of the 16C.

Venice and Murano have long lost their monopoly on the industry but even today, modern glass creations from Murano are considered works of art.

Within everyone's budget are the *murrine*, which sparkle with colour, often set into costume jewellery, and the distinctive discs of kaleidoscopic patterns.

The final effect of this unique glassworking technique is achieved by juxtaposing various coloured rods of glass that have been drawn in length and fused when molten. When the composite rods are then sliced crosswise, the famous discs of colour remain.

Walking Tour

▷ *From the vaporetto stop at Scalo Colonna, follow Fondamenta dei Vetrai.*

San Pietro Martire

Begun in 1363, this brick church was consecrated in 1417. Gravely damaged by fire, it was rebuilt in the Renaissance style before being subjected to further modifications over the ensuing few hundred years. A Renaissance main door is surmounted at the front by a large stained-glass window made of *rui*, small circular sections of Murano glass. Inside, the nave and aisles are apsed and endowed with **paintings**★ by illustrious artists such as Salviati, Veronese, Tintoretto, Bellini and Palma il Giovane.

▷ *Cross the Vivarini Bartolomeo bridge and bear right to reach the glass museum.*

Museo del Vetro★

♿ⓒ*Open year-round Thu–Tue 10am–6pm (Nov–Mar 5pm).* ⓒ*Closed 1 Jan, 1 May, 25 Dec.* €8. ☎041 73 95 86. http://museovetro.visitmuve.it.
Palazzo Giustinian shows the evolution of glassmaking over the centuries. It is a place to see quality before perusing shops. An archaeological section displays embalming tools, cups, utensils and necklaces. On the first floor, the physical processes practised by tradition and modern technology, including coloured glass and *murrine*, are explained with illuminated panels and samples of raw materials. Developments in technique between the 15C and 18C are also defined. The height of artistry attained in the 15C is represented by a wedding cup, traditionally known as the **Barovier Cup**. The museum also houses a fine collection of modern glass and a museum shop.

Seeing through the Glass salesmen

Avoid the offer of a free trip to Murano from sales people around the Piazza San Marco unless you want to be herded into the showroom and subjected to high-pressure sales tactics once on the island.

▷ *Beyond the museum is the Church of Santa Maria e San Donato.*

Basilica dei SS Maria e Donato★★

ⓒ*Open year-round Mon–Sat 9am–noon & 3.30–7pm, Sun 3.30–7pm.* ☎041 73 90 56.
The **apse**, viewed first by most visitors, is a masterpiece of 12C Veneto-Byzantine art. A double series of blind-arched openings resting on coupled columns ripple around the semicircular bay.
Founded in the 7C, the original church was dedicated to the Virgin Mary. The incorporation of San Donato dates from the 12C, when his body, together with what remained of the dragon that he had slain, arrived from Cefalonia (the bones of the "dragon" are stored behind the altar). The church was considerably remodelled in the 12C: the mosaic floor was completed in 1141, and extensively restored during the mid-19C.
Inside, five columns with Veneto-Byzantine capitals separate the nave from the aisles; the striking **mosaic floor**★★ recalls that of the Basilica of St Mark. Among the profusion of decorative, symbolic and figurative elements, there is one particularly significant section between the second and third column on the right depicting two cockerels bearing a fox, and represents the defeat of Cunning by Vigilance.
Above the apse, a 12C mosaic *Virgin in Prayer* stands alone, projected forward by the brilliant gold background. In the left aisle is a wooden panel with *San Donato*, attributed to Paolo Veneziano, and above the door to the baptistery, a lunette by Lazzaro Bastiani depicting the Virgin and Child with John the Almsgiver (1484).

SAN FRANCESCO DEL DESERTO ★

This little island is ideal for anyone seeking respite from commotion and crowds, particularly in high summer when the islands of the lagoon can get very busy.

▪ **Information:** ☎041 528 6863. www.isola-sanfrancescodeldeserto.it.

▸ **Orient Yourself:** The island is situated just south of Burano. The island where St Francis landed is still only accessible by private boat today. Take the vaporetto (12, 14 or 6) to Burano, then water taxi, or negotiate a ride with one of the fishermen. They depart from Burano where the canal meets the lagoon as it laps the water's edge in Piazza Galuppi – not far from the front of San Martino. The cost includes the 10 minute ferry ride and waiting time; ask the boatman, who will make himself known, about the price. It is also possible to spend a few days in retreat with the monastic community by prior arrangement.

🕐 **Organising Your Time:** A complete tour takes about 1hr.

👣 **Also See:** BURANO, TORCELLO.

Monastery

Before St Francis landed on the island on his way back from the Holy Land in 1220, San Francesco del Deserto was known as the *Isola delle due Vigne* (the Island of the Two Vines). Its name was changed when a house for Franciscan novitiates was established on the island in 1224.

Lagoon Life

The Venetian lagoon comprises a variety of active biological ecosystems, and is always an atmospheric sight, whichever time of year you visit. Sea birds rest on *bricole*, the orange-topped beacons that transform the maze of waterways into navigable channels; herons pick their way carefully through the rushes. Most disconcertingly, near Burano, you might see people sheltering from the sun under umbrellas or packing bags with handfuls of mussels, apparently floating in the water. As you get closer you will see that they are standing on barely visible spits of sand.

The term *"deserto"* could be a reference to the island left "deserted" when the monks fled from a malaria epidemic. On four occasions the monastery played host to Bernardino of Siena, who may have paid for the well to be dug to collect water. Set into a wall in the cloisters is a 13C relief of two crossed arms, said to be the arm of Christ and the sleeved arm of St Francis.

Today around seven friars live here, their number augmented by novices who generally stay for a year or so.

Visit

🚣*Visit by guided tour only (1hr) Tue–Sun 9am–11am & 3–5pm.* 💰*Donation requested. www.sanfrancescodeldeserto.it.* A guided tour (1hr) with a Franciscan monk, takes in various paintings depicting the saint arriving on the island and the miracle of St Francis ordering the birds to be quiet and not to move during prayers. Interesting archaeological remains include a cistern.

The island's beautiful and vast cypress-scented **park,** offering an almost pastoral atmosphere, is possibly the most peaceful place in the whole Venetian archipelago. It overlooks the lagoon and affords a clear view of Burano.

SAN LAZZARO DEGLI ARMENI★

This island was especially loved by the Romantic poet Lord Byron, as he found the atmosphere lifted his ascetic spirit in times of melancholy. Today, it is no less evocative to visiting travellers. On arrival by vaporetto, tourists are greeted by charming Armenian monks who chaperone their charges and introduce them to this green, serene island.

▷ **Orient Yourself:** The island is located near the Lido, off the west side. It takes about 30min to get to the island of San Lazzaro degli Armeni on vaporetto line 20 from Riva degli Schiavoni (San Zaccaria). Tours are scheduled to coincide with the vaporetto times – the talk begins on landing and continues through the monastery visit. Should you require more time on the island, catch the vaporetto that leaves at around 2pm and check for the departure time of the second return service.

🕐 **Organising Your Time:** The tour takes about 1hr 15mins.

Monastery

The Armenians and the Mechitar Community

The Armenians are an ancient people whose ancestry has been linked to Noah's Ark, which some believe "ran aground" on Mount Ararat, on the Armenian border. Armenia then extended from the Black Sea to Mesopotamia, where the mountains hide the sources of the River Tigris and River Euphrates. Today the Republic of Armenia is hemmed in between Turkey, Georgia, Azerbaijan and Iran.

The country was conquered on several occasions by the Arabs, Turks, Mongols, Tartars, Ottomans and Persians. During the First World War, its people were persecuted by the Turks, almost to the point of extinction. Subsequent diaspora saw the Armenians flee overseas, particularly to the United States.

From the 14C, the island of San Lazzaro served as a leper colony until the last two leprosy sufferers were transferred to Venice (1600s).

Mechitar was given the island by the Venetian Republic and arrived here in 1717. The church was rebuilt. The pavement was lifted, the arches were made into lancet arches and the vaulted ceiling took the form of a starry sky. The original Romanesque church was built by the Benedictines, who subsequently remodelled it in the Gothic style.

Aerial view of San Lazzaro degli Armeni and the monastery

© Guido Alberto Rossi / Tips Images

Mechitar

Mechitar (1676–1749) was born in Turkey. He was ordained into the Catholic Church before settling in Constantinople, where he founded a community of Uniate Armenian monks based on St Benedict's teachings and precepts of monasticism. The monks were forced to flee the city and take refuge in Morea, a Venetian territory. When Morea was lost to the Turks, the Venetian Republic granted the community the island of San Lazzaro. The Mechitarists devote themselves to education and missionary work. The Armenian liturgy differs from that of the Roman Church in that it does not acknowledge the Pope's primacy or infallibility.

Visit

Visit by guided tours only (1hr 15min), daily 3.25pm. €6. ☎ 041 52 60 104. Cross the simple cloister full of flowering plants, kept neat and tidy, to seek out the historical manuscripts that are a testament not only to the Armenian heritage, but also to the kindly Mechitar monks who dedicate themselves to preserving the Armenian culture. In total there are 10 monks plus 10 seminarians, and around 15 Armenian students who study Italian language and culture.

Visitors are then shown the refectory where the monks and the seminarists eat their meals in silence while the Scriptures are read out in classical Armenian. On ascending the stairs, note the fine Sienese terracotta relief from 1400 and part of a painting by Palma il Giovane depicting the *Martyrdom of St Catherine*: the central section of this painting is in St Petersburg.

As well as being an important centre of Armenian culture, the monastery also owns a collection of Flemish tapestries; paintings by Armenian artists; Greek, Phoenician and Assyro-Babylonian artefacts – there is even an Egyptian sarcophagus and mummy (the latter in a somewhat gruesome state of decay). Other treasures include tapestries, tables, statues, thrones and gold, silver, and jewels that the monks have either bought or received as gifts over the centuries. Indeed the collection is so grand that some visitors tend to raise an eyebrow at its ostentation.

A highlight of the tour comes with a visit to the archive, a modern circular building containing over 150 000 volumes, including 4 000 Armenian Illuminated Manuscripts, some dating back 1 300 years.

The tour ends in a gift shop stocked with religious literature, postcards, and Armenian prints.

Lord Byron (of Venice)

Lord George Gordon Byron (1788–1824) was a handsome youth with a colourful personality. After Cambridge, he took his seat in the House of Lords before travelling to Portugal, Spain, Malta, Greece and the Levant. The experience fired his imagination and he vowed to see Greece freed from Turkish rule. In 1812 *Childe Harold's Pilgrimage* was published, securing his reputation as one of the great Romantic poets. His liaisons with his half-sister and subsequent marriage however led to disrepute. Byron left England in 1816 for the last time. While in Venice he became attracted to the monastic life at San Lazzaro, finding the spiritual quietude he craved and from which he continually transgressed as his passions flared across the water. A plaque in the monastery quotes his thoughts on his time spent here, "the visitor will be convinced that there are other and better things even in this life". Fascinated with the Armenian community, he visited the island twice a week for around 6 months during which time he managed to learn their language in six months. He collaborated with the monks on an English-Armenian dictionary and would swim to San Lazzaro from the Palazzo Mocenigo in Venice.

TORCELLO ★★

The poet and critic, John Ruskin, wrote of the relationship between Torcello and Venice in melancholy terms: "Mother and Daughter, you behold them both in their widowhood". Hemmingway had a favourite retreat here, which is still in operation. A walk along the Fondamenta dei Borgognoni and on by the canal allows a full prospect of the unique lagoon landscape to unfold. Once more important than Venice, these days wild and overgrown, Torcello is an atmospheric near-ghost island, where only the stones can speak of its glorious past.

▶ **Orient Yourself:** Torcello lies about 5.5mi to the northeast of Venice. From Fondamenta Nuove, take the same line (**12**) that goes to Burano, which is only minutes away from Torcello.

🕐 **Organising Your Time:** Allow a minimum of 2hrs to take in the atmosphere.

A Bit of History

Near the **Ponte del Diavolo** (the Devil's Bridge) stands the religious complex of Torcello. Alongside are a handful of restaurants and possibly some itinerant lace sellers. It is incredible to think that in ancient times there were around 20 000 people (some estimates go as high as 50 000) living on the island while the glorious history of Venice was only just beginning.

During the period of barbarian invasions, the Lombards chased out the Byzantines (6C–8C) and established themselves in Aquilea, Padua, Altinum and Oderzo. The bishop and the inhabitants of Altinum moved to Torcello where, in 639, the church and probably the fortifications were built; it is the *torri* (towers) of such fortifications that gave rise to the name of the island. They were not the first inhabitants, however, as the Romans had already discovered the island and records show continuous fishing and glassmaking activities throughout the 5C and 6C.

Torcello's decline started around the 10C and mirrors the pace of the glorious ascent of Venice. When malaria infested the marshes, Torcello was abandoned by its inhabitants, who fled to Venice and Murano. Now there are only around 20 inhabitants who live here year round.

Sights

Basilica di Santa Maria Assunta

♿🕐*Open Mar–Oct 10.30am–6pm, Nov–Feb 10am–5pm.* 🎫*€5 (€7.50 combined ticket with Museo or Campanile; €10 combined ticket with Museo and Campanile).* ☎*041 29 60 630.*

As recorded by the ancient **inscription** on the left of the altar, the cathe-

Locanda Cipriani

In 1934 Giuseppe Cipriani, the founder of Harry's Bar in Venice and the Hotel Cipriani in Giudecca, bought a modest wine and oil shop on Torcello. He transformed the shop into a small inn (*locanda*) with just a few guestrooms and a restaurant surrounded by a garden of flowers and vegetables and an unparalleled view of the churches of Torcello. In 1948 Ernest Hemingway stayed here and, when he wasn't out hunting ducks in the lagoon, was writing *Across the River and Through the Trees*. It may not have been his most famous novel but Hemingway devoted whole pages of it to Torcello and kept a special place in his heart for the island. As a result, the Locanda became a destination of choice for the exclusive world of stars and celebrities who often visited Venice in the post-War era. Six decades on it is still a charming unpretentious place, well worth a visit to eat, drink or stay overnight: www.locandacipriani.com.

dral dedicated to the Assumption was erected in 639, during the reign of Heraclius, Emperor of Byzantium. As such it is the lagoon's oldest building, and a splendid example of the Veneto-Byzantine style. In the 9C and 11C, it underwent modification. Little remains of the 7C baptistry other than fragments of the brick façade and its many pilasters. The 14C portico supported by the columns and pilasters also serves as a link to Santa Fosca.

The interior is divided into nave and aisles by columns. In contrast to the simplicity of structure, the decoration is opulent. The pavement is 11C. The choir, enclosed by Corinthian columns, is separated from the nave by a 15C iconostasis set with 11C Byzantine painted panels depicting the Madonna and Child flanked by the Twelve Apostles with, above, the Crucifixion from the same date. Between the columns nestle delicate Byzantine marble *plutei* carved with semi-symmetrical lions and peacocks. The Roman sarcophagus near the high altar contains the relics of St Heliodorus, the first Bishop of Altinum.

But most striking are the **ancient mosaics**★★ representing the Virgin and Christ. In accordance with Byzan-

© Baviera Guido /Sime / Photononstop

Santa Fosca

tine iconography, the Virgin is portrayed descending from Heaven.

Between the windows are aligned the *Apostles* (12C), and below the window St Heliodorusis. The mosaics of the intersecting vault harbour *Four Angels bearing the Mystic Lamb*, of a type found at Ravenna. The floral mosaic is populated with birds and animals which postdate those at San Vitale in Ravenna (7C), for these are also by artists from Ravenna, who came here while the church was being built.

Campanile

○*Open as Basilica, closes 30min earlier* ☞ *€4 (€7.50 combined ticket with the basilica and museum).* ☏*041 29 60 630.* At the rear of the basilica stands the old bell-tower (12C). The climb is not difficult and the **view**★★ over the lagoon more than compensates for the effort.

Santa Fosca

○*Open daily 10am–4.30pm.* ☏*041 73 00 84.*

This small church, in the form of a Greek cross, was built between the 11C and 12C. Its octagonal exterior is encircled by open arcading with columns capped by Veneto-Byzantine capitals. The interior, imbued with solemn silence, is enclosed below a round wooden roof.

Museo di Torcello

○*Open Mar–Oct Tues–Sun 10.30am–5pm; Nov–Mar, daily except Mon, 10am–4.30pm.* ○*Closed public hols and 21 Nov.* ☞*€7 (enquire about combined ticket with the basilica and the campanile).* ☏*041 26 90 329. http://sbmp. provincia.venezia.it.*

Artifacts associated with the history of Torcello are displayed on two floors. Interesting pieces, some dating to the 9C, include capitals, pateras, tablets, a mid-15C wooden *Pietà* of the Venetian School, paintings from the Church of St Anthony of Torcello, a work from the studio of Veronese, books and documents which recount parts of the island's history, pages from the *Mariegola* and fragments of Venetian ceramics.

The Last Judgement

The Last Judgement is the theme of the mosaics (13C–14C) at the back of the basilica. The main elements of the scene, drawn from the Apocalypse, unfold from top to bottom and are divided into two sections: the Judgement below and the Death and Resurrection of Christ above. From the Crucifixion there follows the Descent into Limbo: Christ tramples over many keys and a devil reduced to miniature proportions while determinedly clutching Adam's hand. Behind is Eve, her hands covered for reasons of propriety; to the right stands John the Baptist, who may easily be recognised by his long hair and camel-hair shirt. Beyond rank the Prophets, and to the left, the two figures with halos are David and Solomon. At the far edges, the Archangels Michael (left) and Gabriel (right) stand guard.

Dominating the central section is the *Deisis*: Christ in glory enclosed within a mandorla, the aura of His divinity, surrounded by the symbols of the Passion. He is flanked by the Virgin and John the Baptist and by two angels.

Arranged symmetrically around the edge are the Apostles, including St Peter (left) and St Paul (right; here St Paul is included among the Twelve Apostles, on a par therefore with St Barnabas).

The lower section recounts the Triumph of the Cross. The angels' trumpets recall the dead from the sea monsters that devoured them. Below the souls are being weighed by St Michael, working to safeguard the salvation of those who deserve to be protected from the demons that burden the scale with bags of sins.

To the left are the saved; to the right the damned. The seven devils portray the seven deadly sins – Pride, Avarice, Lust, Wrath, Gluttony, Envy, Sloth. The main figure is Lucifer, who holds the Antichrist and is sitting on Leviathan, the sea monster described in the Book of Job whose breath sets burning coals ablaze.

Lago di Fedaia and Marmolada, Dolomiti
©Alberto Simonetti/iStockphoto.com

BASSANO DEL GRAPPA★★

POPULATION 41 752
MICHELIN MAP 562 E 17 – VENETO

Bassano del Grappa, a pottery town that also produces brandy (grappa), is built on the banks of the Brenta River. The Old Town is one of the most beautiful in the Veneto, with painted houses and squares bordered by arcades. Its very picturesque covered wooden bridge (Ponte Vecchio or Ponte degli Alpini), designed by Palladio was originally built in the 13C and rebuilt 1751.

- **Information:** Largo Corona d'Italia, 35. ☎0424 52 43 51. www.vicenzae.org.
- **Orient Yourself:** The town lies on the S 47, 53mi/40km northwest of Venice.
- **Don't Miss:** The classic view of the famous covered bridge from just across the river (to the left) and a taste of grappa from the Nardini Distillery (est. 1779) or bars on the bridge.
- **Organising Your Time:** Allow a day.
- **Also See:** PADOVA, TREVISO and VICENZA.

Visit

Museo Civico★
Open Tue–Sat 9am–7pm Sun 10.30am–1pm, 3–6pm. Closed 1 Jan, Easter, 25 Dec. €5. ☎042 45 22 235. www.museobassano.it.

The municipal museum is housed in the monastery next to the church of St Francis. The first floor **picture gallery** has works by the local Da Ponte family. Jacopo da Ponte, otherwise called **Jacopo Bassano** (1510–92), was the best-known. His works were marked by a picturesque realism and contrasts of light and shade. **St Valentine baptising St Lucilla** is his masterpiece.

Other Venetian painters include Guariento, Vivarini, Giambono (14C and 15C), Pietro Longhi, Giambattista Tiepolo and Marco Ricci (18C), Magnasco (18C) and Canova.

Piazza Garibaldi
The square is dominated by the 13C square tower, **Torre di Ezzelino**, and overlooked by the church of San Francesco. The church, which dates from the 12C–14C, has an elegant porch (1306). Inside, the 14C Christ is by Guariento.

Excursions

Monte Grappa★★★
32km/20mi north – alt 1 775m/5 823ft.
The road heads up through forests and mountain pastures to the summit, from where there is a magnificent **panorama** out to Venice and Trieste.

Asolo★
14km/9mi east.
The streets of this beautifully sited charming little hilltop town, dominated by its castle, are lined with palaces painted with frescoes. The town is closely associated with Robert Browning and Eleonora Duse, the famous Italian tragic actress who is buried here.

Marostica★
7km/4mi west.
Every even year (2014, 2016 etc…) in September the **Piazza Castello★**, the main square of this very attractive small medieval city, serves as a giant chessboard for a highly original game of chess. In the **Partita a Scacchi**, costumed people and horses serve as the chess pieces.

Cittadella
13km/8mi south.
This 12C stronghold was built by the Paduans and has fine brick **walls★**.

Possagno

18km/11mi northwest.

This was the birthplace of the sculptor **Antonio Canova** (1757–1822), known for his neo-Classical works. Visit the **house** where he was born and the **Museo Gipsoteca** (sculpture gallery-museum) nearby. (both open Tue–Sun 9am–6pm; closed 1 Jan, Easter, 25 Dec; €8; 042 35 44 323, www.museo-canova.it). The **Tempio di Canova** shows influences of the Parthenon and Pantheon: inside is the sculptor's last work **Descent from the Cross**★ and his tomb (open summer 9am–noon and 3–6pm, rest of the year 9am–noon and 2–5pm; cupola €1.30; 042 35 44 323.

Castelfranco Veneto★

26km/16mi southeast.

This pleasant citadel town contains the **Casa Natale di Giorgione**, where the famous artist was born in 1477 (open Tue–Sun 10am–1pm and 3–7pm; closed 1 Jan, Easter, 15 Aug, 25, 26 and 31 Dec; www.museocasagiorgione.it €5; 042 37 25 022). The cathedral is home to his masterpiece, the **Madonna and Child with Saints**★★.

BELLUNO★

POPULATION 35 077

MICHELIN MAP 562 D 18 – VENETO.

This pleasant town with an attractive historic centre stands at the confluence of the River Piave and River Ardo and enjoys a spectacular mountain backdrop.

- **Information:** Piazza Duomo 2. 043 79 40 083. www.apt-dolomiti-cortina.it.
- **Orient Yourself:** Belluno lies 70mi/112 km north of Venice on the A 27, en-route to the Dolomites.
- **Don't Miss:** Piazza Maggiore in Feltre.
- **Organising Your Time:** Allow half a day.
- **Also See:** DOLOMITI.

Visit

Walk along via Rialto through the 13C gateway, Porta Dojona (remodelled in the 16C), across **Piazza del Mercato**★, bordered with arcaded Renaissance houses and adorned with a 1409 fountain, along via Mezzaterra and Via Santa Croce to the gateway, Porta Rugo. Via del Piave offers an extensive **view**★ of the Piave Valley.

Piazza del Duomo★ is surrounded by the late-15C Venetian-style **Rectors' Palace**★ (Palazzo dei Rettori), the Episcopal Palace (Palazzo dei Vescovi) and the **cathedral** (Duomo), dating from the 16C with its Baroque campanile by Juvara. In the crypt there is a 15C **polyptych**★ by the Rimini school. The Jurists' Palace (Palazzo dei Giuristi) houses the **Museo Civico** (open Tue–Sun 9am–12pm, and 4–7pm; also Wed, Fri 3–6pm; €5; 043 79 44 836, http://museo.comune.belluno.it).

Excursion

Feltre

31km/19mi southwest.

Grouped around its castle, Feltre, has kept part of its ramparts and in **Via Mezzaterra**★, old houses, adorned with frescoes in the Venetian manner. **Piazza Maggiore**★ is a beautiful square with noble buildings, arcades, stairways and balustrades. The **Museo Civico** displays some fine works by artists including Bellini, Cima da Conegliano, Ricci and Jan Massys (open Sat–Sun, holidays 10.30am–12.30pm and 4–7pm; closed 1 Jan and 25–26 Dec; €4; 0439 88 52 41, http://musei.comune.feltre.bl.it/Museo-Civico).

VILLAS OF THE **BRENTA**★★

The Brenta Valley is a bucolic stretch of land where the doges elected to have their lavish country houses. Some Venetian families still follow this tradition today. Reflected in the quiet waters of the river, from Padua to the lagoon, these patrician villas possess that air of an exclusive, cultural country retreat were working farms that were crucial after the loss of trade to the New World.

- ⊞ **Information:** Villa Widmann. Via Nazionale 420, Mira Porte. ☎041 56 00 690. www.riviera-brenta.it.
- ▶ **Orient Yourself:** The Brenta River skirts the city of Padua and arcs south. The villas lie along the Naviglio Brenta section, which empties into the Adriatic Sea at Porto di Brondolo near Fusina, to the south of Chioggia. The River Brenta links Padua to Venice by water, but access from either direction is easiest by road. If you are coming from the west along the A 4, exit at Padova Est. Follow the Noventana road and directions for Stra (SS 11). From Venice–Mestre, follow the signs for Riviera del Brenta and Malcontenta (SS 11).
- ☺ **Don't Miss:** The Salone delle Feste at the Villa Pisani.
- ⏱ **Organising Your Time:** Allow 2 days for the driving itinerary and tour of the villas.

A Bit of History

A Troubled Past

By 1100 the Paduans and the Venetians were locked in conflict over who should have control over the Brenta River's course and therefore the hold on a strategic access point to the lagoon. After 1409, with the annexation of Padua, the Republic of Venice was assured definitive control of the River Brenta and thus started to invest in landed property along its banks. In an effort to limit the threat of damage from flooding, subsidiary canals were built. By the beginning of the 16C, opulent villas, set among extensive gardens, were being designed and built.

In 1840, after a disastrous flood, work was initiated on redirecting the river to flow into the lagoon at Chioggia, but infilling the delta proved so difficult that the water was directed farther down to run straight out to sea, as it does today at Brondolo.

Today the Brenta Valley, like Venice, survives as if by a pact made between nature and architecture. However, many find the area oppressive; heavy swirling mists and flooding exaggerate the cold in winter and the humid atmosphere in summer.

The Villas

The traditional villa was intended to provide the landowner with lodgings and a base for commerce while running his farm estate. Erected near the farm, it was built on a centralised plan, flanked by *barchesse* (☺ See Box, left).

The villa's function as country home to which the landed gentry could retreat was secondary to supervising their tenanted farm, often their main source of income after loss of trade to New World routes that favoured other ports. By the 18C, country houses were all the rage among the Venetian nobility, who basked in luxury, while Venice sang its maritime trade swansong. The most popular holiday periods were the months of June, July, October and November, when the

---

Barchesse

Up until the end of the 17C, the *barchesse* (from *barca* meaning boat) were the outbuildings of the villas used for storing grain and "garaging" the boats, because it was prohibited to leave them moored along the canal.

Frequently, throughout the 17C, the *barchesse* doubled up as sleeping quarters for use by the extra house guests invited to the great parties at the villas, which might go on for days.

Allegorical Painting in the Brenta Villas

Frequent recourse to allegorical subject matter in the art of the 17C and 18C reflects the prevailing wish to assert the Venetian taste in "style": one that was inspired by a *joie de vivre*, a Humanist interest in Classical literature and a predilection for ostentation and luxury. The great battles at sea and on land were now over and Venice was to be celebrated as a proud combatant and conqueror. Now was the time to relish past glories and to enjoy the good life.

balmy evenings might be spent listening to a musical recital or watching a group of players.

Few of the many villas can be attributed to specific architects; however, given their artistic quality, it is generally acknowledged that they must have been designed to satisfy highly sophisticated and aesthetically discerning patrons.

Entertaining along the Brenta

Nobles or peasants, the Venetians shared the same taste for **farce**. Along the riverbanks, where people idled away the time with a good book, puppeteers found an ideal location in which to set up their theatres and animate their characters: Brighella, Harlequin, Columbine and Pantaloon. In the villa gardens, comic plays were staged. The numerous **sagre** (feast days) were always an excuse for throwing a party, when guests could sing and dance the night away in the magnificent villa ballrooms.

Boat Tour

Il Burchiello

The 18C traveller could choose to journey from Venice to Padua by boat or by carriage. The boat was neither comfortable nor quick and fellow passengers would not always have been the most salubrious. The original *Burchiello*, built in Padua c.1700 and adapted from the **burchio** (canal barge) that was used in Venice to transport general goods, heralded an improvement in river transport. Passengers were accommodated on benches arranged around tables and protected by a canopy overhead. Further shelter against driving rain, biting winds or blinding sunshine was provided by decorative panels of inlaid wood and attractive drapes. When travelling upstream, the barge was pulled by a yoke of horses. Travelling aboard the *Burchiello* became a pleasure to be experienced, but the legendary vessel did not survive long: the costly service was suspended when the Republic fell in 1797 and was not revived again until the 1960s when a modest vaporetto was put into service.

The present-day version of the *Burchiello* is modern, and very comfortable - in fact there are no less than 12 *burchielli* presently in service; eight are operated by the I Battelli del Brenta company (☎049 87 60 233, www.battellidelbrenta.it) and three routes by Il Burchiello (☎049 82 06 910, www.ilburchiello.it). Both operators offer various cruises and tours; contact them for details.

Driving Tour

From Padua to Fusina, via Mirano

▸ *Take the A4 to the Padova Est Exit. Follow the Noventana road towards Stra (SS 11).*

Villa Foscarini Rossi

♿ ⏰ *Museum open Apr–Oct Tue–Fri 9am–1pm & 2–6pm. Sat –Sun 2.30–6pm guided tours only. Nov–Mar Mon–Fri 9am–1 pm. ⌨ €5. ☎049 98 01 091. www. villafoscarini.it.*

This villa is named after its most eminent resident, **Marco Foscarini**, who was elected doge in 1762. The current Rossi family are famous for their shoes and several of the rooms open to the public are devoted to a very artistic and stylish display of shoes, past and present. The villa is neo-Classical in style, although modifications were made during the

© Lara Pessina / MICHELIN

Villa Pisani

19C. The adjacent *barchessa* is older and in its hall frescoed allegorical scenes are set among *trompe l'oeil* detailing.

Villa Pisani – La Nazionale ★

🕐 *Open year-round Tue–Sun and hol Mon 8.30am–7pm (9–5pm Oct–Mar).* 🕐 *Closed 1 Jan, 1 May, 25 Dec.* 🍽 . 💶€7.50. ☎049 50 20 74. www.villapisani. beniculturali.it.

The residence of **Alvise Pisani**, elected doge in 1735, comprises a magnificent estate with stables and gardens designed by **Girolamo Frigimelica**, who also submitted plans for the villa. These proved to be too costly and were entrusted to **Francesco Maria Preti**. During the 18C, the villa was endowed with sculpture and paintings, but when the Republic fell in 1797 the Pisani family was forced to sell it to Napoleon who, in turn, gave it to his adopted son Eugène Beauharnais, the Viceroy of Italy. Following the Austrian occupation in 1814, Villa Pisani accommodated several other famous figures, including Francesco Giuseppe, Maximilian of Austria, and Carlos IV of Spain. Soon after the unification of Italy, the villa returned to Italian ownership. It now belongs to the State.

Exterior

At first sight, the house appears to be modelled on a French château. The outside wall, enclosing extensive grounds at the rear, accentuates the horizontal design elements of the façade: the central, projecting Palladian-style bay is charged with decoration; the entrance itself is austerely monumental. Four Atlas figures support the loggia, and silhouetted against the sky, statues and pinnacles punctuate the corners of the pediments.

Beyond the entrance opens a gallery supported by columns, from which there is a magnificent view over the still water and the Palladian-style stables, fronted by their imposing entrance and figures

of Zephyr and Flora, sculpted by **Giovanni Bonazza** and his son Tomaso.

Interior

Villa Pisani has 114 rooms in honour of Alvise Pisani, the 114th Doge of Venice. This most famous member of the Pisani family spent his summers here to keep an eye on the grain harvest and the wine production.

Climb the stairs to the left of the entrance, ornamented with wooden statues attributed to Andrea Brustolon, up to the **Sala del Trionfo delle Arti**s, named after the ceiling decoration executed by Giovan Battista Crosato.

In the next room, dedicated to Bacchus and frescoed by Jacopo Guarana (1770), there is an implausible portrayal of an elephant, painted without first-hand knowledge (*on the wall through which you have come*); watch for the *casone*, a typical peasant dwelling in the Brenta region (*in a panel opposite the windows*). After the room where Hitler and Mussolini met in 1943, comes the Beauharnais suite, furnished with a small bed and the chapel housing an altar by Sansovino, which was brought here by Napoleon from the Church of San Gimignano in Piazza San Marco, which he ordered to be demolished.

The highlight is the vast **Salone delle Feste** in which sumptuous balls were held. The orchestra would play in the long minstrels' gallery. The striking fresco was the last to be painted by Tiepolo in Italy. Look for his signature motif, a parrot (*right corner*).

The Grounds

The great garden extends around a long pond which, although well integrated into the villa's landscape, is a modern addition. It was, in fact, dug in 1911 by the University of Padua to carry out studies on tidal forces. On the west side is the Belvedere folly, its steps seeming to wrap around two columns. The east side is the more animated part of the park: the Café-Haus, built on a mound and surrounded by a ditch, was designed as a summerhouse for relaxation. Beyond, towards the exit, is a gazebo, from which a fine view opens onto the whole villa. Note the nearby maze, a common feature in French and Italian Renaissance gardens that rarely survives.

▶ *Proceed eastwards along the SS 11.*

Villa Soranzo

Villa Soranzo, now a hotel (☎041 58 40 088, *www.villasoranzo.it*), is famous for its façade frescoes painted by Benedetto Caliari, brother of Paolo (Il Veronese). A fine example of *trompe l'oeil*, these depict a balustrade with monochrome characters peeping out from the niches among mythological figures.

▶ *Continue through Dolo and at Mira, follow the directions to Mirano (7km/4mi from Mira) and the road along the canal.*

Mirano

Also known as *Il Musone*, Mirano is a satellite of the Brenta Riviera. Although it is not blessed with all the features of the Riviera proper, it has the usual scenery of mills, aligned houses and villas.

In **Mira Porte** the houses are terraced into long lines and the Brenta loops around them. Once there was a lock here that brought river trade. Today, the place survives as a small but thriving Veneto town, its piazza ringed with local bars. The Villa Widmann Foscari is 1mi/2km from here.

Villa Widmann Foscari Rezzonico

♿ ⏰*Open Tue–Sun 10am–5pm, (Apr–Oct–5pm).* ⏰*1 Jan, 25 Dec.* 🗪. 👓€5. ☎*041 56 00 690 or 041 42 49 73.*

Goldoni, D'Annunzio and Stravinsky all stayed at this 18C villa. The highlight of its magnificent Rococo interior is the ballroom, complete with minstrels' gallery.

Villa Valmarana

♿ ⏰*Open Mar–Oct daily 10am–6pm.* 👓€6. ☎*041 42 66 387. www.villaval marana.net.*

The 18C Villa Valmarana would, at one time, have been flanked by two *barchesse*. The main villa was demolished by the Valmarana family in the 19C to avoid paying a wealth tax on luxury goods. The *barchessa* on the left was divided between six families who modified the original architectural layout of the building. Yet this mere outbuilding is truly monumental. Surrounded by an Italianate rose garden, it is fronted with a fine portico of double Doric columns. In the centre, a giant order of pilasters rises to the cornice.

As usual, the owner's family are glorified in the central **salone** ceiling. The fresco, painted in the second half of the 17C, is attributed to Michelangelo Schiavoni ('Il Chioggotto'), a follower of Tiepolo.

▶ *Continue through Oriago and cross the swing bridge over the river.*

Villa Gradenigo

⏰*Open to B&B guests or by or by appointment* ☎*042 24 46 462. www.villagrad enigo.com.*

One of the oldest villas on the Brenta, Villa Gradenigo has a square floor plan which was typical of the 16C. The frescoes decorating the garden front, despite their poor condition, are still discernible as the work of Benedetto Caliari, brother of Paolo, Il Veronese.

Better preserved although not perfect are the frescoes inside. In the 19C the villa was divided into apartments, and several of the frescoes were irretrievably damaged. At one point in the early 20C, the *palazzo* even served as a laundry, the steam ironically being the coup de grâce for the paintings. Today the villa is a privately owned B&B.

In the reception room on the ground floor, which served as a *portego* – half house, half garden – are murals by Benedetto Caliari. The room is further decorated with friezes of festooned flowers and fruit and painted architectural elements which were first introduced into Venetian villa decoration by Veronese.

▶ *Continue along the SS 11 then turn right, off the Venice road, in the direction of Malcontenta.*

Villa Foscari La Malcontenta★

🕐 *Open May–Oct Tue and Sat 9am–noon.* 🎫 *€8 (€7 Tue and Sun).* 🎫 *€3.* ☎*049 54 70 012 (May–Oct) 049 52 03 966 (Nov–Apr). www.lamalcontenta.com.*

The elegant **Villa Foscari** known as **La Malcontenta** is designated a UNESCO World Heritage Site. The name comes from the controversial excavation of a canal called the *fossa dei malcontenti,* which has lent its name to the area of Malcontenta since 1458.

Since the 16C, the villa has been visited by various illustrious personalities including Henri III, the King of France. Having been used as a military hospital during the First World War, the villa is now back in the hands of the Foscari family, who use it as a summer home.

The House

When Foscari commissioned **Andrea Palladio** (1508–80), the idea was to build a residence in the style of Classical Antiquity: a central square fronted by a temple portico facing the Brenta. This projecting entrance, flanked by Ionic columns, gives the house a formal austerity relieved in part by rustication. The main rooms are accommodated on the *piano nobile*, the first floor, raised above ground level to avoid the risk of flood damage but also to provide

enough space to contain the kitchens and storage areas.

The south-facing "back" overlooks the widest part of the garden: it is less formal than the main front, relieved with decorative touches such as the broken pediment and varied window heights. The arched "thermal" window was an idea borrowed from Roman baths.

It is the precise calculation of geometrical harmonies that is unique to the Villa Foscari, developed by Palladio with all measurements determined by the number four as a unit or as a multiple.

Interior

The main entrance to the villa leads into the Latin-cross shaped *salone*. Space is further enhanced by the fresco decoration by **Giambattista Zelotti**, complete with painted fluted Doric columns.

To the northwest of the *salone* is the **Stanza dell'Aurora** (Aurora Room) containing *Harvest*: a beautiful Venetian lady, the legendary Malcontenta, making her entrance; the dependent *studiolo* is dedicated to Bacchus and Venus. To the northeast, Prometheus is depicted on the ceiling with, on the walls, *Phaethon Struck Down by Jupiter* and *Caco Stealing Arms from Hercules*. The **Stanza dei Giganti** (Room of the Giants) presents a very different, apocalyptic scene of giants being crushed by huge boulders. These frescoes, initiated by **Battista Franco** and completed by Zelotti, recall the influence of the Mannerist painter-architect Giulio Romano (Palazzo del Tè in Mantua 1532–34).

Villa Foscari La Malcontenta

DOLOMITI ★★★
THE DOLOMITES
MICHELIN MAP 562 C 16–19 – VENETO – TRENTINO-ALTO ADIGE

These high, pale-coloured mountains (Monti Pallidi) situated between the Veneto and Trentino-Alto Adige (South Tyrol), straddle the Italian-Austrian border and are legendary for the red tints they take on at sunset. The ski slopes here have long been famous as a winter playground for the Italian jetset, but there is plenty of interest here for less well-heeled visitors all year round.

- **Information:** Veneto: Piazzetta S. Francesco 8, 32043 Cortina d'Ampezzo. ☎043 63 231 or 043 69 119. www.apt-dolomiti-cortina.it. Alto Adige/South Tyrol: Piazza Walther, 8 I Bolzano. ☎047 13 07 000. www.hallo.com.
- **Orient Yourself:** In the Trentino-Alto Adige region, the Dolomites are reached by A 22 off the Brennero transalpine route. From the Veneto region take A 27.
- **Parking:** Leave your car in the car park north of Chiusa if visiting the Convento di Sabiona.
- **Don't Miss:** Val Gardena and the panoramas from Tofana di Mezzo.
- **Organising Your Time:** Allow for 3–4 days of skiing or walking.
- **Also See:** BELLUNO.

A Bit of Geography

The Dolomites are made of a white calcareous rock known as dolomite. Some 150 million years ago this land was submerged by the sea. On its sandy depths coral reefs and limestone began to shape these "Pale Mountains". Then about 70 million years ago the layers were violently compressed and forced to the surface.

The Dolomites were completed about 2 million years ago when glaciers softened and hollowed out the valleys.

The massifs – To the southeast rise the Pelmo (3 168m/10 393ft) and the Civetta (3 220m/10 564ft) massifs. To the south, near the peak of the Vezzana, the Pale di San Martino, streaked by fissures, divide into three chains separated by a plateau. The Latemar (2 842m/9 324ft) and the Catinaccio (2 981m/9 780ft) massifs, together with the Torri del Vaiolet (Towers of Vaiolet), frame the Costalunga Pass. To the north of the pass rise the Sasso Lungo and the vast Sella Massif (Gruppo di Sella).

To the east, the chief summits in the Cortina Dolomites are the Tofane, the Sorapis and the Cristallo. Finally, in the heart of the range, stands the **Marmolada Massif** (Gruppo della Marmolada, 3 342m/10 964ft).

Between Cortina and the Piave Valley the wooded region of **Cadore** boasts the Antelao (3 263m/10 705ft) and the

The Ladin Culture

Ladin is a curious ancient language which has its roots in the Latin language and is spoken by around 30 000 people in and around the Dolomites. It had emerged by the 5C as a direct result of the earlier Roman expansion into the mountainous regions.

At Ciastel de Tor, in San Martino in Badia, the Museum ladin has an impressive exhibition on the Ladin culture. Artistic displays and creative use of the latest communications technology make for an interesting visit: ◷ open Easter–Oct Tue–Sat and Mon Jul–Aug 10am–5pm; Sun 2–6pm; Dec 26–Easter Thu–Sat 3–7pm ; ◷Closed Nov, 25 Dec; ◷€8; ☎047 45 24 020, www.museumladin.it.

Address Book

SPORT AND LEISURE

DOLOMITI – MOUNTAIN FOOTPATHS

The Dolomites have a dense network of footpaths. Whether you are an expert climber or simply want to take a peaceful walk, there is a vast choice of routes for those wishing to get a better look at the Monti Pallidi. Maps and guides listing paths, mountain huts and bivouacs are on sale just about everywhere.

Some mountain pathways include:

No 2 (Bressanone–Feltre): This path crosses the Plose, the Puez Group, the Gardenaccia, the Sella and the Marmolada massif.

No 3 (Villabassa–Longarone): This path winds its way through Val Pusteria, the Croda Rossa, Misurina, the Cristallo, the Sorapis and the Antelao.

No 4 (San Candido–Pieve di Cadore): This track goes through the Sesto Dolomites, the Cadini di Misurina and the Marmarole.

To be fully prepared for a mountain excursion it is advisable to contact the tourist offices listed left.

TREKKING AND CLIMBING

Gruppo Guide Alpine Scuola di Alpinismo – *Corso Italia 69/A – 32043 Cortina d'Ampezzo – ☎043 68 68 505. www.guidecortina.com.*

This company use only experienced mountain guides and offer a wide variety of organised year-round excursions for children and adults alike including hiking, orienteering, climbing courses for all levels, off-piste skiing, ice climbing and trekking.

---

triple peak, Tre Cime di Lavaredo (Drei Zinnen), which it shares with the Parco delle Dolomiti di Sesto in Alto Adige.

Flora and fauna – The Dolomite landscape is coloured by coniferous forests, crocuses, edelweiss, rhododendron, lilies and alpine bluebells. Tourist activity drives away wild animals, but the Dolomites are still a refuge for many, including royal eagles and woodcock.

Driving Tours

1 Strada delle Dolomiti★★★

From Bolzano to Cortina – 210km/131mi – allow at least two days.

This great Dolomite Road is not only a world-famous spectacular route but a perfect example of the science of road engineering.

Bolzano★

Capital of the Alto Adige, Bolzano lies on the A 22, the Brenner transalpine route, at the confluence of the Adige and the Isarco. It anchors one end of the wine road (*Strada di Vino*). The architecture of the town shows a marked Austrian influence, built largely between the 16C and 1918. At its heart centre is the Piazza Walther and the delightful **Via dei Portici**★.

Don't miss the **Museo Archeologico dell'Alto**★ (& ⏱️open Tue–Sun, daily in Jul, Aug, Dec, 8am–6pm; 🕐closed 1 Jan, 1 May, 25 Dec; ⊕€9; ☎047 13 20 100, www.iceman.it), which illustrates the chronology of the South Tyrol from the last Ice Age (15000 BC) to the Carolingian age (AD 800) and houses the "Iceman," known as "Ötzi," whose preserved remains were found by German mountain climbers in the Ötzi Alps, in 1991.

The nearby **Renon Plateau★** (Ritten) is dazzlingly green and fertile, dominating the Isarco Valley (Eisacktal) between Bolzano and Ponte Gardena. It can be reached by car from Bolzano north or the funicular at Soprabolzano in Bolzano.

Gola della Val d'Ega★

This narrow gorge, the Ega Valley, with pink sandstone walls, is guarded by the **Castel Cornedo**.

Passo di Costalunga★

From this pass on the Dolomite Road there is a **view**★ over the Catinaccio on one side and the Latemar on the other.

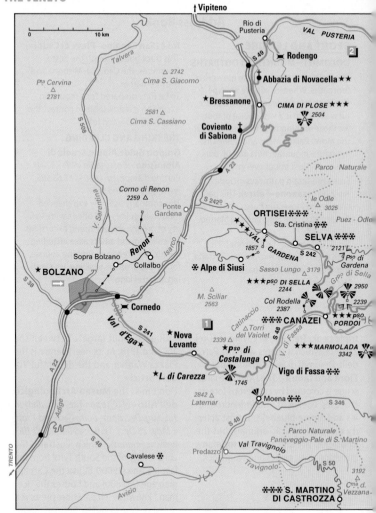

† Vipiteno

VAL PUSTERIA

Rodengo

Abbazia di Novacella ★★

CIMA DI PLOSE ★★★
2504

★ Bressanone

Coviento di Sabiona †

ORTISEI ✳✳✳
Sta. Cristina ✳✳

SELVA ✳✳✳

VAL GARDENA

Pso di Gardena

✳ Alpe di Siusi

Sasso Lungo

★★★Pso DI SELLA
2244

Grpo di Sella

✳✳✳ **CANAZEI**

Col Rodella
2387

★★★ Pso
PORDOI

★ BOLZANO

Sopra Bolzano
Collalbo

■ Cornedo

★ Nova Levante

★Pso di
Costalunga

★★★ **MARMOLADA**
3342

Vigo di Fassa ✳✳

★ L. di Carezza
1745

Moena ✳✳

Latemar
2842

Cavalese ✳

Predazzo

Val Travignolo

Parco Naturale
Paneveggio-Pale di S. Martino

✳✳✳ **S. MARTINO
DI CASTROZZA**

Vigo di Fassa ✳✳
*Strada Rezia 10. ☎046 26 09 700.
www.fassa.com.*

This resort, in a picturesque site★ in the Val di Farsa, is a mountaineering centre in the Catinaccio Massif. The multi-lingual Ski School (*Piazza J.B.Massa; ☎046 27 63 125, www.scuolascivigo.com*) is recommended.

Canazei ✳✳✳
*Piaz G. Marconi, 5. ☎046 26 09 600;
www.fassa.com.*

Canazei lies in the heart of the massif, between the Catinaccio, the Towers of Vaiolet (Torri del Vaiolet), the Sella Massif and the Marmolada. This is the usual

base for excursions in the Marmolada mountain range.

▶ *At Canazei turn right onto the P 641.*

This road affords very fine **views**★★ of the Marmolada range and its glacier. As one comes out of a long tunnel a lake, **Lago di Fedaia**★, suddenly appears.

Marmolada★★★
☎043 77 22 277 www.marmolada.com.
This is the highest massif in the Dolomites, famous for its glacier and fast ski-runs. The **cable car** from Malga Ciapela goes up to 3 265m/10 712ft offering wonderful **panoramas**★★★ of

the Cortina peaks (Tofana and Cristallo), the Sasso Lungo, the enormous tabular mass of the Sella Massif and in the background the summits of the Austrian Alps including the Grossglockner.

▶ *Return to Canazei then after 5.5km/3mi turn left.*

Passo di Sella★★★
Linking the Val di Fassa and Val Gardena this pass offers one of the most extensive **panoramas**★★★ in the Dolomites, including the Sella, Sasso Lungo and Marmolada massifs.

Val Gardena★★★
🔗 www.val-gardena.com.
This is one of the most famous, most beautiful and most visited valleys in the Dolomite. The inhabitants still speak a language which was born during the Roman occupation: the Ladin dialect. Skilful local woodwork can be seen in shops in Selva (Wolkenstein), Santa Cristina and Ortisei (St Ulrich).

Selva Val Gardena★★★
🔗 Wolkenstein Str. Mëisules 213. ☎047 17 77 900. www.val-gardena.com. This resort lies at the Sella Massif base and is a renowned craft centre as well as one of the leading ski resort in the Alps.

The Legend of the Pale Mountains

Legend has it that a prince who lived at the foot of the Alps married the daughter of the King of the Moon. The young girl loved flowers and meadows but she so desperately missed the pale mountains of her home that she felt compelled to return to the Moon. The Prince was unable to go with her because the brightness of the moon would blind him. Some dwarfs came to his aid and made some skeins of thread from the moon's rays, weaving them into nets which they placed on the mountains, turning them into the required pallid shades of the Mountains of the Moon. The princess was thus able to return to her prince.

Ortisei (St Ulrich)★★★
🖪 *Str. Rezia.* ☎*047 17 77 600. www.ortisei. com, www.val-gardena.com.*
From Ortisei (St Ulrich) a cable car climbs up to **Alpe di Siusi**★ (Seiser Alm), a 60km2/23sq mi plateau in a delightful **setting**★★ overlooking the Sasso Lungo and the Sciliar. This is an excellent base for excursions to suit all abilities.

▶ *Return to the Dolomite Road.*

Passo Pordoi★★★
The highest pass (2 239m/7 346ft) on the Dolomite Road lies between huge blocks of rock with sheer sides and shorn-off tops.

Passo del Falzarego
Nearing Cortina the pass cuts through the Tofane and skirts the barren landscape of the Cinque Torri (literally, Five Towers), which are said to have inspired Tolkein when he wrote *The Lord of the Rings.*

Cortina d'Ampezzo★★★
🖪 *www.cortina.dolomiti.com.*
Cortina, the capital of the Dolomites, is a winter sports and summer resort with a worldwide reputation. Set in the heart of the Dolomites at an altitude of 1 210m/4 000ft it is an excellent excursion centre for discovering the magnificent **mountain scenery**★★★.

Tondi di Faloria★★★
🚡 *Cable car service to Faloria from Via Ria di Zeto. From Cortina d'Ampezzo to Tondi di Faloria: in winter, "Tondi," "Girilada," "Vitelli," "Rio Gere" and "Bigontina" chairlifts* 🎿*. ☎043 63 231; www.dolomiti.org.*
From the summit a grand panorama may be enjoyed. Excellent ski slopes.

Tofana di Mezzo★★★ – *"Freccia del Cielo" cable car: for information telephone the tourist office (🚡 see above).* A cable car climbs to 3 244m/10 743ft, for a superb panorama of the mountain.

Belvedere Pocol★★ – 🕐*Open Dec–Easter and 15 Jul–15 Sep. For information* ☎*0436 86 79 21. Hourly bus service from Piazza Roma, Cortina.*
Lying to the southwest, this viewpoint affords a wonderful sunset view of Cortina.

② Val Pusteria and surrounding area

This itinerary begins in Bressanone and continues into the Pusteria Valley.
Val Pusteria, or Pustertal, is bordered to the south by the Dolomites and by the central Alps to the north. From the end of the 13C until the 16C it belonged to the County of Gorizia and formed part of the Strada d'Alemagna, a road which linked Venice and Germany.

Bressanone (Brixen)★★
🖪 *Bahnhofstrasse 9, Bressanone (Brixen).* ☎*047 28 36 401. www.brixen.org.*
Set at the confluence of the Rienza and Isarco rivers, Bressanone is an elegant Tyrolean town that enjoys an exceptionally high number of sunshine hours. Conquered by the Romans in 15 BC, it then belonged to Bavaria and Austria, until 1919 when it became Italian.

Duomo – This Baroque cathedral has a neo-Classical west front and luminous interior decorated with golf leaf frescoes and Romanesque **cloisters.**★

Palazzo vescovile – Commissioned by Prince-Bishop Bruno de Kirchberg after 1250, the palace underwent numerous alterations but retained its superb

courtyard★. It now houses the vast **Museo diocesano**★ (○*open Tue–Sun mid-Mar to Oct 10am–5pm; Nativity display Dec 1–Jan 6 daily;* ○*Closed 24–25 Dec;* ☞*€6 combined ticket, €4 museum only.* ☎*047 28 30 505, www.hofburg. it*) containing a wonderful set of polychrome **wood carvings**★★ (Romanesque and Gothic Tyrolean), **altarpieces**★ carved in the round dating from the Renaissance, the cathedral **treasure**★ and **Nativity scenes**★ dating from the 18C to 20C.

▶ *Head south towards Chiusa (Klausen).*

Convento di Sabiona

○*Church of Our Lady: open mid-Apr to Sept Tue & Fri 2–5pm, Sat 10am–noon. Other areas daily 8am–5pm. www. klausen.it* Ⓟ*If you can, leave the car in the car park north of Chiusa (Klausen), from here it is 30min on foot.* This spectacularly located convent of Benedictine nuns (known as the Acropolis of the Tyrol) dates back to the 17C. It was built on the rock where the bishop's palace had stood, the palace having burnt down after being struck by lightning in 1535.

▶ *Turn around and head in the direction of Bressanone, turning right onto the road for Plose.*

Plose★★

Alt 2 446 m/8 031ft.
A cable car from Valcroce and then another from Plose enable visitors to enjoy a wonderful **panorama**★★★ of the Dolomites and the Austrian mountains.

▶ *Retrace your steps and continue along the S 49. The Abbazia di Novacella is 3km/2mi north of Bressanone.*

Abbazia di Novacella★★

☞*Open by guided tour only (italian and German only) Mon–Sat 10am, 11am, 2pm, 3pm, 4pm. Mid-Jul to mid-Sept also noon, 1pm. Nov–Easter 11am, 3pm only.* ☞*€5.50.* ☎*047 28 36 189. www.abbazi-anovacella.it .*
The abbey, known in German as Kloster Neustift, was founded in 1142 and run by Augustinian monks. The courtyard contains the **Well of Wonders** decorated with "eight" wonders of the world, one of which is the abbey itself. The Bavarian Baroque **church** has an ornate interior and **Rococo** library of 76 000 rare books, and manuscripts.

▶ *Return to the SS 49 and continue north to Rio di Pusteria. Close by stands the Castello di Rodengo.*

Castello di Rodengo

☞*Open by guided tour only (1hr), 1 May–15 Oct Sun–Fri 11am and 3pm, also 4pm 15 Jul 15–31 Aug).* ☞*€4.50.* ☎*047 24 54 056.* The Castle of Rodengo is decorated with the oldest known cycle of Romanesque (13C) frescoes with a profane theme: the epic poem *Iwein* by Hartmann von Aue.

Bruneck (Dietenheim)★★

This is the main town in the Pusteria Valley. The beautiful open-air **Südtiroler Landesmuseum für Volkskunde** (South Tyrol Museum of Folk Traditions) ★ (♿○*Open Easter Mon–Oct Tue–Sat 10am–5pm (Jul–Aug 6pm), Sun and public holidays 2–6pm.* ☞*€6.* ☎*047 45 52 087. www.volkskundemuseum.it*) comprises the stately late 17C residence of Mair am Hof and its grounds of 3ha/7 acres, which includes many and various types of rural buildings brought here from other parts of the region. These include a hayloft, a farm, grain store, and a mill, the oldest building dating as far back as 1497.

▶ *From Bruneck head in the direction of Dobbiaco. After Monguelfo turn right to Lago di Braies (signposted).*

Lago di Braies (Prager Wildsee) ★★★

Alt 1 495m/4 905ft. This shimmering lake can be circumnavigated in around an hour. It is the starting point of some rather arduous mountain footpaths.

▶ *Proceed through the Pusteria Valley. Turn right before Dubbiaco in the direction of Cortina. Follow directions for Misurina and then for Tre Cime di Lavaredo. The last stretch is a toll-road.*

Tre Cime di Lavaredo★★★

From the *rifugio* (refuge) at Auronza the Lavaredo shelter is reached in half an hour. From there the Locatelli shelter is reached in an hour. This last stretch offers spectacular views of the Tre Cime (Three Chimneys) range. The Tre Cime can also be reached from Sesto, along path 102, which leads to Locatelli in two and a half hours.

▶ *On the way back from Tre Cime a stop at Lago di Misurina is recommended.*

Lago di Misurina★★

Alt 1 759m/5 770ft. This lake is set among a plantation of fir trees and is an excellent starting point for excursions to the surrounding mountains, from the Tre Cime di Lavaredo to the Cristallo.

Dobbiaco (Toblach)✳

Dobbiaco was an important town in the Middle Ages, standing at the crossroads with the main Strada dell'Alemagna.

San Candido★

This pretty village has the most important Romanesque church in the Alto Adige. The **collegiata**★ dates from the 13C. Most striking is the *Crucifixion*, a 13C wood sculptural group with Christ's feet resting on Adam's head.

▶ *At San Candido turn right for Sesto leaving the Pusteria, which eventually leads to Austria.*

Sesto★

Sesto overlooks the Dolomites and offers a huge variety of footpaths and alpine excursions. The **Monte Elmo funicular** makes distances shorter. For a peaceful walk, path 4D crosses the forest and high pastures and affords views of the Meridiana del Sesto.

▶ *At San Giuseppe (Moos) the Val Fiscalino leads to **Campo Fiscalinoa**★ offering stunning views of the Meridiana di Sesto and Cima dei Tre Scarperi.*

Visit

Valle del Cordevole★★

The road from Caprile to Belluno is lined with hilltop villages. **Alleghe** on the **lake**★ is a good excursion centre.

San Martino di Castrozza✳✳✳

A good starting point for excursions.

Pieve di Cadore★

🛈*Via Nazionale 45. ☎0435 31644. www. pievedicadore.org.*
The birthplace of the great artist, **Titian**, the town church holds one of his works and his family house **Casa del Tiziano** is now a museum (🕑*open Jun–Sept Mon–Sat 10am–12.30pm and 3–7pm; ☞€3; ☎043 53 22 62, www. magnificacomunitadicadore.it*). Also of interest is the **Cadore Museum** situated in the Palazzo della Magnifica Comunita. Worth a second glance is the unusual but interesting **Museo dell'Occhiale** (Spectacles Museum) (☎*www.museo dellocchiale.it*) displaying over 2 600 examples of reading glasses, dating from the Middle Ages to the modern day.

Tre Cime di Lavaredo

© Lara Pessina / MICHELIN

PADOVA ★★
PADUA
POPULATION 210 821
MICHELIN MAP 562 F 17 – VENETO

Padua is home to some of the finest historical and artistic sights in the Veneto. The city's cultural and artistic heritage dates back to the 13C and 14C when its university was one of the very best in Europe, the Scrovegni Chapel had become a landmark in Renaissance Art and the Basilica di Sant'Antonio (Basilica del Santo) was founded as a major site of pilgrimage.

- **Information:** Galleria Pedrocchi. ☎049 87 67 927. Stazione Ferrovie dello Stato. ☎049 87 52 077. www.turismopadova.it.
- **Orient Yourself:** Padua is 24mi/40km west of Venice.
- **Don't Miss:** Giotto's frescoes in the Scrovengni Chapel, the Basilica del Santo, the University.
- **Organising Your Time:** Allow at least two day to explore Padua.
- **Also See:** Riviera del BRENTA, TREVISO, VENEZIA, VICENZA.

A Bit of History

There are few traces of ancient *Patavium*, which was one of the most prosperous Roman cities in the Veneto during the 1C BC owing to its river trade, its agriculture and the sale of horses. In the 7C Padua was destroyed by the Lombards, and from the 11C to 13C it became an independent city-state. The city underwent its greatest period of economic and cultural prosperity under the enlightened rule of the lords of Carrara (1337–1405). In 1405 Padua came under the sway of the Venetian Republic and remained a loyal subject until 1797 when the Venetian Constitution was abolished by Napoleon.

The City of St Anthony the Hermit – This Franciscan monk was born in Lisbon in 1195 and died at the age of 36 in the environs of Padua. He was a forceful preacher and is generally represented holding a book and a lily. St Anthony is buried in the Basilica which has long been one of Italy's major pilgrimage sites.

A Famous University – The University of Padua, founded in 1222, is the second oldest in Italy after Bologna. Galileo was a professor and its students included Renaissance scholar Pico della Mirandola, the astronomer Copernicus and the poet Tasso.

Art in Padua – In 1304, **Giotto** came to Padua to decorate the Scrovegni Chapel, with a superlative cycle of frescoes.

In the 15C the Renaissance in Padua was marked by **Donatello**, another Florentine, who stayed in the city from 1444 to 1453. Also in the 15C, Paduan art flourished under the influence of the Paduan artist, **Andrea Mantegna** (1431–1506), a powerful painter and an innovator in the field of perspective.

Sights

Scrovegni Chapel (Capella degli Scrovegni) ★★★

Open year-round daily 9am–7pm. The chapel may only be visited by supervised tour (20min allowed in chapel). Reservations compulsory. On-line reservations must be made at least 24hrs in advance. (See Box below for more details on visiting). Closed 1 Jan, 1 May, 25 & 26 Dec. €13. ☎ 049 20 10 020. www.cappelladegliscrovegni.it.

The chapel was built in 1303 by Enrico degli Scrovegni. His father had been an infamous usurer, condemned to eternal damnation by Dante (in the Inferno) and this monumental offering was his son's attempt to save his soul. In 1303 he commissioned Giotto (1267–1327), then at the height of his career, to fresco the building from top to bottom in religious

Visiting the Scrovegni Chapel – Practicalities

The Scrovegni Chapel is one of the most precious places in all Italy and strict visiting rules are in place to preserve it for future generations. For centuries visitors to the chapel were inadvertently accelerating the decaying process of the frescoes simply by breathing and perspiring in here. In May 2000 an access building was installed, with a special air-conditioned waiting-room which reduces the body temperature of visitors (and filters out other pollutants), while they watch a short introductory film. This means that they can enter the chapel without further jeopardizing its fragile condition and the condition of the frescoes is now stable though restoration is an ongoing process.

The number of visitors each day is strictly limited to timed tickets and only 25 people per visit. Pre-booking is advisable though at quiet times you can just buy a ticket and almost walk straight in. You can pay by credit card up until the previous day. You must collect pre-paid booked tickets at the Eremitani Museum ticket office (100 metres away) one hour before the assigned time of entry, then arrive at the entrance of the air-conditioned waiting-room outside the Scrovegni Chapel five minutes before the allotted visiting time. Late visitors will not be admitted into the chapel, and will have to pay again and re-book.

To buy tickets on the day and collect prepaid tickets, go to the office at Piazza Eremitani.

imagery; the result is widely recognised as one of the milestones in the history of art. Before the Scrovegni Chapel such images were stylised icon-like representations; Giotto brought life and humanity to his subjects.

To get the most out of your visit it is highly recommended that you see the excellent Sala Multimediale (multimedia room) in the Eremitani Museum complex (&see below) before the chapel. A short film and interactive computer screens give the background to the project and shows how frescoes are created. There are no guides or interpretation in the chapel itself so you need to answer all your questions here.

The remarkable cycle of 39 frescoes, with colours still as bright as the day they were painted, illustrates episodes in the lives of Joachim and Anna (the parents of the Virgin), episodes in the Virgin Mary's life, and Christ's life and death. Highlights are *Flight into Egypt, Judas' Kiss,* the *Entombment* and the saturated cobalt-blue ceiling sprinkled with golden stars. On the lower register powerful monochrome figures depict the Vices and Virtues. A powerful and graphic *Last Judgement* on the west wall completes the cycle. On the altar stands an often overlooked masterpiece

of a **Virgin**★ by the Tuscan sculptor Giovanni Pisano.

Chiesa degli Eremitani ★★
www.cappelladegliscrovegni.it.
In the Cappella Ovetari of the 13C church of the Hermits (*the second on the right of the Cappella Maggiore*) are fragments of frescoes by **Mantegna**; *Martyrdom of St James on the north wall, Assumption in the apse and Martyrdom of St Christoper on the south wall.* The Lady Chapel (Cappella Maggiore) has splendid frescoes by **Guariento**, Giotto's pupil.

Museo Civici agli Eremitani★
&&Open Tue–Sun and hol Mons 9am–7pm. &Closed Mon, 1 Jan, 1 May, 25 & 26 Dec. &*€10 museums and multimedia room only, €13 with Cappella degli Scrovegni ticket* &049 82 04 551. *www.cappelladegliscrovegni.it.*
The Civic Museums complex is a collection of three separate museums and the **Sala Multimediale** (&see above).
The main building, which includes the Scrovegni Chapel ticket office, is in the cloisters of the former Eremetani monastery. This houses the extensive **Museo Archeologico** (Archealogoical Museum) with its superb Roman section, and above the three thousand paintings

or so that make up the **Museo d'Arte-Medioevale e Moderna** (Medieval and Modern Art Museum). These span the period from the 14C to 19C and include works by Giotto, Bellini, Giorgione, Titian, Bassano, Veronese, Tintoretto and Tiepolo alongside a large Flemish and Dutch collection.

Across the road, housed in the Palazzo Zuckermann, is the **Museo Arti Applicate e Decorative & Museo Bottacin**, which is split between and the famous numismatic Bottacin collection.

The former contains more than 2 000 Applied and Decorative Arts pieces: glass, intaglio and inlay work, ceramics, silver, ivory, jewellery, Oriental antiquities, textiles and fabrics, and furniture. Many of these are on display for the very first time since recently being transferred from the storeroom of the Museum of Medieval and Modern Art. They illustrate the various types of artefacts made and used in Padova between the Middle Ages and second half of the 19C,

The Bottacin Collection comprises some 50,000 coins, medals and seals making it one of the most important collections of its kind in the world.

Basilica del Santo (Sant'Antonion)★★

&. ⏱⚲*Open: Basilica year-round daily 6.20am–7pm (Mar–Oct 7.45pm). Anthonian Museum, Scuola di Sant Antonio, Oratorio di San Giorgio: Apr–Sept daily 9am–1pm and 2–6pm. Oct–Mar Tue–Fri 9am–1pm and 2–6pm, Sat–Sun 9am–1pm and 2–6pm. ⚲€2.50. ☏049 82 25 655. www.saintanthonyofpadua.net.*

In front of the basilica Donatello erected an **equestrian statue**★★ of the Venetian leader **Gattamelata** (the nickname of Erasmo di Narni). This bronze was the first of its size to be cast in Italy.

This lavish building, often described as a poor man's St Mark's, began construction immediately after the death of "Il Santo" in 1231. The exterior is an imposing sight in Romanesque Gothic style with eight domes and spires of eastern inspiration that make it look almost like a mosque.

The **interior**★★ is equally impressive, sumptuously decorated with a multitude of monuments. The magnificent nave is divided by huge pillars and the main attraction is the **Cappella del Santo**★★, location of the tomb/altar of St Anthony (Arca di Sant'Antonio) by Tiziano Aspetti (1594).

The magnificent nave is divided by huge pillars and the main attraction, the Capella del Santo, lies to the left. This 16th-century marble confection is mostly the work of Tullio Lombardo and Jacopo Sansovino, adorned with 21st century photographs of healed limbs and various other votive offerings which attest to the ongoing miraculous powers of St Antonio. Next to this is the Chapel of the Black Madonna, the Saint's original resting place.

The main altar is decorated with acclaimed bronze statues and reliefs by Donatello. Behind here is the **Treasury Chapel** with some of the church's most valuable relics. These include a thorn from Christ's crown and the tongue, jawbone and larynx (labelled, *apparato vocal*) of St Anthony. Apparently when his body was removed to the basilica 32 years after his death, the tongue had remained completely intact – a miracle attributed to his great oratorical skills. On the walls are 16C **high reliefs**★★. In the chancel the **high altar**★★ has bronze panels (1450) by Donatello. The third chapel has **frescoes**★ by Altichiero (14C), a Veronese artist.

There is a fine **view**★ of the building from the cloisters, to the south, which are chock-a-block with tombs, monuments and plaques. The **Magnolia (Chapter) Courtyard** with its 200-year old magnolia tree is particularly beautiful.

The **Oratorio di San Giorgio** (St George's Oratory) is decorated with 21 **frescoes**★ (1377) by Altichiero.

In the adjacent **Scuola di Sant'Antonio**, are 18 16C frescoes★ relating the life of St Anthony. Four of these are by Titian. (To visit the Oratory you may have ask one of the guardians, who can be found in the adjacent building which connects the Oratory to the little church on the right, the 'Scoletta'.)

Palazzo della Ragione★

Enter by the Scala delle Erbe off the Piazza delle Erbe. ♿ *Entrance on via VIII Febbraio* 🕐 *Open Feb–Oct Tue–Sun 9am–7pm (Nov–Jan 6pm).* 🕐 *Closed 1 Jan, 1 May, 25 & 26 Dec.* 💶€4. ☎049 82 05 006. www.padovanet.it.

The former Law Courts are set between two of the city's liveliest squares, the **Piazza della Frutta**★ and the **Piazza delle Erbe**★, named after the colourful daily markets that take place.

Built in 1218–19 the Palazzo boasts the largest undivided hall in Europe. Known as the **Salone**★★ the hall measures 79m long, 27m wide and 26m high, with a magnificent upturned wooden ships-keel style roof. The four walls are covered by a beautiful intriguing cycle of 333 astrological and religious frescoes designed by Nicola Miretto in 1425–40. In total they stretch some 217 linear metres. Pick up a leaflet at the front desk. There is also a Foucault pendulum (Italian author Umberto Eco wrote a book entitled *Foucault's Pendulum*, although not about this one).

Unmissable is the hall's largest permanent exhibit, **Il Cavallo Ligneo**★ (The Wooden Horse). This magnificent equine giant stands over 4m tall (5.75m including its plinth) and dates from 1466. It is thought to have been made for a fair or joust, perhaps on the Prato dell Valle next to the Basilica del Santo and is probably modelled after Donatello's Gattemelata monument, though the architect is unknown.

Piazza dei Signori

This is one of the city's most beautiful squares, headed by the Palazzo del Capitanio, built 1599–1605, with a **Torre dell'Orologioa** (astronomical clock tower) made in 1344. On the corner of the square with Via Monte de Pieta is the Loggia della Gran Guardia, completed in 1523.

Università★★

🗣*Visit by guided tours only. Mar–Oct: Mon, Wed and Fri 3.15pm, 4.15pm and 5.15pm; Tue, Thu and Sat 9.15am, 10.15am and 11.15am. Nov–Feb: Mon, Wed and Fri 3.15pm and 4.15pm; Tue, Thu and Sat 10.15am and 11.15am.* 🕐*Closed Sun and public holidays.* 💶€5. ☎049 82 75 111. www.unipd.it.

Established in 1222, the University of Padua was among the first in Europe. Its main block, right in the centre of town, is known as the Palazzo del Bo (or to its students, simply Il Bo) – bo meaning ox, after an inn that once stood here.

As you ascend the stairs the statue of Elena Cornaro Piscopia (1646–84) is a reminder how enlightened the university was for its time, in allowing her to become the very first woman in the world to receive a doctorate degree. Upstairs is an ancient relic of the University's most famous lecturer, the raised desk-cum lectern from which Galileo taught physics from 1592 to 1610. Even this is eclipsed however by the first permanent **Teatro Anatomico**★★ (Anatomy Theatre) in the world, built for the university in 1594, by Fabricius. His student William Harvey studied at Padua in 1602 and formulated the (then) very controversial theory of the circulation of the blood from the heart, after watching dissections in the University theatre. Another famous Padua graduate was Fallopius (of Fallopian tubes fame) who attended here in 1561. The structure – a round wooden amphitheatre that once held up to 250 students – is still perfectly intact though no longer strong enough to stand on. Visitors are offered a curious worm's-eye view, looking up through a hole from beneath the theatre.

Caffè Pedrocchi★

This beautiful landmark neo-Classical café, established 1831, is famous as being the place where the student rebellion against the Austrians was played out in 1848. The lower floor is a grand cafe while upstairs (*piano nobile*) is the **Museo del Risorgimeno** (Museum of Independence) (🕐 *open year-round. Upstairs museum Tue–Sun and hol Mons 9.30am–12.30pm and 3.30–6pm;* 🕐*Closed 1 Jan, 1 May, 25–26 Dec;* 💶€4; ☎049 87 81 231, www.caffepedrocchi.it).*

Chiesa Santa Giustina

This 16C church, dedicated to St Justina boasts an **altarpiece**★ by Veronese.

Orto Botanico

🕐 *Open daily Apr–Oct 9am–1pm, 3–7pm. Nov–Mar 9am–1pm.* 🎫 *€4.* ☎ *049 82 72 119. www.ortobotanico.unipd.it.*

These botanical gardens, laid out in 1545, contain many exotic species including a palm tree, planted in 1585, made famous by Goethe who was apparently inspired by it to write essays and scientific works on plants.

Excursions

Colli Euganei★

The Euganean hills, south of Padua, are of volcanic origin and were appreciated in Roman times for their hot springs and wines.

Abano Terme♦♦♦

11km/7mi southwest.
www.abanomontegrotto.it.
Shaded by pines, this is one of Italy's most famous thermal spa towns. The adjacent resort of **Montegrotto Terme** is also a first-class spa resort.

Monselice★

27km/17mi southwest.
This town (Latin name *Mons Silicis*; granite mountain) was an ancient Roman mining community. The upper terrace of the Villa Balbi with its Italian garden affords a lovely **view**★ of the region.

Arquà Petrarca★

27km/17mi southwest.
It was here that the poet **Petrarch** (1304–74) died. **Petrarch's house**★ is open to the public. Exhibits include memorabilia and autographs of visitors such as Carducci and Byron. 🕐 *Open Mar–Oct daily 9am–12.30pm and 3–7pm. Nov–Feb 9am–noon and 2.30–5.30pm.* 🕐 *Closed 1 Jan, 1 May, 25–26 Dec.* 🎫 *€3.* ☎ *042 97 18 294. www.arquapetrarca.com.*

Montagnana★

47km/29mi southwest.
Impressive 14C **ramparts**★★ reinforce this town. The **Duomo**, by Sansovino, contains a *Transfiguration* by Veronese.

Delta del Po★

Once a malaria-infested marshy district, this is now a fertile agricultural area and a designated nature reserve. The Chioggia–Ravenna road traverses flat expanses stretching away to the horizon. Clumps of poplars and umbrella pines, canals (where eel fishing is still common) spanned by curious bridges, and fishing boats add touches of colour and a special charm. The area to the south of the Valli di Comacchio lagoons has a melancholy beauty.

Abbazia di Pomposa★★

96km/60mi southeast.
🕐 *Open year-round daily 9.30am–1pm and 2.30–5.30pm.* 🕐 *Closed 1 Jan, 1 May, 25 Dec.* ☎ *053 39 99 523. www.pomposa.info.*

This Benedictine abbey was founded in the 6C and enjoyed fame in the Middle Ages due to its musical heritage. The fine pre-Romanesque **church** in the style typical of Ravenna is preceded by a narthex whose decoration exemplifies the Byzantine style. The nave has some magnificent **mosaic flooring** and two holy water stoups, one in the Romanesque style and the other in the Byzantine style. The walls bear an exceptional cycle of 14C **frescoes** based on the illuminator's art. From right to left the upper band is devoted to the Old Testament while the lower band has scenes from the Life of Christ; the corner pieces of the arches depict the *Apocalypse*. On the west wall are a *Last Judgement* and in the apsidal chapel *Christ in Majesty*.

Padova Cards

The Padova Card (48hrs or 72hrs) gives free admission to the Scrovegni Chapel, to 12 important sights and museums, free public transport and many other discounts for €16 or €21, little more than the cost of the standard ticket for the Scrovegni Chapel. Alternatively there is the Museums All Year Long Card which is cheaper, but does not include transport. Valid for one adult plus one under age 14 years.

TREVISO★

POPULATION 82 112
MICHELIN MAP 562 E–F 18

Treviso sits at the heart of an important agricultural and industrial area. The old centre, surrounded by waterways and what remains of the city walls, is a delight and includes an area of Venetian-style canals.

- **Information:** Palazzo Scotti, Via Andrea 3. ☎042 25 47 632. http://turismo. provincia.treviso.it.
- ▶ **Orient Yourself:** Treviso is 23 mi/37km north of Venice, linked by the SS 13.
- **Don't Miss:** Chiesa di San Nicolo and the Villa Maser.
- **Organising Your Time:** Allow at least a day to visit the city.
- **Also See:** PADOVA, VENEZIA.

A Bit of History

Treviso flourished under Carolingian rule in the early Middle Ages. However, in 1237 the city fell under the tyranny of Ezzelino da Romano and subsequently endured over a century of torment and civil war as authority passed from hand to hand. Treviso made a pact with Venice in 1389, which heralded a long period of prosperity and saw another period of construction, this time in the Venetian Gothic style. In 1509 the city began to play a key role in Venice's defence of the south. The current walls and gates date back to this period.

In 1797 Treviso – and Venice itself – fell to Napoleon, and was subsequently subsumed into the Austrian domain until 15 July 1866.

Allied bombings in 1944 killed thousands and many historic landmarks were destroyed.

Visit

Piazza dei Signori★

Alongside the piazza, the centre of town is landmarked by the monumental medieval **Palazzo dei Trecento**★ (1207) complex which also includes the **Palazzo del Podestà**, with its huge Torre Civica, and the Palazzo Pretorio. The effect of the devastating air raid on the city in 1944 is illustrated by photographs in the arcades below the buildings and a dark line marked on the side of the Palazzo dei Trecentro shows the level at which it had to be painstakingly reconstructed. Restaurants and cafes now cluster around here. Behind these buildings, almost hidden from view are the former **Monte di Pietà** (old pawn shop, closed to the public) and the two atmospheric **medieval churches** of Santa Lucia and San Vito (*open daily year-round 9am–noon*). The former contains frescoes by Tomaso da Modena.

Just the other side of the Piazza Indipendenza is another seamlessly reconstructed medieval structure, the **Loggia dei Cavaliere**, with some of its original 13th-century frescoes still intact.

Chiesa di San Nicolò★

This large Romanesque-Gothic church contains interesting frescoes, especially those on the columns by Tommaso da Modena. In the Onigo Chapel there are portraits of people from Treviso by Lorenzo Lotto (16C). The *Virgin in Majesty* at the far end of the chancel is by Savoldo (16C). The adjoining **monastery** has portraits of famous Dominicans by Tomaso da Modena.

Museo di Santa Caterina★

Via S. Caterina. Open Tue–Sun 9am–12.30pm, 2.30pm–6pm. €3. ☎042 25 44 864.

Housed in the former convent of Santa Caterina is a fine exhibition of art and archaeology from the 5C BC up to the 1900s, with outstanding paintings by Bellini, Titian, Lorenzo Lotto, Jacopo Bassano and other masters. The star attraction however is in the deconsecrated church next door which houses the **Santa Orsola (Ursula) cycle of frescoes** and the **Capella degli Innocenti frescoes**, both masterpieces by Tomaso da Modena.

Duomo

The 15–16C cathedral has seven domes and a Romanesque crypt. In the Chapel of the Annunciation (Cappella dell'Annunziata) there are frescoes by Pordenone and on the altarpiece an *Annunciation* by Titian.

Chiesa di San Francesco

Viale Sant'Antonio da Padova.
This church in the transitional Romanesque-Gothic style has a fine wooden ceiling, the tombstone of Petrarch's daughter and includes the tomb of one of Dante's sons, as well as frescoes by Tommaso da Modena.

Excursions

Villa di Maser (Villa Barbaro)★★★

29km/18mi northwest on the SS 348.
⏰*Open Apr–Jun daily 10am–6pm. Jul–Oct Tue, Sat, Sun and public holidays, 3–6pm; Nov–Feb Sat–Sun and public holidays only, 2.30–5pm.* ⏰*Closed Easter Sun, 24 Dec–6 Jan.* €6. ☎042 39 23 004; *www.villadimaser.it.*
This famous villa was built in 1560 by Palladio for the Barbaro brothers: Daniele, Patriarch of Aquileia, and Marcantonio, ambassador of the Venetian Republic. The interior was decorated 1566–8 with a splendid cycle of **frescoes**★★★ by Veronese and has been declared a World Heritage Site and has a winery.

Conegliano

28km/17mi north. 🛈*via XX Settembre, 61.* ☎0438 21230. *www.conegliano2000.it.*
Conegliano is surrounded by hills clad with vineyards famous for producing excellent Prosecco white wine. This was the birthplace of **Cima da Conegliano** (1459–1518), a gifted colourist. The **Duomo** has a fine **Sacra Conversazione**★ by the artist. ⏰*Open Mon–Fri, by appointment*

only. ☎043 82 26 06. The **castello** houses the Museo Civico (⏰*open Apr–Sept daily 10am–12.30pm and 4–7.30pm; Oct–Mar 10am–12.30pm and 2.30–6pm (Nov Sat–Sun only);* €2.50; ☎043 82 28 71) and affords a lovely **panorama**★of the town By the cathedral the **Sala dei Battuti** (⏰*open year-round Sat 3–6pm, Sun and Hols 10–12, 3–6pm; donation*) has 15C and 16C Venetian and Lombardstyle **frescoes**★.

Vittorio Veneto

41km/26mi north. 🛈*Viale Della Vittoria, 110* ☎043 85 72 43.
The name of this town recalls the great victory of the Italians over the Austrians in 1918. To celebrate, the two separate, but adjacent towns of Ceneda (now the southern half) and Serravalle (the northern half) were unified into a single town. In Ceneda the **Museo della Battaglia** is installed in a 16C loggia with a frescoed portico by Sansovino (⏰*closed until 2014 for restoration;* ☎043 85 76 95; *www.museobattaglia.it*). Serravalle is the older town and has retained its period charm. The church of **San Giovanni** has 15C **frescoes**★.

Portogruaro★

56km/35mi east.
www.comune.portogruaro.ve.it.
Two fine main streets lined with attractive porticoes flank the river banks and there are numerous palaces. On the **Corso Martiri della Libertà**★★ (the busiest of the shopping streets) not far from the 19C cathedral and its leaning Romanesque campanile is the strange **Palazzo Municipale**★, built in a late-Gothic style (14C). Behind the palace is the river with two 15C watermills and a small 17C fishermen's chapel with its own landing-stage. In the Via del Seminario stands the **Museo Nazionale Concordiese** (⏰*open year-round daily 8.30am–7pm;* ⏰*closed 1 Jan, 1 May, 25 Dec;* €3; ☎042 17 26 74. *www.archeopd.beniculturali.it*) with fine Roman exhibits and palaeo-Christian artefacts from Concordia Sagittaria (*3km/2mi south*), a Roman colony founded in 40 BC.

VERONA★★★

POPULATION 259 068
MICHELIN MAPS 561, 562 F 14–15

Verona stands on the banks of the Adige against a hilly backdrop. It is the second most important art centre in the Veneto region after Venice. The fashionable Piazza Bra is linked by Via Mazzini to the heart of the old town.

- **Information:** Via degli Alpini, 9. ☎045 80 68 680. www.tourism.verona.it. The Verona Card (two- or five- day) offers a savings on multiple sights.
- ▶ **Orient Yourself:** Verona lies between Venice (120km/75mi east) and Lake Garda (30km/19mi) west.
- **Don't Miss:** The Arena (catch a summer opera performance if possible); Castelvecchio and Ponte Scaligero; San Zeno Maggiore.
- **Also See:** PADOVA.

A Bit of History

Verona reached the peak of its glory under the Scaligers who governed for the Holy Roman Emperor from 1260 to 1387. It then passed to the Visconti of Milan before submitting to Venetian rule from 1405. Verona was occupied by Austria in 1814 and became part of the Veneto with Italy in 1866.

Pisanello – Artists of the Veronese school were influenced by Northern art from the Rhine Valley and they developed a Gothic art which combined flowing lines with a meticulous attention to detail. Antonio Pisanello (c.1395–c.1450), a great traveller, active painter, prodigious medal-maker and enthusiastic draughtsman, was the greatest exponent of this school. His painting, with soft colours, meticulous details and flowing lines, was reminiscent of the rapidly disappearing medieval world.

Walking Tour

Arena di Verona★★

⏱Tue–Sun 10am–7.30pm, Mon 1.30-7.30. Schedule may vary performance days. ✖Closed 1 Jan, 25 Dec. €6. ☎045 80 05 151; www.arena.it.
This magnificent amphitheatre, among the largest in the Roman world, was built to accommodate 25 000 spectators in 44 tiers. It is built of blocks of pink marble, flint and brick and thus probably dates from the late 1C. Mid-June to September it is the venue for a world-famous opera season. The topmost row offers

Aerial view of Verona with the Arena

© Guido Alberto Rossi / Tips / Photononstop

a **panorama**★★ of the town in its hilly setting, which on a clear day reaches as far as the Alps.

Castelvecchio and Ponte Scaligero★★

◷*Open Tue–Sun 8.30am–7.30pm, Mon 1.30–7.30pm).* ◉*€6.* ☏*045 80 62 611. www.comune.verona.it.*

This splendid fortified complex was built in 1354 by Cangrande II Scaliger. It is now home to the superb **Museo d'Arte** collection★★, with Veronese art from the 12C to the 16C, showing links with Venice and the International Gothic movement. There are frescoes by local artists and canvases by Stefano da Verona, Pisanello, Giambono, Carlo Crivelli (a splendid Madonna of the Passion), Mantegna and Carpaccio as well as the Bellinis.

The rooms on the upper floor contain works from the Renaissance period by Veronese artists: Morone, Liberale da Verona (Virgin with a Goldfinch), Girolamo dai Libri and Veronese. There are also Venetian works by Tintoretto, Guardi, Tiepolo and Longhi. Also on display are jewellery and sculpture.

▸ *Follow Corso Cavour, home to the church of San Lorenzo, then continue to the Porta dei Borsari (1C AD). Continue along Corso Porta Borsari.*

Piazza delle Erbe★★

The "Square of Herbs" was the former Roman forum. Markets still take place mornings, though in recent years they have become very touristy. In the middle of the square stand the market column; the *capitello* (a rostrum from which

decrees and sentences were proclaimed) by the 16C governors (*podestà*). Also look for the fountain known as the Verona Madonna, with a Roman statue symbolising the town, and a Venetian column surmounted by the winged Lion of St Mark (1523).

Palaces and old houses, some with pink marble columns and frescoes, frame the square: on the north side is the Baroque **Palazzo Maffei**.

In Via Cappello (No 23) is the **Casa di Giulietta** (Juliet's House); in fact it is a Gothic palace which is said to have belonged to the Capulet family; the famous balcony is in the inner courtyard (free access). ◷*Open Tue–Sun 8.30am–7.30pm, Mon 1.30pm–7.30pm.* ◷*Closed, 1 Jan, 25 Dec.* ◉*€6 (with Tomba di Giulietta €7).* ☏*045 80 34 303.*

Piazza dei Signori★★

Take Via della Costa to reach this elegant square. On the right is the 12C **Palazzo del Comune** (Town Hall), also known as the Palazzo della Ragione, dominated by the **Torre dei Lamberti** (◷*open year round 8.30am–8.30pm, Fri 11pm;* ◷*closed 1 Jan, 25 Dec;* ◉*€6;* ☏*045 92 73 027, www.comune.verona.it*), a tower built of brick and stone and with an octagonal upper storey. This building is connected by an arch with the **Palazzo dei Tribunali** (Law Courts), formerly the Palazzo del Capitano (Governor's Residence) which is also flanked by a massive brick tower, the Torrione Scaligero. The **Loggia del Consiglio** on the opposite side is an elegant edifice in the Venetian-Renaissance style. At the far end of the square, the late-13C **Palazzo del Governo** with its machicolations and fine Classical doorway (1533) by Sammicheli was initially a Scaliger residence.

Arche Scaligere★★

◷*Open Tue–Sun 10am–1pm, 2–6pm.* ◉*€2. www.comune.verona.it.*

The Scaliger built their tombs between their palace and their church. The sarcophagi bear the arms of the family, with the symbolic ladder (*scala*). Theses elegant Gothic mausolea are surrounded by marble balustrades and wrought-iron rails, and are decorated with carvings

Romeo and Juliet

The setting for this apocryphal drama was Verona in 1302, when political conflict raged. The tragic young couple immortalised by Shakespeare belonged to rival families: Romeo to the Montecchi (Montagues), who were Guelphs and supported the Pope, and Juliet to the Capuleti (Capulets), who were Ghibellines and supported the Emperor.

Roma V.	AVX	46	S. Francesco V.	BX	54	SS. Trinità V.	BX	56
S. Anastasia Cso	BV	50	S. Tomaso Pza	BV	55	Stella V.	BV	59
S. Chiara V.	BV	52	Signori Pza dei	BV		Tezone V.	BX	60
S. Cosimo V.	BV	53	Sottoriva V.	BV	58			

| Loggia del Consiglio | BV | E | Palazzo Maffei | BV | B | Palazzo del Comune | BV | D |
| Museo Archeologico | BV | M¹ | Palazzo dei Tribunali | BV | J¹ | Palazzo del Governo | BV | P |

of religious scenes and statues of saints in niches.

Over the door of the Romanesque church of **Santa Maria Antica** is the tomb of one of the more infamous of the family "Cangrande" I (d.1329) with his equestrian statue above.

Teatro Romano and Museo Archeologico★

⏱ *Open daily 8.30am (Mon 1.30pm)– 7.30pm.* ⊗ *€4.50.* ☎ *045 80 00 360. www. comune.verona.it.*

The Roman theatre dates from the time of Augustus but has been heavily restored. Regular summer theatrical performances are staged here.

Above the theatre a former monastery houses the small archaeological museum with a lovely view over the city.

Castel San Pietro

Take the stairway which leads off Regaste Redentore. St Peter's Castle dates back to the Visconti and the period of Venetian rule. The terraces afford splendid **views**★★ of Verona.

Verona's Churches

All the churches below belong to the *Associazione Chiese Vive Verona.* ⏱ *See individual churches.* ⏱ *Closed Monday in winter.* ⊗ *€2.50; combined ticket to four churches (also San Fermo) €6.* ☎ *045 59 28 13. www.chieseverona.it.*

Sant'Anastasia★

⏱ *Open Mar–Oct Tue–Sat 9am–6pm, Sun 1–6pm. Winter Tue–Sat 10am–1pm & 1.30–5pm, Sun 1–5pm.*

This church was begun at the end of the 13C and completed in the 15C. The campanile is remarkable and the façade is pierced with a 14C double doorway adorned with frescoes and sculpture. The lofty interior contains several masterpieces: four figures of the Apostles by Michele da Verona; Pisanello's famous **fresco**★ (above the Pellegrini Chapel, to the right of the high altar) of St George delivering the Princess of Trebizondaa (1436), which has an almost surreal combination of realistic precision and Gothic fantasy; 17 **terracottas**★ by Michele da Firenze in the Cappella Pellegrini; and the **fresco**★ showing Knights of the Cavalli family being presented to the Virgin (1380) by the Veronese artist, Altichero (first chapel in the south transept).

Duomo★

⏱ *Open summer Tue–Sat 10am–5.30pm, Sun 1.30–5.30pm. Winter Tue–Sat 10am–1pm & 1.30–4pm, Sun 1–5pm.* ⊗ *€2.50*

The cathedral has a 12C Romanesque chancel, a Gothic nave and a Classical-style tower. The remarkable main doorway in the Lombard-Romanesque style is adorned with sculptures and low reliefs by Maestro Nicolò. The interior has pink marble pillars. The altarpiece (*first altar on the left*) is decorated with an *Assumption* by Titian. The marble chancel screen is by Sammicheli (16C).

San Zeno Maggiore★★

Access via Largo D. Bosco. ⏱ *Open summer Tue–Sat 8.30am–6pm, Sun 1–6pm. Winter Tue–Sat 10am–1pm & 1.30–5pm, Sun 12.30–5pm.* ⊗ *€2.50.*

St Zeno is one of the finest Romanesque churches in northern Italy. It was built on the basilical plan in the Lombard style in the 12C. The façade is decorated with Lombard bands and arcading; the side walls and campanile have alternate brick and stone courses. In the entrance porch resting on two lions, there are admirable bronze **doors**★★★ (11C–12C) with scenes from the Old and New Testaments. On either side are low reliefs by the master sculptors Nicolò and Guglielmo (12C). On the tympanum of the doorway is a statue of St Zeno, patron saint of Verona.

The imposing interior has a lofty, bare nave with a cradle roof flanked by aisles with shallow roofing. On the high altar is a splendid **triptych**★★ (1459) by Mantegna. There are 14C statues on the chancel screen and a curious polychrome statue of St Zeno laughing in the north apse.

San Fermo Maggiore★
ⓒ*Open summer Tue–Sat 10am–6pm, Sun 1–6pm. Winter Tue–Sat 10am–1pm & 1.30–5pm, Sun 1–5pm.* ⌷ *€2.50.*
The church, dedicated to St Firmanus Major, was built in the 11C–12C and remodelled at a later date. The façade is in the Romanesque and Gothic styles. The aisleless church is covered by a stepped, keel-shaped roof. By the west door the Brenzoni mausoleum (1430) is framed by a **fresco**★ of the Annunciation by Pisanello.

▶ *Follow the river south for 800m, passing the Ponte Aleardi.*

Tomba di Giulietta (Juliet's Tomb)
Via del Pontiere, 35. ⓒ*Open year-round daily 8.30am (Mon 1.30pm)–7.30pm.* ⌷*€4.50 (joint ticket with Casa di Giulietta €7).* ☏*045 80 00 361.*
Juliet's supposed tomb is in the atmospheric cloisters of the church of San Francesco al Corso. On display in the adjoining **Museo degli Affreschi G.B. Cavalcaselle** are cycles of frescoes coming from buildings dating from the Middle Ages to the 16C century.

VICENZA★★

POPULATION 113 483
MICHELIN MAP 562 F 16

Strategically located at the crossroads of the routes that link the Veneto with the Trentino, Vicenza is now a busy commercial and industrial centre, renowned for its textile industry and as a gold-working and trading centre. But above all it is the home of the great Renaissance architect, Palladio.

▯ **Information:** Piazza Matteotti 12. ☏044 43 20 854. Piazza dei Signori, 8. ☏044 45 44 122. www.vicenzae.org.
▶ **Orient Yourself:** Vicenza lies 75km/47mi west of Venice along the A 4.
☺ **Don't Miss:** Piazza dei Signori, the Teatro Olimpico and the frescoes by Giovanni Battista at the Villa Valmarana ai Nani.
ⓒ **Organising Your Time:** Allow a day for a visit.
ⓑ **Also See:** LAGUNA VENETA, PADOVA, VERONA.

A Bit of History

The ancient Roman town of Vicetia became an independent city state in the 12C. After several conflicts with the neighbouring cities of Padua and Verona, Vicenza sought Venetian protection at the beginning of the 15C. This was a period of great prosperity, when Vicenza counted many rich and generous art patrons among its citizens and it was embellished with an amazing number of palaces.

Andrea Palladio
Andrea di Pietro della Gondola (1508–80) was born in Padua and apprenticed at the age of 13 as a stonemason. He came to Vicenze three years later and worked for two of the most eminent stone cutters in the city, mingling with the city's leading architects. One of these, Giangiorgio Trissini took him under his wing and named him Palladio, after the goddess Pallas Athene (representing Strength and Wisdom). Given the enormous wealth of the Vene-

tian Empire these were fertile times for architects with a plentiful supply of rich citizens who wanted to affirm their status through the outward appearance of their city houses and country villas (💡 *see VILLAS OF THE BRENTA*). It was in the latter area where Palladio was to achieve his greatest fame though remarkably he didn't receive his first public commission (the Basilica at Vicenza) until the relatively advanced age of 38. His *Quattro Libri dell' Architettura*, Four Books on Architecture was later to become the profession's bible. In Britain, Inigo Jones and Sir Christopher Wren were close followers.

In addition to palazzi and villas he was also to find fame in Venice designing the churches of San Giorgio Maggiore and the Redentore.

In total there are 66 bodies of work that Palladio designed and completed during his lifetime, with many more collaborations, and projects finished after his death. His pupil, Vicenzo Scamozzi (1552–1616), completed several of these works and carried on his style.

Visit

Piazza dei Signori★★

Like St Mark's Square in Venice, this is an open-air meeting-place recalling the forum of Antiquity. As in the Piazzetta in Venice, there are two columns, here bearing effigies of the Lion of St Mark and the Redeemer.

With the lofty **Torre Bissara**★, a 12C belfry, the **Basilica Palladiana** ★★ (💡*open only for exhibitions.* ☎*044 42 22 101; www.museicivicivicenza.it*), built 1549–1617, occupies one whole side of the square. The elevation is one of Palladio's masterpieces, with two superimposed galleries in the Doric and Ionic orders, admirable for their power, proportion and purity of line. The great keel-shaped roof, destroyed by bombing, has been rebuilt. Despite its name the building was *not* a church but a meeting-place for the Vicenzan notables. The 15C **Monte di Pietà** (municipal pawn shop) opposite, its buildings framing the Baroque façade of the church of

San Vincenzo, is adorned with frescoes. The **Loggia del Capitano**★, formerly the residence of the Venetian Governor, which stands to the left, at the corner of the Contrà del Monte, was begun to the plans of Palladio in 1571 but left unfinished.

Teatro Olimpico★★

Piazza Giacomo Matteotti. ♿💡*Open Tue –Sun Jul and Aug 9am–7pm, rest of year 9am–5pm.* 💶*€8 (includes Museo Civico and Museo Naturalistico-Archeologico.* ☎*044 42 22 800. www.vicenzae.org.*

This splendid building in wood and stucco was designed by Palladio in 1580 on the model of the theatres of Antiquity. The tiers of seats are laid out in a hemicycle and surmounted by a lovely **colonnade** with a balustrade crowned with statues. The **stage**★★★is one of the finest in existence with its superimposed niches, columns and statues and its amazing perspectives painted in *trompe l'oeil* by Scamozzi who completed the work.

Corso Andrea Palladio★

This, the main street of Vicenza, and several neighbouring streets, are embellished by many palaces designed by Palladio and his pupils. At the beginning is the **Palazzo Chiericati**, an imposing work by Palladio; at No 147 the 15C **Palazzo Da Schio** in the Venetian-Gothic style was formerly known as the Ca d'Oro (Golden House) because it was covered with frescoes with gilded backgrounds. The west front of **Palazzo Thiene** overlooking Contrà S. Gaetano Thiene was by Palladio, while the entrance front at No 12 Contrà Porti is Renaissance, dating from the late 15C. The **Palazzo Porto-Barbaran** opposite is also by Palladio. At No 98 the **Palazzo Trissino** (1592) is one of Scamozzi's most successful works. Next is the Corso Fogazzaro, where the **Palazzo Valamarana** (1566) at No 16 is another work by Palladio.

Museo Civico★

Palazzo Chiericati. ♿💡*Open Sept–Jun Tue–Sun 9am–5pm, Jul–Aug Tue–Sun 10am–6pm.* 💶*€8.50 (includes Teatro*

Olimpico and Museo Naturalistico-Archeologico. ☎044 43 21 348. www.museicivicivicenza.it.

The collection of paintings includes Venetian Primitives (*The Dormition of the Virgin* by Paolo Veneziano); a **Crucifixion**★★ by Hans Memling; canvases by Bartolomeo Montagna (pupil of Giovanni Bellini), Mantegna and Carpaccio, one of the most active artists in Vicenza. There are Venetian works by Lorenzo Lotto, Veronese, Bassano, Piazzetta, Tiepolo and Tintoretto as well as Flemish works by Brueghel the Elder and Van Dyck.

Santa Corona

The church was built in the 13C. Works of art include: a **Baptism of Christ**★★ by Giovanni Bellini (*fifth altar on the left*) and an **Adoration of the Magi**★★ (1573) by Veronese (*third chapel on the right*). The fourth chapel on the right has a coffered **ceiling**★, adorned with gilded stucco, and a *Mary Magdalene and Saints* by Bartolomeo Montagna.

The cloisters house the small **Museo Naturalistico-Archeologico** (Museum of Natural History and Archaeology) (◷ *open Sept–Jun Tue–Sun 9am–5pm, Jul–Aug Tue–Sun 10am–6pm;* ◷ *€8.50 (includes Teatro Olimpico and Museo Civico);* ☎044 43 20 440, www.museicivicivicenza.it).

Duomo

◷ *Open Mon–Fri 10.30am–noon & 3.30–5.30pm, Sat 10.30am–noon.* ☎044 43 20 99.

Built between the 14C and 16C, the cathedral has an attractive colourful Gothic façade and a Renaissance east end. Inside is a fine **polyptch**★ (1356) by Lorenzo Veneziano.

Excursions

Villa Valmarana ai Nani★★

2km/1mi south by the Este road and then the first road to the right. ◷ *Open mid-Mar through Oct 10am–noon and 3–6pm. Nov to Jan Sat–Sun 10am–12.30pm and 2–4.30pm.* ◷ *€9.* ☎044 43 21 803. www.villavalmarana.com.

The villa dates from the 17C. Both the mainhouse and the Forestiera buildings are adorned with splendid **frescoes**★★★ by Giovanni Battista (Giambattista) Tiepolo and his son Giovanni Domenico.

La Rotonda★

2km/1mi southeast, off the Este road. ◷ *Open mid-Mar–Nov daily 10am–noon and 3–6pm. Nov to mid-Mar Tue–Sun 10am–noon & 2.30–5pm.* ◷ *€10 interior (Wed&Sat only); garden only, €5.* ☎044 43 21 793. www.villalarotonda.it.

The Rotonda is one of Palladio's most famous creations and has inspired many other masterpieces worldwide. The gracefully proportioned square building is roofed with a dome and fronted on each side by a pedimented portico, making it look like an ancient temple.

Basilica di Monte Berico and Monti Berici★

2km/1mi south by Viale Venezia. ◷ *Open year-round daily 6am–12.30pm & 2.30–7pm (winter 6pm).* ☎044 43 20 998. www.monteberico.it.

As the Viale X Giugno climbs uphill, it is lined with an 18C portico and chapels. On the summit is the Baroque basilica roofed with a dome. Inside, there is a Pietà (1500) by Bartolomeo Montagna. From the esplanade there is a wonderful **panorama**★★ of Vicenza, the Venetian plain and the Alps.

Montecchio Maggiore

13km/8mi southwest on the S 11. www.comune.montecchio-maggiore.vi.it.

Novelist Luigi del Porta of Vicenza set the original story of Romeo and Juliet in Montecchio Maggiore in 1552 and the town's two adjacent ruined 10C castles are known as the castles of Romeo and Juliet respectively. From here there are **views**★ of the Po Plain and Vicenza.

On the outskirts, on the Tavernelle road, the **Villa Cordellina-Lombardi** has one room entirely covered with **frescoes**★ by Tiepolo. ♿◷ *Open Apr–Oct Tue–Sun 9am–1pm; Wed–Sun also 3–6pm. Nov–Mar Wed–Thu.* ◷ *€3.* ☎044 49 08 111. www.provincia.vicenza.it.

Gondolas and view of
Isola di S. Giorgio Maggiore
© Gwen Cannon / MICHELIN

WHERE TO STAY

Although Venice has a wide range of accommodation, visitors should be aware that prices can be high and value for money difficult to find. Venice is now a travel destination throughout the year. The city officially defined high season for 2013 as 1 Feb–30 Nov. Although summer weather can be hot and damp, which makes sightseeing extremely tiring, don't expect discounts. **It is advisable to book as far in advance as possible,** especially for dates during Carnival. Like Rome and Florence, Venice and some other Veneto cities have instituted a hotel tax, which applies to each occupant per night at fees that range from €0.40 to €5 based on type of accommodation, location, and season. Information on accommodation in Venice is available from the official tourist board website, www.turismovenezia.it. The red **Michelin Guide Italy**, updated on a yearly basis, also provides a detailed list of recommended hotels and restaurants in Venice.

Prices and Amenities

We have provided below a number of hotels and guest houses located in various parts of the city, classified according to price for a **double room** (for coin ranges see the Legend for large cities on the cover flap). However, as **these prices often vary quite considerably throughout the year,** you are strongly advised to enquire beforehand and to check the rates during the period chosen for your stay. Most prices quoted include breakfast, but not the hotel tax. These hotels accept major credit cards unless otherwise indicated. In the summer,

visitors are advised to choose lodgings with air-conditioning (only basic premises do not include it), as it is particularly hot during this period. The number of establishments run by religious orders has dwindled, but some still take in paying guests in their casa per ferie ("holiday homes"), some at budget rates, without any need for religious qualification. Accommodation is generally spartan (with no air conditioning) though invariably spotlessly clean. Note that very few of these places take credit cards, some impose a curfew, and don't always accommodate couples. The main visitor season may vary.

Address Book

VENICE

RELIGIOUS ESTABLISHMENTS

Casa Cardinal Piazza – Cannaregio 3539/A, vicino alla Madonna dell'Orto. ☎041 721 388. 24 rooms.

Casa Murialdo-Circolo ANSPI – Cannaregio 3512; ☎041 719 933. 12 rooms.

Domus Civica – San Polo 3082. ☎041 721 103. www.domuscivica.com. 65 rooms.

Istituto San Giuseppe – Ponte della Guerra 5402. ☎ 041 522 5352. 11 rooms.

Santa Fosca – Cannaregio 2372. ☎041 715 775; www.santafosca.it. 30 beds. 2 rooms.

Casa Caburlotto – Fondamenta Rizzi, Santa Croce 316. ☎041 710 877.

Domus Ciliota – Calle delle Muneghe 2976, San Marco. ☎041 520 4888. www.ciliota.it. 100 beds.

Foresteria Valdese – Castello 5170. ☎041 528 6797. www.foresteriavenezia.it.

HOSTELS, PENSIONS AND HOTELS

Ostello Venezia – Fondamenta Zitelle 86, Giudecca. ☎041 523 8211. www.ostellionline.org. 260 beds. This youth hostel (IYHF or AIG card required) is located in an old, refurbished grain store, across the lagoon on Guidecca, on the canal overlooking the city.

Pensione Seguso – Zattere 779. ☎041 528 6858. www.pensioneseguso.it.

34 rooms. Wooden panelling, round windows and antique furnishings and fittings lend a pleasantly old-fashioned feel to this hotel which has long been popular with English and American guests including Ezra Pound.

Ai Do Mori – *Calle Larga, S Marco 658. ☎041 520 8177. www.hotelaidomori.com. 11 rooms.* Friendly and intimate hotel steps from San Marco is simply furnished and offers reasonable rates. A very lively neighbourhood.

Hotel Bernardi Semenzato – *Calle dell'Oca 4366 – Vaporetto Ca d'Oro. ☎041 522 7257. www.hotelbernardi.com. 25 rooms.* Situated at the heart of the city in a secluded street behind Campo S.S. Apostoli, offering good value in an excellent location.

Venice Certosa Hotel – *Isola della Certosa 30141 – vaporetto Certosa. ☎041 277 8632. www.ventodivenezia.it. 18 rooms.* Easy access to boats, accommodation for bicyclists, and plenty of space to run. Good for families or those who like a good dose of nature with art. Ristorante Certosino serves lunch and dinner. Bar.

Locanda Cà Foscari – *Calle della Frescade 3887/B – Vaporetto San Tomas. ☎041 710 401. www.locandacafoscari.com. 11 rooms.* A simple but pleasant establishment with light, airy good value rooms and a family atmosphere.

Ostello Venissa – *Fondamenta Santa Caterina, 3, 30170 Isola di Mazzorbo – Vaporetto Mazzorbo. ☎041 527 2281. www.venissa.it. 6 rooms.* Delightfully situated between the waterfront and a vineyard that produces Dorona wine, this inn offers either budget rooms with shared bath or more deluxe expensive rooms. The restaurant merits a visit for its creative cuisine.

Hotel Abbazia – *Calle Priuli 68, Cannaregio. ☎041 717 333. www.abbaziahotel.com. 50 rooms.* This atmospheric hotel near the railway station was originally a Carmelite monastery and retains many of its original features. The bar is the former refectory, complete with pulpit and pews.

Centro Culturale Don Orione Artigianelli – *Dorsoduro 909, vaporetto Zattere ☎041 522 4077. www.donorione-venezia.it. 50 rooms.* This restored monastery, well-situated on the Zattere, runs a religious guest house offering clean, modern accommodation. Rooms are air-conditioned and adequately but simply furnished.

Pensione La Calcina – *Dorsoduro 780, vaporetto Zattere. ☎041 520 6466. www.lacalcina.com. 32 rooms.* This *pensione*, with great views along the Canale della Giudecca is sited where the historic La Calcina inn stood (where Ruskin stayed and praised in 1876). The quality of the service has remained high

Pensione La Calcina

ever since and it is fully renovated. Their La Piscina restaurant is good value and quality, with terrace tables over the Giudecca Canal.

○○⊜⊜**Hotel Falier** – *Salizzada San Pantalon 130, Santa Croce.* ☎041 710 882. *www.hotelfalier.com. 19 rooms.* Close to I Frari but away from the bustling town centre, this hotel is a haven of peace and quiet with a small but delightful back garden.

○○⊜⊜**Metropole** – *Riva degli Schiavoni 4187, Castello.* ☎041 520 6044. *www.hotelmetropole.com. 69 rooms.* A a fine hotel with attentive service. Family antique clocks are on display throughout, as are antique fans, which must have fluttered through fascinating scenes. Met Restaurant, one of the city's best, merits a visit for the chef's creative cuisine, fine service, and tranquil atmosphere.

○○⊜⊜**Antica Locanda Sturion** – *Calle del Sturion San Polo 679.* ☎041 523 6243. *www.locandasturion.com. 11 rooms.* Overlooking the Grand Canal next to the Rialto Bridge, this has been an inn for more than four centuries. (On the third floor, no lift). Venetian style decor.

○○⊜⊜**Hotel Paganelli** – *Riva degli Schiavoni 4687, Castello.* ☎041 522 4324. *www.hotelpaganelli.com. 22 rooms.* Some rooms of this family-run, Venetian style hotel front the Bacino di San Marco while others in a separate building afford good views of Campo San Zaccaria.

○○⊜⊜**Hotel Serenissima** – *Calle Goldoni 4486.* ☎041 520 0011. *www. hotelserenissima.it.* Situated between St Mark's Square and the Goldoni Theatre, this charming, unpretentious hotel offers a convenient location within a busy shopping area. Walls are hung with paintings by modern artists, but Old World atmosphere prevails.

○○⊜⊜**Ca' Pisani Hotel** – *Dorsoduro 979A.* ☎041 240 1411. *www.capisani hotel.it. 29 rooms.* This stunning modern Design Hotel celebrates cutting-edge art and technology at every turn.

○○⊜⊜**Hotel Danieli** – *Riva degli Schiavoni 4196, Castello.* ☎041 522 6480. *www.starwoodhotels.com. 233 rooms, 12 suites.* Housed in the Palazzo Dandolo since 1822, the Danieli calls

to mind the Baroque vision of Venice that drew so many Romantic authors and musicians to the city. The top-level terrace, used for dining and cocktails, enjoys a marvellous view.

○○⊜⊜**Hotel Cipriani** – *Giudecca.* ☎041 520 7744. *www.hotelcipriani.it. 70 rooms, 24 suites.* Housed in the Palazzo Vendramin evokes elegance and good taste. In a quiet, secluded spot. Impeccable style extends to its spa and beautiful grounds with swimming pool.

○○⊜⊜**Hotel Des Bains** – *Lido, Lungomare Marconi 17.* ☎041 526 5921. *www.venice-hotel-desbains.com.* Under renovation through 2014. On the Lido, Hotel Excelsior is open Spring–Autumn *www.hotelexcelsiorvenezia.com.*

○○⊜⊜**Hotel Flora** – *Calle Larga XXII Marzo 2283/A.* ☎041 520 5844. *www.hotelflora.it. 40 rooms.* Art enhances early-20C charm. Careful attention has been lavished on every detail in the room decor, the 1920s staircase and the delightful garden, ideal for taking breakfast. It enjoys the perfect location, central but also quiet. Gym.

○○⊜⊜**Hotel Gritti Palace** – *Campo Santa Maria del Giglio 2467.* ☎041 794 611. *www.starwoodhotels.com. rooms, 21 suites.* An extensive restoration, completed 2013, renewed this superb 16C *palazzo,* the former private residence of

Hotel Danieli

© Gwen Cannon / MICHELIN

the Doge Gritti, bestowed with minute detail and lavish ornamentation.

THE VENETO

DOLOMITI

The Dolomites have two seasons, winter and summer. The foothills, however, stay busy year-round with wineries and other activites.

⊜⊜**Alice Relais nelle Vigne** – *Via Giardino 94, Loc. Carpesica 31029- Vittorio Veneto.* ☎*0438 561 173 .www.alice-relais.com. 10 rooms.* In the foothills of the Dolomites in Prosecco wine territory, the friendly owners of Bellenda and Alice wineries own this tastefully furnished stylish 19C farmhouse. Daily *aperitivo* with plenty of bubbles.

⊜⊜**Hotel Gran Ancëi** – *39030 San Cassiano (26.5km/16mi west of Cortina d'Ampezzo).* ☎*0471 84 95 40 . www.granancei.com. 29 rooms .* Surrounded by woodland and near the ski slopes. Classic mountain style wood decor. Spacious with wonderful views over the Dolomites. Outdoor pool.

⊜⊜⊜ **Hotel Erika** – *Via Braies di Fuori 66, Braies (5km/3mi north of Lago di Braies).* ☎*0474 74 86 84. www.hotelerika. net. 28 rooms.* Friendly and family-run cosy Alpine-style rooms in the Dolomites whatever the season. Typically South Tyrolean food is excellent.

⊜⊜ **Hotel Cavallino d'Oro** – *Piazza Kraus, Castelrotto (26km/16mi northeast of Bolzano).* ☎*0471 70 63 37. www. cavallino.it. 21 rooms.* Romantic four-poster beds, elegant antique Tyrolean-style furniture, open bar and fireplace. Dine in a traditional 17C *stuben* serving Tyrol, Italian and Mediterranean cuisine. Wellness centre.

⊜⊜⊜⊜ **Monika Hotel** – *Via del Parco 2 – 39030 Sesto/Sexten – ☎0474 71 03 84. www.monika.it. 49 rooms.* This well-being hotel in the Dolomites features comfortable modern rooms in oak and larch wood. Indoor pool, outdoor whirlpool, saunas, large stylish relaxation rooms and all kinds of treatments.

⊜⊜⊜ **Hotel Lavaredo** – *Via M. Piana 11. Misurina.* ☎*0435 39 227. www.lavaredohotel.it.* This family-run traditional chalet hotel has a wellness centre and enjoys a lakeside setting by the magnificent mountain peaks of the Cime di Lavaredo. Comfortable rooms with spacious public areas. Tyrolese and Italian cuisine.

⊜⊜⊜⊜**Hotel Kolfuschgerhof** – *Via Ronn 7, Corvara in Badia (2km/1.2mi east of Passo Gardena).* ☎*0471 83 61 88. www.kolfuschgerhof.com. 44 rooms.* Family-owned and run hotel in the heart of the Ladin mountains. Skiing in winter, walking trails in summer, and a wellness centre with swimming pool. Typically Tyrolean with delicious cuisine.

VERONA

Verona plays host to the world famous operas at the Arena amphitheatre from June to early September, and is close to the summer playground of Lake Garda, and to Amarone and Valpolicella wineries. During trade fairs and exhibitions most hotels increase their prices.

⊜⊜**Cavour** – *Vicolo Chiodo 4 – Verona.* ☎*045 59 01 66, fax 045 59 05 08. 19 rooms.* The main benefit of this hotel is its quiet, central location, except when the opera season is on and then you are so close that you could probably stay in your room and listen to it. Simple rooms with modern furnishings. Small patio.

⊜⊜ **Hotel Torcolo** – *Vicolo Listone 3* ☎*045 80 07 512. www.hoteltorcolo. it. 19 rooms.* Pleasant rooms with an endearingly retro feel in a traditional hotel where the staff are keen to please, located a stone's throw from the Arena.

⊜⊜⊜ **Villa del Quar** – *Via Quar 12, 37029 - Pedemonte* ☎*045 680 0681. www. hotelvilladelquar.it. 25 rooms.* Luxuriate in this 15-16C villa situated on the family vineyard 6km from Verona. Don't miss a meal at Ristorante Arquada. Great attention to detail in service and furnishing. Swimming pool, heliport.

VICENZA

⊜⊜**Hotel Victoria** – *Strada Padana Padua road) 52 (7km/4mi east of Vicenza on SS 11).* ☎*0444 91 22 99. www.hotel victoriavicenza.com. 120 rooms.* This modern hotel on the outskirts of town combines reasonable prices with comfortable surroundings. Pool, gym.

⊜⊜⊜⊜**G Boutique** – *Via Giuriolo 10.* ☎*0444 32 64 58. www.gboutiquehotel. com. 17 rooms.* A stone's throw from the Teatro Olimpico, the former Giardini hotel has gone upscale with design and artisan touches in silk and glass.

⊜⊜⊜⊜**Hotel Villa Michelangelo** – Via Sacco, 35, Arcugnano (6km south of city centre). ☎*0444 550 300. www.hotel-villamichelangelo.com.* Set in a former monastery with a panorama over the Berici Hills. Outdoor swimming pool.

PADOVA

⊜⊜**Hotel Al Fagiano** – *Via Locatelli 45.* ☎*049 87 53 396. www.alfagiano.com.* Only 100m from the Basilica di Sant'Antonio this attractive eclectic modern hotel with stylish good-sized bedrooms enjoys a central location and offers excellent value.

⊜⊜⊜⊜**Grand' Italia** – Corso del Popolo, 81. ☎*049 876 1111. www.hotelgranditalia.it.* This beautiful 1909 art nouveau-building has a sweeping ornate staircase and gilded, stuccoed public areas. Bedrooms are minimalist style with modern facilities. Good central location by the railway station.

CAMPING FACILITIES

Camp sites dot the Cavallino coastline. www.turismovenezia.it.

WHERE TO EAT

The city's finest restaurants are listed in the **Michelin Guide Italy**, which is updated annually. Venice also has a wide choice of less formal establishments serving light meals, drinks and snacks (⊜ *for assistance with local dishes, see Introduction: Food and Wine*). Visitors should be aware that it is nearly always cheaper to stand at the bar than to sit at a table; be sure to check prices before ordering.

Provided below is a selection of *osterie*, trattorias and *pasticcerie* grouped under their respective neighbourhoods.
The coin symbols here denote the price of a dinner meal consisting of an appetizer, an entree and a dessert (without drinks). Note that most restaurants in Venice include a *coperto*, a small charge (€2–€3 perhaps) for incidentals such as bread. Tips are sometimes, but not always included in the bill – always check to avoid tipping twice!

When in Venice

The Piazza San Marco is famous for its *gran caffès* and almost equally infamous for the prices they charge. Just bear in mind that when you pull up a chair in one of these establishments, that you are not *just* buying a drink or a meal; rather you are taking up an exalted position in what Napoleon (supposedly) once called Europe's finest drawing room. There are several cafes around the square but two are world famous: the **Caffè**

Florian (*www.caffeflorian.com*) and the **Caffè Quadri** (*www.quadrivenice*). Opened in 1720, Caffè Florian is not only Venice's most venerable cafe but the oldest in the country. The Quadri, in its present incarnation, opened in 1830, though a coffee shop once traded on the same site – perhaps the first ever in Venice – and is thought to have dated back to 1683. If you really want to push the boat out, take a seat outside either of these aristocratic *grand dames* (not forgetting to have a good look inside to admire their magnificent interiors) , and enjoy the music of a live orchestra. Dancing in the piazza is encouraged, and many would argue it is the best way to get your money's worth. The best cuisine on the piazza is at Quadri.

A few steps away from the piazza on Calle Vallaresso, is Venice's most famous watering hole, **Harry's Bar** (*041 528 5777. www.cipriani.com*). The haunt of Hemingway, this stylish bar and restaurant continues to be the stamping ground of the glitterati, who come here for the trademark Bellini cocktail (sparkling prosecco and white peach juice) as well as its good traditional cuisine. Like the Caffès in the square, it is ferociously expensive, but sometimes money isn't everything.

© Gwen Cannon / MICHELIN

Caffè Florian in Piazza San Marco

'La Dolce Vita'

Venice is full of little spots for sitting back and quite literally enjoying "*La Dolce Vita*":

SAN MARCO

Paolin – *Campo Santo Stefano* *041 522 0710. Closed Sat*. Imaginative and-delicious ice creams, a Venice favourite. Outside tables.

Le Cafè – *Campo Santo Stefano 2797*. *041 523 7201*. This excellent *pasticceria* has outside tables and light lunch fare.

DORSODURO

La Piscina – *Dorsoduro 780, Zattere 30123*. *041 520 6466*. The homemade ice cream is better than in most of the gelaterie. Watch water vessels on the Giudecca Canal. Pleasant for lunch, dinner, or snacks.

LA GIUDECCA

Harry's Dolci – *Fondamenta S. Biagio 773*. *041 522 4844; www.cipriani.com. Closed Tue and Nov–Mar*. This restaurant-cum-*pasticceria* is a little less expensive than Harry's Bar.

Address Book

For coin ranges, see the Legend for large cities on the cover flap.

VENICE

SAN MARCO

A la Campana – *Calle dei Fabbri 4720*. *041 528 5170. Closed Sun*. This typically Venetian restaurant is situated a stone's throw from the Rialto Bridge.

Ai Rusteghi – *Campo San Bartolomeo 5529; *041 523 2205. Closed Sun*. The well chosen wines are the main draw, with some quality *panini*.

Al Volto – *Calle Cavalli 4081*. *041 522 8945*. This wine bar, close to Campo Manin, is an ideal spot to sample typical Venetian snacks (*cichetti*).

Chat Qui Rit – *Calle Tron, Angolo Frezzeria*. *041 522 9086. Closed Sat mid-Oct–Jun*. This self-service cafeteria offers a wide selection of entrees, salads and sides at reasonable prices. Courtyard and indoor dining.

Leon Bianco – *Salizida San Luca 4153*. *041 522 1180*. This small restaurant has seafood specialities and quick service.

© Grancaffè Quadri

Grancaffè Quadri

⊜⊜**Antica Carbonera** – *Calle Bembo 4648.* ☎*041 522 5479. www.antica carbonera.it. Closed Tue.* Historic trattoria serving typical Venetian fare.

⊜**Trattoria Da Fiore** – *Calle delle Botteghe 3461.* ☎*041 523 5310. www. dafiore.it. Closed Tue.* On a narrow, yet bustling street off Campo S. Stefano, this charming trattoria offers fine food in an intimate setting and remains a favourite with locals, too.

⊜⊜**Bistrot de Venice** – *Calle Calle dei Fabbri 4685.* ☎*041 523 6651 www.bistrotdevenise.com.* Historical Venetian cuisine, a vast selection of superb wines (also by the glass), local events and later serving hours make for a lively mix.

⊜⊜⊜**Grancaffe Quadri** – *Piazza San Marco 120.* ☎*041 522 2105. www.quadrivenice.com. Closed Mon.* Elegant drinking and dining in Venice in a triumph of stucco, Murano glass and precious tapestries in this beautiful historic site. Enjoy superb creative and Venetian cuisine at its finest under chef Alajmo's team, albeit at a hefty price.

DORSODURO

⊜**Il Caffè (Caffè Rosso)** – *Campo Santa Margherita 2963.* ☎*041 528 7988. Closed Sun.* This historic cafe in the Dorsoduro district is a popular meeting place with the avant-garde and bohemian set.

⊜⊜**Antica Locanda Montin** – *Fondamenta Borgo, Dorsoduro 1147.* ☎*041 522 7151. www.locandamontin.com.* A Venetian institution, this charming trattoria serves excellent cuisine.

⊜⊜**Dona Onesta** – *Ponte de la Dona Onesta 3922.* ☎*041 710 586. www.donaonesta.com.* Typical trattoria, near the Ca' Foscari, serves mostly fish.

⊜⊜**San Trovaso** – *Rio di San Trovaso, Dorsoduro 1016.* ☎*041 520 3703. Closed Mon.* An attractive taverna near the Galleria dell'Accademia, which serves good pizzas. Popular with tourists and Venetians, booking advised. Outdoor terrace.

⊜⊜⊜**Lineadombra** – *Dorsoduro 19, just past the Dogana.* ☎*041 241 1881. www.ristorantelineadombra.com.* Traditional Venetian cuisine with a touch of creative fusion, is served in sleek modern minimalist restaurant behind La Salute

SANTA CROCE

⊜⊜**Al Ponte** – *Ponte del Megio 1666.* ☎*041 719 777. Closed Sat evening and Sun.* This canalside trattoria is renowned for its fish dishes.

⊜⊜**Vecio Fritolin** – *Calle della Regina 2262.* ☎*041 522 28. www.veciofritolin.it. Closed Sun evening and Mon.* Situated near Ca' Corner, the famous Vecio Fritoin specialises in Venetian *cicheti* (snacks) and dishes.

⊜⊜**La Zucca** – *Ponte del Megio 1762.*
☎*041 524 1570. www.lazucca.it. Closed*
Sun. Reservations highly recommended.
This friendly restaurant near the Church
of San Giacomo dall'Orio. Varied,
innovative cuisine at reasonable prices;
meat and many vegetarian dishes like
pumpkin (*zucca*) flan and desserts are
highly recommended. Popular with
locals and visitors.

CANNAREGIO

⊜**Algiubagiò** – *Fondamenta Nuove
5039.* ☎*041 523 6084. www.algiubagio.
com. Closed Tue.* This romantic and
rustic bar and restaurant is an ideal spot
for a drink near the vaporetto. Tables
outside have a view of the lagoon.

⊜**Alla Fontana** – *Fondamenta 1102.*
☎*041 715 077. Closed Sun evening and
Mon.* An attractive bar serving a good
selection of Venetian snacks (*cicheti*).

⊜**Gam-Gam** – *Sottoportego del
Ghetoo Vecchio 1122.* ☎*041 523 1495.
Closed Fri evening, Sat and Jewish hols.*
Kosher meals in the Old Ghetto.
Many vegetarian options and a few
exotic dishes.

⊜**La Perla** – *Rio Terà dei Franceschi.*
☎*041 528 5175.* Choose from a wide
selection of pizzas in this restaurant
situated behind Campo SS Apostoli.

⊜**Ai Promessi Sposi** – *Calle dell'Oca
4367.* ☎*041 241 2747. Closed Wed.* This
typical Venetian bar (*bacaro*) is found
in the district of Campo SS. Apostoli.

⊜⊜**Alla Vedova** – *Calle del Pistor
3912.* ☎*041 528 5324. Closed Thu and
Sun lunchtime.* This popular *bacaro*

and restaurant can get very busy.
Booking is highly recommended.

⊜⊜⊜**Anice Stellato** – *Fondamenta
della Sensa 3272.* ☎*041 720 744. Closed
Mon–Tue. Reservations essential.* Humble
exterior, but this osteria has a direct link
to the sea. Venetians frequent the "Star
Anise" for its innovation and tradition,
informal ambience at reasonable prices.

⊜⊜⊜**Fiaschetteria Toscana** – *F S
Giovanni Crisostomo Cannaregio 5719.*
☎*041 528 5281. Closed Tue, lunch Wed.*
Delicious meat and seafood, but fish is
the main feature. Don't miss *moeche*
(soft-shell lagoon crab) in season.

SAN POLO

⊜**All'Arco** – *San Polo 436.* ☎*041
520 5666. Closed Sun.* This bar serves
numerous wines by the glass, delicious
snacks, and daily market dishes.

⊜**Ai Nomboli** – *Calle Goldoni 2717.*
☎*041 523 0995. Closed Sun.* A good bar
for sandwiches and snacks.

⊜**Alla Patatina** – *Calle Saoneri 2741.*
☎*041 523 7238.* This busy, friendly café
serves a wide selection of vegetable
dishes at the bar, including the
eponymous fried potatoes. Or at tables,
choose from mostly fish with some
meat dishes.

⊜**Dai Tosi** – *Seco Marina, Castello 738.*
☎*041 523 7102.* An excellent pizzeria
that also serves pasta and other dishes.

⊜**Vini Da Pinto** – *Campo delle Becarie
367.* ☎*041 522 4599.* This popular,
typically Venetian bar near the market is
a good place for a quick drink.

⊜⊜**All'Aciugheta** – *Campo Santi
Filippo e Giacomo 4357.* ☎*041 522 4292.*
A varied menu but quality fluctuates;
good *cichetti* and extensive wine list.

⊜⊜⊜**Al Mascaròn** – *Calle Lunga
S. Maria Formosa 5225.* ☎*041 522
5995. Closed Sun.* A popular *osteria*. Try
spaghetti in seppia or *bacalà* (salt cod) a
variety of ways.

CASTELLO AND SANT'ELENA

⊜⊜**Rivetta** – *Ponte S. Provolo, Castello
4625.* ☎*041 528 7302. Closed Mon.* This
typical trattoria also serves snacks
at the bar. Gnocchi with crab are a
speciality.

© Paolo della Corte / Vecio Fritolin

*Scampi tails and pasta with drops
of coffee at Vecio Fritolin*

Outdoor seating at Lineadombra

🍽️🍽️🍽️**Antico Dolo** – *Ruga Rialto 778, Rialto.* ☎*041 522 6546. www.antico dolo.it.* The *osteria* serves a range of local delicacies, such as tripe, *crostini*, polenta and *bacalà* (salt cod).

🍽️🍽️🍽️🍽️**Alle Testiere** – *Calle del Mondo Novo, Castello 5801.* ☎ *041 522 7220. Closed Sun–Mon.* This attractive *osteria* many claim serves the best seafood in Venice. Always busy, reservations are a must.

🍽️🍽️🍽️🍽️ **Corte Sconta** – *Castello 3886 Calle del Pestrin.* ☎*041 522 7024.* A good assortment of fish dishes, all well prepared. Lucia offers good wines.

🍽️🍽️🍽️🍽️**L'Osteria di Santa Marina** – *Castello 5911 Campo Santa Marina.* ☎*041 528 5239.* Creative and unexpected food pairings and attentive service.

🍽️🍽️🍽️🍽️ **Met** – *Castello 4149 Riva degli Schiavoni.* ☎*041 520 5044.* Traditional or highly creative cuisine, all served with great flair and attentive service.

🍽️🍽️🍽️🍽️**Osteria da Fiore** (Zanetti) – *Calle del Scaleter 2202/A.* ☎*041 721 308. reservation@dafiore.com. Closed Sun, Mon. Reservations essential.* Always in vogue with both tourists and locals, this fine establishment excels at everyday Italian cuisine with a twist. Signature dishes include *capesante gratinate al timo* (grilled scallops with thyme) and an eye-popping *frittura mista di pesce.*

🍽️🍽️**Al Pampo** – *Calle Chinotto 24, Isola di Sant'Elena.* ☎*041 520 8419.* An excellent value traditional Italian trattoria.

OUTLYING ISLANDS

BURANO

🍽️🍽️🍽️ **Trattoria Da Romano** – *Via Galuppi 221 Burano.* ☎*041 730 030. Closed Tue.* A tradition for risotto and fish dishes, right on the main street.

🍽️🍽️🍽️ **Il Gatto Nero** – *Via Giudecca 88 Burano.* ☎*041 730 120.* Good seafood and wines in this refined trattoria.

MAZZORBO

🍽️🍽️ **Trattoria Maddalena** – *Mazzorbo 7C, 30141 Mazzorbo.* ☎*041 730 151. Closed Thu.* Run by the same friendly family since 1954, enjoy pastas, fish, game and their fresh garden vegetables.

🍽️🍽️🍽️🍽️**Venissa** – *CFondamenta Santa Caterina 3* ☎*041 527 2281. www. venissa.it. Closed Nov=Mar. Reservations essential.* Set at the edge of an island vineyard, chef Budel deliciously blends tradition and innovation.

MURANO

🍽️🍽️ **Ai Frati** – *Fondamenta Venier 4, 30141 Murano.* ☎*041 736 694. 8am-3.30pm. Lunch only. Closed Thu.* A mid-19C wine shop that has been serving good, authentic home cooking for more than half a century. Try to get a terrace table overlooking the canal.

THE VENETO

VICENZA

Al Pestello – *Contrà Santo Stefano 3. ☎0444 32 37 21. www. ristorantealpestello.it. Closed Sun. Vincentina cuisine is served this small restaurant adorned with lovely country scenes of Villa Pisani. Small outdoor area.*

Antica Osteria da Penacio – *Via Soghe 22, località Soghe, 36077 Arcugnano (10km/6mi south of Vicenza on S 247). ☎0444 27 30 81. Closed Wed, Thu lunchtime.* From the outside this looks like a rather old taverna but the interior is surprisingly elegant. Both dining rooms are modern in style and there is a small but well-stocked wine cellar which adds to the atmosphere. The cuisine is of a high standard.

DOLOMITI

Unterwirt – *Località Gudon – 39043 Chiusa d'Isarco – 34km/20mi northeast of Bolzano on S 12. ☎0472 84 40 00. www.unterwirt-gufidaun. com. Closed Sun and Mon, Jan–Mar.* In a charming village, traditional cooking has an imaginative slant.

Al Borgo – *Via Via Ancoretta 8 Belluno. Closed Mon eve, Tue. ☎0437 926 755. www.alborgo.to.* Locals head here for a special night out with cuisine typical of the Veneto in 18C Villa Doglioni. Much of the food they raise themselves in the attached garden. They also have 4 guest rooms.

Rifugio Larin – *Località Senes, 32046 San Vito di Cadore (9km/5mi south of Cortina d'Ampezzo on S 51) ☎0436 91 12. Closed Oct–May.* An atmospheric classic mountain hut with hearty food. Accessible by car, but it makes for a pleasant stroll. Wonderful views.

Enoteca – *Via Mercato 5, 32043 Cortina d'Ampezzo. ☎0436 86 20 40. Closed lunch, Sun.* A beautiful old door opens onto this lovely wine bar with its wooden ceiling. Great to try local wines.

VERONA

Just a short distance from the Valpolicella and Amarone winemaking area, here are a few suggested wineries to try: Stefano Accordini, Igino Accordini, Antolini, Dal Bosco Giulietta, Trabucchi d'Illasi, Buglioni, Le Maragnole, Roccolo Grassi, Tommasi, Valentina Cubi, and Zenato.

San Basilio alla Pergola – *Via Pisano 9, Verona. ☎045 52 04 75.* Rustic-style dining rooms lend a country feel to the chef's traditional but imaginative cooking. Good value.

Osteria del Bugiardo – *Via Casette 19, Santa Maria di Negrar (15km/9mi north of Verona on SS12). ☎045 602 0808. www.buglioni.it.* The Buglioni winery offers traditional country fare served with their Amarone and Valpolicella wines.

Ciccarelli – *Via Mantovana 171, Località Madonna di Dossobuono (8km/5mi southwest of Verona). ☎045 95 39 86. www.ristoranteciccarelli.it. Closed Sat.* The speciality of this traditional trattoria (est. 1865) is boiled meats.

Ristorante Arquada – *Via Quar 12, 37029 - Pedemonte ☎045 680 0681. www. hotelvilladelquar.it.* In Villa Quar (see Where to Stay). Refined cuisine and service in an historic setting.

PADOVA

Le Calandre – *Via Liguria 1 Sarmeola I - 35030 Rubano (7km/4mi northwest of Padua on SS11). ☎049 630 303. www.alajmo.it. Closd Sun Mon.* Chef Max Alajmo's creativity has made this one of Italy's top food destinations for inventions such as cuttlefish cappuccino or saffron risotto dusted with licorice powder. Tasting menu ranges €175-240. For a more economical experience, next door their pastry shop and bistrot Il Calandrino is open 7 days, serving breakfast- dinner. Tasting menus, also very sophisticated, begin at about €45.

Trattoria la Ragnatela – *Via Caltana 79. 30030 Scaltenigo di Mirano (13km/8mi northeast of Padua). ☎41 43 60 50. www.ristorantelaragnatela.com.* Simple, informal cooperative, where the clientele ranges from decorators in their overalls to businessmen. Authentic regional cooking.

ENTERTAINMENT

Venice at night is magically romantic and atmospheric. The play of lights on the lamplit canals and floodlit *palazzi* is a special sight to remember, especially from the vantage point of a slow gliding gondola.

Evening entertainment is low key, though widespread in venues from theatres to churches. Few bars and cafes stay open past 11pm. Since the time of Goldoni and Pietro Longhi, Venice has been the perfect backdrop for theatre. Festivals and drama are still very much a part of life in this scenic city.

Information

The tourist office has a free calendar of Shows and Events on a monthly basis (&see *Planning Your Trip*): evening performances are listed day by day. The office also offers a free, event-packed booklet entitled **un Ospite di Venezia**: see the Venice by Night section. Information is also available online at www.unospitedivenezia.it and www.turismovenezia.it (click on Events); both sites are also in English. At the weekend the magazine of the daily newspaper, **Il Gazettino,** provides comprehensive coverage of the shows, exhibitions and festivals held in Venice, as well as concerts and recitals in churches and public buildings. Information on theatre, cinema and concerts in Venice is also available at www.culturaspettacolovenezia.it. Simplest of all, large posters announcing events are plastered throughout the streets so keep your eyes peeled.

Address Book

VENICE

LATE BARS, LOUNGES AND PUBS

Bacaro Jazz – *Campo S Bartolomo.* ☎041 528 249. www.bacarojazz.com. *Noon–2am.* Jazz is the theme at this lively cocktail bar. Near the Rialto Bridge, it serves panini in and simple Venetian specialities like *fegato*.

Birreria Forst – *Calle delle Rasse, 4540.* ☎041 523 0557. *9am-10pm.* A typical brasserie where gondoliers meet, with a range of beers and German-style black-bread sandwiches.

Bistrot de Venice – *Calle Calle dei Fabbri 4685.* ☎041 523 6651 www.bistrotdevenise.com. *Open to 1am* (also see Restaurants). The kitchen serves to midnight and a savvy sommelier offers a few hundred wines by the glass

Centrale – *Piscina Frezzeria, San Marco,* ☎041 296 0664. www.caffecentrale venezia.com. *Closed Tue.* A glamorous nightspot near La Fenice (before- or after-theatre dining) in the atmospheric 16C Palazzo Cocco Melin, with soft lighting, designer armchairs, sofas, Mediterranean cuisine and cocktails.

Devil's Forest – *Calle degli Stagneri 5185.* ☎041 520 0623. www.devilsforest. com. *Closed Mon.* A pleasant brasserie for a glass of beer and *panini*.

Dogado – *Via Cannaregio 3660A.* ☎041 520 8544. Good value food by

Mimes

© Gwen Cannon / MICHELIN

day in a smart cafe downstairs, while by night it is a smart wine bar, with a full a la carte restaurant and roof terrace with garden-style swing loungers.

Antico Martini – *Calle del Cafetier, 1007 San Marco.* ☎*041 522 4121. Closed Tue.* Drinks and restaurant with inside garden. Runs nearby **Vino Vino** wine bar.

Al Paradiso Perduto – *Fondamenta de la Misericordia 2540.* ☎*041 720 581. 6–11pm. Closed Mon–Tue.* Enjoy homemade *primi* (first courses), *fritti* (fried) and grilled fish in this long-term favourite *osteria*.

HOTEL BARS

A way to enjoy the ambience of the city's great hotels without the high cost of a room is to have a drink at the Hotel Bauer, Danieli, Metropole, or the Gritti Palace. Enjoy your cocktail in the bar or on the outdoor terrace, offering stunning nighttime views with royal service.

PERFORMING ARTS

The main theatres are:

Gran Teatro La Fenice *Campo San Fantin, San Marco.* ☎*041 78 65 11. www.teatrolafenice.it.* The city's beloved opera house also hosts ballet and jazz concerts.

Teatro Goldoni (*Calle del Teatro.* ☎*041 24 02 011. www.teatrostabileveneto.it/ Goldoni.* Plays and occasional concerts

Teatro Fondamenta Nuove *Fondamenta Nuove, Cannaregio.* ☎*041 522 44 98. www.teatrofondamentanuove. it.* Programme includes jazz, contemporary music and dance.

Teatro Goldoni

Teatro Malibran *behind the church of San Giovanni Grisostomo, Cannaregio.* ☎*041 78 66 01. www.teatrolafenice.it.* Plays, operas and classical concerts.

OTHER CLASSICAL CONCERT VENUES
Churches and Scuoli

A Vivaldi concert in one of the city's historic **churches** is a highlight of any visit. Get the tourist office's Shows and Events calendar and watch the street posters. Churches holding performances usually display a printed announcement at the entrance steps a few days in advance of the event. Many of the **scuoli,** such as Grande di San Teodoro, San Giovanni Evangelista, and San Rocco, offer evening

Street musicians

Aida performed at the Arena di Verona

performances of classical music, often in masks and period costumes. Be prepared to pay in cash, as credit cards are generally not accepted. Plan to arrive early to get good seats and to admire the wall and ceiling art.

STREET MUSIC
One of the delights of Venice is the variety of live classical music heard on so many streets and church entrance steps, both day and night.

CINEMA
The Venice International Film Festival is the world's oldest film festival (www.labiennale.org). The Lido and the city's squares host open-air cinemas showing films competing in the festival; the 70th in 2013 held Aug 28-Sept 7 also added sections on restored classic films and documentaries. Year-round the small **Casa del Cinema-Videoteca Pasinetti** (Palazzo Mocenigo,San Stae 1990; ☎041 5241320; www.comune.venezia.it) shows some films in their original language.

VERONA

OPERA
The opera seasons draw large crowds to the famous Arena to watch famous perennials such as Aida, Carmen and Madame Butterfly, from June to September. Ticket prices range from over €150 for the front row of the stalls, to just over €100 for numbered seats on the steps. Numbered seats low down are more comfortable than the stone steps but on hot nights it can be airless and stuffy and your view of the stage may be restricted. Sit high up for a breath of air and of course a grandstand view. As may be expected in an open-air venue acoustics are imperfect – the best sound is reckoned to be halfway down the tiers. An unreserved seat on the stone steps (gradinata) starts at under €20. ☎045 8005151. www.arena.it.

Other venues to check for performances are churches throughout the Veneto region, historic *palazzi*, and the Palladian and other historic villas.

SHOPPING

Shopping in Venice is a treat. So many small shops greet visitors, showcasing glass, textiles, masks and other products that are unique to the area. In some, it is possible to watch specialists at work, such as the glassmakers on the island of Murano. Most shops are open Mon–Sat, 8am–1pm and 3.30–7.30pm. Credit cards are accepted in most stores. Venice has never been a place to seek out bargains, but remains a wonderful place for fine craftsmanship for the observant visitor to discover amidst the many tourist-oriented shops (many do not permit photos.)

Venice Streets

Calle Larga 22 Marzo – *West of Piazza San Marco.* Designer boutiques, glitzy shops, including shoe and handbag.
Mercerie – *Between Pizza San Marco and the Rialto Bridge.* Upscale boutiques selling leather goods, luggage, clothing, housewares and other merchandise.
Rio Terà Lista di Spagna – *Just east of the train station.* Here you'll find a wide variety of glass, clothing and souvenir shops.
Strada Nuova – *Near Ca' d'Oro in the Cannaregio district.* Bakeries and restaurants intermingle with souvenir stalls, gift, food and clothing stores. Pricey gift and clothing shops dot the **Procuratie Nuovo** bordering Piazza San Marco and heavyweight designer boutiques along **Calle Vallaresso,** just west of the Piazza, leading to Harry's Bar**.**

Address Book

VENICE

COSTUMES AND MASKS

To hire a typical Venetian Carnival costume contact **Il Prato**, Frezzeria 1771, San Marco, ☎041 520 33 75, or **Nicoloa Atelier**, Cannaregio 5565, ☎041 520 70 51.
Masks are sold everywhere; if you are looking for a good quality Venetian-mask, opt for one made of *carta pesta* (papier-mâché). Reputable shops include **Ca' Macana**, the original is at Dorsoduro 3172, another at 1169, and by appointment a workshop for individuals or families to make their own masks at 3215 ☎041 27 76 142, www.camacana.com; **La pietra filosofale**, San Marco 1735 (Frezzeria, near Fenice Theatre); and **Tragicomica**, San Polo 2800 (Calle dei Nomboli, near Campo San Tomà, between San Polo and I Frari), ☎041 72 11 02, www.tragi-comica.it. **Carta Alta** (www.cartaalta.it) mask worshop (not open to visitors) is on the Giudecca; their masks are sold in various shops including **Fabris Leda** (S. Marco 702).

TRADITIONAL STATIONERY

Quality paper can be bought in many shops in the city, including **Alberto Valese's** (3471 Santo Stefano, San Marco, www.albertovalese-ebru.com). Everything a graphomaniac could want can be found in the shops in Calle della Mandola, between Campo Manin and Campo Sant'Angelo, and Calle del Piovan, between Campo San Maurizio

Costumed for Carnival

© R. Mattes / MICHELIN

Venitian paper and pencils

and Campo Santo Stefano. The **Legatoria Piazzesi** (Campiello della Feltrina, between Santa Maria del Giglio and San Maurizio, www.legatoriapiazzesi. it) stocks beautiful cards printed using old-fashioned Venetian methods. **Gianni Basso's** (Calle del Fumo 5306, Cannaregio), near the Fondamenta Nuove, where the vaporettos leave for the islands, produces a range of quality stationery, personal bookplates and business cards, embossed and printed using traditional methods.

TEXTILES, GLASS, LEATHER

Shops specialising in textiles, glassworks, dolls and puppets abound in Venice. In business since 1700, **Mario Bevilacqua** (Campo S. Maria del Giglio, S. Marco 2520) has gorgeous textiles and decorative trimmings, tie-backs, embroidery and velvet in the great tradition of Venetian fabrics; some are still woven on period looms. A collector, too, they even have some vintage Fortuny textiles here; another shop is in Castello, this is most atmospheric. Venice has fine textile shops that specialise in velvets, silks, and brocades, for clothing or interior design. **Giuliana Longo** (Calle del Lovo, S. Marco 4813) in the family trade since 1901, is wedged into her tiny hat shop with a lovely variety, from wool felt or velvet with feathers, to hand-made Montecristi panama hats, or a reasonably priced doge's hat for Carnival. **Bottega Veneta** (San Marco 30124) crafts some of Italy's finest leather purses and bags near Vicenza, their trademark being their artisans' complex *intrecciato* (braided) weave. On a more economical scale, **Benetton** shops abound and clothes are manufactured worldwide, but the company still operates out of Treviso.

Glass stores are common in Venice, although quality varies greatly and much of it comes from Asia. These 11 companies make their glass exclusively on Murano: Anfora, DinoRosin Arte Studio, Effe, Formia, Galliano Ferro, Gino Cenedese, Linea Vetro, NasonMoretti, Nuova Biemmeci, S.a.l.i.r, Seguso Viro. The Museo del Vetro can help locate some of the local glass artists; the small museum shop often displays their work.

MODEL BOATS

The shop window of **Gilberto Penzo's** near I Frari (Calle Seconda dei Saoneri 2681, San Polo, 041 524 6139, www. veniceboats.com) specialises in historic Venetian model boats, gondolas and *bricole* made from wood. The shop sells model kits, construction plans, reliefs, rowlocks and nautical ex-votos.

COFFEE

Venice has several excellent *torrefazioni* (coffee roasters). **Marchi** (Cannaregio 1337) roasts beans several times a day, sells them whole or ground, also has a small bar. Other brands are **Girani** (Castello 3727), **Doge** (bar at Calle dei Cinque San Polo 609) and **India** (bar at Campo Santa Margherita).

CONFECTIONERY

Volpe (in the Ghetto, Cannaregio) sells Jewish bread and pastries. **VizioVirtù Cioccolateria** (S. Polo 2898/A) makes chocolates.

VERONA

Via Mazzini and **Corso Porta Borsari** display top quality clothing and shoes. On the former look for **Libreria Ghelfi & Barbato** (at no 21) with its beautiful shopfront, a fine selection of books and, less expected, fine food and wine. An old shop **La Salumeria** (Corso Sant'Anastasia) is crammed with Italian foodstuffs. **Rossi** bakes excellent breads and has enough treats to concoct a gourmet picnic. **Stradone Porta Palio** is known for its antique shops. The once-famous **Mercato di Piazza Erbe** (fruit, vegetables, and increasingly, tourist fripperies) is a shadow of its former self.

PADOVA

Designer fashions are found around the **Piazza Cavour** and particularly on **Via San Fermo** with prices going stratospheric around the **Galleria Borghese**.

Rinascente, on Piazza Garibaldi, is a mid-range department store. On via P F Calvi, just off Piazza Cavour, is **Racca**, a wonderful little confectioners and ice cream seller established 1933.

The town's other main shopping street is **Via Roma** with a selection of general shops for most budgets.

Between the Piazza delle Erbe and the Duomo, **Via Daniele Manin** is a pretty arcaded street, lined with shops selling cut-price clothes, shoes and accessories, popular with the university students. Padova is famous for its goldsmiths. On **Via Davila** are jewellers and silversmiths including **Roberto Callegari** at no 8, and at no 6 **L'Antiquario Gemmologo**. Other fine goldsmiths are **Alberta Vita**, **Mario Pinton**, and **Paolo Marcolongo**. Padua is excellent for **markets**. Its daily fruit and vegetable markets are renowned for their quality. The weekly general market is each Saturday on the Prato della Valle; on the third Sunday of every month, some 200 antiques and collectibles vendors set out their stalls.

MOLO (PROVINCE OF VICENZA)

Guerrino Lovato moved his mask collection from Venice (🔊 *see photo*) to set up a museum **Museo Mondonovo Maschere** (www.museialtovicentino. it). He made masks for Stanley Kubrik's *Eyes Wide Shut*, as well as for Branaugh, Zeffirelli and La Fenice. Mask workshop at www.maskedart.com.

Silverware in the antique market on the Prato della Valle, Padova

© veslivio / iStockphoto.com

INDEX

INDEX

INDEX

INDEX

MAPS AND PLANS

THEMATIC MAPS

MAPS AND PLANS

Maps

COMPANION PUBLICATIONS

INTERNET

Users can access personalised route plans, Michelin mapping on line, addresses of hotels and restaurants featured in the *Michelin Guide* collection, and practical and tourist information through the website
www.viamichelin.com
www.travel.viamichelin.com

For planning in-depth trips in the Venice region, this guide may be used in conjunction with:

♦ **Michelin map 562 Italy**, which covers the northeast of Italy and includes an index of towns. Scale 1:400 000.

For visitors travelling throughout Italy, we recommend:

♦ **Michelin Road Atlas Italy**, a useful spiral-bound atlas with an alphabetical index of 70 towns and cities. Scale 1:300 000.

♦ **Michelin map 735 Italy**, a practical map which provides the visitor with a complete picture of Italy's road network. Scale 1:1 000 000.

MAP LEGEND

	Sight	Seaside Resort	Winter Sports Resort	Spa
Highly recommended	★★★	≋≋≋	❄❄❄	♯♯♯
Recommended	★★	≋≋	❄❄	♯♯
Interesting	★	≋	❄	♯

Tourism

◉⊐ Sightseeing route with departure point indicated	AZ B Map co-ordinates locating sights
⌂♱⌂♱ Ecclesiastical building	🛈 Tourist information
✡ ☪ Synagogue – Mosque	⊷ ♣ Historic house, castle – Ruins
⊡ Building (with main entrance)	⌣ ☼ Dam – Factory or power station
■ Statue, small building	☆ ∩ Fort – Cave
♱ Wayside cross	♜ Prehistoric site
◎ Fountain	▼ ᐯ Viewing table – View
●━●━● Fortified walls – Tower – Gate	▲ Miscellaneous sight

Recreation

Racecourse	🏃 Waymarked footpath
Skating rink	◈ Outdoor leisure park/centre
Outdoor, indoor swimming pool	⛯ Theme/Amusement park
Marina, moorings	⋎ Wildlife/Safari park, zoo
⌂ Mountain refuge hut	⊛ Gardens, park, arboretum
▫━▪━▫ Overhead cable-car	⊙ Aviary, bird sanctuary
🚂 Tourist or steam railway	

Additional symbols

══ ══ Motorway (unclassified)	⊠ ◎ Post office – Telephone centre
❶ ❶ Junction: complete, limited	⊠ Covered market
⊏══⊐ Pedestrian street	⁘ Barracks
⊏═══⊐ Unsuitable for traffic, street subject to restrictions	△ Swing bridge
⊏⊏⊏⊏ Steps – Footpath	∪ ✗ Quarry – Mine
🚊 Railway – Coach station	Ⓑ Ⓕ Ferry (river and lake crossings)
▫++++▫ Funicular – Rack-railway	⛴ Ferry services: Passengers and cars
━━ ⊙ Tram – Metro, underground	⛴ Foot passengers only
Bert (R.)... Main shopping street	③ Access route number common to MICHELIN maps and town plans

Abbreviations and special symbols

H	Town hall (Municipio)	**T**	Theatre (Teatro)
J	Law courts (Palazzo di Giustizia)	**U**	University (Università)
M	Museum (Museo)	🏛	Palace, villa
P	Local authority offices (Prefettura)		
POL.	Police station (Polizia) (in large towns: Questura)	8 EX	Map number and grid reference locating sights on maps 2 - 11

The Michelin Adventure

It all started with rubber balls! This was the product made by a small company based in Clermont-Ferrand that André and Edouard Michelin inherited, back in 1880. The brothers quickly saw the potential for a new means of transport and their first success was the invention of detachable pneumatic tires for bicycles. However, the automobile was to provide the greatest scope for their creative talents. Throughout the 20th century, Michelin never ceased developing and creating ever more reliable and high-performance tires, not only for vehicles ranging from trucks to F1 but also for underground transit systems and airplanes.

From early on, Michelin provided its customers with tools and services to facilitate mobility and make traveling a more pleasurable and more frequent experience. As early as 1900, the Michelin Guide supplied motorists with a host of useful information related to vehicle maintenance, accommodation and restaurants, and was to become a benchmark for good food. At the same time, the Travel Information Bureau offered travelers personalised tips and itineraries.

The publication of the first collection of roadmaps, in 1910, was an instant hit! In 1926, the first regional guide to France was published, devoted to the principal sites of Brittany, and before long each region of France had its own Green Guide. The collection was later extended to more far-flung destinations, including New York in 1968 and Taiwan in 2011.

In the 21st century, with the growth of digital technology, the challenge for Michelin maps and guides is to continue to develop alongside the company's tire activities. Now, as before, Michelin is committed to improving the mobility of travelers.

MICHELIN TODAY

WORLD NUMBER ONE TIRE MANUFACTURER
- 70 production sites in 18 countries
- 111,000 employees from all cultures and on every continent
- 6,000 people employed in research and development

Moving
for a world

Moving forward means developing tires with better road grip and shorter braking distances, whatever the state of the road.

CORRECT TIRE PRESSURE

RIGHT PRESSURE

- Safety
- Longevity
- Optimum fuel consumption

-0,5 bar

- Durability reduced by 20% (- 8,000 km)

-1 bar

- Risk of blowouts
- Increased fuel consumption
- Longer braking distances on wet surfaces

forward together
where mobility is safer

It also involves helping motorists take care of their safety and their tires. To do so, Michelin organises "Fill Up With Air" campaigns all over the world to remind us that correct tire pressure is vital.

WEAR

DETECTING TIRE WEAR

The legal minimum depth of tire tread is 1.6mm. Tire manufacturers equip their tires with tread wear indicators, which are small blocks of rubber moulded into the base of the main grooves at a depth of 1.6mm.

Tires are the only point of contact between the vehicle and road.

The photo below shows the actual contact zone.

If the tread depth is less than 1.6mm, tires are considered to be worn and dangerous on wet surfaces.

NEW TIRE

WORN TIRE
(1,6 mm tread)

Moving forward
means sustainable mobility

By 2050, Michelin aims to cut the quantity of raw materials used in its tire manufacturing process by half and to have developed renewable energy in its facilities. The design of MICHELIN tires has already saved billions of litres of fuel and, by extension, billions of tons of CO2.

Similarly, Michelin prints its maps and guides on paper produced from sustainably managed forests and is diversifying its publishing media by offering digital solutions to make traveling easier, more fuel efficient and more enjoyable!

The group's whole-hearted commitment to eco-design on a daily basis is demonstrated by ISO 14001 certification.

Like you, Michelin is committed to preserving our planet.

Chat with Bibendum

Go to
www.michelin.com/corporate/en
Find out more about
Michelin's history and the
latest news.

QUIZ

Michelin develops tires for all types of vehicles.
See if you can match the right tire with the right vehicle...